The Economics of Urban Transportation

Kenneth A. Small's *Urban Transportation Economics* went on to become *the* textbook on the economics of transportation. Fifteen years after its original publication, as local and national authorities are increasingly turning to economic principles to cope with urban transportation problems, a second edition could not be more timely. This time co-authored with Erik T. Verhoef, this newly expanded edition has been fully updated, covering such new areas as parking policies, reliability of travel times, and the privatization of transportation services, as well as updated treatments of congestion modeling, environmental costs, and transit subsidies.

The book covers the basic topics needed for any application of economics to transportation: forecasting the demand for transportation services under alternative policies, measuring all the costs including those incurred by users, setting prices under practical constraints, choosing and evaluating investments in basic facilities, and designing ways in which the private and public sectors interact to provide services. Among the specific new topics in this edition are statistical models that better account for the variety of types of users in assessing their demands, measurement of users' perception of reliability of service, criteria for choosing prices and investment under specified financial or practical constraints, and market structures in which private companies operate with some but not full competition.

This book will be of great interest to students with basic calculus and some knowledge of economic theory who are engaged with transportation economics, planning and/or engineering, travel demand analysis, and many related fields. It will also be essential reading for researchers in any aspect of urban transportation.

Kenneth A. Small is Research Professor and Professor Emeritus of Economics at the University of California at Irvine.

Erik T. Verhoef is Professor of Spatial Economics at VU University, Amsterdam.

The Economics of Urban Transportation

Kenneth A. Small and Erik T. Verhoef

Routledge
Taylor & Francis Group

LONDON AND NEW YORK

First published 2007 by Routledge
2 Park Square, Milton Park, Abingdon, OX14 4RN

Simultaneously published in the USA and Canada
by Routledge
270 Madison Ave, New York, NY 10016

Routledge is an imprint of the Taylor & Francis Group an informa business

© 2007 Kenneth A. Small and Erik T. Verhoef

Typeset in Times New Roman by Keyword Group Ltd
Printed and bound in Great Britain by
TJ International Ltd, Padstow, Cornwall

British Library Cataloguing in Publication Data
A catalogue record for this book is available from the British Library

Library of Congress Cataloging in Publication Data
Small, Kenneth A.
   The economics of urban transportation/Kenneth A. Small and Erik T. Verhoef.
   p. cm.
   Includes bibliographical references and index.
   1. Urban transportation–Economic aspects. 2. Urban transportation–
   Research. 3. Transportation, Automotive. I. Verhoef, E. T. II. Title.
   HE305.S585 2007
   388.4–dc22
   2007014080

ISBN10: 0–415–28514–3 (hbk)
ISBN10: 0–415–28515–1 (pbk)
ISBN10: 0–203–64230–9 (ebk)

ISBN13: 978–0–415–28514–8 (hbk)
ISBN13: 978–0–415–28515–5 (pbk)
ISBN13: 978–0–203–64230–6 (ebk)

Contents

Tables

Figures

Acknowledgments

We are indebted to Richard Arnott, Robin Lindsey, Stef Proost, and Clifford Winston for extensive comments on earlier drafts of this second edition. In addition, we thank the many people who have provided suggestions and answered questions related to both editions of this book. They include Alex Anas, John Bates, David Brownstone, Xuehao Chu, Bruno De Borger, André de Palma, John Dodgson, Gordon J. Fielding, Stephenie Frederick, Marc Gaudry, Stephen Glaister, Amihai Glazer, David Hensher, Sergio Jara-Díaz, Marvin Kraus, Charles Lave, Herbert Mohring, Juan de Dios Ortúzar, Ian Parry, Seiji Steimetz, Kenneth Train, and Kurt Van Dender. We also are grateful to Lyn Long for assistance in editing, and Chunkon Kim and Chen Feng Ng for research and proofreading assistance. Of course, none of these people shares responsibility for any deficiencies.

Selected symbols and abbreviations

$A(t)$	Cumulative queue-entries
a	Exponent in Cobb–Douglas utility function of goods and leisure; Parameter in BPR congestion function
ac	Average cost
B	Total benefits (willingness to pay including actual payments)
$B(q)$	Benefit function: total willingness to pay (function of outputs)
$B(t)$	Cumulative queue-exits (function of clock time)
b	Parameter (exponent) in BPR congestion function
C	Total cost
$\tilde{C}$	Long-run cost (when distinction with short-run is relevant)
C_B	Cost to bus agency
C_g	Congestion-related part of total cost, including capacity cost
$\tilde{C}_g$	Congestion-related part of long-run total cost, including capacity cost
C_W	Cost of waiting time to bus passengers
c	Short-run average variable cost (SRAVC)
c_0	SRAVC on an uncongested road
c_{00}	SRAVC on an uncongested road exclusive of the value of free-flow travel time
c_1–c_5	Other cost parameters (definition may vary with context)
c_b, c_p	Cost per vehicle-mile of base and peak bus service, respectively
c_{bpr}, c_{bot}	Shorthand (derived) cost parameters in analytical long-run highway cost analysis
c_g	Congestion-related part of SRAVC
$\bar{c}_g$	Time-averaged congestion-related equilibrium SRAVC in dynamic models
c_l	SRAVC on link l of a network
c_S, c_T	Parts of congestion-related SRAVC attributable to schedule delay and travel time (*i.e.*, queuing delay), respectively
$\bar{c}_S, \bar{c}_T$	Parts of congestion-related time-averaged SRAVC attributable to schedule delay and travel time (*i.e.*, queuing delay), respectively
cdf	Cumulative distribution function
D	Density of vehicle traffic
D^i	Alternative-specific dummy variable for alternative i
D_j	Jam density
DL	Dummy variable equal to 1 for late arrival, 0 otherwise
D_m	Density consistent with maximum flow

d	Inverse demand function, giving generalized price as a function of quantity of travel (in highway cost analysis);
	Average passenger trip length (in transit cost analysis)
d_{jn}	Choice variable (=1 if decision-maker n chooses alternative j)
d_m	Inverse demand function for market m (defined by an origin-destination pair)
e, exp	Exponential function
$F(t)$	Cumulative desired queue-exits
G	Function for generating GEV models of discrete choice
GEV	Generalized extreme value
H	Number of time periods per weekday
h	Time period
I_r	Inclusive value for alternative group r
iid	Identically and independently distributed
J	Number of dependent variables (aggregate models) or alternatives (disaggregate models)
J_a	Delay parameter in Akçelik's travel-time function
J_r	Number of alternatives in alternative group r
K	Capital cost (present value)
K_0	Fixed part of capital cost
K_1	Coefficient of capacity in variable part of capital cost
L	Leisure (in disaggregate demand analysis);
	Length of a road (in highway cost analysis)
log	Natural logarithm
MB_K	Marginal benefit of capacity expansion
mc	Marginal cost
mec	Marginal external cost
$mecc$	Marginal external congestion cost
N	Total number of people a bus can pick up and drop off along its entire route, equal to bus capacity times length of route divided by average passenger trip length (bus cost analysis);
	Number of vehicles in queue (highway queuing analysis)
n	Bus capacity
P	Price vector of other goods (in aggregate demand analysis);
	Choice probability (in disaggregate demand analysis);
	Inflow period (in duration-dependent congestion functions)
PV	Present value
p	Price of a good, or generalized price of travel to user
Q	Total number of travelers (=qV_d when V_d is constant)
q	Output (in general cost analysis);
	Bus passenger volume (in bus cost analysis);
	Duration of period of desired queue entries = $t_{p'}-t_p$ (in highway queuing analysis)
$\boldsymbol{q}$	Vector of durations of different time periods
R	Revenue

r	Interest rate
S	Speed
S_D	Schedule delay $(= t' - t_d)$
SDE	Schedule delay early
SDL	Schedule delay late
S_f	Free-flow speed
S_m	Speed consistent with maximum flow
s	Returns to scale: ratio of average to marginal cost
s_K	Returns to scale in producing highway capacity
s_n	Vector of socioeconomic or other characteristics of decision-maker n
T	Time (or vector of times) spent in activities; Travel time (usually in-vehicle) if used as scalar without subscripts or superscripts
T^0	Out-of-vehicle travel time
T_0	Free-flow travel time
T_D	Queuing-delay portion of travel time
T_f	Free-flow travel time
t_i^k	kth travel-time component on ith mode
T_w	Time spent at work (in value-of-time analysis)
t	Time of day (in queuing analysis)
t'	Time of queue exit
t_d	Desired time of queue exit
$t_p, t_{p'}$	Beginning and end of desired period of queue exits
$t_q, t_{q'}$	Beginning and end of actual period of queue exits
t^*	Time for which actual and desired queue-exit times coincide
$\tilde{t}$	Queue-entry time leading to maximum queuing delay
U	Utility function
V	Indirect utility function (in travel-demand analysis); Volume (flow) of vehicle traffic (vehicles per hour) (in highway cost analysis); Frequency of transit service (vehicles per hour) (in transit cost analysis)
$\mathbf{V}$	Vector of vehicle flows in different time periods
V_a	Rate (volume) of actual entries to queue (vehicles per hour)
V_b	Rate (volume) of actual exits from bottleneck (vehicles per hour)
V_d	Rate (volume) of desired exits from bottleneck (vehicles per hour)
V_h	Volume (flow) of vehicle traffic during time period h
V_i	Rate (volume) of actual entries to road
V_o	Rate (volume) of actual exits from road
V_K	Capacity of highway or bottleneck (vehicles per hour)
$V_l(V_r)$	Flow of traffic on link l (route r) of a network
v_T	Value of time (usually in-vehicle time)
W	Welfare measure (usually consumer surplus); Aggregate waiting time
w	Wage rate (in travel-demand analysis); Input-price vector (in general cost-function analysis); Width of a road (in speed–flow functions)
X	Vector of other goods or a single generalized consumption good

x	Consumption good or vector of goods (in demand analysis); Input vector (in general cost-function analysis)
x_n	Fixed input in short-run cost function (in cost analysis); Location of nth vehicle (in car-following model)
Y	Unearned income
y	Total income (in aggregate demand analysis); Generalized argument for function G generating GEV models (in disaggregate demand analysis)
Z	Characteristics of travel choices and travelers
z	Independent variables for travel-demand models
α	Value of travel time (in highway cost analysis)
α_i	Alternative-specific constant for alternative i in discrete-choice indirect utility function
β	Parameter vector in demand function (in travel demand analysis); Shadow price of schedule delay early (in highway cost analysis)
γ	Shadow price of schedule delay late
γ_i	Coefficient of an independent variable interacted with an alternative-specific constant for alternative i in discrete-choice utility function
δ	$\beta\gamma/(\beta+\gamma)$ (in highway cost analysis)
δ_{lr}	Dummy variable indicating route-link incidence ($=1$ if link l is part of route r)
δ_{rm}	Dummy variable indicating route-market incidence ($=1$ if route r can serve market m)
ε	Error term
ε_h	Elasticity of demand in period h
ε_i	Stochastic term for alternative i in discrete-choice indirect utility function
Θ	Meta-parameters describing densities of random parameters
θ	Parameter vector (in general cost-function analysis); Fixed cost of arriving late (in highway cost analysis)
Λ	Lagrangian function
λ	Lagrange multiplier; Marginal utility of income
μ	Scale parameter for probability density function (in discrete-choice analysis); Lagrange multiplier (in value-of-time analysis)
Π	Profit
π	Annual rate of inflation
ρ	Parameter of GEV functions (in discrete-choice analysis); Capital recovery factor divided by number of weekdays per year (converts capital cost to an ongoing daily cost) (in cost analysis)
σ	Standard deviation (in statistical estimates); Parameter of GEV function ($=1-\rho$) (in travel demand analysis); Fraction of travelers exiting queue prior to t^* (in highway cost analysis)
τ	Congestion fee ($ per vehicle-mile or per passage; depending on context)
Φ	Cumulative normal distribution function
ϕ	Normal probability density function
ψ	Lagrange multiplier
ω	Weight on a representative individual when aggregating

1 Introduction

At the heart of all modern economic activity is trade. People trade labor and ideas for cash, and cash for goods and services; firms trade technology, expertise, financial capacity, intermediate goods, administrative functions, and many other things with each other, with individuals, and with governments. All these transactions require communications and most require transportation of goods or people – to work, shopping, tourist sites, meeting locations. Thus it is fair to say that transportation is central to economic activity.

Cities exist when there are special advantages to carrying out economic activities in proximity, advantages often called "economies of agglomeration" because costs are lower when certain groups of activities locate close to each other. The primary reason for agglomeration economies, especially in a world with low communication costs, is that transportation costs are still significant and proximity reduces them. A corollary is that anything that reduces transportation costs within an urban area increases the extent to which its activities are easily linked to each other, and thus takes further advantage of agglomeration economies. In a world of many competing urban centers, those with more efficient transportation systems have an advantage.

The study of transportation involves researchers trained in many disciplines, including engineering, economics, geography, planning, psychology, business, and regional science. Regardless of its disciplinary origin, transportation research has become increasingly sophisticated in its use of economics. This trend has brought a solid practical footing to policy analysis, by showing how the ideas and goals generated within various analytical frameworks can be reconciled with the actual behavior of users of transportation systems and with the resource constraints of a real economy.

This book reviews the contributions that economics can make to the analysis of urban transportation. It concentrates mainly on industrialized nations, but many of the principles are equally applicable to developing nations. This is especially true in light of the ubiquitous rise in travel by private automobile. Because of the predominance of this trend, we place heavy emphasis on highway transportation and use it as a topic in which to present a comprehensive set of formal models.

The scope of urban transportation economics

The boundaries of transportation economics are neither well defined nor static. Nevertheless, the reader is entitled to know what principles we use to limit the scope of this review. Aside from the inevitable one that we try to write about what we know best, the following observations are guidelines.

Transportation economics is, of course, a branch of economics. Hence it focuses on resource allocation and how the interactions among independent agents bring about a self-consistent outcome. It draws from and interacts closely with transportation engineering, urban planning, and other disciplines, but has a somewhat different emphasis. Engineering emphasizes facility design and implementation, while economics emphasizes behavioral principles and resource allocation. The disciplines of management, public administration, and urban planning are concerned with the formulation of workable transportation policies, for example by studying decision processes and organizational structures. An important role of economics is to inform these disciplines about the complex ways in which transportation policies exert their influence. Economics is well suited to predict the ultimate results of behavioral shifts among interacting economic actors in response to policy implementations or exogenous events. It also can identify tradeoffs between efficiency and other goals.

These orientations toward the subject give it certain characteristics that are evident in this review. Transportation economics tends to focus on models that illustrate concepts, as opposed to those whose output is the actual design of facilities or regulations. Hence its models are usually at a coarse rather than a fine geographical scale, lending themselves to "sketch planning" of the broad features of a transportation system.

Analysis often proceeds by defining a demand structure and a supply structure for a set of goods or services, then searching for an outcome that is consistent with both structures. This is a normal microeconomic approach, although the nature of transportation creates ambiguities in the boundary between demand and supply: for example, is the time required for a trip an attribute affecting demand, or is it part of the cost? Either viewpoint is valid so long as demand and cost are consistently defined; doing so is the task of Chapters 2 and 3, respectively. Their interconnection is made explicit in the discussion of the "value of time" in Section 2.6.

Demand and supply structures are complex, involving many types of people, modes, locations, and times. For this reason, finding a consistent solution – an equilibrium, in economics parlance – requires considerable analytical sophistication. A pioneering study by Beckmann, McGuire and Winsten (1956) showed how to do this for arbitrary transportation networks given certain assumptions. In the presence of increasing returns to scale and lack of efficient pricing (conditions which, as we shall see, often characterize urban transportation), this equilibrium may differ in drastic and surprising ways from a configuration satisfying optimality conditions. In other words, what happens when people make decisions out of self-interest is not necessarily what they would choose collectively and cooperatively. A common thread throughout this review is that transportation economics should provide the tools to understand and quantify such differences, and to design policies that address them.

Three important types of policies to consider are pricing, investment, and industrial organization (including regulations contingent on the form of organization). Pricing and investment have long been the hallmark of urban transportation economics, and are accorded full treatment here (in Chapters 4 and 5). Industrial organization has likewise been of great concern, and recent changes throughout the world have brought to the fore questions of oligopolistic markets, regulation, and government versus private provision of services. Chapter 6 considers a number of these questions.

Transportation potentially affects the nature of the urban area itself. If transportation were costless, participants in an economy would have no economic reason to locate close to one another. The study of this influence is clearly germane to transportation policy. To analyze it fully requires the full power of disciplines such as urban geography, urban economics, and regional science, which seek to explain the shape of urban development. Important as this is, it is too ambitious for this book and we limit ourselves to a brief summary in Section 2.1.6.

The scope of this book

The aim of this book is to provide a self-contained introduction to major research themes in contemporary transportation economics. We have chosen to explore certain topics in great detail, in order to illustrate how the analysis can be put to practical use, and others much more cursorily. In both cases, extensive citations provide the reader opportunities to expand on any particular theme. Thus we aim to make the book suitable both as an initial textbook for students with a good technical background and as a reference work for practicing researchers and professionals.

Above all, we attempt to show how to construct a set of workable models that can be adapted, refined, and combined in subsequent research. In the sections on highway congestion, for example, the models presented incorporate critical features that are often omitted in transportation analyses, such as queuing, trip scheduling, peak shifting, and reliability. There is evidence that these phenomena greatly affect the outcomes from policies to relieve congestion, and their analysis has been made tractable by recent technical advances. It is our hope that such models will provide a common language for researchers in urban transportation, facilitating comparisons among theoretical innovations and among empirical applications.

2 Travel demand

In order to plan transportation facilities, it is necessary to forecast how much they will be used. In order to price them rationally and determine the best operating policies, it is necessary to know how users respond to prices and service characteristics. In order to evaluate whether a project is worthwhile at all, it is necessary to have a measure of the benefits it produces. All these requirements are in the province of travel demand analysis.

The demand for travel takes place in a multi-dimensional setting. The traditional sequential framework used by many metropolitan transportation planning agencies considers four choice dimensions: trip generation (the total number of trips originating from an area); trip distribution (the locations of the trips' destinations); modal choice (the means of travel, such as car, bus, train, bicycle, or walking); and trip assignment (the exact route used). More recently, researchers have paid greater attention to other dimensions of choice, such as residential and job location, household automobile ownership, the time of day at which trips are taken, parking locations, and the duration of activities for which travel is undertaken.

These multiple decisions are often envisioned as a sequence, typically starting with residential and job locations, then vehicle ownership, then other aspects. This sequence is in decreasing order of the time span over which the decision can be changed easily. However, it does not imply a sequential decision procedure whereby one decision is made without regard to its implications for later decisions. Rather, each decision is affected by others and so can be fully understood only as part of a simultaneous choice process. A given study may isolate just a few of these decisions for tractability; it is then all the more important to remember, in interpreting results, that other decisions are lurking in the background.

Furthermore, travel is a derived demand, usually undertaken not for its own sake but rather to facilitate a spatially varied set of activities such as work, recreation, shopping, and home life. This observation links the study of travel demand to studies of labor supply, firms' choices of technologies, and urban development. It also calls attention to an increasingly common form of travel: the linking together of several trip purposes into one integrated itinerary or *tour*, a process known as *trip chaining*.

The chapter begins (Section 2.1) by asking what can be learned from aggregate data about travel and how conventional economic demand theory is applied to such data. It then moves on to disaggregate models (Section 2.2), also known as "behavioral" because they depict individual decision-making explicitly. Section 2.3 presents examples of models explaining some key travel choices: mode, time of day, and route. More specialized topics are then discussed (Sections 2.4–2.5). Finally, Section 2.6 analyzes two quantities of special interest to policy: travelers' willingness to pay for travel-time savings and for improved reliability. We mostly discuss passenger transportation, in part because more data are available than for freight; however, studies of the demand for urban freight transportation tend to use similar methods.[1]

2.1 Aggregate tabulations and models

Much can be learned simply from cross-tabulating survey data. For the United States, there are two very useful sources. One, covering all trips, is the National Personal Transportation Survey (NPTS), collected at approximately six-year intervals; for the single year 2001 it was subsumed into a broader survey called the National Household Travel Survey (NHTS). The other useful source is the journey-to-work portion of the US Census, taken every 10 years. This consists of responses to questions about work travel, asked on the Census "long form," which is administered to about 17% of all households. Pisarski (2006) provides a comprehensive analysis of the 2000 journey-to-work census and compares it to earlier censuses and to the 2001 NHTS.

The NHTS shows that work trips in the US continue to decline as a proportion of all trips, amounting to about 16% in 2001.[2] However, it would be a mistake to conclude that work trips are no longer important for urban transportation. Two-thirds of US work trips in 2000 occurred during the hours 6–9 a.m., and work trips account for about half of all person-miles of travel during those hours. Trips to work have been found to account for more than half of all trips in selected Belgian cities, and a very high fraction of peak-period trips on some of the most notoriously congested Los Angeles freeways.[3] Thus work trips remain predominant contributors to congestion.

Private vehicles dominate all categories of trips in the US, and increasingly so. They account for 91% of all work trips in 2000, up from 89% in 1990. The share of work trips that use public transit is just 4.7%, down from 5.3% in 1990. However, transit share is much larger in large metropolitan areas, averaging 5.7% and reaching 11.5% in those areas with over 5 million residents. Carpooling accounts for 12.6% of all metropolitan work trips. Automobile ownership is high and continues to grow faster than the population. Yet many US households owned no car in 2001: roughly 8% of all households and 26% of those with incomes below $20,000.[4]

The geography of commuting continues to become more dispersed. Commuting within the main central cities of US metropolitan areas accounted for about one-fourth of all work trips by metropolitan residents, and those from suburbs to central cities another 17%; the rest are trips within or between suburbs (41%), reverse commuting from central city to suburbs (8%), and trips to workplaces outside the metropolitan areas (10%).[5] The increased dispersion of work trips shows up as longer distances traveled at somewhat higher speeds: average commuting distance has risen by about 14% over the decade (to 12.1 miles), while average commuting time has risen by only 9% (to 25.5 minutes).[6] Commuting times are slightly higher in metropolitan areas than in the US as a whole – 26.1 minutes in 2000 – and higher still in larger metropolitan areas, reaching 34 minutes in New York (where the percentage using public transit is especially high). Several metropolitan areas, all of them with high population growth, had a 20% increase in average commuting time over the decade 1990–2000; yet in only one of them, Atlanta, did the average commute exceed 30 minutes in 2000.[7] If we look just at commutes by private vehicles, their duration averaged 26 minutes in metropolitan areas over 3 million in population and considerably less in smaller areas (Hu and Reuscher 2004, Fig. 11).

Most of these trends apply to other parts of the world as well, although the actual numbers may be quite different. For example, rather different modal splits are observed for the Netherlands: 38% of all trips are by car as driver, 12% by car as passenger, 5% by public transport, 26% by bicycle, and 17% walking.[8] Of course, heavily urbanized areas have a much bigger proportion of trips by public transport – accounting for 23% of person-kilometers, compared to just 12% for the entire nation.[9] Total travel per person (in kilometers per day) is also about 7% less in the heavily urbanized areas, probably reflecting greater accessibility and possibly also the impact of congestion.

Work trips in the Netherlands account for 26% of person-kilometers, with car driver accounting for a higher proportion of them than is the case for all trips (66% *vs.* 54%), while car passenger accounts for a lower proportion of work trips than of all trips (8% *vs.* 21%). Public transport in the Netherlands captures a higher proportion of person-kilometers for work trips than for all trips (16% *vs.* 12%), but this may be because work trips are longer.

The stereotype of the US being more car-dependent than a European country like the Netherlands thus seems confirmed by these figures, and by other information about the European Union in Strelow (2006). It is also reflected in car ownership: 23% of the Dutch households have no car and 56% have one car; in heavily urbanized areas these shares are 40% and 50%, respectively. Local circumstances—including cultural, geographical, and historical differences, but also more "conventional" economic factors such as fuel prices, vehicle taxes, and parking policies—are among the factors commonly thought to explain such differences; more systematic analyses will be discussed below.

2.1.1 *Aggregate demand models*

For more formal analysis, the approach most similar to standard economic analysis of consumer demand is an aggregate one. The demand for some portion of the travel market is explained as a function of variables that describe the product or its consumers. For example, total transit demand in a city might be related to the amounts of residential and industrial development, the average transit fare, the costs of alternative modes, some simple measures of service quality, and average income. Because behavior cannot be predicted precisely, an "error term" is added to represent behavior that, to the researcher at least, appears random. Thus a demand function might be represented as:

$$x = f(Z) + \varepsilon, \tag{2.1}$$

where x is the quantity demanded, Z is a vector of values of all the relevant characteristics of the good and its potential consumers, $f(\cdot)$ is some mathematical function, and ε is the random error term. Statistical data on x and Z can be used to estimate the function f and the probability distribution of ε.

It is possible to estimate f using *non-parametric methods* that impose no prior assumptions about its shape. More commonly, f is *specified* to be a particular functional form with parameters whose values are to be determined from statistical data. For example, f might be specified as a general quadratic function:

$$f(Z) = \beta_0 + \sum_k \beta_{1k} Z_k + \sum_k \beta_{2k} Z_k^2 + \sum_k \sum_{l \neq k} \beta_{3kl} Z_k Z_l, \tag{2.2}$$

where Z_k and Z_l are characteristics included in vector Z, and the β parameters are to be estimated empirically. This is an example of an equation that is *linear in parameters*. To see why, define variables $z_0 \equiv 1$, $z_{1k} = Z_k$, $z_2 = Z_k^2$ and $z_{3kl} = Z_k Z_l$, for all values of k and of $l \neq k$. Combining all these variables into a single vector z and all the corresponding parameters into a single vector β, we can write (2.1) as:

$$x = \beta'z + \varepsilon, \tag{2.3}$$

where the prime on β indicates transposition (changing it from a column vector to a row vector); thus $\beta'z$ is the inner product between β and z.[10]

Equation (2.3) is known as a *regression* of x on z. When it is linear in β, as in this example, one can very easily estimate the unknown parameters. Indeed, we chose this example to illustrate that even a quite complex relationship between x and Z can often be represented as a linear regression.[11] The most common way of estimating the unknown parameters in (2.3) is *ordinary least squares*, in which the value of β is found that minimizes the sum of squared residuals for a set of observations labeled $n = 1, \dots , N$:

$$\hat{\beta} = \arg\min_{\beta} \sum_{n=1}^{N} (x_n - \beta'z_n)^2,$$

where now we have indexed each observed data point (x_n, z_n) by its observation label n. Ordinary least squares has particularly nice properties when the random error ε is assumed to have a normal (bell-shaped) distribution. However, it is quite possible to estimate regression models with non-linear functional forms or with other error distributions.[12]

The non-random part of the demand equation (2.1) is often based on an explicit theory of consumer choice. Such a theory is not necessary in order to specify and estimate a demand function, but it may help by suggesting likely functional forms for f and it is useful for interpreting the results. The most common such theory postulates that a consumer or group of consumers maximizes a *utility function*, $u(x, X)$; this function expresses preferences over the quantities of the good x under consideration and of other goods represented by the vector X. The consumer is limited by a budget constraint, expressed in terms of the price p of x and a price vector P consisting of prices of all the other goods X. Mathematically, then, consumption is determined as a solution to the following constrained maximization problem:

$$\underset{x,X}{\text{Max}}\ u(x, X) \quad \text{subject to: } px + P'X = y, \tag{2.4}$$

where y is income and again the prime on P transposes it so that $P'X$ is an inner product, expressing the cost of consuming all the goods in vector X. Denoting the solution to (2.4) by vector (x^*, X^*), we note that it depends on prices and income:

$$x^* = x^*(p, P, y)$$
$$X^* = X^*(p, P, y). \tag{2.5}$$

Thus if we knew, or were willing to postulate, a form for the function u, and if we could solve the maximization problem, we would know the form of the demand function (2.1) except for its random term.[13]

The demand functions (2.5), when derived in this way, can be used to define a very useful quantity. We simply substitute them into the utility function to see how much utility can be achieved with a given set of prices and income. The result is known as the *indirect utility function*, often written as *V*:

$$V(p, P, y) = u(x^*(p, P, y), X^*(p, P, y)).$$

The indirect utility function has a property known as *Roy's identity*:

$$x^* = -\frac{\partial V/\partial p}{\partial V/\partial y}, \tag{2.6}$$

where it is understood that all quantities in (2.6) depend on *p*, *P*, and *y*. We will make use of the indirect utility function and Roy's identity when we discuss disaggregate demand analysis in Section 2.2. For simplicity, our notation for demand functions will omit the asterisks in (2.5) and (2.6).

The demand functions (2.5) were defined as resulting from an individual consumer's optimization. An aggregate demand function can simply be derived from individuals' demands by summing quantities demanded over consumers. Under some quite restrictive conditions, the resulting aggregate demand function may look as if it could have resulted from optimization by a single "representative" consumer, which can be convenient in analyses. Specifically, a necessary and sufficient condition for this to be true is that individuals' indirect utility functions take the "Gorman form," meaning that for an individual *i* it can be written as $V_i(p, P, y) = a_i(p, P) + b(p, P) \cdot y_i$, where the a_i-term can vary across consumers but the *b*-term cannot (Varian 1992, p. 154). This condition is satisfied for several utility functions commonly used for theoretical analysis, but not for those underlying most empirical work.

2.1.2 Cross-sectional studies of metropolitan areas

Many studies have used aggregate data, such as are commonly reported by transit authorities or local governments, to study influences on travel behavior across cities. We illustrate here with three.

Gordon and Willson (1984) compile an international data set of 91 cities with light-rail systems, and estimate simple regression equations explaining the ridership (per kilometer of line) on those systems. They show that ridership is positively related to city population density and gross national product per capita. Applying this model to five North American cities with light-rail systems then under construction, they predict far lower ridership than the official forecasts – about half in most cases, but less than one-seventh in the case of Detroit. It has been shown subsequently by Pickrell (1992) that nearly every modern rail system built in the US has in fact attained less than half the originally forecast patronage.

Winston and Shirley (1998) examine the shares of US work trips across metropolitan areas made by any of five different modes (two private, two public, plus taxi) within any of 10 different time-of-day intervals. Their data are from the 1990 journey-to-work census. Among the many interesting findings are these: travel time has the largest effect on choice for trips of moderate distance, being less important for both short and long trips; route coverage and service frequency is important for public transit use, especially for commuters making long trips; and workers in the finance, real estate, and insurance industries tend to travel earlier in the day if they live further west, suggesting that they need to overlap with the operating hours of New York or other East Coast banking and financial markets.

Black (1990) uses regression analysis on data from 120 US metropolitan areas to see what factors influence the fraction of metropolitan workers who walk to work. This fraction varies from 1.9% to 15.7%, averaging 5.4%. It is higher in cities with military bases or universities, in small cities, and where incomes are low. Black's study is a useful reminder that walking can be an important journey-to-work mode, its prevalence being sensitive to land uses and demographics. Plaut (2004) reports that in Tel Aviv, 9.4% of workers walk to work, a fraction that varies by gender, age, and household status.[14]

2.1.3 Cross-sectional studies within a metropolitan area

Statistical analysis can also be used to analyze trip-making in different parts of one metropolitan area. This approach, known as *direct demand modeling*, was introduced by Domencich and Kraft (1970) to explain the number of round trips between zone pairs, by purpose and mode, in the Boston area. An example is the analysis by Kain and Liu (2002, Table 5-10) of mode share to work in Santiago, Chile. The share is measured for each of 34 districts ("*communas*"); its logarithm is regressed on variables such as travel time, transit availability, and household income. The most powerful predictors for automobile share are vehicle ownership and household income, both of which increase the share. (Unfortunately, this does not control for the possibility that vehicle ownership is influenced by automobile share itself – an "endogeneity problem" that we discuss later.) The share for the Metro rail system is strongly increased, quite naturally, by presence of a Metro station in the district, and is strongly decreased by high household income.

Dagenais and Gaudry (1986), analyzing Montreal data on trip-making, find it important to include observations of zone pairs with zero reported trips, using the standard "tobit" model for limited dependent variables to account for the fact that the number of trips between two zones cannot be negative.[15] This illustrates a pervasive feature of travel-demand analysis: many of the variables to be explained are limited in range, making ordinary regression analysis inappropriate. For this reason, travel-demand researchers have contributed importantly to the development of techniques, discussed later in this chapter, that are appropriate for such data (McFadden 2001). Here we describe one such technique that is applicable to aggregate data.

Suppose the dependent variable of a model can logically take values only within a certain range. For example, if the dependent variable x is the modal share of transit, it must lie between zero and one. If one or both of these limits is actually observed in the data, we can explain the observations using a single- or double-censored tobit model, which explicitly allows for non-zero probabilities of such observations.[16] If neither limit is observed in the data, an alternative would be, instead of explaining x directly, to explain the logistic transformation of x as follows:

$$\log\left(\frac{x}{1-x}\right) = \beta'z + \varepsilon, \tag{2.7}$$

where β is a vector of parameters, z is a vector of independent variables, and ε is an error term with infinite range. Equivalently,

$$x = \frac{\exp(\beta'z + \varepsilon)}{1 + \exp(\beta'z + \varepsilon)}. \tag{2.8}$$

Except for how ε enters, this is an *aggregate logit* model for a single dependent variable.

In many applications, several dependent variables x_i are related to each other, each associated with particular values z_i of some independent variables. For example, x_i might be the share of trips made by mode i, and z_i a vector of service characteristics of mode i. If the characteristics in the z variables encompass all the systematic influences on mode shares, then a simple extension of equation (2.8) ensures that they sum to one:

$$x_i = \frac{\exp\left(\beta'z_i + \varepsilon_i\right)}{\displaystyle\sum_{j=1}^{J} \exp\left(\beta'z_j + \varepsilon_j\right)}, \tag{2.9}$$

where J is the number of modes.[17] Anas (1981) and Mackett (1985) use counts of interzonal flows to estimate models similar to this, in order to explain location and mode choice in Chicago and in Hertfordshire (England), respectively. The study by Winston and Shirley (1998), mentioned in the previous subsection, also uses a formula like this.

2.1.4 Studies using time-series data

One can estimate demand equations from aggregate time-series data from a single area. For example, Greene (1992) uses US nationwide data on vehicle-miles traveled (VMT) to examine the effects of fuel prices. Several studies have examined transit ridership using data over time from a single metropolitan area or even a single transit corridor – for example, Gaudry (1975) and Gómez-Ibáñez (1996) use this method to study Montreal and Boston, respectively. Time-series studies are quite sensitive to the handling of autocorrelation among the error terms, which refers to the tendency for unobserved influences on the measured dependent variable to persist over time. They may also postulate "inertia" by including among the explanatory variables one or more lagged values of the variable being explained. For example, Greene considers the possibility that once people have established the travel patterns that produce a particular level of VMT, they change them only gradually if conditions such as fuel prices suddenly change. The coefficients on the lagged dependent variables then enable one to measure the difference between short- and long-run responses. This measured difference is especially sensitive to the treatment of autocorrelation.

It is common to combine cross-sectional and time-series variation, for example using observations from many separate locations and two or more time periods. Voith (1997) analyzes ridership data from 118 commuter-rail stations in metropolitan Philadelphia over the years 1978–91 to ascertain the effects of level of service and of demographics on rail ridership. Surprisingly, he finds that demographic characteristics have little independent effect; rather, he suggests that much of the observed correlation between demographic factors and rail ridership arises from reverse causation. For example, a neighborhood with good rail connections to the central business district (CBD) will attract residents who work in the CBD. A corollary of this finding is that the long-run effects of changes in fares or service levels, allowing for induced changes in residential location, are considerably greater than the short-run effects. Another study using cross-sectional time series is that by Petitte (2001), who estimates fare elasticities from station-level data on Metrorail ridership in Washington, DC.

Studies using cross-sectional time series need to account for the fact that, even aside from autocorrelation, the error terms for observations from the same location at different points in time cannot plausibly be assumed to be independent. Neglecting this fact will result in an unnecessary loss of efficiency and an over-statement of the precision of the estimates; for non-linear models, it may also bias the estimates. To account for the error structure, at least three approaches are available. One is to "first difference" all variables, so that the variable explained describes *changes* in some quantity rather than the quantity itself; this reduces the size of the data set by N if N is the number of locations.[18] A second is to estimate a "fixed-effects" model, in which a separate constant is estimated for every location; this retains all observations but adds $N - 1$ new coefficients to be estimated (assuming one constant would be estimated in any case). A third is a "random effects" model, in which a separate random-error term is specified that varies only by location (not time), usually with an assumed normal distribution; this specification adds only one parameter to be estimated (the standard deviation of the new error term) and so is especially useful where only a few time periods are available. Statistical tests are available to determine whether the more restrictive random-effects model is justified. Voith (1997) uses both the first-difference and fixed-effects approaches.

2.1.5 Summary of key results of aggregate studies

Several literature surveys have compiled estimates of summary measures such as own- and cross-elasticities of demand for auto or public transit with respect to cost and service quality. Service quality is typically proxied by annual vehicle-miles or vehicle-hours of service. Goodwin (1992) and Pratt *et al.* (2000, Chapter 12) provide thorough reviews, which also include some studies using the disaggregate techniques described later in this chapter.

As a rough rule of thumb, a 10% increase in transit fare reduces transit demand by 4%: that is, transit's own-price elasticity is approximately –0.4 on average (Pratt *et al.* 2000, p. 12–9). This elasticity is higher for trips to a central business district, trips on buses (compared to urban rail), and off-peak trips (Lago, Mayworm and McEnroe 1981). Transit elasticities with respect to service quality tend to be higher, especially where service quality is poor (Chan and Ou 1978). Unfortunately, the time period over which these elasticities apply varies from study to study and is often unstated; usually the elasticities are measured using data covering a period of a few months to about two years.

Demand for automobile work trips is similarly more sensitive to service quality than to cost. For example, time- and cost-elasticities are measured at -0.8 and -0.5, respectively, for Boston; and at -0.4 and -0.1 for Louisville, Kentucky (Chan and Ou 1978, p. 43). Overall demand for travel in personal vehicles has more often been measured as a function of fuel price and/or fuel cost per mile; typical results show elasticities between -0.1 and -0.3, with short-run elasticities typically smaller (in absolute values) than long-run elasticities. The demand elasticity for fuel itself is apparently two to three times as large, indicating that changes in fuel price affect the composition of the motor-vehicle fleet more than its usage.[19]

Several studies have found intriguing regularities in the per-capita or per-household expenditures of time and money on travel. In a series of papers and reports, Yacov Zahavi has made these regularities the centerpiece of a model of travel demand known as Unified Mechanism of Travel. However, most scholars have concluded that the regularities can be explained by more conventional models and, furthermore, that the regularities are only approximations and that violations of them occur as predicted by economic theory (Schafer 2000). For example, Kockelman (2001) rejects the hypothesis of fixed travel-time budgets using data from the San Francisco Bay Area. She finds rather that total time spent traveling declines as nearby activities are made more accessible and as distant activities are made less accessible, the latter suggesting that substitution (of nearby for distant destinations) more than offsets the direct effects of increased travel time to distant locations.

2.1.6 Transportation and land use

Transportation is defined with respect to particular locations. Naturally, the way the land at those locations is used – the types and densities of buildings occupying them and the activities that occur there – are among the most important factors influencing travel decisions. For example, researchers have found that public transit ridership in a city is more heavily influenced by the number of jobs in the city's downtown area than by almost any other factor (Barnes 2005). Furthermore, transportation facilities have significant effects on land use. Thus, the two-way inter-relationship is important analytically and, because transportation and land use have significant spillover effects on quality of life for nearby residents, it fuels contentious policy debates.[20] Here, we consider just one of the two-way directions of influence: from land use to travel.

One approach to understanding this influence is to study the relationships among aggregate land-use and travel measures, typically at the level of a metropolitan area. One needs to keep track of which is causing which, and to carefully disentangle related factors. For example, one obviously must control for variables like income and fuel price, which are correlated with land-use characteristics and which independently affect travel. Some influential studies claiming far-reaching effects of urban density on travel, such Newman and Kenworthy (1989), have been severely criticized for neglecting this fundamental requirement of statistical analysis.

But several other pitfalls afflict such aggregate studies. Most importantly, because the interaction is two-way, land-use patterns are not exogenous; instead, they respond strongly to transportation systems. As a result, trying to explain travel decisions with land-use patterns risks confusing cause with effect. Statistical techniques exist to handle this type of "endogeneity problem," notably the use of "instrumental variables," in this case variables related to land use but believed to be exogenous (see any of the econometrics texts listed in Section 2.1.1). An example might be the age of the city, or a measure of its density several decades earlier. Roughly speaking, the variable feared to be endogenous (land use) is replaced, in the equation explaining travel, by a predicted version formed by regressing the land-use variable on all exogenous variables in the system, including the instrumental variables. We discuss instrumental variables further in Section 2.4.5.

Even when the two directions of causality between transportation and land use are correctly measured, they can produce surprising policy paradoxes. For example, expanding highways to relieve congestion may attract development that undermines the intended effect; this is just one of many examples of "induced demand," discussed in Chapter 5. Expanding mass transit can even exacerbate highway congestion because the induced development, even if relatively transit-oriented, still generates many automobile trips. For example, the Bay Area Rapid Transit system in San Francisco is credited with causing Walnut Creek, an outlying station, to develop into a major center of office employment – but despite its good transit access, 95% of commuting trips to this center are by automobile (Cervero and Wu 1996, Table 5).

A similar endogeneity problem afflicts measures of transportation infrastructure or service provision, such as the extent of roadways and rail transit lines or the amount of bus service provided. Presumably policy makers provide infrastructure and services at least partly in response to actual or expected travel. Therefore any factors, unaccounted for by the model, that increase a particular type of travel may also tend to increase the associated infrastructure and service provision. Ignoring this reverse causality could lead to an overstatement of the effect of infrastructure or service provision on travel and, because infrastructure is closely related to urban density, an understatement of the effect of land-use patterns (since some of their effects would be attributed instead to the transportation service variables).

Another problem is that land-use patterns cannot be modified by fiat. Even in countries with strong land-use authority, such as the Netherlands, land-use policies do not always bring about the changes that were intended (Schwanen, Dijst and Dieleman 2004). In others, such as the US, the changes in land use that can feasibly be accomplished through policy are quite limited. The urbanized area of Portland, Oregon, remains relatively low density despite three decades of stringent policies aimed at increasing urban density; one reason is that Portland's policies have apparently diverted urban development to more outlying jurisdictions outside its control (Downs 2004; Jun 2004). Thus, even when it can be established that a certain type of land-use pattern has favorable effects on travel, there may be no way to bring about the desired change.

We turn now to empirical findings on how land use affects travel demand at an aggregate level. At the level of an entire metropolitan area, modest effects have been documented. Within a cross-section of 49 US metropolitan areas, Keyes (1982) shows that per-capita gasoline consumption rises with total urban population and with the fraction of jobs located in the central business district, and falls with the fraction of people living in high-density census tracts. These effects are estimated to be even larger if transportation infrastructure and services are omitted on the grounds that they are endogenous. Gordon, Kumar and Richardson (1989) examine average commuting time among individual respondents to the 1980 National Personal Transportation Study. Commuting time, unlike gasoline consumption, goes *up* with residential density; presumably this reflects longer or more congested commutes. But commuting time goes *down* with the proportion of the metropolitan population that lives outside the central city. This last finding suggests that polycentric or dispersed land-use patterns enable people to bypass central congestion, which in turn may explain a paradox: average commuting times have risen much more slowly than the amount of congestion on any given road.

Bento *et al.* (2005) ask how various land-use and transportation variables, intended to measure "urban sprawl," influence travel choices across 114 US metropolitan areas. While no one factor explains very much of the variation, all of them taken together make a significant difference. To illustrate, the authors predict annual vehicle use for a national sample of households if they all lived in metropolitan areas with specified characteristics related to land use and transportation supply. If the characteristics are those of Atlanta, their model predicts 16,900 vehicle-miles per household; if the characteristics are changed to those of Boston, the same households would travel 25% less. While many characteristics contribute to this difference, the most important is population centrality, which indicates that a higher proportion of Boston's population than Atlanta's lives within the central portions of the total urbanized land area. Boston also has a higher urban population density and a more even balance between jobs and households at the zip-code level, both of which contribute to its lower vehicle use. This limiting effect of density upon vehicle-miles traveled is consistent with the Dutch figures quoted in the introduction to Section 2.1.

Other contexts, or more precise breakdowns, may yield different results. Schwanen, Dijst and Dieleman (2004) examine the effects of urban size and form on travel for commuting and shopping trips in the Netherlands. For any given mode (auto or transit), they find that the largest cities have the shortest and fastest commutes, medium-sized cities and outlying "growth centers" have the longest, while suburbs are in between. They also report exceptionally high use of walking and bicycling, amounting to 40% of work trips and 67% of shopping trips, in the three largest cities, with lower rates in other areas.

Turning to the neighborhood level, the evidence on how land use affects travel is quite mixed. Crane (2000) provides a useful review. It is clear that high-density neighborhoods near transit stops support higher use of public transit. It is less clear how much of this is due simply to sorting of households: those who want to use transit choose transit-oriented neighborhoods. This is not a concern if one simply wants to predict transit patronage in a proposed isolated transit-oriented development; but if one wants to know the aggregate effects of building many such developments, one needs to control statistically for sorting. When this is done, the effects of land use on the travel behavior are found to be much more modest, and to depend on a number of collateral factors such as how centralized the entire urban area is. For example, Cervero and Gorham (1995) find that transit-oriented development encourages more walking and bicycling in local areas within the San Francisco region, but not in those within the Los Angeles region. Recent work has suggested that the neighborhood-level effects of land use on travel can be understood by examining how trip costs are affected (Boarnet and Crane 2001); this observation opens the door to research explaining more specifically why land use has impacts in some settings and not others.

One of the factors limiting the influence of land use is that people travel far greater distances than are required by land-use patterns alone. Even when jobs–housing balance is achieved within a community, people do not predominately choose nearby jobs. Thus, for example, new ex-urban communities intended to be relatively self-contained have generally discovered that most residents work elsewhere.[21]

A quite different approach to the linkage between land use and transportation is to build detailed computer models that simulate both land-use decisions, such as whether to develop a property and at what density, and travel decisions. Typically this is done at the level of small- to moderate-sized zones within an urban area. Because the potential number of relevant decisions is enormous, it has proven difficult to simultaneously meet the goals of theoretical rigor (generally based on microeconomic theory), adequate spatial detail, computational tractability, data availability, and comprehensibility. Nevertheless such models have achieved some success. Anas (1982) describes a model, known as the Chicago Area Transportation/Land Use Analysis System (CATLAS), calibrated for Chicago and used for a number of interesting policy evaluations. One of them was to predict impacts of a new transit line from downtown Chicago to Midway Airport. Subsequent studies by other researchers have verified two of its predictions: substantial impacts on housing prices for properties within half a mile of the line, and virtually no price impact on housing more than 1.5 miles distant. Another notable result is that much of the impact appeared during the several years after the line was approved but not yet constructed.[22]

More recently, Anas and Liu (2007) describe a model that attempts to more fully represent economic decision-making with computational tractability. The land-use portion of the model keeps track of product prices, wages, housing rents and prices, and stocks of buildings, allowing for dynamic decision-making and accounting for the durability of decisions about buildings. The transportation portion of the model contains the usual components of a complete travel model as described earlier in Section 2.1, including equilibration of route choices on networks representing available transit lines and roads. Safirova *et al.* (2006) combine the same underlying land-use model with a different transportation model, known as START, and use it for policy analysis for the Washington, DC area. Another significant recent model system is UrbanSim, which adopts an open computer architecture to facilitate adaptation by other researchers for specific purposes. It is described by Waddell (2002), who also provides a useful review of older models and of modeling strategies specifically designed for the needs of transportation agencies.

2.2 Disaggregate models: methods

An alternative approach, known as *disaggregate* or *behavioral* travel-demand modeling, is now far more common for travel demand research. Made possible by micro data (data on individual decision-making units), this approach explains behavior directly at the level of a person, household, or firm. Disaggregate models are more efficient in their use of survey data when such data are available, and are based on a more satisfactory microeconomic theory of demand, a feature that is particularly useful when applying welfare economics. Most such models analyze choices among discrete rather than continuous alternatives and so are called *discrete-choice models*.[23]

2.2.1 Basic discrete-choice models

The most widely used theoretical foundation for these models is the additive random-utility model of McFadden (1974). Suppose a decision maker n facing discrete alternatives $j = 1, \ldots, J$ chooses the one that maximizes utility as given by

$$U_{jn} = V(z_{jn}, s_n; \beta) + \varepsilon_{jn}, \tag{2.10}$$

where $V(\cdot)$ is a function known as the *systematic utility*, z_{jn} is a vector of attributes of the alternatives as they apply to this decision maker, s_n is a vector of characteristics of the decision maker (effectively allowing different utility structures for different identifiable groups of decision makers), β is a vector of unknown parameters, and ε_{jn} is an unobservable component of utility which captures idiosyncratic preferences. U_{jn} and V are known as *conditional indirect utility* functions, since they are conditional on choice j and, just like the indirect utility function of standard consumer theory, may depend on income and prices and thus implicitly incorporate a budget constraint.

The choice is probabilistic because the measured variables do not include everything relevant to the individual's decision. This fact is represented by the random terms ε_{jn}. Once a functional form for V is specified, the model becomes complete by specifying a joint cumulative distribution function (cdf) for the random terms, $F(\varepsilon_{1n}, \ldots, \varepsilon_{Jn})$. Denoting $V(z_{jn}, s_n, \beta)$ by V_{jn}, the choice probability for alternative i is then

$$
\begin{aligned}
P_{in} &= \Pr[U_{in} > U_{jn} \text{ for all } j \neq i] \\
&= \Pr[\varepsilon_{jn} - \varepsilon_{in} < V_{in} - V_{jn} \text{ for all } j \neq i] \\
&= \int_{-\infty}^{\infty} F_i(V_{in} - V_{1n} + \varepsilon_{in}, \ldots, V_{in} - V_{jn} + \varepsilon_{in}) d\varepsilon_{in},
\end{aligned}
\tag{2.11}
$$

where F_i is the partial derivative of F with respect to its ith argument. F_i is thus the probability density function of ε_{in}, conditional on the inequalities in (2.1).

Suppose the cdf $F(\cdot)$ is multivariate normal. Then (2.11) is the *multinomial probit* model with general covariance structure. However, neither F nor F_i can be expressed in closed form; instead, equation (2.11) is usually written as a $(J - 1)$-dimensional integral of the normal density function. In the special case where the random terms are identically and independently distributed (iid) with the univariate normal distribution, F is the product of J

univariate normal cdfs, and we have the *iid probit* model, which still requires computation of a $(J-1)$-dimensional integral. For example, in the iid probit model for binary choice $(J=2)$, (2.11) becomes

$$P_{1n} = \Phi\left(\frac{V_{1n}-V_{2n}}{\sigma}\right), \tag{2.12}$$

where Φ is the cumulative standard normal distribution function (a one-dimensional integral) and σ is the standard deviation of $\varepsilon_{1n}-\varepsilon_{2n}$. In equation (2.12), σ cannot be distinguished empirically from the scale of utility, which is arbitrary; for example, doubling σ has the same effect as halving both V_1 and V_2. Hence it is conventional to normalize by setting $\sigma=1$.

The *logit* model (also known as multinomial logit or conditional logit) arises when the J random terms are iid with the *extreme-value distribution*, sometimes called the Gumbel, Weibull, or double-exponential distribution. This distribution is defined by

$$\Pr\left[\varepsilon_{jn}< x\right]= \exp\left(-e^{-\mu x}\right) \tag{2.13}$$

for all real numbers x, where μ is a scale parameter. Here the convention is to normalize by setting $\mu=1$. With this normalization, McFadden (1974) shows that the resulting probabilities calculated from (2.11) have the logit form:

$$P_{in} = \frac{\exp(V_{in})}{\sum\limits_{j=1}^{J}\exp(V_{jn})}. \tag{2.14}$$

This formula is easily seen to have the celebrated and restrictive property of *independence from irrelevant alternatives*: namely, that the odds ratio (P_{in}/P_{jn}) depends on the utilities V_{in} and V_{jn} but not on the utilities for any other alternatives. This property implies, for example, that adding a new alternative k (equivalent to increasing its systematic utility V_{kn} from $-\infty$ to some finite value) will not affect the relative proportions of people using previously existing alternatives. It also implies that for a given alternative k, the cross-elasticities $\partial\log P_{jn}/\partial\log V_{kn}$ are identical for all $j\neq k$: hence if the attractiveness of alternative k is increased, the probabilities of all the other alternatives $j\neq k$ will be reduced by identical percentages. These properties apply only to a group of consumers with a common value for V_{in}; they do not apply to heterogeneous populations.

The binary form of (2.14), *i.e.*, the form with $J=2$, is:

$$P_{1n} = \frac{1}{1+\exp[-(V_{1n}-V_{2n})]}.$$

If graphed as a function of $(V_{1n}-V_{2n})$, this equation looks quite similar to (2.12).

It is really the iid assumption – identically and independently distributed error terms – that is restrictive, whether or not it entails independence of irrelevant alternatives. Hence there is no basis for the widespread belief that iid probit is more general than logit. In fact, the logit and iid probit models have been found empirically to give virtually identical results when normalized comparably (Horowitz 1980).[24] Furthermore, both probit and logit may be generalized by defining non-iid distributions. In the probit case the generalization uses the multivariate normal distribution, whereas in the logit case it can take a number of forms to be discussed later.

As for the functional form of V, by far the most common is linear in unknown parameters β. More general forms such as Box-Cox and Box-Tukey transformations are studied by Gaudry and Wills (1978). Just as with regression analysis, V can be linear in *parameters* while still non-linear in *variables*, just by specifying new variables equal to non-linear functions of the original ones. For example, the utility (2.10) on mode i of a traveler n with wage w_n facing travel costs c_{in} and times T_{in} could be specified as:

$$V_{in}(c_{in}, T_{in}, w_n; \beta) = \beta_1 \cdot (c_{in}/w_n) + \beta_2 T_{in} + \beta_3 T_{in}^2. \tag{2.15}$$

This is non-linear in travel time and in wage rate. If we redefine z_{in} as the vector of all such combinations of the original variables,[25] then the linear-in-parameters specification is simply written as

$$V_{in} = \beta' z_{in}, \tag{2.16}$$

where β' is the transpose of column vector β.

2.2.2 Estimation

For a given model, data on actual choices, along with traits z_{jn}, can be used to estimate the unknown parameter vector β in (2.16) and to carry out statistical tests of the specification (*i.e.*, tests of whether the assumed functional form of V and the assumed error distribution are valid). Parameters are usually estimated by maximizing the log-likelihood function:

$$L(\beta) = \sum_{n=1}^{N} \sum_{i=1}^{J} d_{in} \log P_{in}(\beta), \tag{2.17}$$

where N is the sample size. In this equation, d_{in} is the choice variable, defined as 1 if decision-maker n chooses alternative i and 0 otherwise, and $P_{in}(\beta)$ is the choice probability. Not only does maximizing this function give us the *maximum-likelihood estimates* of parameters, often written as $\hat{\beta}$; the derivatives of L also provide information about the statistical uncertainty in $\hat{\beta}$, usually summarized as its *variance–covariance matrix*, denoted $\text{Var}(\hat{\beta})$. The diagonal elements of this matrix give the variances (*i.e.*, the squares of the standard deviations) of the individual parameters, while the off-diagonal elements give the covariances between pairs of parameters. This information is crucial to knowing how firm we can be in making quantitative statements about the parameters based on the particular data set used.

A correction to (2.17) is available for choice-based samples, *i.e.*, those in which the sampling frequencies depend on the choices made. Choice-based samples often are available for practical reasons, such as the convenience of conducting a mode-choice survey at train stations and bus stops. The correction simply multiplies each term in the second summation by the inverse of the sampling probability for that sample member (Manski and Lerman 1977). This correction does not, however, make efficient use of the information on aggregate mode shares that it requires; Imbens and Lancaster (1994) show how to incorporate aggregate information to improve efficiency.

Recent work has shown that demand functions built up from discrete-choice models at the individual consumer level can be estimated using data solely on aggregate market shares. Bresnahan, Stern and Trajtenberg (1997) provide a particularly clear exposition. Basically, they use an extension of the idea, described earlier in connection with regression analysis, of minimizing the sum of squared residuals. Recall that a residual is the discrepancy between an observed quantity (such as amount of a good consumed) and that predicted by the model at any particular set of parameters; it is those parameters that are adjusted to minimize the sum of squared residuals. In the treatment by Bresnahan, Stern and Trajtenberg, the sum of squared residuals is generalized to a quadratic form in the vector of residuals, a common procedure in econometric models. The innovation, derived from Berry (1994), is in constructing the residuals themselves, one for each alternative j; they are formed as the differences between the indirect utility V_j (as computed from the discrete-choice model at a trial set of parameter values) and the indirect utility δ_j that is implied by its observed market share. (The authors assume that the discrete-choice model contains no variables describing characteristics of consumers, which enables us to omit subscript n from indirect utility.) The values of δ_j used in this procedure are determined (again for a given set of trial parameters) by solving the equation for probabilities, *e.g.*, (2.14), so as to give each indirect utility V_j as a function of the probabilities P_i ($i = 1, \ldots, J$); the solution is interpreted as giving δ_j in terms of the observed market shares.[26]

One of the major attractions of logit is the computational simplicity of its log-likelihood function, due to taking the logarithm of the numerator in equation (2.14). With V linear in β, the logit log-likelihood function is globally concave in β, so finding a local maximum assures finding the global maximum. Fast computer routines to do this are widely available. In contrast, computing the log-likelihood function for multinomial probit with J alternatives entails computing for each member of the sample the $(J-1)$-dimensional integral implicit in equation (2.11). This has generally proven difficult for J larger than 3 or 4, despite the development of computational-intensive simulation methods (Train 2003).

It is possible that the likelihood function is unbounded in one of the coefficients, making it impossible to maximize. This happens if one includes a variable that is a perfect predictor of choice within the sample. For example, suppose one is predicting car ownership (yes or no) and wants to include among variables s_n in (2.10) a dummy variable for high income. If it happens that within the sample everyone with high income owns a car, the likelihood function increases without limit in the coefficient of this dummy variable. The problem is that income does too good a job as an explanatory variable: within this data set, the model exuberantly declares high income to make the alternative of owning a car infinitely desirable relative to not owning one. We know of course that this is not true and that a larger sample would contain counter-examples – even in the US, 1.5% of the highest-income households owned no car in 2001 (Pucher and Renne 2003). Given the sample we have, we might solve the problem by respecifying the model with more broadly defined income groups or more narrowly defined alternatives. Alternatively, we could postulate a *linear probability model*, in which probability rather than utility is a linear function of coefficients; despite certain statistical disadvantages, this model is able to measure the coefficient in question (Caudill 1988) because there is a limit to how strongly income can affect probability.

2.2.3 *Interpreting coefficient estimates*

It is useful for interpreting empirical results to note that a change in $\beta'z_{in}$ in (2.16) by an amount of ±1 increases or decreases the relative odds of alternative i, compared to each other alternative, by a factor $\exp(1) = 2.72$. Thus a quick gauge of the behavioral significance of any particular variable can be obtained by considering the size of typical variations in that variable, multiplied by its relevant coefficient—if the result is on the order of 1.0 or larger, such variations have large effects on the relative odds. In fact some authors prefer to provide this information by listing, in addition to or instead of the coefficient estimates, the marginal effect of a specified change in the independent variable on the probabilities; this marginal effect, however, depends on the values of the variables.

The parameter vector may contain *alternative-specific constants* for one or more alternatives i. That is, the systematic utility may be of the form

$$V_{in} = \alpha_i + \beta'z_{in}. \tag{2.18}$$

Since only utility differences matter, at least one of the alternative-specific constants α_i must be normalized, usually to zero: that alternative then serves as a "base alternative" for comparisons.

The constant α_i may be interpreted as the average utility of the unobserved characteristics of the ith alternative, relative to the base alternative. In a sense, specifying these constants is admitting the inadequacy of variables z_{in} to explain choice; hence the constants' estimated values are especially likely to reflect circumstances of a particular sample rather than universal behavior. The use of alternative-specific constants also makes it impossible to forecast the result of adding a new alternative, unless there is some basis for a guess as to what its alternative-specific constant would be. Quandt and Baumol (1966) coined the term "abstract mode" to indicate the desire to describe a travel mode entirely by its objective characteristics, rather than relying on alternative-specific constants. In practice, however, this goal is rarely achieved.

Equation (2.18) is really a special case of (2.16) in which one or more of the variables Z are *alternative-specific dummy variables*, D^k, defined by $D^k_{jn} = 1$ if $j = k$ and 0 otherwise (for each $j = 1, ..., J$). (Such a variable does not depend on n.) In this notation, parameter α_i in (2.18) is viewed as the coefficient of variable D^i included among the z variables in (2.16). Such dummy variables can also be interacted with (*i.e.*, multiplied by) any other variable, making it possible for the latter variable to affect utility in a different way for each alternative. All such variables and interactions may be included in z, and their coefficients in β, thus allowing (2.16) still to represent the linear-in-parameters specification.

The most economically meaningful quantities obtained from estimating a discrete-choice model are often ratios of coefficients, which represent marginal rates of substitution – that is, the rates at which two variables can be traded against each other without changing utility. By interacting the variables of interest with socioeconomic characteristics or alternative-specific constants, these ratios can be specified quite flexibly so as to vary in a manner thought to be *a priori* plausible.

A particularly important example is the marginal rate of substitution between time and money in the conditional indirect utility function, often called the *value of travel-time savings*, or *value of time* for short. It represents the monetary value that the traveler places on time savings, and is very important in evaluating the benefits of transportation improvements whose primary effects are to improve people's mobility. The value of time in the model (2.15) is

$$(v_T)_{in} \equiv -\left(\frac{dc_{in}}{dT_{in}}\right)_{V_{in}} \equiv \frac{\partial V_{in}/\partial T_{in}}{\partial V_{in}/\partial c_{in}} = \left(\frac{\beta_2 + 2\beta_3 T_{in}}{\beta_1}\right) \cdot w_n, \tag{2.19}$$

which varies across individuals since it depends on w_n and T_{in}. We emphasize that this is a marginal concept: it is a measure, per unit of time, that applies to small time savings. For a larger time saving, say from T_{in}^0 to T_{in}^1, the total value to travelers would be the integral of (2.19), which can be computed analytically:

$$\int_{T_{in}^0}^{T_{in}^1} (v_T)_{in} \, dT = \left(\frac{\beta_2 + 2\beta_3 \bar{T}}{\beta_1}\right) \cdot w_n \cdot \Delta T,$$

where $\bar{T} = (T_{in}^0 + T_{in}^1)/2$ and $\Delta T = T_{in}^1 - T_{in}^0$. Thus, in this example, the value of a finite time saving is computed as the time saving multiplied by the marginal value of time, with the latter evaluated at the average trip duration before and after the change.

As a more complex example, suppose we extend equation (2.15) by adding alternative-specific dummies, both separately (with coefficients α_i) and interacted with travel time (with coefficients γ_i):

$$V_{in} = \alpha_i + \beta_1 \cdot (c_{in}/w_n) + \beta_2 T_{in} + \beta_3 T_{in}^2 + \gamma_i T_{in}, \tag{2.20}$$

where one of the α_i and one of the γ_i are normalized to zero. This yields the following value of time applicable when individual n chooses alternative i:

$$(v_T)_{in} = \left(\frac{\beta_2 + 2\beta_3 T_{in} + \gamma_i}{\beta_1}\right) \cdot w_n. \tag{2.21}$$

Now the value of time varies across modes even with identical travel times, due to the presence of γ_i. There is a danger, however, in interpreting such a model. What appears to be variation in value of time across modes may just reflect selection bias: people who, for reasons we cannot observe, have high values of time will tend to self-select onto the faster modes (MVA Consultancy *et al.* 1987, pp. 90–92). This possibility can be modeled explicitly using a random-coefficient model, described later in this chapter.

Confidence bounds for a ratio of coefficients, or for more complex functions of coefficients, can be estimated by standard approximations for transformations of normal variates. Specifically, if vector β is asymptotically normally distributed (as sample size increases) with mean b and variance–covariance matrix Σ, then a function $f(\beta - b)$ is asymptotically normally distributed with mean zero and variance-covariance matrix $(\nabla f)\Sigma(\nabla f)'$, where ∇f is the vector of partial derivatives of f.[27] A more accurate estimate may be obtained by taking repeated random draws from the probability distribution of β (that distribution being estimated along with β itself), and then examining the values of f corresponding to these draws. As an example, the 5th and 95th percentile values of those values of f define a 90% confidence interval for f.[28]

2.2.4 Data

Some of the most important variables for travel demand modeling are determined endogenously within a larger model of which the demand model is just one component. The most common example is that travel times depend on congestion, which depends on the amount of travel, which depends on travel times. Thus the application of a travel demand model may require a process of *equilibration* in which a solution is sought to a set of simultaneous relationships. An elegant formulation of supply–demand equilibration on a congested network is provided in the remarkable study by Beckmann, McGuire and Winsten (1956). Boyce, Mahmassani and Nagurney (2005) provide a readable review of its history and subsequent impact.

With aggregate data, the endogeneity of travel characteristics is an important issue for obtaining valid statistical estimates of demand parameters. In most cases, endogeneity can be ignored when using disaggregate data because, from the point of view of individual decision-making, the travel environment does not depend appreciably on that one individual's decisions. (See Section 2.4.5 for an important exception.) Nevertheless, measuring the values of attributes z_{in}, which typically vary by alternative, is more difficult than it may first appear. How does one know the attributes that a traveler would have encountered on an alternative that was not in fact used?

One possibility is to use objective estimates, such as the *engineering values* produced by network models of the transportation system. Another is to use *reported values* obtained directly from survey respondents. Each is subject to problems. Reported values measure people's perceptions of travel conditions, which, even for alternatives they choose regularly, may be quite different from the measures employed in policy analysis or forecasting. People know even less about alternatives they do not choose. Hence even if reported values accurately measure the perceptions that determine choice, the resulting models cannot be used for prediction unless one can predict how a given change will alter those perceptions. Worse still, the reports may be systematically biased so as to justify the choice, thereby exaggerating the advantages of the alternative chosen and the disadvantages of other alternatives. The study by MVA Consultancy *et al.* (1987, pp. 159–63) finds such bias to be severe in a study of the Tyne River crossing in England. In this case the measured values for explanatory variables are endogenous to the choice, which makes the estimated model appear to fit very well (a typical finding for studies using reported values) but which renders it useless for prediction.

Objective estimates of travel attributes, on the other hand, may be very expensive and not necessarily accurate. Even something as simple as the travel time for driving on a particular highway segment at a particular time of day is quite difficult to ascertain. Measuring the day-to-day variability of that travel time is even more difficult. Three recent studies in California have accomplished this, one by applying sophisticated algorithms to data from loop detectors placed in the highway and two by using the floating-car method, in which a vehicle with a stopwatch is driven so as to blend in with the traffic stream.[29]

Ideally, one might formulate a model in which perceived attributes and actual choice are jointly determined, each influencing the other and both influenced by objective attributes and personal characteristics. This type of model most faithfully replicates the actual decision process. However, it is doubtful that the results would be worth the extra complexity unless there is inherent interest in perception formation for marketing purposes. For purposes of transportation planning, we care mainly about the relationship between objective values and actual choices. A model limited to this relationship may be interpreted as the reduced form of a more complex model including perceptions, so it is theoretically valid even though perception formation is only implicit. Hence the most fruitful expenditure of research effort is usually on finding ways to measure objective values as accurately as possible.

In a large sample, a cheaper way to compute objective values may be to assign values for a given alternative according to averages reported by people in the sample in similar circumstances who use that alternative. While subject to some inaccuracy, this at least eliminates endogeneity bias by using an identical procedure to assign values to chosen and unchosen alternatives.

The type of data described thus far measures *revealed preference* (RP) information, that reflected in actual choices. There is growing interest in using *stated preference* (SP) data, based on responses to hypothetical situations (Hensher 1994). SP data permit more control over the ranges of and correlations among the independent variables by applying an appropriate experimental design (see, for example, Louviere, Hensher and Swait 2000). If administered in interviews using a portable computer, the questions posed can be adapted to information about the respondent collected in an earlier portion of the survey – as, for example, in the study of freight mode choice in India by Shinghal and Fowkes (2002). SP surveys also can elicit information about potential travel options not now available. It is still an open question, however, how accurately they describe what people really do.

It is possible to combine data from both revealed and stated preferences in a single estimation procedure in order to take advantage of the strengths of each (Ben-Akiva and Morikawa 1990; Louviere and Hensher 2001). As long as observations are independent of each other, the log-likelihood functions simply add. To prevent SP survey bias from contaminating inferences from RP, or more generally just to account for differences in surveys, it is recommended to estimate certain parameters separately in the two portions of the data: the scale factors μ for the two parts of the sample (with one but not both normalized), any alternative-specific constants (see next subsection), and any critical behavioral coefficients that may differ. For example, in the logit model of (2.14) and (2.18), one might constrain all parameters to be the same for RP and SP observations except for the scale, alternative-specific constants, and the first variable z_{1in}. Letting $\beta'_2 z_{2in}$ represent the rest of $\beta' z_{in}$, adding superscripts for the parameters assumed distinct in the two data subsamples, and normalizing the RP scale parameter to one, the log-likelihood function (2.17) becomes the following:

$$L(\alpha,\beta,\mu^{SP}) = \sum_{n \in RP} \sum_{i=1}^{J} d_{in} \left\{ \alpha_i^{RP} + \beta_1^{RP} z_{1in} + \beta'_2 z_{2in} - \log \sum_{j=1}^{J} \exp(\alpha_j^{RP} + \beta_1^{RP} z_{1jn} + \beta'_2 z_{2jn}) \right\}$$

$$+ \sum_{n \in SP} \sum_{i=1}^{J} d_{in} \left\{ \mu^{SP} \cdot (\alpha_i^{SP} + \beta_1^{SP} z_{1in} + \beta'_2 z_{2in}) - \log \sum_{j=1}^{J} \exp \left[\mu^{SP} \cdot (\alpha_j^{SP} + \beta_1^{SP} z_{1jn} + \beta'_2 z_{2jn}) \right] \right\},$$

where $(\alpha, \beta, \mu^{SP})$ denotes the entire set of parameters shown on the right-hand side (excluding α_1^{RP} and α_1^{SP}, which can be normalized to zero). This expression is not as complicated as it looks: the first term in curly brackets is just the logarithm of the logit probability (2.14) for RP observations, while the second is the same thing for SP observations except utility V_{in} is multiplied by scale factor μ^{SP}.

Discrete-choice modeling of travel demand has mostly taken advantage of data from large and expensive transportation surveys. Deaton (1985) shows that it can also be used with household-expenditure surveys, which are often conducted for other purposes and are frequently available in developing nations.

2.2.5 *Randomness, scale of utility, and measures of benefit*

The variance of the random utility term in equation (2.10) reflects randomness in behavior of individuals or, more likely, heterogeneity among observationally identical individuals. Hence it plays a key role in determining how sensitive travel behavior is to observable quantities such as price, service quality, and demographic traits. Little randomness implies a nearly deterministic model, one in which behavior suddenly changes at some crucial switching point (for example, when transit service becomes as fast as a car). Conversely, if there is a lot of randomness, behavior changes only gradually as the values of independent variables are varied.

When the variance of the random component is normalized, however, the degree of randomness becomes represented by the inverse of the scale of the systematic utility function. For example, in the logit model (2.14), suppose systematic utility is linear in parameter vector β as in (2.16). If all the elements of β are small in magnitude, the corresponding variables have little effect on probabilities so choices are dominated by randomness. If the elements of β are large, most of the variation in choice behavior is explained by variation in observable variables.

Randomness in individual behavior can also be viewed as producing variety, or *entropy*, in aggregate behavior. Indeed, it can be measured by the entropy-like quantity $-\Sigma_n\Sigma_j P_{jn} \log P_{jn}$, which is larger when the choice probability is divided evenly among the alternatives than when one alternative is very likely and others very unlikely. Anderson, de Palma and Thisse (1988) show that the aggregate logit model can be derived by maximizing a utility function for a representative traveler that includes an entropy term, subject to a consistency constraint on aggregate choice shares. Thus entropy is a link between aggregate and disaggregate models: at the aggregate level we can say the system tends to favor entropy or that a representative consumer craves variety, whereas at the disaggregate level we represent the same phenomenon as randomness in utility.

It is sometimes useful to have a measure of the overall desirability of the choice set being offered to a decision maker. Such a measure must account both for the utility of the individual choices being offered and for the variety of choices offered. The value of variety is directly related to randomness because both arise from unobserved idiosyncrasies in preferences. If choice were deterministic, *i.e.*, determined solely by the ranking of V_{in} across alternatives i, the decision maker would care only about the traits of the best alternative; improving or offering inferior alternatives would have no value. But with random utilities, there is some chance that an alternative with a low value of V_{in} will nevertheless be chosen; so it is desirable for such an alternative to be offered and to be made as attractive as possible. A natural measure of the desirability of choice set J is the expected maximum utility of that set, which for the logit model has the convenient form:

$$\mathrm{E}\max_j(V_j + \varepsilon_j) = \mu^{-1} \log \sum_{j=1}^{J} \exp(\mu V_j) + \gamma, \tag{2.22}$$

where $\gamma = 0.5772$ is Euler's constant (it accounts for the non-zero mean of the error terms ε_j in the standard normalization). Here we have retained the parameter μ from (2.13), rather than normalizing it, to make clear how randomness affects expected utility. When the amount of randomness is small (large μ), the summation on the right-hand side is dominated by its largest term (let's denote its index by j^*); expected utility is then approximately

$\mu^{-1} \cdot \log[\exp(\mu V_{j*})] = V_{j*}$, the utility of the dominating alternative. When randomness dominates (small μ), all terms contribute more or less equally (let's denote their average utility value by V); then expected utility is approximately $\mu^{-1} \cdot \log[J \cdot \exp(\mu V)] = V + \mu^{-1} \cdot \log(J)$, which is the average utility plus a term reflecting the desirability of having many choices.

Expected utility is, naturally enough, directly related to measures of consumer welfare. Small and Rosen (1981) show that provided price is included among the variables in V_{jn}, changes in aggregate consumer surplus (the area to the left of the demand curve and above the current price)[30] are appropriate measures of consumer welfare even when the demand function is generated by a set of individuals making discrete choices. For a set of ω_n individuals characterized by systematic utilities V_{jn}, changes in consumer surplus are proportional to changes in this expected maximum utility. The proportionality constant is ω_n divided by λ_n, the marginal utility of income; thus a useful welfare measure for such a set of individuals, with normalization $\mu = 1$, is:

$$W = \frac{\omega_n}{\lambda_n} \log \sum_{j=1}^{J} \exp(V_{jn}), \tag{2.23}$$

a formula also derived by Williams (1977). (The constant γ drops out of welfare comparisons so is omitted.) Because portions of the utility V_i that are common to all alternatives cannot be estimated from the choice model, λ_n cannot be estimated directly. However, if a price or cost variable c is included in the specification, λ_n can be determined from Roy's Identity (2.6):

$$\lambda_n = -\frac{1}{x_{jn}} \cdot \frac{\partial V_{jn}}{\partial c_{jn}}, \tag{2.24}$$

where x_{jn} is consumption of good j conditional on choosing it among the discrete alternatives.[31] In the case of commuting-mode choice, for example, x_{jn} is just the individual's number of work trips per year (assuming income and hence welfare are measured in annual units). Expression (2.24) is valid provided that its right-hand-side is independent of j; when it is not, tractable approximations are available (Chattopadhyay 2001).

There is an important condition for the validity of (2.23), which is that any *income effects* in the response of transportation demand be small. Changes in transportation costs or service quality exert most of their influence directly: travelers respond by shifting toward or away from the particular choices that have become more or less desirable. However, there is also a somewhat indirect effect caused by travelers being made more or less well off overall in terms of their standard of living. For example, suppose the price of gasoline rises by 50%, and gasoline accounts for 2% of total expenditures by a particular group of people. The price increase makes activities that use gasoline somewhat less attractive than before, and so tilts consumers toward choosing fewer of them. (They might travel less, or they might buy smaller cars with fewer energy-consuming options.) This is sometimes expressed as a *compensated price elasticity*: the responsiveness to price they would exhibit if their incomes were supplemented so as to leave them just as well off as before. But presuming they are not so compensated, the price increase makes them worse off overall by reducing their discretionary income for other consumption. As a first-order approximation, in the above example people would behave as though they had 1% less discretionary income (50% of 2%).

If gasoline is a *normal* good – one whose consumption increases with income – then this indirect effect also reduces gasoline consumption, by an amount proportional to the product of the income elasticity of gasoline and the fraction of income spent on gasoline.[32] This indirect effect is called an *income effect*. The combined direct and indirect effects may be expressed as the total price elasticity, sometimes called the *uncompensated price elasticity* to distinguish it from the compensated elasticity. For normal goods the two effects reinforce each other, so the uncompensated price elasticity is larger in magnitude than the compensated one.[33]

Equation (2.23) is valid when λ_n, the marginal income of utility, is the same before and after the change under consideration. This condition is as assured as a close approximation if any income effects of the change are small – as is likely for transportation analysis because the fraction of income spent on any one transportation activity is usually quite small.

2.2.6 Aggregation and forecasting

Once we have estimated a disaggregate travel-demand model, we face the question of how to predict aggregate quantities such as total transit ridership or total travel flows between zones. Ben-Akiva and Lerman (1985, Chapter 6) discuss several methods.

The most straightforward and common is *sample enumeration*. A sample of consumers is drawn, each assumed to represent a subpopulation with identical observable characteristics. (The estimation sample itself may satisfy this criterion and hence be usable as an enumeration sample.) Each individual's choice probabilities, computed using the estimated parameters, predict the shares of that subpopulation choosing the various alternatives. These predictions can then simply be added, weighting each sample member according to the corresponding subpopulation size – just as we did using weight ω_n when computing welfare changes in (2.23). Standard deviations of forecast values can be estimated by Monte Carlo simulation methods.

One can simulate the effects of a policy by determining how it changes the values of independent variables for each sample member, and recomputing the predicted probabilities accordingly. Doing so requires that these variables be explicitly included in the model. For example, to simulate the effect of better schedule coordination at transfer points on a transit system, the model must include a variable for waiting time at the transfer points. Such a specification is called *policy-sensitive*, and its absence in earlier aggregate models was one of the main objections to the traditional travel-demand modeling framework. The ability to examine complex policies by computing their effects on an enumeration sample is one of the major advantages of disaggregate models.

Aggregate forecasts may display a sensitivity to policy variables that is quite different from a naïve calculation based on a representative individual. For example, suppose the choice between travel by automobile (alternative 1) and bus (alternative 2) is determined by a logit model with utilities given by equation (2.15) with $\beta_3 = 0$. Then the probability of choosing bus travel is:

$$P_{2n} = \frac{1}{1 + \exp[(\beta_1/w_n) \cdot (c_{1n} - c_{2n}) + \beta_2 \cdot (T_{1n} - T_{2n})]}. \tag{2.25}$$

Suppose everyone's bus fare is c_2 and everyone's wage is w. Then

$$\frac{\partial P_{2n}}{\partial c_2} = (\beta_1/w) \cdot P_{2n} \cdot (1 - P_{2n}). \tag{2.26}$$

Now suppose half the population has conditions favorable to bus travel, such that $P_{2n} = 0.9$; whereas the other half has $P_{2n} = 0.1$. Aggregate bus share is then 0.5. Applying (2.26) to each half of the population, we see that the rate of change of aggregate bus share with respect to bus fare is $(\beta_1/w) [\frac{1}{2}(0.9)(0.1) + \frac{1}{2}(0.1)(0.9)] = 0.09 (\beta_1/w)$. But if we were to apply (2.26) as though there were a single representative traveler with $P_2 = 0.5$, we would get $(\beta_1/w)(0.5)(0.5) = 0.25(\beta_1/w)$, more than twice the true value. Again, the existence of variety reduces the actual sensitivity to changes in independent variables, in this case because there are only a few travelers (those with extreme values of $\varepsilon_{1n} - \varepsilon_{2n}$) who have a close enough decision to be affected.

McFadden and Reid (1976) derive a more formal result illustrating this phenomenon in the case of a binary probit model where the independent variables are normally distributed in the population. They show that if a single individual's choice probability (2.12) is written in the form $P_1 = \Phi(\beta'z)$, then the expected aggregate share is

$$\bar{P}_1 = \Phi\left(\frac{\beta'\bar{z}}{\sqrt{1+\sigma^2}}\right), \tag{2.27}$$

where $\bar{z}$ and σ^2 are the average of z and the variance of $\beta'z$, respectively, within the population. Once again, the existence of population variance reduces policy sensitivity and causes the naïve calculation using an average traveler (equivalent to setting $\sigma = 0$) to overestimate that sensitivity.

Equation (2.27) illustrates a danger in using aggregate models for policy forecasts. If an aggregate probit model fitting $\bar{P}_1$ to $\bar{z}$ were estimated, its coefficients would correspond to $\beta/\sqrt{(1+\sigma^2)}$. If a policy being investigated changed σ, these coefficients would no longer accurately represent behavior under the new policy.

2.2.7 Specification

Like most applied statistical work, travel demand analysis requires balancing completeness against tractability. A model that includes every relevant influence on behavior may require too much data to estimate with adequate precision, or it may be too complex to serve as a practical guide to policy analysis. A related problem, also common to most empirical work, is that the statistical properties of the model, such as standard errors of estimated coefficients, are valid only when the model's basic assumptions are known in advance to be correct. But in practice the researcher normally chooses a model's specification (*i.e.,* its functional form and set of included variables) using guidance from the same data as those from which its parameters are estimated.

A good way to handle both problems is to base empirical models on an explicit behavioral theory. Rather than try out dozens of specifications to see what fits, one gives preference to relationships that are predicted by a plausible theory. For example, a specification like (2.15) would be chosen if there is good theoretical reason to think the value of time is proportional to the wage rate – a question explored later in this chapter. We discuss some other specification issues in connection with an example in Section 2.3.3.

Bayesian methods offer a more formal approach to using prior information or judgments when specifying empirical models. Instead of all-or-nothing decisions about model structure, they allow one to explicitly describe prior uncertainty and to calculate the manner in which prior beliefs need to be modified in light of the data. Such methods have recently been developed for parameter estimation in discrete-choice models (Train 2003, Chapter 12) and for selection among competing model specifications (Berger and Pericchi 2001).

One of the goals of disaggregate travel-demand modeling is to describe behavioral tendencies that are reasonably general. This would enable a model estimated in one time and place to be used for another. The progress toward this goal of *transferability* has been disappointing, but some limited success has been achieved by making certain adjustments. Notably, the alternative-specific constants and the scale of the utility function are often found to be different in a new location, presumably because they reflect our degree of ignorance, which may vary from one setting to another. Such adjustments can be made relatively inexpensively by using limited data collection in a new location or, in the case of alternative-specific constants, just by adjusting them to match known aggregate choice shares (Koppelman and Rose 1985). The adjustment procedure is sometimes called calibration, and requires an iterative algorithm for matching the choice shares predicted by the model to observed shares; the match is exact so the algorithm is numerical rather than statistical.[34]

2.2.8 *Ordered and rank-ordered models*

Sometimes there is a natural ordering to the alternatives that can be exploited to guide specification. For example, suppose one wants to explain a household's choice among owning no vehicle, one vehicle, or two or more vehicles. It is perhaps plausible that there is a single index of propensity to own many vehicles, and that this index is determined in part by observable variables like household size and employment status.

In such a case, an *ordered response* model might be assumed. In this model, the choice of individual n is determined by the size of a "latent variable" $y_n^* = \beta' z_n + \varepsilon_n$, with choice j occurring if this latent variable falls in a particular interval $[\mu_{j-1}, \mu_j]$ of the real line, where $\mu_0 = -\infty$ and $\mu_J = \infty$. The interval boundaries $\mu_1, \ldots, \mu_{J-1}$ are estimated along with β, except that one of them can be normalized arbitrarily if $\beta' z_n$ contains a constant term. The probability of choice j is then

$$P_{jn} = \Pr[\mu_{j-1} < \beta' z_n + \varepsilon_n < \mu_j] = F(\mu_j - \beta' z_n) - F(\mu_{j-1} - \beta' z_n), \tag{2.28}$$

where $F(\cdot)$ is the cumulative distribution function assumed for ε_n. In the *ordered probit* model $F(\cdot)$ is standard normal, while in the *ordered logit* model it is logistic, *i.e.*, $F(x) = [1 + \exp(-x)]^{-1}$. Thus probabilities depend entirely on a single index, $\beta' z_n$, calculated for individual n. When this index is strongly positive, all the terms $F(\mu_j - \beta' z_n)$ are small except for the last, $F(\mu_J - \beta' z_n) = F(\infty) = 1$, so the most likely choice will be alternative J. When the index is strongly negative, the most likely choice will be alternative 1. At intermediate values it becomes more likely that alternatives between 1 and J will be chosen. Note that all the variables in this model are characteristics of individuals, not of the alternatives, and thus if the latter information is available this model cannot easily take advantage of it.

In some cases the alternatives are integers indicating the number of times some random event occurs. An example would be the number of trips per month by a given household to a particular destination. For such cases, a set of models based on Poisson and negative binomial regressions is available (Washington, Karlaftis and Mannering 2003, Chapter 10).

Sometimes information is available not only on the most preferred alternative, but on the individual's ranking of other alternatives. In this case, we effectively observe "choices" for numerous situations. Efficient use can be made of such data through the *rank-ordered logit* model.[35] In the case where a complete ranking of *J* alternatives is obtained, the probability formula for rank-ordered logit is a product of *J* logit probability formulas, one for each ranked alternative, giving the probability of choosing that alternative from the set of itself and all lower-ranked alternatives. One may want to ignore the stated ordering among some low-ranked alternatives, or alternatively to estimate a separate scale factor for those choices, to allow for the possibility that a respondent pays less attention when answering questions about alternatives of little interest.

2.3 Disaggregate models: examples

Discrete-choice models have been estimated for nearly every conceivable travel decision, forming a body of research that cannot possibly be reviewed here.[36] In some cases, these models have been linked into large simultaneous systems requiring extensive computer simulation. An example is the system of models developed to analyze a proposal for congestion pricing in London (Bates *et al.* 1996).

In this section we present three very modest disaggregate models, each chosen for its compact representation of a behavioral factor that is central to urban transportation policy as analyzed in later chapters.

2.3.1 Mode choice

Kenneth Train (1978, 1980) and colleagues have developed a series of models explaining automobile ownership and commuting mode, estimated from survey data collected before and after the opening of the Bay Area Rapid Transit (BART) system in the San Francisco area. Here we present one of the simplest, explaining only mode choice: the "naïve model" reported by McFadden *et al.* (1977, pp. 121–23). It assumes choice among four modes: (1) auto alone, (2) bus with walk access, (3) bus with auto access, and (4) carpool (two or more occupants). The model's parameters are estimated from a sample of 771 commuters to San Francisco or Oakland who were surveyed prior to opening of the BART system.

Mode choice is explained by just three independent variables plus three alternative-specific constants. The three variables are: c_{in}/w_n, the round-trip variable cost (in US\$) of mode *i* for traveler *n* divided by the traveler's post-tax wage rate (in \$ per minute); T_{in}, the in-vehicle travel time (in minutes); and T_{in}^0, the out-of-vehicle travel time including walking, waiting, and transferring. Cost c_{in} includes parking, tolls, gasoline, and maintenance (Train 1980, p. 362). The estimated utility function is:

$$V = -0.0412 \cdot c/w - 0.0201 \cdot T - 0.0531 \cdot T^o - 0.89 \cdot D^1 - 1.78 \cdot D^3 - 2.15 \cdot D^4, \qquad (2.29)$$
$$(0.0054) \quad (0.0072) \quad (0.0070) \quad (0.26) \quad (0.24) \quad (0.25)$$

where the subscripts denoting mode and individual have been omitted, and standard errors of coefficient estimates are given in parentheses. Variables D^j are alternative-specific dummies.

This utility function is a simplification of (2.20) (with $\beta_3 = \gamma_i = 0$), except that travel time is broken into two components, T and T^o. Adapting (2.21), we see that the "value of time" for each of these two components is assumed to be proportional to the post-tax wage rate, the proportionality constant being the ratio of the corresponding time-coefficient to the coefficient of c/w. Hence the values of in-vehicle and out-of-vehicle time are 49% and 129% of the after-tax wage. The negative alternative-specific constants indicate that the hypothetical traveler facing equal times and operating costs by all four modes will prefer bus with walk access (mode 2, the base mode); this is probably because each of the other three modes requires owning an automobile, which entails fixed costs not included in variable c. The strongly negative constants for bus with auto access (mode 3) and carpool (mode 4) probably reflect unmeasured inconvenience associated with getting from car to bus stop and with arranging carpools.

The fit of Train's model's could undoubtedly be improved by including automobile ownership, perhaps interacted with $(D^1 + D^3 + D^4)$ to indicate a common effect on modes that use an automobile. However, there is good reason to exclude such a variable because it is endogenous – people choosing one of those modes for other reasons are likely to buy an extra car as a result. This in fact is demonstrated by the more complete model of Train (1980), which considers both choices simultaneously. The way to interpret (2.29), then, is as a "reduced-form" model that implicitly incorporates the automobile ownership decision. It is thus applicable to a time frame long enough for automobile ownership to adjust to changes in the variables included in the model.

More complete models typically aim to directly measure some of the preferences indicated here by coefficients of alternative-specific dummy variables. Currie (2005) compares results of 10 mode-choice studies that estimate a "transfer penalty," *i.e.*, that include a dummy variable indicating if a transfer was necessary (or how many were necessary) for the trip being explained. The studies measure the penalty in terms of the equivalent number of minutes of in-vehicle time, which means they are measuring the rate of substitution between additional travel time and the saving of one transfer. The average penalty ranges from eight minutes for transfers between subway lines to 22 minutes for transfers between bus lines, with intermediate values for transfers where one or both modes is suburban rail or light rail. Currie also compares alternative-specific constants, finding that "bus rapid transit," a type of bus service designed to mimic rail in convenience, does indeed achieve mode-specific constants comparable to those of rail.

2.3.2 Trip-scheduling choice

One of the key decisions affecting congestion is the timing or scheduling of work trips. There is now a substantial body of empirical work on this subject, reviewed by Mahmassani (2000).

Although the scheduling decision is inherently continuous, most authors model it as a discrete choice among time intervals. There are two reasons for this: survey responses are rounded off to a few even numbers, and disaggregate models can easily portray the complex manner in which travel time varies across possible schedules. Small (1982) estimates the choice among 12 possible five-minute intervals for work arrival time, using a set of auto commuters from the San Francisco Bay Area who have an official work-start time. The data set includes characteristics of the workers and a network-based engineering calculation of the travel time that each would encounter at each arrival time. Commuters are assumed to have full information; reliability of arrival is not considered except that the specification assumes the consumer needs to arrive *before* the work-start time in order to avoid a penalty.

The utility specification postulates a linear penalty for arriving early, on the assumption that time spent before work is relatively unproductive; and a much larger linear penalty for arriving late, on the assumption that employer sanctions take hold with gradually increasing severity. Define *schedule delay*, S_D, as the difference (in minutes, rounded to nearest five minutes) between the arrival time represented by a given alternative and the official work-start time. Define "Schedule Delay Late," *SDL*, as Max$\{S_D, 0\}$ and "Schedule Delay Early," *SDE*, as Max$\{-S_D, 0\}$. Define a "late dummy," *DL*, equal to one for the on-time and all later alternatives and equal to 0 for the early alternatives. Define *T* as the travel time (in minutes) encountered at each alternative.

The utility function estimated by Small (1982, Table 2, Model 1), with estimated standard errors in parentheses, is:

$$V = -0.106 \cdot T - 0.065 \cdot SDE - 0.254 \cdot SDL - 0.58 \cdot DL. \qquad (2.30)$$
$$\quad (0.038) \quad (0.007) \quad\quad (0.030) \quad\quad (0.21)$$

Here we exclude two variables used by Small to represent a tendency of respondents to round off answers to the nearest 10 or 15 minutes. More complex models are also estimated, in which the various penalties are non-linear or depend upon such factors as the worker's family status, occupation, car occupancy, and stated work-hour flexibility.

Figure 2.1 shows utility function (2.30), divided by the coefficient of travel time. The marginal rates of substitution indicate that the commuter is willing to suffer an extra 0.61 minutes of congestion to reduce the amount of early arrival by one minute;[37] and 2.40 minutes of congestion to reduce late arrival by one minute, plus an extra 5.47 minutes of congestion to avoid any of the just-on-time or late alternatives. These turn out to be key parameters in models, to be presented in the next chapter, which describe equilibrium when congestion occurs in the form of queuing behind a bottleneck. They also can be used to formulate models of traveler response to network unreliability, as we describe in Section 2.6.4.

The 12 alternatives in the choice model just described have a natural ordering in terms of chronological time; so why is the ordered response model not used? There are two reasons. First, as already noted, the ordered response model cannot take advantage of information that varies by alternative, such as travel time. Second, there is no plausible combination of

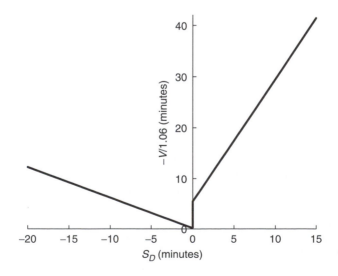

Figure 2.1 Disutility of schedule delay.

variables that would exert a monotonic influence on the time of day; rather, there are likely to be some variables that favor peak times, others that favor earlier or later times, others still that would affect the strength of preference for low travel times, and so forth. Such richness can be incorporated into the specification of a discrete-choice model based on random utility maximization, one of its great advantages.

2.3.3 Choice of free or express lanes

Lam and Small (2001) analyze data from commuters with an option of paying to travel in a set of express lanes on a very congested freeway, State Route 91 (SR91), in southern California. The toll depends on time of day and on car occupancy, both of which differ across respondents. Travel time also varies by time of day – fortunately in a manner not too highly correlated with the toll. The authors construct a measure of the unreliability of travel time by obtaining data on travel times across many different days, all at the same time of day. After some experimentation, they choose the median travel time (across days) as the best measure of travel time, and the difference between 90th and 50th percentile travel times (also across days) as the best measure of unreliability. This latter choice is based on the idea, documented in the previous subsection, that people are more averse to unexpected delays than to unexpected early arrivals.

The model explains a pair of related decisions: (a) whether to acquire an electronic toll-collection transponder (required for any use of the express lanes), and (b) which lanes to take on the day in question. A natural way to view these decisions is as a hierarchical set, with transponder choice governed by the potential benefits of express-lane travel and other factors. As we will see in the next section, a model known as "nested logit" has been developed precisely for this type of situation, and indeed Lam and Small estimate such a model. However, they obtain virtually identical results with a simpler "joint logit" model with three choice alternatives: (1) no transponder; (2) have a transponder but travel in the free lanes on the day in question; and (3) have a transponder and travel in the express lanes on the day in question. The model that Lam and Small estimate is:[38]

$$V = -0.862 \cdot D^{\text{tag}} + 0.0239 \cdot Inc \cdot D^{\text{tag}} - 0.766 \cdot ForLang \cdot D^{\text{tag}} - 0.789 \cdot D^3$$
$$\quad (0.411) \qquad (0.0058) \qquad\qquad (0.412) \qquad\qquad\qquad (0.853)$$
$$\quad - 0.357 \cdot c - 0.109 \cdot T - 0.159 \cdot R + 0.074 \cdot Male \cdot R + (\text{other terms}) \qquad (2.31)$$
$$\quad (0.138) \quad (0.056) \quad (0.048) \quad (0.046)$$

Here $D^{\text{tag}} \equiv D^2 + D^3$ is a composite of alternative-specific dummy variables for those choices involving a transponder, or "toll tag"; its negative coefficient presumably reflects the hassle and cost of obtaining one. Getting a transponder is apparently more attractive to people with high annual incomes (*Inc*, in $1000s per year) and less attractive to those speaking a foreign language (dummy variable *ForLang*). The statistical insignificance of the coefficient of D^3, an alternative-specific dummy for using the express lanes, suggests that the most important explanatory factors are included explicitly in the model.

The coefficients on per-person cost c, median travel time T, and unreliability R can be used to compute dollar values of time and reliability. Here we focus on two aspects of the resulting valuations. First, reliability is highly valued, achieving coefficients of similar magnitudes as travel time (recall that both variables are measured in units of time). Second, men seem to care less about reliability than women; their value is only 53% as high according to the point estimates,[39] although the difference (*i.e.*, the coefficient of $Male \cdot R$) is not quite statistically significant even at a 10% significance level.

This provides a good opportunity to consider how one chooses the list of variables to be included in a travel-demand model. In this case, the model is specified to yield a constant value of time and a constant value of reliability. Although theory suggests these values might vary by income or other factors, prior experimentation showed that including such variations (through interactions as in Section 2.3.1) resulted in imprecise and ambiguous results. However, the authors did find that those same factors strongly affect the alternative-specific constants (as determined by interacting these variables with alternative-specific dummies, part of "other terms" in the results shown here). Furthermore, the hierarchical nature of the decision process, already mentioned, suggests that certain alternatives are likely to fall within groups subject to common influences. Specifically, one might assume that certain unobserved factors would influence the extent to which the requirement to get a "toll tag," specific to two of the alternatives, is regarded as onerous. For example, the financial set-up arrangements for a toll tag might be of lesser significance to people with high incomes and of greater significance for people who have difficulty communicating in English – precisely what is indicated by the signs of the second and third coefficients in equation (2.31). The additional alternative-specific constant D^3 is included on the grounds that yet other unmeasured factors could affect the actual decision to pay for the express lanes. The variable $Male \cdot R$ is included because several studies of this particular toll facility have found women noticeably more likely to use the express lanes than men. This could be accounted for with a simple interaction variable $Male \cdot D^3$, but experimentation shows that the formulation shown here fits better. It is more specific about why men use the express lanes less often: apparently, the reason is less aversion to the unreliability of the free lanes. To be specific, reliability enters women's utility with the negative coefficient -0.159, whereas it enters men's utility with the more weakly negative coefficient $(-0.159 + 0.074) = -0.085$. One could attempt to be even more specific: perhaps the gender difference is due to differing responsibility for children; the authors investigated this by including a variable equal to R multiplied by a dummy for women with children, but they were unsuccessful in pinpointing the effect in this manner.[40]

Equation (2.31) also makes it easy to define a quantity used often in demand and cost analysis: the *generalized price* of a particular type of travel.[41] The idea is that if a traveler considers cost and other aspects of travel, such as time and reliability, in fixed proportions, it may be analytically useful to combine them into a single index denominated in money. The conditional indirect utility function, V in this example, summarizes the relative weights the traveler puts on these various aspects of travel. Thus in (2.31), the generalized price p for females would be defined as

$$p = c + \frac{0.109}{0.357} T + \frac{0.159}{0.357} R \qquad (2.32)$$

and the same for males except the coefficient of R would have numerator $(0.159 - 0.074)$. It is not hard to see that the first ratio of coefficients is just the value of time defined earlier (perhaps in different units); and the second will be defined later as the value of reliability. The concept of generalized price is most straightforward if the price is the same for everyone;

it is somewhat less straightforward in this example since there are two groups with two different generalized prices. It would be even more complicated in our mode-choice example of (2.29), where the value of time depends on the traveler's wage rate.

The generalized price could also incorporate more than one component of travel time, as in (2.29), and it could incorporate scheduling costs, as in (2.30). Note that (2.30) itself is insufficient to define a generalized price because it does not contain a cost variable. However, it gives the rates of tradeoff between schedule delay and time, and (2.31) gives the tradeoff between time and cost, so by combining the two studies we could extend (2.32) as follows:

$$p = c + \frac{0.109}{0.357} \cdot \left[T + \frac{0.065}{0.106} SDE + \frac{0.254}{0.106} SDL + \frac{0.58}{0.106} DL \right] + \frac{0.159}{0.357} R. \tag{2.33}$$

In Chapter 3, we will see that a generalized price based on those parts of (2.33) involving c, T, SDE, and SDL has been used extensively to analyze equilibria with travelers individually choosing their trip schedules in response to time-varying congestion.

2.4 Advanced discrete-choice modeling

2.4.1 Generalized extreme value models

Often it is implausible that the additive random utility components ε_j be independent, especially if important variables are omitted from the model's specification. This will make either logit or iid probit predict poorly.

A simple example is mode choice among automobile, bus transit, and rail transit. The two public-transit modes have many unmeasured attributes in common, such as occasional crowding. Suppose a traveler initially has available only auto ($j = 1$) and bus ($j = 2$), with equal systematic utilities V_j so that the choice probabilities are each one-half. Now suppose we want to predict the effects of adding a rail service ($j = 3$) with measurable characteristics identical to those for bus. The iid models would predict that all three modes would then have choice probabilities of one-third; in reality, the probability of choosing auto would most likely remain near one-half while the two transit modes divide the rest of the probability equally between them. The argument is even stronger if we imagine instead that the newly added mode is simply a bus of a different color: this is the famous "red bus, blue bus" example.

The probit model generalizes naturally, as already noted, by allowing the distribution function in equation (2.11) to be multivariate normal with an arbitrary variance-covariance matrix. It must be remembered that not all the elements of this matrix can be distinguished (*identified*, in econometric terminology) because, as already noted, it is only the $(J-1)$ utility differences that affect behavior.[42]

The logit model generalizes in a comparable manner, as shown by McFadden (1978, 1981). The distribution function is postulated to be *generalized extreme value* (GEV), given by

$$F(\varepsilon_1, \dots, \varepsilon_J) = \exp\left[-G(e^{-\varepsilon_1}, \dots, e^{-\varepsilon_J}) \right],$$

where G is a function satisfying certain technical conditions. With this distribution, the choice probabilities are of the form

$$P_i = \frac{e^{V_i} \cdot G_i(e^{V_1}, \ldots, e^{V_J})}{G(e^{V_1}, \ldots, e^{V_J})},$$ (2.34)

where G_i is the ith partial derivative of G. (The technical conditions assure that these probabilities add to one.) The expected maximum utility is

$$\mathrm{E} \max_j (V_j + \varepsilon_j) = \log G(e^{V_1}, \ldots, e^{V_J}) + \gamma,$$ (2.35)

where (again) γ is Euler's constant.[43] Logit is the special case $G(y_1, \ldots, y_J) = y_1 + \cdots + y_J$.

The best known GEV model, other than logit itself, is *nested logit*, also called *structured logit* or *tree logit* and first developed by Ben-Akiva (1974). McFadden (1981) discusses its theoretical roots and computational characteristics. In this model, certain groups of alternatives are postulated to have correlated random terms. This is accomplished by grouping the corresponding alternatives in G in a manner we can illustrate using the auto-bus-rail example, with auto the first alternative:

$$G(y_1, y_2, y_3) = y_1 + (y_2^{1/\rho} + y_3^{1/\rho})^\rho.$$ (2.36)

In this equation, ρ is a parameter between 0 and 1 that indicates the degree of dissimilarity between bus and rail; more precisely, $1 - \rho^2$ is the correlation between ε_1 and ε_2 (Daganzo and Kusnic 1993). The choice probability for this example, computed from (2.34), may be written:

$$P_i = P(B_{r(i)}) \cdot P(i \mid B_{r(i)})$$ (2.37)

$$P(B_r) = \frac{\exp(\rho \cdot I_r)}{\sum_{s=1}^{2} \exp(\rho \cdot I_s)}$$ (2.38)

$$P(i \mid B_r) = \frac{\exp(V_i/\rho)}{\sum_{j \in B_r} \exp(V_j/\rho)},$$ (2.39)

where $B_1 = \{1\}$ and $B_2 = \{2, 3\}$ are a partition of the choice set into groups; $r(i)$ indexes the group containing alternative i; and I_r denotes the *inclusive value* of set B_r, defined as the logarithm of the denominator of (2.39):

$$I_r = \log \sum_{j \in B_r} \exp(V_j/\rho).$$ (2.40)

When $\rho = 1$ in this model, ε_2 and ε_3 are independent and we have the logit model. As $\rho \downarrow 0$, ε_2 and ε_3 become perfectly correlated and we have an extreme form of the "red bus, blue bus" example, in which auto is pitted against the better (as measured by V_i) of the two transit alternatives; in this case $\rho I_1 = V_1$ and $\rho I_2 \to \max\{V_2, V_3\}$.

The model just described can be generalized to any partition $\{B_r, r = 1, \dots, R\}$ of alternatives, and each group B_r can have its own parameter ρ_r in equations (2.36)–(2.40), leading to the form:

$$G(y_1, \dots, y_J) = \sum_r \left(\sum_{j \in B_r} y_j^{1/\rho_r} \right)^{\rho_r}. \tag{2.41}$$

This is the general two-level nested logit model. It has choice probabilities (2.37)–(2.40) except that the index s in the denominator of (2.38) now runs from 1 to R. Like logit, it can be also derived from an entropy formulation (Brice 1989). The groups B_r can themselves be grouped, and those groupings further grouped, and so on, giving rise to even more general "tree structures" of three or more levels.

As in the logit model, the inclusive value is a summary measure of the overall desirability (expected maximum utility) of the relevant group of alternatives. This fact gives the "upper-level" probability (2.38) a natural interpretation as a choice among groups, taking the logit form with I_r playing the role of the independent variable and ρ_r its coefficient. Thus, for example, in a destination-choice model the inclusive value of a set of shopping destinations (from a given origin) can serve as a measure of accessibility of that origin to shopping (Ben-Akiva and Lerman 1979). The welfare measure for a representative individual following the two-level nested logit model is, from (2.35), (2.40), and (2.41):

$$W = \frac{1}{\lambda} \log \sum_r \exp(\rho_r \cdot I_r), \tag{2.42}$$

where again λ is the marginal utility of income and the constant γ is omitted.

In nested logit, $\{B_r\}$ is an exhaustive partition of the choice set into mutually exclusive subsets. Therefore equation (2.39) is a true conditional probability, and the model can be estimated sequentially: first estimate the parameters (β/ρ) from (2.39), use them to form the inclusive values (2.40), then estimate ρ from (2.38). Each estimation step uses an ordinary logit log-likelihood function, so it can be carried out with a logit algorithm. However, this sequential method is not statistically efficient, nor does it produce consistent estimates of the standard errors of the coefficients. Several studies show that maximum-likelihood estimation, although computationally more difficult, gives more accurate results (Hensher 1986; Brownstone and Small 1989).[44]

Most other GEV models that have been studied generalize (2.41) by not requiring the subsets B_r to be mutually exclusive. Small (1987) defines subsets each encompassing two or more alternatives that lie close to each other on some ordering. Vovsha (1997) defines a *cross-nested logit* model with nests that can overlap in a general way and with alternatives that can belong to a nest in a partial sense, with weights to be estimated. Chu (1981) and Koppelman and Wen (2000) define a model in which the subsets B_r include all possible pairs of alternatives:

$$G(y_1, \dots, y_J) = \sum_{j=1}^{J-1} \sum_{k=j+1}^{J} \left(y_j^{1/\rho_{jk}} + y_k^{1/\rho_{jk}} \right)^{\rho_{jk}}. \tag{2.43}$$

This model, known as *paired combinatorial logit*, has error terms whose variance–covariance matrix contains the same number of estimable parameters as does multinomial probit with a general covariance structure (again, the arbitrary scale requires one more normalization); thus the two models can be expected to have comparable degrees of generality, although in practice paired combinatorial logit seems to be easier to estimate.

Nevertheless, estimation of GEV models is often difficult because of the highly non-linear manner in which ρ_r enters the equation for choice probabilities. When the true model is GEV but differs only moderately from logit, a reasonable approximation can be estimated using two steps of a standard logit estimation routine, a procedure that appears to be considerably more stable than maximum-likelihood estimation (Small 1994).

A different direction for generalizing the logit model is to maintain independence between error terms while allowing each error term to have a unique variance. This is the heteroscedastic extreme value model of Bhat (1995); it is a random-utility model but not in the GEV class, and its probabilities cannot be written in closed form so require numerical integration.[45]

2.4.2 Combined discrete and continuous choice

In many situations, the choice among discrete alternatives is made simultaneously with some related continuous quantity. For example, a household's choice of type of automobile is closely intertwined with its choice of how much to drive. One can formulate an equation to explain usage, conditional on ownership, but it is subject to *sample selection bias* (Heckman 1979). To illustrate, suppose that people who drive a lot tend to select themselves into the category of owners of nice cars; the conditional model would overstate the independent effect of nice cars on driving by ignoring this reverse causality (a form of endogeneity).[46] A variety of methods are available to remove this bias.

The essence of the problem can be illustrated within an example of binary choice: that of owning a new or used automobile, denoted $j = 1$ or 2. Each type of car has a fixed measurable quality level Q_j that we can assume is higher for new cars, *i.e.*, $Q_1 > Q_2$. For example, Q could be the number of safety features offered from a particular list, or simply an alternative-specific dummy variable equal to 1 for a new car. Let us suppose that the decision of how much to drive depends on car quality Q, income Y, and other explanatory variables X as follows:

$$x = \beta_X X + \beta_Q Q + \beta_Y Y + u, \tag{2.44}$$

where u is a random error term. For simplicity we have omitted the subscript n denoting the individual in the sample. Car quality can be written in terms of the choice variable d_{1n} defined earlier, as follows (again omitting subscript n):

$$Q = d_1 Q_1 + (1 - d_1) Q_2. \tag{2.45}$$

Substituting (2.45) into (2.44) makes explicit the dependence of the usage decision (x) on the ownership decision (d_1).

Suppose also that the ownership decision (which type of car to own) depends on some set of observable variables Z, which might include Y, some elements of X, and/or the quality difference $(Q_1 - Q_2)$:

$$d_1 = 1 \quad \text{if } U_1 > U_2, \ 0 \text{ otherwise};$$
$$U_1 - U_2 = \beta_Z' Z + \varepsilon. \tag{2.46}$$

This equation defines a binary probit model if ε is assumed normal, binary logit if ε is assumed logistic.

Selection bias is present if u and ε are correlated, which is likely because unobservable factors may affect both usage and the relative desirability of a new car. (An example of such a factor is how much this individual likes listening to a high-quality car stereo.) If u is correlated with ε, it is also correlated with the car-type indicator d_1, via (2.46), and therefore with car quality Q, via (2.45). This biases the estimated coefficients in (2.44) – especially that of β_Q, – because Q is an explanatory variable for usage and thus needs to be uncorrelated with the error term for usage.

If we can find an exogenous proxy for Q, we can use it instead of Q in estimating (2.44) and solve the problem. This can be accomplished using the following two-step procedure proposed by Heckman (1979).

Step 1 consists of estimating (2.46). Its explanatory variables are presumed exogenous so there is no bias at this stage. From the estimated coefficient vector $\hat{\beta}_Z$, we can compute a predicted probability $\hat{P}_1$ of choosing a new car, equal to $\Phi(\hat{\beta}_Z' Z)$ if the model is probit or $[1 + \exp(-\hat{\beta}_Z' Z)]^{-1}$ if the model is logit.

Step 2 consists of estimating a variant of (2.44) that is purged of endogeneity. There are two alternative strategies for doing this:

Step 2 Version (a): replace Q by an exogenous predictor $\hat{Q}$
We look for an unbiased estimate of Q that does not use the observed ownership choice, d_1, as does (2.45). There are at least three possibilities, which are Methods II, I, and III, respectively, of Train (1986, p. 90):

(i)   Compute $\hat{Q}$ as $E(Q) \equiv \hat{P}_1 \cdot Q_1 + (1 - \hat{P}_1) \cdot Q_2$.
(ii) Compute $\hat{Q}$ as the predicted value from an auxiliary regression of observed Q on all the exogenous variables of the system, namely X, Y, and Z. (This method does not actually require that Step 1 be carried out.)
(iii) Compute $\hat{Q}$ from an auxiliary regression as in (ii) with $E(Q)$, calculated as in (i), as an additional variable in the regression. This procedure is more statistically efficient than either (i) or (ii) because it incorporates data on actual choices (via the process for computing $\hat{P}_1$) as well as on variables X, Y, and Z.

Method (iii) is probably the best choice in most cases, although like (ii) it requires one to arbitrarily specify the exact functional form of the auxiliary regression.

Step 2 Version (b): add a "correction term" to the error term in (2.44) to make it independent of u
One way to look at selection bias is that observed Q is conditional on the individual's ownership decision. Therefore using Q as a variable in (2.44) would be appropriate if (2.44) could be transformed into an equation describing usage *conditional on* ownership. This can be done by making its error term conditional on ownership. If u is assumed to be normal, as is usual, the required transformation is accomplished by subtracting the conditional expectation of a normal variable, given its link to ownership via (2.46), from u; the remaining error term is independent of Q and so (2.44) is purged of selectivity bias. A recent application of this technique in transportation is West's (2004) model of automobile type choice and amount of use.

The conditional expectation just mentioned can be computed explicitly for binary probit and logit models.[47] We write the result as a term γC to be added to (2.44), where γ is a parameter to be estimated and C is a "correction variable" computed from the results of Step 1. The correction variable is included in an ordinary regression as though it were a real variable, and its coefficient is an estimate of γ. The estimated value of γ will be proportional to the correlation between u and ε, which we denote by ρ. It is this correlation that causes the problem, so we can test for selection bias by testing whether γ is different from zero. Furthermore, error term u may be regarded as consisting of γC plus a new error that is uncorrelated with Q; hence the other coefficients in the model are now estimated without bias.

Table 2.1 gives formulas for the correction variable $C = d_1 C_1 + (1 - d_1) C_2$; it also shows how parameter γ is related to correlation ρ. In this table, ϕ denotes the probability density function of a standard normal random variable, σ_u is the standard deviation of u, and $\hat{P}_2 = 1 - \hat{P}_1$. Sometimes data are lacking on people making choice $j = 2$, in which case the correction factor is simply C_1 and the usage equation is estimated on just the subsample of new car owners.[48]

What this procedure does is add correction γC_1 for those individuals in the sample who chose a new car and γC_2 for the others. Note that in each row, C_1 is positive and C_2 is negative. Thus if ρ is positive, indicating that people choosing new cars are likely to drive more for unobserved reasons, the adjustment γC is positive for those individuals who choose new cars and negative for those who choose used cars – exactly the pattern we want for γC to replace the part of error term u that is correlated with Q.

More elaborate systems of equations can be handled with the tools of *structural equations modeling*. These methods are quite flexible and allow one to try out different patterns of mutual causality, testing for the presence of particular causal links. They are often used when large data sets are available describing mutually related decisions. Golob (2003) provides a review.

2.4.3 Disaggregate panel data

When observations from individual respondents are collected repeatedly over time, the set of respondents is called a *panel* and the information on them is called *panel data* or *longitudinal data*. A good example is the Dutch National Mobility Panel, in which travel-diary information was obtained from the same individuals (with some attrition and replacement) at 10 different times over the years 1984–89. The resulting data have been widely used to analyze time lags and other dynamic aspects of travel behavior (Van Wissen and Meurs 1989).

Table 2.1 Selectivity correction terms $\gamma \cdot (d_1 C_1 + d_2 C_2)$ for (2.44)

Model	Correction variable		Coefficient
	C_1	C_2	γ
Probit	$\dfrac{\phi(\hat{\beta}_z' Z)}{\hat{P}_1}$	$-\dfrac{\phi(\hat{\beta}_z' Z)}{\hat{P}_2}$	$\rho \sigma_u$
Logit	$-\left[\dfrac{\hat{P}_2 \ln \hat{P}_2}{1 - \hat{P}_2} + \ln \hat{P}_1 \right]$	$\left[\dfrac{\hat{P}_1 \ln \hat{P}_1}{1 - \hat{P}_1} + \ln \hat{P}_2 \right]$	$(\sqrt{6}/\pi) \cdot \rho \sigma_u$

The methods described earlier for aggregate cross-sectional time series are applicable to disaggregate panel data as well. In addition, attrition becomes a statistical issue: over time, some respondents will be lost from the sample and the reasons need not be independent of the behavior being investigated. The solution is to create an explicit model of what causes an individual to leave the sample, and to estimate it simultaneously with the choice process being considered.[49]

2.4.4 Random parameters and mixed logit

In the random utility model of (2.10)–(2.11), randomness in individual behavior is limited to an additive error term in the utility function. Other parameters, and functions of them, are deterministic: that is, the only variation in them is due to observed variables. Thus, for example, the value of time defined by (2.19) varies with observed travel time and wage rate but otherwise is the same for everyone.

Experience has shown, however, that parameters of critical interest to transportation policy vary among individuals for reasons that we do not observe. Such reasons could be missing socioeconomic characteristics, personality, special features of the travel environment, and data errors. These, of course, are the same reasons for the inclusion of the additive error term in utility function (2.10). So the question is, why not also include randomness in the other parameters?

The only reason is tractability, and that has largely been overcome by advances in computing power. Boyd and Mellman (1980) and Cardell and Dunbar (1980) showed how one could allow a parameter in the logit model to vary randomly across individuals. The idea is to specify a distribution, such as normal with unknown mean and variance, for the parameter in question; the overall probability is determined by embedding the integral in (2.11) within another integral over the density function of that distribution. Subsequently, this simple idea was generalized to allow for general forms of randomness in all the parameters – even alternative-specific constants, where further randomness might seem redundant, yet it proves a simple way to produce correlation patterns like those in GEV without the complexity of the GEV probability formulas. Such models are tractable because the outer integration (over the distribution defining random parameters) can be performed using simulation methods based on random draws, while the inner integration (that over the remaining additive errors ε_{jn}) is unnecessary because, conditional on the values of random parameters, it yields the logit formula (2.14). The model is called *mixed logit* because the combined error term has a distribution that is a mixture of the extreme value distribution with the distribution of the random parameters.

The mixed logit model is not difficult to write out. Using the logit formulation of (2.14) and (2.16), the choice probability conditional on random parameters is

$$P_{in|\beta} = \frac{\exp(\beta' z_{in})}{\sum_j \exp(\beta' z_{jn})}. \tag{2.47}$$

Let $f(\beta|\Theta)$ denote the density function defining the distribution of random parameters, which depends on some unknown "meta-parameters" Θ (such as means and variances of β). The unconditional choice probability is then the multi-dimensional integral:

$$P_{in} = \int P_{in|\beta} \cdot f(\beta|\Theta) d\beta. \tag{2.48}$$

Integration by simulation consists of taking R random draws β^r, $r = 1, \ldots, R$, from distribution $f(\beta|\Theta)$, calculating $P_{in|\beta}$ each time, and averaging over the resulting values:

$$P_{in}^{sim} = (1/R)\sum_{r=1}^{R} P_{in|\beta}^r .$$
(2.49)

Doing so requires, of course, assuming some trial value of Θ, just as calculating the usual logit probability requires assuming some trial value of β. Under reasonable conditions, maximizing the likelihood function defined by this simulated probability yields statistically consistent estimates of the meta-parameters Θ. Details are provided by Train (2003).

Brownstone and Train (1999) demonstrate how one can shape the model to capture anticipated patterns by specifying which parameters are random and what form their distribution takes–in particular, whether some of them are correlated with each other.[50] In their application, consumers state their willingness to purchase various makes and models of cars, each specified to be powered by one of four fuel types: gasoline (G), natural gas (N), methanol (M), or electricity (E). Respondents were asked to choose among hypothetical vehicles with specified characteristics. A partial listing of estimation results is as follows:

$$V = -0.264 \cdot [p/\log(inc)] + 0.517 \cdot range + (1.43 + 7.45\phi_1) \cdot size + (1.70 + 5.99\phi_2) \cdot luggage$$
$$+ 2.46\phi_3 \cdot nonE + 1.07\phi_4 \cdot nonN + \text{(other terms)},$$

where p (vehicle price) and inc (income) are in thousands of dollars; the *range* between refueling (or recharging) is in hundreds of miles; *luggage* is luggage space relative to a comparably sized gasoline vehicle; *nonE* is a dummy variable for cars running on a fuel that must be purchased outside the home (in contrast to electric cars); *nonN* is a dummy for cars running on a fuel stored at atmospheric pressure (in contrast to natural gas); and ϕ_1–ϕ_4 are independent random variables with the standard normal distribution. All parameters shown above are estimated with enough precision to easily pass tests of statistical significance.

This model provides for observed heterogeneity in the effect of price p on utility, since $(\partial V/\partial p)$ varies with *inc*. It provides for random coefficients on *size* and *luggage*, and for random constants as defined by *nonE* and *nonN*. This can be understood by examining the results term by term.

The terms in parentheses involving ϕ_1 and ϕ_2 represent the random coefficients. The coefficient of *size* is random with mean 1.43 and standard deviation 7.45. Similarly, the coefficient of *luggage* has mean 1.70 and standard deviation 5.99. These estimates indicate a wide variation in people's evaluation of these characteristics. For example, it implies that many people actually prefer less luggage space, namely those for whom $\phi_2 < -1.70/5.99$; presumably they do so because a smaller luggage compartment allows more interior room for the same size of vehicle. Similarly, preference for vehicle size ranges from negative (perhaps due to easier parking for small cars) to substantially positive.

The terms involving ϕ_3 and ϕ_4 represent random alternative-specific constants with a particular correlation pattern, predicated on the assumption that groups of alternatives share common features for which people have idiosyncratic preferences – very similar to the rationale for nested logit. Each of the dummy variables *nonE* and *nonN* is simply a sum of alternative-specific constants for those car models falling into a particular group. The two groups overlap: any gasoline-powered or methanol-powered car falls into both. If the coefficients of ϕ_3 and ϕ_4 had turned out to be negligible, then these terms would play no role and we would have the usual logit probability conditional on the values of ϕ_1 and ϕ_2. But the coefficients are not negligible, so each produces a correlation among utilities for alternatives within the corresponding group. For example, all cars that are not electric share a random utility component $2.46\phi_3$, which has standard deviation 2.46; this is in addition to other random utility components including ε_{in} in (2.10). Thus the combined additive random term in utility,[51] $(\varepsilon_{in} + 2.46\phi_{3n} \cdot nonE_i + 1.07\phi_{4n} \cdot nonN_i)$, exhibits correlation across those alternatives i representing cars that are not electric and, by similar argument involving ϕ_4, across those alternatives representing cars that are not natural gas. The two alternatives falling into *both* the *nonE* and *nonN* groups, namely alternatives G and M, are even more highly correlated with each other. Note that because the distributions of ϕ_3 and ϕ_4 are centered at zero, this combined random term does not imply any overall average preference for or against various types of vehicles; such absolute preferences are in fact included in *other terms*.

The lesson from this example is that mixed logit can be used not only to specify unobserved randomness in the coefficients of certain variables, but also to mimic the kinds of correlation patterns among the random constants for which the GEV model was developed. Indeed, McFadden and Train (2000) show that it can closely approximate virtually any choice model based on random utility. The model described above acts much like a GEV model with overlapping nests for alternatives in groups *nonE* and *nonN*, and with random parameters for *size* and *luggage*. It is probably easier to estimate than such a nested logit model, especially if one is already committed to random parameters. Even more complicated error structures can be accommodated within this framework; for example, one designating repeated observations from a given individual (Small, Winston and Yan 2005) or spatial correlation related to geographical location (Bhat and Guo 2004).

In principle, the mixing idea can be applied to any choice model, not just logit, in order to randomize its parameters. Indeed, it happens that the multinomial probit model was first developed with a random-parameters formulation (Hausman and Wise 1978), a fact that has caused some confusion about the relationship between probit and logit. There may be cases where it is easier to estimate a random-parameters multinomial probit than a mixed logit model, but usually it is harder because one needs to simulate not only the explicit integral in (2.48) but also the integral that, for probit, is part of the definition of the conditional choice probability $P_{in|\beta}$.

2.4.5 Endogenous prices

We have already mentioned the biases that can be introduced by including, as an explanatory variable, one that is not really independent of what is being explained. For example, the level of automobile ownership does a great job of "explaining" mode choice, but is it really an independent factor or does it, at least partly, respond to the mode choice decision? If the latter, automobile ownership is *endogenous* to mode choice; including it to explain mode choice then overstates its effect and also biases the coefficients of other variables that are correlated with it. This is called *endogeneity bias*.

There is a more subtle source of endogeneity bias that can occur with a variable measuring the price of an alternative. This has long been recognized as a problem in aggregate demand studies, where the demand curve is understood to be just one side of a simultaneous system determining price and quantity. But it can also afflict disaggregate studies if price is determined in a market setting where unobserved quality attributes are important and if those unobserved attributes are not controlled for in the model.

For example, Train and Winston (2007) seek to explain individual consumers' choices among 200 different makes and models of cars. Naturally they want to include the price of the car as a variable. The trouble is, manufacturers' pricing decisions take account of the car's quality, including some aspects of quality that the investigators are unable to measure. If some makes and models have higher unmeasured quality than others, and their prices reflect this, it can appear as though consumers are drawn to high prices whereas they are really drawn to high unobserved quality. Thus, the strength of the usual negative effect of price on choice probability will tend to be underestimated or even not discerned at all.

Unobserved quality attributes are not a problem if the model includes a full set of alternative-specific dummy variables, because then the attributes are accounted for by the coefficients of those dummy variables (*i.e.*, by the alternative-specific constants). But that solution is not always satisfactory for at least two reasons. First, the data set might be too small to estimate all the alternative-specific constants, especially when there are many of them; for example, if it happens that some alternative is not chosen by anyone in the sample, its alternative-specific constant cannot be estimated. Second, including all alternative-specific constants makes it impossible to include any other variable that varies across alternatives but not across sample members.[52] Thus, for example, if for any given product all sample members face the same price, the price alone cannot be included as an explanatory variable along with a full set of alternative-specific dummies; price can only be included by interacting it with some characteristic of consumers such as income, so that it varies in some manner different from what can be absorbed into the alternative-specific constants. Thus the alternative-specific constants, if included in the model, may hide important information.

A solution to this problem is available whether or not alternative-specific constants have been estimated. The key is to either estimate or calibrate alternative-specific constants and then regress them on price (and any other variables that vary only by alternative) using an *instrumental-variables estimator* – a procedure noted briefly in Section 2.1.6. If the alternative-specific constants are not estimated statistically, one can obtain them using the calibration procedure described earlier for updating a model to a new location (Section 2.2.7). That procedure finds the values that equate the choice shares predicted by the discrete-choice model to the observed choice shares. (Presumably the latter are based on large enough samples so that they are all strictly positive.)[53]

We now describe the instrumental-variables estimator more fully, using the example of an endogenous price variable in Train and Winston (2007). The instrumental variables are any set of variables that do a good job of predicting price but are independent of unmeasured quality attributes that might be correlated with price. The instrumental-variables estimator effectively replaces "price" in the regression equation by its predicted value based on all exogenous variables in the model, including the instrumental variables. In this way price is purged of its endogeneity but otherwise still carries information relevant to understanding consumer choice. The procedure works only in a linear model, which is why it cannot be applied directly to the discrete-choice model itself.

The full Train–Winston procedure, then, looks like this. The conditional indirect utility function V_{in} is decomposed into two parts, one varying across consumers and the other not:

$$V_{in} = \beta' z_{in} + (\gamma' x_i + \xi_i), \tag{2.50}$$

where z_{in} and x_i are vectors of explanatory variables, the latter varying only across alternatives, not individuals. The first part of this decomposition, $\beta'z_{in}$, has exactly the same meaning as in the mixed logit model of (2.47), including the fact that β can vary randomly across consumers. The second part, which we write as

$$\delta_i = \gamma'x_i + \xi_i, \tag{2.51}$$

varies only across products and has a constant parameter vector γ. Price is included among variables x; it may also be included in z if it is interacted with a consumer characteristic such as income.

The model is estimated iteratively. Starting with a guess or a preliminary estimate of constants $\{\delta_i^{old}\}$, β is estimated using the mixed-logit estimator with utility (2.50), holding the part in parentheses (δ_i) constant. Predicted choice shares $\hat{s}_i$ (conditional on $\{\delta_i^{old}\}$) are then obtained by aggregating the mixed-logit probabilities (2.49) over the sample. Finally, using the observed choice shares s_i, δ_i is updated according to the rule described in a note to Section 2.2.7:

$$\delta_i^{new} = \delta_i^{old} + \log(s_i) - \log(\hat{s}_i).$$

These steps are iterated until they converge.[54] Finally, γ is estimated by regressing the resulting values of $\{\delta_i\}$ on x_i according to (2.51), using instrumental variables.

What sort of variable would make a good instrument for price? The value of such a variable, for a given make/model of automobile, needs to be reasonably well correlated with the price of that make/model but not with its unmeasured characteristics. A key insight of Berry (1994) is that a good instrument can be constructed as an index of the measured characteristics of *other* makes and models. This is because automobile prices are presumed to be determined in an oligopoly setting, in which each firm sets product prices while taking account of all the other products in the market, including its own. Hence price is influenced by the instrumental variable, as required. Furthermore, because there are many other makes and models, it is reasonable to assume that an index of such characteristics is not significantly influenced by the price of the make/model under consideration, thus meeting the other requirement for an instrument.[55]

Fortunately, this procedure is unnecessary for most problems in urban transportation because either the model contains alternative-specific constants or prices can be considered exogenous (for example, they may be set by a public agency). The procedure has been used mainly to study the demand for automobiles, computers, and other products characterized by significant and measurable product variety.[56]

2.5 Activity patterns and trip chaining

A more fundamental approach to the demand for travel would be to explain the entire structure of decision-making about what activities to undertake in what locations. This idea has proven difficult to translate into workable models that use available data. For example, early theories based on shopping strategies in the face of multiple products and storage costs yielded rich insights but no practical predictive models, whereas *ad hoc* empirical models were theoretically unsatisfactory and also not very accurate (Thill and Thomas 1987). Nevertheless, important progress has been made. Descriptive information on activity patterns is now extensive, often showing surprising similarities across nations.[57] Surveys now elicit multi-day diaries describing all activities and travel undertaken during a period of time. And newer theoretical work more fully integrates shopping and trip chaining into conventional consumption theory (Anas 2007). One intriguing result: making it easier to chain trips together may result in more destinations visited rather than less travel.

As for models that are fully activity-based, two main classes have emerged.[58] One consists of econometric models that extend the basic framework of this chapter to deal with additional choice dimensions such as trip frequency, destination, and type and duration of activities undertaken. The other consists of simulation models that enumerate feasible combinations of activities, based on logical constraints relating activities at different locations to travel between those locations.

Turning to the first class of models, one significant advance has been to model an entire tour (a round trip visiting one or more destinations in sequence) as an object of choice. The problem with this is that it leads to enormous numbers of possible choice alternatives, especially when one considers a daily schedule containing several possible tours. Bowman and Ben-Akiva (2001) improve tractability by breaking the overall decision about the daily schedule into parts, including a primary tour type, secondary tour type(s), and destinations and modes of travel for each tour. Such a model lends itself to a structured choice model such as nested logit. Illustrating the difficulty of designing realistic models, the authors acknowledge that the results in their example are able to explain only a small part of variations in observed activity patterns.

Fundamental to describing trips are the locations and the starting and ending times of activities that the trips are intended to connect. Yet few if any formal activity models, whether of the econometric or simulation variety, have been able to satisfactorily account for the varying degrees of flexibility in locations and times of day. Moreover, to fully understand the processes generating travel, one needs to model the substitution between in-home and out-of-home activities, adding further to the sheer number of possibilities to consider.

As an example of what can be accomplished, Shiftan and Suhrbier (2002) utilize one of the best data sets for activity analysis – a 1994 household survey in Portland, Oregon – to analyze several policies classified as "travel demand management." One result is illustrative. A policy to encourage telecommuting is predicted to reduce long-distance work trips to downtown Portland, just as one would expect. But the policy *increases* the number of short tours, as people make special-purpose trips for activities that previously were handled as part of a tour from home to work and back. This result is consistent with several studies of telecommuting, which have found only a very small net reduction in travel; indeed many types of telecommunication appear to be complements to, rather than substitutes for, travel.[59]

2.6 Value of time and reliability

Among the most important quantities inferred from travel demand studies are the monetary values that people place on saving various forms of travel time or on improving the predictability of travel time. The first, loosely known as the *value of time* (VOT), is a key parameter in cost–benefit analyses that measure the benefits brought about by transportation policies or projects. The second, the *value of reliability* (VOR), also appears important, but accurate measurement is a science in its infancy.

The main reason these quantities are so important is that they account for a large portion of the benefits (positive or negative) of changes in the transportation environment. For this reason, analysts are generally not satisfied to merely have these benefits captured implicitly as part of consumer surplus as, for example, in equation (2.23); rather, they would like to separate them explicitly in order to illuminate the nature of the changes being considered. In this section, we consider the theory behind consumers' response to time and reliability and our empirical knowledge about those responses; in Chapter 5, we discuss how that knowledge is used in the evaluation of projects or policies.

2.6.1 Value of time: basic theory

The most natural definition of value of time is in terms of "compensating variation" (Varian 1992). The value of saving a given amount and type of travel time by a particular person is the amount that person could pay, after receiving the saving, and be just as well off as before. This amount, divided by the time saving, is that person's average value of time saved for that particular change. Aggregating over a class of people yields the *average value of time* for those people in that situation. The limit of this average value, as the time saving shrinks to zero, is called the *marginal value of time*, or just "value of time."[60]

Value of time may depend on many aspects of the trip-maker and of the trip itself. To name just a few, it depends on trip purpose (*e.g.*, work or recreation), demographic and socioeconomic characteristics, time of day, physical or psychological amenities available during travel, and the total duration of the trip. There are two main approaches to specifying a travel-demand model so it can measure such variations. One is known as *market segmentation*: the sample is divided according to criteria such as income and type of household, and a separate model is estimated for each segment. This has the advantage of imposing no potentially erroneous constraints, but the disadvantage of requiring many parameters to be estimated, with no guarantee that these estimates will follow a reasonable pattern. The second approach uses theoretical reasoning to postulate a functional form for utility that determines how VOT varies. This second approach is pursued here.

A useful theoretical framework builds on that of Becker (1965), in which utility is maximized subject to a time constraint. Becker's theory has been elaborated in many directions; here, we present ideas developed mainly by Oort (1969) and DeSerpa (1971), adapting the exposition of MVA Consultancy *et al.* (1987).

Let utility U depend on consumption of goods G, time T_w spent at work, and times T_k spent in various other activities k. We can normalize the price of consumption to one. Utility is maximized subject to several constraints. First, the usual budget constraint requires that expenditures are no greater than the sum of unearned income Y and earned income wT_w, where w is the wage rate. Second, a time constraint requires that time spent on all activities be within total time available, $\overline{T}$. Finally, certain activities (such as travel) have technological features (such as maximum speeds) that impose a minimum $\overline{T}_k$ on time T_k spent in activity k. (We will consider later an extension where T_w is also so constrained.) We assume that the first two constraints are binding, so they can be expressed as equalities.

This problem can be solved by maximizing the following Lagrangian function with respect to G, T_w, and $\{T_k\}$:

$$\Lambda = U(G, T_w, \{T_k\}) + \lambda \cdot \left[Y + wT_w - G \right] + \mu \cdot \left[\overline{T} - T_w - \sum_k T_k \right] + \sum_k \phi_k \cdot \left[T_k - \overline{T}_k \right], \quad (2.52)$$

where λ, μ, and $\{\phi_k\}$ are Lagrange multipliers that indicate how tightly each of the corresponding constraints limits utility. The first-order condition for maximizing (2.52) with respect to one activity time T_k is

$$U_{Tk} - \mu + \phi_k = 0, \tag{2.53}$$

while that with respect to T_w is

$$U_{Tw} + \lambda \cdot \left[w + T_w \cdot (\mathrm{d}w/\mathrm{d}T_w) \right] - \mu = 0, \tag{2.54}$$

where subscripts on U indicate partial derivatives. We have allowed for a non-linear compensation schedule by letting w depend on T_w.

We can denote the value of utility at the solution to this maximization problem by V, the indirect utility function; it depends on Y, $\bar{T}$, wage schedule $w(T_w)$, and minimum activity times $\{\bar{T}_k\}$. The rate at which utility increases as the kth minimum-time constraint is relaxed is given by its Lagrange multiplier, ϕ_k; the increase of utility with respect to unearned income is λ. Hence the marginal value of time for the kth time component is their ratio:

$$v_T^k \equiv \left(\frac{\partial Y}{\partial \bar{\bar{T}}_k} \right)_V = -\frac{\partial V / \partial \bar{T}_k}{\partial V / \partial Y} = \frac{\phi_k}{\lambda}. \tag{2.55}$$

Those activities for which the minimum-time constraint is not binding, *i.e.*, those for which $\phi_k = 0$, are called by DeSerpa *pure leisure activities*. The others, which presumably include most travel, are *intermediate activities*.

Equations (2.53)–(2.55) imply that for a travel activity k,

$$v_T^k = \frac{\mu}{\lambda} - \frac{U_{Tk}}{\lambda} = w + T_w \cdot \frac{\mathrm{d}w}{\mathrm{d}T_w} + \frac{U_{Tw}}{\lambda} - \frac{U_{Tk}}{\lambda}. \tag{2.56}$$

This equation decomposes the value of travel-time savings into the opportunity cost of time that could be used for work, μ/λ, less the value of the marginal utility of time spent in travel. The opportunity cost μ/λ is both pecuniary (the first two terms after the last equality) and non-pecuniary (the third term, which could be positive or negative).

Most of the theoretical literature assumes that the wage rate is fixed, in which case equation (2.56) gives the result noted by Oort (1969): the value of time exceeds the wage rate if time spent at work is enjoyed relative to that spent traveling, and falls short of it if time at work is relatively disliked. This is a fundamental insight into how the value of time, even for non-work trips, depends on conditions of the job. It suggests a modeling strategy that interacts variables believed to be related to compensation and work enjoyment with those measuring time or cost. In addition, we might expect v_T^k to rise with total trip time because the total time constraint in (2.52) will bind more tightly, causing μ, the marginal utility of leisure, to rise.[61]

2.6.2 Empirical specifications

The most common situation for measuring values of time empirically is one where a discrete choice is being made, such as among modes or between routes. To clarify how the general theory just presented corresponds to empirical specifications, assume that there is only one pure leisure activity, $k = 0$, and that the other activities are all mutually exclusive travel activities, each consisting of one trip. We can also add travel cost $c_k \delta_k$ to the budget constraint, where δ_k is one if travel activity k is chosen and zero otherwise. The indirect utility function has the same derivatives with respect to exogenous variables c_k and $\overline{T}_k$ as does the Lagrangian function, which under the assumptions just stated can be written as:

$$\frac{\partial V}{\partial c_k} = -\lambda \delta_k; \quad \frac{\partial V}{\partial \overline{T}_k} = -\phi_k \delta_k.$$

Equivalently, writing V_k as the conditional indirect utility function:

$$\frac{\partial V_k}{\partial c_k} = -\lambda; \quad \frac{\partial V_k}{\partial \overline{T}_k} = -\phi_k. \tag{2.57}$$

Then our definition of value of time in (2.55) is identical to that in (2.19):

$$v_T^k \equiv \frac{\phi_k}{\lambda} = \frac{\partial V_k / \partial \overline{T}_k}{\partial V_k / \partial c_k}.$$

Note also that the first of equations (2.57) is identical to (2.24) since we assume just one trip per time period. (It is easy to generalize to allow for an endogenously chosen number of trips per time period.)

Our theory provides some guidance about how to specify the systematic utilities V_k in a discrete-choice model. Suppose, for example, one believes that work is disliked (relative to travel) and that its relative marginal disutility is a fixed fraction of the wage rate. Suppose further that the wage rate is fixed, so the second term in the right-hand side of (2.56) disappears. Then (2.56) implies that the value of time is a fraction of the wage rate, as for example with specification (2.15) with $\beta_3 = 0$. Alternatively, one might think that work enjoyment varies non-linearly with the observed wage rate: perhaps negatively due to wage differentials that compensate for working conditions, or perhaps positively due to employers' responses to an income-elastic demand for job amenities. Then (2.56) implies that value of time is a non-linear function of the wage rate, which could suggest using (2.15) with a non-zero term β_3 or with additional terms involving cost divided by some other power of the wage. Train and McFadden (1978) demonstrate how specific forms of the utility function in (2.52) can lead to operational specifications for the conditional indirect utility function.

2.6.3 Extensions

Human behavior is complex, and many additional factors may affect how people allocate their time. No analytical model can account for all of them, but we can mention several interesting extensions to the theory just presented. They account for constraints on work hours, variable commuting times, technologies of home production, and psychological bias against losses from the status quo.

First, consider work-hour constraints. People cannot always change the amount of time they spend at work, perhaps because they are locked into a particular job with fixed hours.

To some extent this is handled by allowing w to depend on T_w; but we could also consider a stricter constraint that T_w be fixed, say at $\overline{T}_w$. This adds a term $\phi_w \cdot [T_w - \overline{T}_w]$ to (2.52), where ϕ_w is another Lagrangian multiplier whose sign indicates whether this person would prefer to work fewer ($\phi_w > 0$) or more ($\phi_w < 0$) hours. This modification adds a term ϕ_w / λ to the value of time as given by (2.56), thus raising or lowering the value of time depending on the sign of ϕ_w. Indeed, MVA Consultancy *et al.* (1987, pp. 149–50) find that people who are required to work extra hours at short notice have 15%–20% higher values of travel time than other workers, suggesting that for them such a model may apply with $\phi_w > 0$.

Second, consider the situation where the amount of time devoted to consuming goods is proportional to the amount of goods – as, for example, occurs if the "good" is watching a movie. For simplicity, let's label this as activity 0 and consider it a generalized leisure activity, whose consumption time is proportional to all goods consumption G. Then the term $\phi_0 \cdot [T_0 - \overline{T}_0]$ in (2.52) must be changed to $\phi_0 \cdot [T_0 - \ell \cdot G]$, where ℓ is the unit time requirement for consumption. The constraint is binding if $\phi_0 > 0$. While this modification does not alter the formulas derived for value of time, it does change the meaning of λ (the marginal utility of income) in those formulas, as shown by Jara-Díaz (2000, 2003). Previously, the solution required that $\lambda = U_G$, the marginal utility of consumption, as is easily seen from the first-order condition for maximizing (2.52) with respect to G. But now that first-order condition implies $\lambda = U_G - \phi_0 \cdot \ell$. Since λ appears in the denominator of expressions for value of time, this change would tend to raise the value of time if the constraint is binding. Consumers are pressed for time in all their activities because of the time needed for ordinary consumption.

Third, suppose that working more hours requires spending more time commuting. This would be the case, for example, if it requires a secondary worker entering the work force or a part-time worker increasing the number of days worked. Following De Borger and Van Dender (2003), suppose commuting is activity c and commuting time is proportional to the amount of time worked: $T_c = a \cdot T_w$ for fixed parameter a. Substituting this equality into the overall time constraint in (2.52), the value μ in (2.54) becomes multiplied by $(1 + a)$ and all terms on the right-hand side of (2.56) are therefore divided by $(1 + a)$. Thus greater commuting time (larger a) causes the value of time to *decrease* – opposite to the effect noted earlier from a rising marginal utility of leisure. One way to understand this is that a larger value of a reduces the effective hourly wage rate, *i.e.*, the wage rate net of commuting cost. De Borger and Van Dender suggest in numerical simulations that the effect can be quite large.

Finally, consider the well-known phenomenon of loss aversion. People often display asymmetric preferences regarding gains or losses from the status quo (more generally, from a reference situation), assigning far more weight to losses than to gains. Kahneman and Tversky (1979) develop a general theory of such behavior known as prospect theory. This behavior may create a large gap between "willingness to pay" (WTP) for a time savings and "willingness to accept" (WTA) for an identical time increase, each being defined as the amount of money paid or received so as to leave the traveler indifferent to the change. De Borger and Fosgerau (2006) apply the following "reference-dependent" utility function, adapted from the literature on prospect theory:

$$V(c,t) = V^c(-c) + V^t(-v_T t),$$

where c and t are deviations in cost and time, respectively, from the reference situation, v_T is a fixed parameter for a given traveler known as the "reference-free value of time," and the "value function" $V^i(\cdot)$ is an increasing function of its argument with $V^i(0) = 0$, $i = c, t$.

Loss aversion is represented by assuming that V^i slopes downward from zero more steeply than it slopes upward from zero: $V^i(x) < -V^i(-x)$ for $x > 0$. Specifically, De Borger and Fosgerau assume the following value functions postulated by Tversky and Kahneman (1991):

$$V^i(x) = xe^{-\eta_i S(x)},$$

where $S(x) \equiv x/|x|$ is the sign of x, with $S(0) = 0$, and η^c and η^t are fixed parameters. We have loss aversion in V^i if $\eta^i > 0$. We define willingness to pay $WTP(t)$ as the amount the consumer would pay and remain indifferent in light of a time saving of $t > 0$; *i.e.*, it is the solution to

$$V^c(-WTP) + V^t(v_T t) = 0.$$

Similarly, $WTA(t)$ is the amount the consumer would have to receive to be willing to accept a time increase of t:

$$V^c(WTA) + V^t(-v_T t) = 0.$$

These definitions imply that $WTP(t) = v_T e^{-(\eta^c + \eta^t)} \cdot t$ and $WTA(t) = v_T e^{(\eta^c + \eta^t)} \cdot t$, again for $t > 0$. If there is loss aversion ($\eta > 0$), we immediately see that $WTP < WTA$ and both WTP and WTA differ from $v_T t$. In terms of our previous definitions, the marginal value of time $(\partial V / \partial t)/(\partial V / \partial c)$ falls short of v_T for a time saving and it rises above v_T for a time increase. Furthermore, if values of (WTP/t) and (WTA/t) can be measured from experimental data, then v_T can be determined simply as their geometric mean. De Borger and Fosgerau, using a considerably more general model than this one, estimate values of $\eta^c = 0.24$ and $\eta^t = 0.50$ from stated preference data from over 2000 individuals, implying that WTA exceeds WTP by a factor of four.

We caution that the kind of loss aversion applied to an individual, in a hypothetical situation with a very clear reference scenario (a recent actual trip), need not apply to a proposed change to a transportation system affecting thousands of people in varying and changing circumstances. If you improve a traffic signal and wait a few months, many users' situations will have changed since before the improvement and their reference situations are unclear; indeed, other events simultaneously affecting their travel might make them quite unaware of the signal improvement, even if they pay close attention to the overall time of their commute. Therefore it is not appropriate to use distinct values for WTP and WTA in most welfare analyses of public policies. Rather, we view the model just described as useful for interpreting stated-preference results. Nevertheless it illustrates that the standard assumption of rational behavior need not hold literally in all situations, and sometimes this must be taken into account in empirical work.

Other theoretical extensions to the theory of value of time include those showing how it depends on tax rates (Forsyth 1980) and on scheduling considerations (Small 1982).

2.6.4 *Value of reliability: theory*

It is well known that uncertainty in travel time, which may result from congestion or poor adherence to transit schedules, is a major perceived cost of travel (*e.g.*, MVA Consultancy *et al.* 1987, pp. 61–62). This conclusion is supported by attitudinal surveys (Prashker 1979), and perhaps by the frequent finding that time spent in congestion is more onerous than other in-vehicle time.[62] How can this aversion to unreliability be captured in a theoretical model of travel?

One approach, adapting Noland and Small (1995), is to begin with the model of trip-scheduling choice presented in equation (2.30). Dividing utility by minus the marginal utility of income, we can write this model in terms of trip cost, in a conventional notation that we will use extensively in the next chapter:

$$C(t_d, T_r) = \alpha \cdot T + \beta \cdot SDE + \gamma \cdot SDL + \theta \cdot DL, \tag{2.58}$$

where $\alpha \equiv v_T/60$ is the per-minute value of travel time, β and γ are per-minute costs of early and late arrival, and θ is a fixed cost of arriving late. Travel time T is disaggregated into a value T_f that represents the lowest possible travel time for this particular trip, plus a random (unpredictable) component of travel time, $T_r \geq 0$. Since T_f is simply a given for the traveler, we use the functional notation $C(t_d, T_r)$ to focus attention on two variables: departure time t_d and stochastic delay T_r. Specifically, our objective is to measure the increase in expected cost C due to the dispersion in T_r, given that t_d is subject to choice by the traveler. Letting C^* denote this expected cost after the user chooses t_d optimally, we have

$$C^* = \operatorname*{Min}_{t_d} \mathrm{E}\left[C(t_d, t_r)\right] = \operatorname*{Min}_{t_d}\left[\alpha \cdot \mathrm{E}(T) + \beta \cdot \mathrm{E}(SDE) + \gamma \cdot \mathrm{E}(SDL) + \theta \cdot P_L\right], \tag{2.59}$$

where E denotes an expected value taken over the distribution of T_r, conditional on t_d; and where $P_L \equiv \mathrm{E}(DL)$ is the probability of being late, again conditional on t_d. This equation can form the basis for specifying the reliability term in a model like (2.31). It captures the effect of travel time uncertainty upon expected schedule delay costs, but may omit other reasons why uncertainty could cause disutility.

To focus just on reliability, let's ignore the dynamics of congestion for now by assuming that T_f and hence $\mathrm{E}(T)$ are independent of departure time. To find the optimal departure time, let $f(T_r)$ be the probability density function for T_r and let t^* be the preferred arrival time at the destination. The next-to-last term in the square brackets of (2.59) can then be written as

$$\gamma \cdot \mathrm{E}(SDL) = \gamma \cdot \mathrm{E}(t_d + T_r - \tilde{t} \mid T_r > \tilde{t} - t_d)$$

$$= \gamma \cdot \int_{\tilde{t}-t_d}^{\infty} (t_d + T_r - \tilde{t}) \cdot f(T_r) \mathrm{d}T_r,$$

where $\tilde{t} \equiv t^* - T_f$ is the time the traveler would depart if T_r were equal to zero with certainty. Differentiating yields:

$$\frac{\mathrm{d}}{\mathrm{d}t_d} \gamma \cdot \mathrm{E}(SDL) = 0 + \gamma \cdot \int_{\tilde{t}-t_d}^{\infty} \left[\frac{\mathrm{d}}{\mathrm{d}t_d}(t_d + T_r - \tilde{t}) \cdot f(T_r)\right] \mathrm{d}T_r = \gamma P_L^*,$$

where P_L^* is the probability of being late given the optimal departure time.[63] Similarly, differentiating the term involving β in (2.59) yields $-\beta \cdot (1 - P_L^*)$. Finally, differentiating the last term yields $-\theta f^0$ where $f^0 \equiv f(\tilde{t} - t_d^*)$ is the probability density at the point where the traveler is neither early nor late. What these three derivatives tell us is that departing later will lower the expected cost of early arrival but raise the expected costs of late arrival (involving γ and θ). Combining all three terms and setting them equal to zero gives the first-order condition for optimal departure time:

$$P_L^* = \frac{\beta + \theta f^0}{\beta + \gamma}.$$ (2.60)

In the special case $\theta = 0$, equation (2.60) yields the very intuitive rule $P_L^* = \beta / (\beta + \gamma)$, noted by Bates *et al.* (2001, p. 202).

Equation (2.60) is only an implicit equation for the optimal departure time, t_d^*, because both P_L and f^0 depend on t_d. The equation can be regarded as a rule for setting a "buffer" to allow for occasional delays, a buffer whose size balances the aversions to early and late arrival. If T_r has a tight distribution (low variance), then the desired probability P_L^* can be achieved by a small time buffer; but as the distribution of T_r becomes more dispersed (more unreliability), a larger time buffer is required, causing the usual early arrivals to be of greater magnitude and therefore to incur greater costs. Lomax, Turner and Margiotta (2003) estimate buffers in 21 US cities using an assumed value $P_L^* = 0.05$, obtaining results that are substantial fractions of average travel time.

The cost function itself has been derived in closed form for two cases: a uniform distribution and an exponential distribution for T_r. In the case of a uniform distribution with range b, (2.60) again simplifies to a closed form:

$$P_L^* = \frac{\beta + (\theta / b)}{\beta + \gamma}.$$

The value of C^* in this case is given by Noland and Small (1995) and Bates *et al.* (2001). In the special case $\theta = 0$, it is equal to the cost of expected travel time, $\alpha \cdot E(T)$, plus the following cost of unreliability:

$$v_R R = \left(\frac{\beta \gamma}{\beta + \gamma} \right) \cdot \frac{b}{2}.$$ (2.61)

The quantity in parenthesis is a composite measure of the unit costs of scheduling mismatch, which plays a central role in the cost functions considered in the next chapter. Thus (2.61) indicates that reliability cost derives from the combination of costly scheduling mismatches and dispersion in travel time. The specific value for v_R depends on how unreliability R is defined; if it is defined as half the possible range of travel times, then v_R is just the term in parenthesis in (2.61).

More generally, the last two terms in (2.59) are potentially important if $\gamma > \beta$ or if θ is large, conditions that are in fact true according to the empirical findings in (2.30). Because they contain $E(SDL)$ and P_L, these terms depend especially on the shape of the distribution of

T_r in its upper ranges, which governs the likelihood that T_r takes a high enough value to make the traveler late. Thus we might expect the expected cost of unreliability to depend more on this part of the distribution (its "upper tail") than on other parts.

Equation (2.61) applies equally to the expected cost of schedule mismatches on a transit trip, under the common assumption that people arrive at a transit stop at a steady rate and with b now defined as the headway between transit vehicles.[64] Although under that interpretation $v_R R$ is proportional to expected waiting time, it is *not* a representation of waiting-time cost but rather must be added to it. In the case where the transit headway is itself uncertain, or where the vehicle might be too full to accommodate another passenger, the derivation of reliability cost for transit becomes much more complicated (Bates *et al.* 2001).

2.6.5 Empirical results

Research has generated an enormous literature on empirical estimates of value of time, and a much smaller one on value of reliability. Here we rely mainly on reviews of these literatures by others.

Waters (1996) reviews 56 value-of-time estimates from 14 nations. Each is stated as a fraction of the gross wage rate. Focusing on those where the context is commuting by automobile, he finds an average ratio of VOT to wage rate of 48%, and a median ratio of 42%. He suggests that "a representative [VOT] for auto commuting would be in the 35% to 50% range, probably at the upper end of this range for North America." Consistent with this last statement, both Transport Canada (1994, Section 7.3.2) and US Department of Transportation (1997) currently recommend using a value for personal travel by automobile equal to 50% of the average wage rate.

Reviewing studies for the UK, Wardman (1998, Table 6) finds an average VOT of £3.58/hour in late 1994 prices, which is 52% of the corresponding wage rate.[65] Mackie *et al.* (2003), reviewing a larger set of UK studies, recommend best hourly values for VOT of £3.96 for commuting and £3.54 for other trips at 1997 prices; the average of these two values is 51% of the relevant wage rate.[66] Gunn (2001) finds that Dutch values used in 1988, differentiated by level of household income, compare well with various British results for a similar time. However, Gunn reports that there was a substantial unexplained downward shift in the profile for 1997 – a phenomenon possibly resulting from better amenities in vehicles. Another Dutch study – using a novel methodology in which the "choice" is to leave a job rather than to pick a mode or route – finds a ratio of VOT to wage rate of one-third for shorter commutes (less than one hour round trip) and two-thirds for longer ones, for an average of "almost half" (Van Ommeren, Van den Berg and Gorter 2000). A French review by the Commissariat Général du Plan (2001, p. 42) finds VOT to be 77% and 42% of the wage for commuting and other urban trips, respectively, for an average of 59%. Finally, a Japanese review suggests using ¥2333/hour for weekday automobile travel in 1999, which was 84% of the wage rate.[67]

There is considerable evidence that value of time rises with income but less than proportionally, which makes the expression of VOT as a fraction of the wage rate, as above, somewhat of an approximation.[68] The easiest way to summarize this evidence is as an elasticity of value of time with respect to income. Wardman (2001, p. 116), using a formal meta-analysis, finds that elasticity to be 0.51 when income is measured as gross domestic product per capita; with a larger sample he obtains 0.72 (Wardman 2004, p. 373), and he is part of a group that recommends using an elasticity of 0.8 (Mackie *et al.* 2003). These elasticities could be subject to a downward bias if there is indeed a downward trend, independent of income, as suggested by Gunn.

Wardman's (2001) meta-analysis is especially useful for tracking the effects of various trip attributes on value of time. For example, there is a 16% differential between value of time for commuting and leisure trips. There are also considerable differences across modes, with bus riders having a lower than average value and rail riders a higher than average value – possibly due to self-selection by speed.

Most important, walking and waiting time are valued much higher than in-vehicle time – a universal finding conventionally summarized as 2.0 to 2.5 times as high. Wardman actually gets a smaller differential, namely a ratio of 1.62, which is quite precisely estimated; nevertheless he joins Mackie *et al*. (2003) in recommending a ratio of 2.0. There is considerable dispersion in the reported estimates of these relative valuations, especially in the relative value of waiting time (MVA Consultancy *et al*., 1987, p. 130). This may indicate that the disutility of transfers (which entail waiting as well as other possible difficulties) is quite variable, and suggests a payoff from research into the sources of this variation.

A number of studies have been carried out using Chilean data. Munizaga *et al*. (2006), using an innovative model that combines choices of activities and travel modes by residents of Santiago, obtain average VOT equal to 46% and 67% of the wage rate for middle- and upper-income groups, respectively.

Stated preference (SP) data often yield considerably smaller values of time than revealed preference (RP) data. For example, Hensher (1997) and Calfee and Winston (1998) obtain values using SP surveys of car commuters of 19% and 20%, respectively, of the wage rate.[69] Brownstone and Small (2005) take advantage of three data sets, all from "high occupancy toll lane" facilities in southern California, that obtained RP and SP data from comparable populations, in some cases from the same individuals. They find that SP results for VOT are one-third to one-half the corresponding RP results,[70] the latter being 50%–90% of the wage rate. One possible explanation for this difference is hinted at by the finding, from other studies of these same corridors, that people overestimate the actual time savings from the toll roads by roughly a factor of two; thus when answering SP survey questions, they may indicate a per-minute willingness to pay for *perceived* time savings that is lower than their willingness to pay for *actual* time savings. If one wants to use a VOT for purposes of policy analysis, one needs it to correspond to actual travel time since that is typically the variable considered in the analysis. Therefore if RP and SP values differ when both are accurately measured, it is the RP values that are relevant for most purposes.

From this evidence, we conclude that the value of time for personal journeys varies widely by circumstance, usually between 20% and 90% of the gross wage rate and averaging around 50%. Although it varies somewhat less than proportionally with income or wages, expressing it as a fraction of the wage rate is a good approximation and is more useful than expressing it as an absolute amount. (This is not to prejudge whether it may be desirable to use a constant absolute amount in cost–benefit analysis for political or distributional reasons.) The value of time is much higher for business travel, generally taken as 100% of total compensation including benefits. The value of walking and waiting time for transit trips is 1.6 to 2.0 times that of in-vehicle time, not counting some context-specific disutilities of having to transfer from one vehicle to another.

Several studies have applied mixed logit to measure variation from unobserved sources in the disutility of time and reliability. Hensher (2001) allows for random coefficients of three types of travel time, using SP data on New Zealand commuters, resulting in standard deviations of VOT equal to 41%–58% of the corresponding mean VOT.[71] The California studies reviewed by Brownstone and Small (2005) measure heterogeneity as the inter-quartile range (75th minus 25th percentile values) of the distribution of VOT or VOR. With that measure, they find that unobserved heterogeneity in VOT–that is, heterogeneity due just to random coefficients–is 55%–144% of median VOT.

There has been far less empirical research on value of reliability. Almost all of it has been based on SP data, for at least two reasons: it is difficult to measure unreliability in actual situations, and unreliability tends to be correlated with travel time itself. However, a few recent studies have had some success with RP data. One key development is to measure unreliability as a property of the upper percentiles of the distribution of travel times, as suggested by the theory discussed earlier. It turns out that such a measure is less correlated with travel time than is a symmetric measure like standard deviation, because the upper-percentile travel times (*i.e.*, travel times that occur only rarely) tend to arise from incidents such as accidents or stalled vehicles. The occurrence of such incidents is closely correlated to congestion, but the delays they cause are less so because the effects of the incident persist long after it occurs.

Bates *et al.* (2001) review several SP studies of car travel that define unreliability as the standard deviation of travel time. Those that they deem most free of methodological problems produce a value of reliability (VOR), expressed in units of money per unit increase in that standard deviation, on the order of 0.8 to 1.3 times the value of time (VOT). Brownstone and Small (2005) review studies in which unreliability is defined as the difference between the 90th and 50th percentile of the travel-time distribution across days, or some similar measure. In these studies also, VOR tends to be of about the same magnitude as VOT. One of these studies, using data from the high-occupancy toll (HOT) lane on State Route 91 in the Los Angeles region, finds that roughly two-thirds of the advantage of the HOT lane to the average traveler is due to its lower travel time and one-third is due to its higher reliability.[72]

If reliability is not controlled for in studies of value of time, the estimated VOT may include some aversion to unreliability to the extent that time and unreliability are correlated. Nevertheless, the studies of automobile users reviewed by Brownstone and Small (2005) obtain high VOT for automobile users even when simultaneously measuring VOR.

Turning to freight transportation, it is clear that values of time and reliability are important, but empirical evidence is sparse and definitions inconsistent. Most studies use SP methodology and place primary emphasis on inter-city travel. De Jong (2000) provides a recent review of studies; they suggest that for countries like the Netherlands, where a high proportion of travel is urban, values of time are quite high. This finding is consistent with the common belief that travel time for freight vehicles is viewed as similar to business time for the driver plus some inventory value for equipment and payload. Kawamura (2000), Wigan *et al.* (2000), and Fowkes *et al.* (2004) provide evidence on values of both travel time and reliability.

2.7 Conclusions

All tractable approaches to travel-demand analysis are based on greatly simplified portrayals of behavior. This is necessary because the variety of purposes and available choices make travel behavior very complex. As a result, distinct or even mutually contradictory analytical approaches may each provide useful information for particular circumstances, and the sophisticated planner will want to understand several different approaches.

Both aggregate and disaggregate models can be instructive, the choice between them depending on availability of micro data and on how important it is to have an explicit representation of individual decision-making processes. Many of the problems plaguing the traditional planning process are not inherent in aggregate models, but rather in simplifications that obscure important feedback effects. Disaggregate models have performed well in many but not all circumstances, and have enabled researchers to undertake new and sophisticated types of policy analysis. They have also enriched our understanding of how variability affects travel behavior, and have given new insights into aggregate measures of attractiveness, accessibility, and welfare.

The theory of time allocation is well developed and permits us to rigorously address conceptual issues concerning value of time and reliability. Despite uncertainty, a consensus has developed over many of the most important empirical magnitudes for values of time, permitting them to be used confidently in benefit assessment. Another decade should bring similar consensus to value of reliability.

3 Costs

Having surveyed the demand for travel in the previous chapter, we now turn to its supply: that is, the conditions that determine how much travel of various types can be accomplished at what costs and prices. Just as travel demand is multi-dimensional, so a full analysis of the supply of transportation involves many facets, including multiple outputs, complex price structures, dimensions of service quality, and alternative forms of industrial organization.

It is useful to separate supply analysis into different parts. The first part, the subject of this chapter, consists of describing the technologies and factor supplies faced by transportation providers, information that is usefully summarized as cost functions. Other parts, in Chapters 4 through 6, consist of pricing, investment, and strategic decisions; these analyses involve transportation providers' economic behavior, resulting market outcomes, and normative criteria by which policy makers might like to influence those outcomes.

Because service quality is so important to the demand for transportation, we must also include it in any supply analysis. One way to do so is to define quality dimensions for each output. This is conceptually natural, but cumbersome. Another way is to view consumers as part of the production process, as in Becker's (1965) theory of household production; the level of service quality, like any other productive input, is then determined by conditions for efficient production. This approach, adopted here, treats user-supplied inputs, such as time, as if purchased in markets at prices equal to the values that are determined from demand analysis. In doing so, it moves such user inputs from the demand side to the supply side of the analysis and embeds them directly into cost functions.

Knowledge of cost functions enables us to answer questions about the relative efficiency of various types of transportation and about the relative importance of various parts of the production process such as capital, user time, operator wages, public facilities, and even unintended spillovers to non-users. The discussion begins in the next section with basic cost concepts. Section 3.2 then surveys our knowledge of cost functions for public transit service. Sections 3.3 through 3.5 do the same for highway transportation, with an emphasis on private automobiles and congestion; these sections provide a variety of models of congestion and synthesize our knowledge of key quantitative parameters affecting the social cost of automobile transportation. Section 3.6 briefly compares the average costs of particular types of trips by various private and public modes.

3.1 The nature of cost functions

The literature on transportation cost contains much confusion that can be avoided by using standard economic concepts and terminology as presented in, for example, Varian (1992).

Useful reviews include Jara-Díaz (1982), Braeutigam (1999), and Pels and Rietveld (2000). What follows is our own synthesis.

General definitions

A general description of technology, allowing for multiple outputs and inputs, is the *transformation function*:

$$F(q, x; \theta) = 0, \tag{3.1}$$

where q and x are vectors of outputs and inputs, respectively, and θ is a vector of parameters which may include service-quality descriptors. (Alternatively, services of different quality may be considered as different outputs in the vector q.) When there is just one output, (3.1) can be rewritten as a *production function* $q(x;\theta)$, giving q as a function of inputs and θ.

The *cost function* for a given producer gives the minimum cost C of producing output vector q, given the transformation function and the supply relations for inputs. Usually, these supply relations are assumed to consist of a fixed price vector w, so that the firm is a "price taker" in the input markets, in which case the problem becomes minimizing input expenditures $w'x$ subject to the technology constraint (3.1). The solution, if unique, determines an optimal input vector x^*. The resulting minimum cost, $w'x^*$, depends on q, w, and θ, so the cost function is written as $C(q,w;\theta)$. If input prices w are not independent of the producer's input choices and can therefore not be treated as fixed parameters, the vector w in the cost function should be redefined to represent parameters of these more elaborate factor-supply equations.

If all inputs are included in x, including those that can be varied only over a long time period, we obtain a *long-run cost function*, which will be denoted $\tilde{C}$ when the distinction between short and long run is relevant. If instead one or more inputs are held fixed during the minimization, the resulting cost is called a *short-run cost function*. Typically, the fixed input is a measure of capital stock, say x_n; its fixed value $\bar{x}_n$ becomes another argument of the resulting short-run cost function, which we may write as $C(q,w;\theta,\bar{x}_n)$. By definition,

$$\tilde{C}(q, w; \theta) = \min_{x_n} C(q, w; \theta, x_n). \tag{3.2}$$

Either the short- or long-run cost function may approach a positive constant C^0 as $q \to 0$. If so, C^0 is called the *fixed cost* and $C - C^0$ the *variable cost*. A short-run cost function always contains a fixed cost because it includes the carrying cost of fixed capital (*e.g.*, $w_n\bar{x}_n$); the rest of the short-run cost is called *operating cost*, since it characterizes ongoing operations. But operating cost may again contain a fixed component, independent of q: for example, the cost of maintaining the air supply in a subway tunnel or of repainting an automobile stored outdoors. Fixed cost should furthermore not be confused with *sunk cost*, a dynamic concept that expresses irreversibility in starting a business: for example, the cost of the marketing analysis and initial advertising campaign that might precede the introduction of a new transit service. A fixed operating cost can be eliminated by closing down the service entirely, whereas a sunk cost cannot.

Letting C denote either a short- or long-run cost function, we may define marginal cost with respect to output q_i as $mc_i = \partial C/\partial q_i$. One can see from (3.2) that, as follows from the envelope theorem (*e.g.*, Varian 1992), the long-run marginal cost is equal to the short-run marginal cost with $\bar{x}_n$ set to x_n^*; this implies that if capital stock is optimal, the cost of producing a small increment of output is the same whether or not capital stock is allowed to vary.

Economies of scale

Interest often centers on the degree of *scale economies, s*, which summarizes how fast costs rise with respect to output(s). If output q is a scalar, s is defined simply as the inverse of the output-elasticity of cost: letting $ac = C/q$ be average cost,

$$s \equiv \frac{ac}{mc} = \frac{C}{q \cdot (\partial C/\partial q)}.$$
(3.3)

If $mc < ac$ so that $s > 1$ (equivalently, if ac is falling in q), we have *economies of scale*. The opposite case ($s < 1$) is *diseconomies of scale*; and $s = 1$ defines a situation of *neither economies nor diseconomies of scale* or, more simply, *neutral scale economies*. Because a short-run cost function has a larger fixed cost than the corresponding long-run cost function, it is more likely to show scale economies.

Sometimes we want to consider cases where input prices w are functions of the amount of them that is purchased, thus indirectly of output, $w(q)$. In that case we can define scale economies using the total rather than partial derivative in (3.3); we may then call the (total) relationship between C and q the *general-equilibrium supply function* and the corresponding scale economies *general-equilibrium scale economies*. If all input prices w are constant, then (dis)economies of scale, which are properties of cost functions, are equivalent to *increasing (decreasing) returns to scale*, which are properties of the transformation function (3.1) and the production function implied by it. (The term "returns to scale" refers to whether production rises more or less than proportionally when all inputs are increased together by the same proportion.) As a result, scale economies and returns to scale are often treated as synonymous. However, for a general-equilibrium supply function, a rising or falling supply price of a factor input can upset this relationship.

If a firm sells output q at a price equal to its marginal cost, revenue is

$$R = q \cdot (\partial C/\partial q) = C/s.$$
(3.4)

Hence revenue will exactly cover total cost if there are neutral scale economies ($s = 1$); scale diseconomies will produce a profit, while scale economies will produce a deficit. This observation makes it clear that an analysis of scale economies has significant implications for the financial terms at which marginal-cost pricing can take place, which makes it of interest in the study of regulation, competition, and public pricing – as we shall see in later chapters.

This relationship between cost coverage and economies of scale generalizes readily to many outputs, provided the degree-of-scale indicator s is redefined in a particular but natural way. Following Bailey and Friedlaender (1982), define s by the last equality in (3.3) but with the denominator replaced by $\sum_i q_i \cdot \partial C/\partial q_i$. (This version of s is a measure of *multiproduct scale economies*.) Then (3.4) again holds under marginal-cost pricing for all outputs i.

In this case *s* can be related to a combination of individual-product scale economies and *economies of scope*, which measure the extent to which it is cheaper to produce several products within the same firm rather than in separate firms.

Definition of outputs

The definitions just given can be made operational only by simplifying the complex production processes encountered in real life. For example, a transit agency does many things, only a few of which can be measured and analytically manipulated as outputs; it draws on many resources, only a few of which find their way into formal analysis as inputs. There is no one correct set of definitions; what matters is that the definitions chosen to study a particular phenomenon facilitate understanding and prediction.

For transportation cost analysis, it is useful to consider two classes of output. One, which we can call *final* or *demand-related outputs*, measures the quantity and/or extent of trips taken. This type of output corresponds to the variables studied in travel-demand analysis. A complete cost analysis would distinguish all the various kinds of trips produced, such as trips from central London to Heathrow airport during the afternoon rush-hour. In practice, final outputs are usually aggregated in some manner for tractability – expressed for example as total passenger trips, revenue passengers (the number of distinct fares paid), unlinked passenger trips (the number of passenger boardings of distinct vehicles), passenger-miles, vehicle-miles, or even total revenues (a valid output measure if the fare structure is held constant in the analysis).

From the point of view of the transportation provider, however, final outputs are not under its control in the same way that, say, the number of chairs produced is under the control of a furniture manufacturer. No one would analyze a furniture manufacturer by counting as its output the number of its chairs that are occupied at any moment. Similarly, the transit firm may be more interested in the cost of producing the potential for trips – as measured, for example, by vehicle-miles, vehicle-hours, or seat-miles of service. We may consider such measures to be *intermediate outputs*, because they are combined with user time to produce the final outputs; they are also called *supply-related outputs*. Intermediate outputs are sometimes bought and sold as intermediate goods – for example, when a public transit agency contracts to pay a private firm for a particular amount and type of bus service on a particular route – while the agency itself undertakes to use its marketing abilities to convert this service into actual trips taken.

Whether one measures cost functions in terms of final or intermediate outputs depends upon the purpose of the analysis. A study of the technical efficiency of firms' production would use intermediate outputs, whereas a study of the effectiveness of the firms' service offerings and marketing policies would use final outputs. One may also include both in a multi-output analysis.

Implicit in the definition of a cost function for producing *final* outputs is a decision rule for choosing *intermediate* outputs. For example, determining the minimum cost of producing passenger trips along a given bus route entails finding the cost-minimizing headway (the time interval between buses). This suggests a two-step strategy for analyzing transit service. In the first step, a cost function is defined in terms of intermediate outputs such as vehicle-miles, vehicle-hours, and peak vehicles in service. In the second step, a model is constructed to represent optimal choice of intermediate outputs, given the environment and final output demands. A description of this environment might include the length of a corridor, the area from which it draws patronage, densities of trip origins and destinations, and possible methods by which passengers can access the system and reach their final destinations. This two-step model makes explicit the optimization of intermediate outputs, and thereby makes it possible to analyze a firm's operating policies as well as its technical production process.

Whatever the type of outputs considered, care should be taken when aggregating them into a manageable number of empirical measures. A pragmatic way of handling multiple outputs parsimoniously in cost functions is to choose aggregate measures of output (*e.g.*, vehicle-miles) while allowing the function to depend also on descriptors of the operating environment (*e.g.*, traffic speeds). It is especially important to retain the distinction between expanding the *density* of output – for example, by adding more vehicle-miles on a given route network – and expanding the *spatial scale* of output: for example, by extending service to new suburban locations. The former often allows more intense use of equipment, thereby lowering average cost – a form of scale economies called *economies of density*. In contrast, extending service to new locations may or may not involve scale economies: if it does they are called *economies of size*. Many transportation industries have been found to have economies of density but not of size (Braeutigam 1999). However, some have argued that the usual forms of network aggregation defining economies of size are ambiguous and do not correspond to useful policy questions (Basso and Jara-Díaz 2006).

Methods of measurement

There are at least three general approaches to empirically measuring cost functions. The *accounting* approach examines the budgetary accounts of one or more enterprises, adjusts as needed to match economic concepts of opportunity cost, and then attributes specific accounts to specific outputs. The *engineering* approach builds a production function from technical descriptions of the production process and adds information about input prices. The *statistical* approach infers how cost varies with levels of output and other variables by observing the costs actually incurred in many different situations: for example, over many time periods or over a cross-section of firms. The generality of the statistical approach has been greatly enlarged by techniques, pioneered by Christensen, Jorgenson and Lau (1973) and Spady and Friedlaender (1978), for estimating flexible functional forms such as the trans-log function (which is quadratic in logarithms of all variables). There is considerable overlap among these three approaches, and any given study may make use of more than one.

External, social, and full costs

Recent years have seen increased attention to costs that are borne not by the providing agency or the individual users of a given service, but by other parties. Examples abound: air pollution, noise, ground-water contamination, and wildlife disruption, to name a few. Such costs are called "external" because they fall on parties who are not part of the decision resulting in that cost (for example, a decision to make a trip by car worsens the air quality along the route taken). Those parties might be people who have themselves made similar decisions, but unless they do so as part of a collective (*e.g.*, a tour operator), it can be presumed for the most part that each person disregards such external effects when deciding on travel arrangements. External costs drive a wedge between the private costs, as faced by the decision maker, and the social costs, as incurred by society at large. We shall see later that this wedge implies that the market will fail to produce an efficient outcome. External costs like these should not be confused with so-called *pecuniary externalities*, which arise when one actor's market behavior affects – perhaps marginally – the prevailing market prices. Pecuniary externalities are not, by themselves, a source of market failure.

There are other reasons why observable factor prices do not exactly reflect an input's true cost to society. Some factor prices may reflect subsidies, taxes, or regulations, and therefore may cause someone beside the factor owners to be affected by their use. Likewise, when the supplier of the input holds market power, the input's price will generally exceed the supplier's true cost, with the difference reflecting the supplier's mark-up and giving rise to supernormal profits. In such cases, part of the cost to the purchaser of the input is not a cost to society but rather a transfer to someone else, and so again there is a discrepancy between private and social cost.

Social or *full costs* are the total costs to society, including any external costs and correcting for transfers as described just above. We may next define the *marginal social cost (msc)* of a particular travel movement (such as a vehicle-mile in an automobile) as the derivative of social cost with respect to that movement. Most often when studying divergences between private and social costs, we are interested in external costs rather than distorted factor pricing; the *msc* therefore includes both the marginal private cost as defined from a private cost function (excluding taxes and subsidies) and the *marginal external cost (mec)*: *i.e.*, the effect of that movement on other parties. If consumers are atomistic price-takers and ignore their own impact on cost levels, then perceived marginal private cost equals average private cost. If furthermore the externality is fully mutual, in the sense that external costs are borne entirely by other travelers making the same kind of decision, then the average private cost must be the same as average social cost (*ac*), so that $mec = msc - ac$. Congestion is usually modeled this way.

With a mutual externality, costs do not divide up neatly between the perpetrators and the recipients of the externality, because they are the same people. Therefore, measures of "total external cost," for example obtained by multiplying *mec* by quantity, are not easy to interpret and generally not very useful. This is especially true because many externalities are only partly mutual. For example, carbon monoxide emissions from motor vehicles tend to remain close to the highway so their damage is borne partly by the parties producing it (drivers on that highway) and partly by third parties (pedestrians or nearby residents). As another example, motor vehicle injuries involve a complex mix of private costs, mutual external costs, and external costs borne by non-motorists. Note that for the determination of *mec*, relevant for the formulation of efficient (tax) policies, it is immaterial whether or not the externality is mutual.

Numerous studies have attempted to quantify social costs; some also identify those costs that are external and/or those costs that are marginal to a particular movement.[1] Section 3.4.6 incorporates results of many such studies.

3.2 Cost functions for public transit

This section examines some of the many attempts to measure the cost of providing bus or rail transit service. We adopt the two-step strategy described earlier: first we analyze the cost of producing intermediate outputs, then we use the results in explicit optimization models of the production of final outputs. The first three subsections that follow are mainly about the first step, describing three approaches to measuring cost functions; the last subsection covers the second step.

3.2.1 Accounting cost studies

Accounting cost studies seek to determine the relation between cost and intermediate outputs by examining cost accounts of transit agencies. Studies using this approach usually assume that cost is a linear function of a few measures of intermediate outputs such as route-miles RM, peak vehicles in service PV, vehicle-hours VH, and vehicle-miles VM:

$$C = c_1 \cdot RM + c_2 \cdot PV + c_3 \cdot VH + c_4 \cdot VM. \tag{3.5}$$

This approach involves "fully allocated costs," in the sense that all cost items are allocated to one and only one of the outputs: there are no fixed costs and no joint costs.[2]

We can use the outputs in this model to distinguish between economies of density and of size, by noting that RM is a measure of network size. If all four outputs are expanded together, cost rises by the same percentage; so the cost function shows neither economies nor diseconomies of size by assumption. If route-miles are held fixed, however, cost rises less than proportionally to a simultaneous increase in the other three outputs (assuming $c_1 > 0$); so there are economies of density.

Many accounting studies were developed during the 1970s and 1980s due to the need for more fine-tuned cost information as part of policy developments involving deregulation and privatization of transit (Savage 1988, 1989). Table 3.1 compares the results of two such studies that use equation (3.5). They attempt to provide figures that are comparable across modes, although only one (Boyd, Asher and Wetzler 1973, 1978) includes any infrastructure for bus (an exclusive busway). Each study has a different strength: Allport (1981) draws from the accounts of a single agency providing three types of transit (in Rotterdam, the Netherlands), thereby eliminating some sources of difference in comparing across modes; whereas Boyd, Asher and Wetzler draw from many transit agencies in Canada, the US, and Mexico, thereby providing a more representative sample. From both studies, it is clear that capital costs for rail vehicles are much higher than for buses. The Allport study suggests that, for Rotterdam, any cost advantage of light rail (running on city streets) over heavy rail (with fully separated right of way) is confined primarily to lower capital and maintenance costs for its tracks; it is uncertain whether even this is a real cost advantage or a failure to account for the opportunity cost of public street space.

Naturally the cost of providing transit service depends on the balance of peak and off-peak service. The model of equation (3.5) portrays this dependence in two ways. First, peak service obviously determines the value of PV. Second, peak operations require a larger number of vehicle-hours VH to provide the same frequency of service because peak congestion slows those vehicles. In addition, one would expect driver costs per vehicle-hour to differ between peak and off-peak service, because peak periods are too short to constitute a full workday and therefore result in unproductive time and/or overtime pay for full-time drivers. To represent this, it is common to divide vehicle-hours into *base service*, VH_b, and *peak service*, VH_p, the former representing service at a constant rate over most of the day (including peak hours) and the latter representing additional service during peak hours only. (One could distinguish night or weekend service as well, but we forgo that complication.) This suggests the following modification of (3.5):

$$C = c_1 \cdot RM + c_2 \cdot PV + c_b \cdot VH_b + c_p \cdot VH_p + c_4 \cdot VM.$$

Table 3.1 Accounting cost functions for public transit: incremental costs

	Rapid rail		Light rail	Bus	
	Boyd[a]	Allport[b]	Allport	Allport	Boyd
Capital cost:[c]					
Per route-mile ($M/yr)	6.57	3.84	0.77	NA	0.99[d]
Per peak vehicle ($K/yr)	104.1	63.2	83.9	16.0	28.4
Operating cost:					
Per route-mile ($M/year)	0	0.920	0.231	0.009	0
Per peak vehicle ($K/yr)	0	63.9	45.2	29.2	0
Per convoy-hour[e] ($)	7.92	41.59	54.55	52.35	30.07
Per vehicle-mile[e] ($)	8.15	2.95	3.12	1.39	1.32

Notes:

All figures are in 2005 US$, updated using the transportation component of the Consumer Price Index for all urban consumers (US CEA 2006, Table B-60).

NA means the costs in this category were excluded by the author(s); in contrast to 0, which indicates the costs were included but allocated to other outputs.

a   Boyd, Asher and Wetzler (1978, pp. 5–6) and (1973, pp. 29, A-47, and E-1). Figures given by the authors are projected 1980 costs in 1972 US prices.

b   Allport (1981). Figures given by the author are estimates from accounts of the Rotterdam system in 1978 but adjusted to British conditions in 1980; we have converted to US dollars at the average 1978–80 exchange rate of £1 = $2.12, then updated as noted above. Distances are converted using 1 km = 0.6214 mile. Costs per station or stop are converted to costs per route-mile using the average spacings given for Rotterdam (Allport 1981, p. 633).

c   Annualized capital cost of way, structures, and rolling stock. Allport computes them using an interest rate of 5% per year, and appropriate lifetimes; for rapid rail we average his figures for underground and elevated systems and for different vehicle specifications, while for light rail we use his "high demand" figures, which apply to peak-direction peak-hour passenger demand volumes "considerably higher" than Rotterdam's 450–1010 (p. 633). Boyd *et al.* give capital outlay; we annualize it using their assumptions of: 5% interest; 30-year lifetime for way, structures, and rail cars (hence capital recovery factor 0.0651); 12-year lifetime for bus (capital recovery factor 0.1128). Also, we add a 20% "spare ratio" to their vehicle costs to account for vehicles not in service (this ratio was used by the US Urban Mass Transportation Administration for its funding formulas: *Metro Magazine*, July/August 1990, p. 16).

d   Cost of a two-lane exclusive busway, using land cost in 1972 prices of $0.68M/route-mile (Boyd *et al.* 1978, p. 6) plus construction cost of $1.40M/lane-mile (Boyd *et al.* 1973, p. 29), both annualized as in the previous note.

e   A "vehicle" is one rail car or bus. A "convoy" consists of one train (rapid rail), one light-rail vehicle, or one bus. The trains considered by Allport are 2–6 vehicles (1981, p. 633), while those considered by Boyd *et al.* are 2–10 vehicles (1973, pp. E-2 and E-3); we assume a four-car train.

Analysis of staffing requirements in British and US transit agencies has suggested to several authors that the ratio c_p/c_b is about 2.0 for bus systems;[3] empirical estimates range from 1.1 to 2.5.[4] Simulation studies of driver schedules, given work rules and overtime pay rates, suggest an approximate value of $c_p/c_b = 1.5$ for typical conditions.[5] This figure is probably the best estimate currently available.

Since the extra cost incurred in peak service depends on work rules, it might be reduced through labor negotiations. Chomitz and Lave (1984) find that work-rule changes, especially hiring part-time drivers, could reduce total bus operating costs modestly, in most cases between 3% and 8%. (More generally, of course, the magnitudes of the all-important parameters c_p and c_b depend on negotiated wage rates whenever unions are involved, and may be quite sensitive to the laws governing unionization and contract negotiations.)

Abbas and Abd-Allah (1999) demonstrate how the cost accounts of a transit agency can be dissected to allocate costs among output categories, using accounts of the primary public transit provider for Cairo, Egypt. To aid in allocation, they use information about the activity (operation, maintenance, or administration) and travel mode(s) to which a given cost item pertains. Some of their results are summarized in Table 3.2. It is notable that nearly every type of unit cost is much higher for full-size bus than for minibus, and higher still for tram (streetcar). These differences are reduced but not eliminated if we divide by average capacity, as shown in the second panel. The aggregate percentages shown in the third panel portray a surprisingly high proportion of costs depending on peak vehicles in service, which effectively are fixed in the short run; this result is attributed by the authors to "overstaffing" of the transit system, the extent of which is suggested by the figures in the last row. (However, Egyptian wage rates are far lower than those in highly developed nations, so it is appropriate that capital equipment be used more intensively.)

We caution that accounting practices vary from agency to agency, and do not always accurately reflect the economic costs that are the real concern of the transportation analyst.

3.2.2 Engineering cost studies

Engineering cost studies use detailed engineering information to construct cost functions in a "bottom-up" fashion. The classic study by Meyer, Kain and Wohl (1965) is a masterful example of engineering costing, supplemented by accounting and statistical methods. They estimate cost functions for several forms of public transit, as well as for automobile travel. The authors specify in great detail the characteristics of each mode, including engineering specifications and lifetimes for the physical infrastructure and vehicles, precise operational characteristics such as headways and station dwell times, and prices for all components. Many of these parameters are specified as functions of passenger volume and urban residential density.

Table 3.2 Accounting cost model for Cairo, Egypt

	Minibus	*Regular bus*	*Tram*
Unit costs:[a]			
Per peak convoy[b] per year (*PV*)	196	557	1782
Per convoy-hour (*VH*)	3.4	13.8	44.6
Per convoy-mile (*VM*)	0.35	0.48	3.57
Unit costs divided by capacity *n* (for seated plus standing people):			
Per person per year (*PV·n*)	7.84	16.88	23.45
Per person-hour (*VH·n*)	0.14	0.42	0.59
Per person-mile (*VM·n*)	0.0142	0.0146	0.0470
Percentage of category in total cost:			
$c_2 \cdot PV$	66.0	65.2	61.2
$c_3 \cdot VH$	16.5	24.8	23.4
$c_4 \cdot VM$	17.5	10.0	15.4
Employees per convoy	7.5	16.7	51.9

Source: Abbas and Abd-Allah (1999, Tables 1, 4).

Notes:
a   Monetary units are Egyptian pounds (EGP) for fiscal year 1996–97. The exchange rate was 3.4 EGP = US$1.
b   A convoy means one or more vehicles traveling together. It consists of one minibus, one regular bus, or two tram cars.

Some of the costs are estimated from firms' accounts and others from statistical analysis, but most come from actual price quotes; for example, the prices of vehicles.

Meyer, Kain and Wohl's cost estimates for highway construction are discussed in Section 3.5.3, and their overall results comparing costs for different modes are considered in Section 3.6.

3.2.3 Statistical cost studies

Statistical cost studies pool information from various transit agencies and/or time periods and use statistical inference to estimate the parameters of cost functions. These studies permit relaxing the assumption of linearity in cost functions, and so are especially useful for their results on scale economies.

Viton (1980) uses "translog" functions (*i.e.*, functions that are quadratic in the logarithms of the variables) to estimate a short-run operating-cost function for rapid rail operations, with vehicle-miles as output, using annual data for seven North American agencies in the years 1970–80. Cost is specified as a function of output, input prices, and fixed capital stock. Because track length is fixed, the ratio of average to marginal cost is a measure of the degree of economies of density. The results are firm-specific, but generally suggest a U-shaped average cost curve, with strong economies of density for some smaller agencies (maximum $s = 2.04$) and strong diseconomies for some large ones ($s = 0.30$ for New York).[6] The diseconomies found for New York, Chicago, and Philadelphia are evidence of congested operations on a too-small system of tracks. According to Viton's estimated model, the median agency's short-run average operating cost, in 2005 prices, is US\$5.34 per vehicle-mile.[7] Savage (1997) distinguishes between economies of density and size, finding that 22 US light- and heavy-rail systems operate with strong economies of density but close to neutral economies of size.

Turning to bus providers, Viton (1981b) estimates a short-run cost function on a 1975 cross-section of 54 US city bus systems, using vehicle-miles as output. He then uses the results, along with engineering estimates of capital costs, to construct long-run costs under optimal capital utilization. The results again indicate a U-shaped average cost function, but a much flatter one than for rail: he finds mild scale economies for small firms (maximum $s = 1.16$ for the smallest) and mild scale diseconomies for large firms ($s = 0.87$ for the largest, Chicago). Long-run average cost, restated in 2005 prices, ranges from US\$2.90 to US\$4.94 per vehicle-mile.[8] Viton finds that most bus providers have a fleet that is considerably larger than the one he computes as optimal. Button and O'Donnell (1985), using 55 UK bus agencies and passenger revenues as output, similarly find mild scale economies (up to 1.43) for small firms and diseconomies (down to 0.89) for large firms.[9]

Berechman (1993) and De Borger and Kerstens (2000) review these and other statistical studies, reaching several conclusions. First, for bus providers, statistical evidence supports the conclusion of Viton (1981b): intermediate outputs such as vehicle-miles are produced with a mildly U-shaped relationship between average cost and output. Second, producing final outputs such as passenger trips is much more likely to entail scale economies. Third, rail systems exhibit much greater variability in scale economies; this is especially true in the short run because their capital stock may be too large or too small for the current operations. Fourth, however, there seems to be a bias toward operating with a larger than optimal capital stock, possibly due to incentives built into capital subsidy programs.

Wunsch (1996) provides a nice example of how knowledge from previous studies can guide a statistical specification to derive the greatest amount of information from a limited data set. Wunsch compiles cost data from a cross-section of 178 separate operating agencies throughout western and northern Europe. Rather than estimate flexible functional forms from this rather small data set, he uses earlier work to justify the assumptions that (a) there are no scale economies in producing convoy-miles VM (where a convoy is one or more vehicles operated by a single driver: *e.g.*, a train or bus); (b) labor costs follow a linear form, something like (3.5), and are proportional to the local wage rate; and (c) non-labor costs are allocable entirely to convoy-miles. The variant of (3.5) used for labor cost is:

$$LC^j = \left[c_{1a}^j \cdot TM^j + c_{1b}^3 \cdot Stations^j + c_3 \cdot VH^j + (c_{4a}^j + c_{4b}^j \cdot n^j) \cdot VM^j \right] \cdot (w/\overline{w}), \qquad (3.6)$$

where $j = 1, 2, 3$ is a modal indicator representing bus, streetcar, or subway; TM is the number of track-miles in the streetcar or subway system (0 for bus); $Stations$ is the number of subway stations (0 for bus and streetcar); n is the capacity of a convoy in persons (measured as square meters of floor space divided by four); w is the local wage rate; and $\overline{w}$ is the average wage rate over the sample. The study does not distinguish between peak and off-peak service. Because an agency's bus and streetcar operations, and sometimes its subways, are consolidated into a single account, this equation is estimated by simultaneously estimating one equation for total labor cost, $LC = \Sigma_j S^j LC^j$ (where S^j is the j th modal share in convoy-miles), and another just for subway cost, LC^3, where separate observations on subway cost are available (16 agencies).[10] In order to avoid heteroscedasticity (differing variances across observations), equation (3.6) is divided by VM^j before aggregation and estimation.

An example will help clarify how to interpret the coefficients. Parameter c_3 is the cost of a vehicle-hour of service at wage rate $\overline{w}$; its estimate of 598 BF (Belgian francs) per convoy-hour, compared to $\overline{w} = 520$ BF per hour, suggests that labor costing the same as 1.15 hours of driver time is required for every incremental convoy-hour of service provided. Furthermore, the relative size of $c_3 \cdot VH^j$ compared to the other terms in (3.6) determines the labor-cost elasticity with respect to speed, *i.e.*, the percentage change in labor cost brought about by a 1% increase in speed. If all labor cost were proportional to VH and thus inversely proportional to speed, this elasticity would be -1; the actual elasticities estimated for average conditions are very different: -0.392 for bus, -0.121 for streetcar, and -0.047 for subway. These values are important in knowing how congestion affects transit costs, but their absolute values may be underestimates because of the assumption that all non-labor cost (for those properties where it could be isolated) is independent of speed.

Wunsch's (1996) results can also be used to estimate scale economies in providing vehicle capacity – which are the root source of economies of density. Thus, the results help us understand what passenger densities are required for rail modes (streetcar, subway, or a mixture of the two which Wunsch calls "light rail") to be cheaper than bus. As it happens, the coefficients c_{4b}^j giving the *incremental* operating cost of expanding passenger capacity are estimated to be very similar among the three modes. However, due to the other terms, the *average* operating cost of passenger capacity declines with capacity, in a manner that turns out to be nearly identical for the two rail modes but very different for bus. In the case of bus, it declines to a value equivalent to about US$0.073/person-mile (at 2005 prices) at the maximum bus capacity, shown by Wunsch as about 110. In the case of rail, average capacity cost starts higher but declines throughout a larger range of capacities, with subways reaching the value just stated when capacity is about 400 potential passengers per convoy. In other words, a subway has a lower operating cost than bus if there is enough passenger density to require trains holding 400 or more people. This capacity is greater than that observed for any streetcar system, causing Wunsch to conclude that, in terms of operating costs, "streetcars do not fill a significant gap between buses and underground rail" (p. 171). Of course, to complete the comparison, we need to consider capital costs as well, which we take up in Sections 3.5 and 3.6.

3.2.4 Cost functions including user inputs

As already noted, travelers must supply some inputs, especially their time, as part of producing final outputs such as trips. We illustrate here with public transit users, and in Sections 3.4–3.5 with users of private vehicles.

Transit users spend time accessing the system, waiting for vehicles, riding in vehicles, possibly transferring between vehicles, and getting to final destinations. This section considers just waiting time. The consequences of including waiting time as an input to the production of trips are dramatic, and similar consequences would follow from including time spent walking or transferring. Specifically, Mohring (1972) shows that when waiting-time costs are included, transit service is subject to strong economies of density in producing final outputs, even if such economies are absent for producing intermediate outputs.

We can demonstrate this proposition with a simplified version of Mohring's model for peak-period bus transit on a single route.[11] The measure of final output, q, is the number of passengers per peak hour on the route. It is produced using two inputs. First is the intermediate good V defined as vehicles passing a given bus stop per peak hour, produced at unit cost c_p. Second is a user-supplied input, aggregate waiting time per peak hour W, valued at unit cost α^W. Suppose average waiting time per passenger, W/q, is equal to half the headway, $1/V$; this would reflect arrivals at the stop independent of the schedule. Aggregate costs to the bus agency and to the users, respectively, are then:

$$C_B = c_p V; \quad C_W = \frac{\alpha^W q}{2V}.$$

We choose V to minimize the sum of these costs, subject to a constraint imposed by bus capacity:

$$q \leq NV,$$

where N is the total number of passengers a bus can pick up and drop off as it travels the entire route. That is, $N = nL/d$ where n is the physical capacity of the bus (maximum number of passengers at any time); d is the average passenger's trip length; and L is the length of the route.

Letting λ be the Lagrangian multiplier of the constraint, the first-order condition is:

$$c_p - \frac{\alpha^W q}{2V^2} - N\lambda = 0.$$

There are two possible solutions. If $\lambda=0$, indicating that buses are not full, the solution is (with a star denoting optimized choices):

$$V^* = \sqrt{\frac{\alpha^W}{2c_p}} \cdot \sqrt{q}; \quad W^* = \frac{q}{2V^*} = \sqrt{\frac{c_p}{2\alpha^W}} \cdot \sqrt{q};$$

$$C_B^* = c_P \cdot V^* = \sqrt{\frac{\alpha^W \cdot c_p}{2}} \cdot \sqrt{q}; \quad C_W^* = \alpha^W \cdot W^* = \sqrt{\frac{\alpha^W \cdot c_p}{2}} \cdot \sqrt{q}.$$

Two properties of this solution are worth noting. First, the optimal bus frequency V^* is proportional to the square root of the passenger density q; this is known as the *square root rule* for operating policy. Second, the cost function is also proportional to $\sqrt{q}$, which gives it economies of scale (*i.e.*, of density): specifically, $s = 2$. This implies that a generalized price set equal to marginal cost will involve a fare that is insufficient for the transit provider to cover its average cost. In fact, that fare is zero, which is the difference between the marginal cost $\partial C/\partial q$ and the value of the inputs supplied by users, C_W/q. The intuition here is simple: if buses are not full, then it costs nothing to take another passenger. We derive optimal fares more formally in the next chapter.

If $\lambda>0$, indicating the capacity constraint is binding, the solution is $V^*= q/N$, $W^*=q/(2\cdot V^*) = N/2$, $C_B^* = c_p \cdot q/N$, and $C_W^*= \alpha^W N/2$. Over the range of output for which this solution holds, the total cost function is linear in output and has fixed cost C_W^*. It thus again exhibits density economies, namely $s=1+(C_W^*/C_B^*)$.[12] Once again, setting generalized price equal to marginal cost will not make the fare high enough for the transit provider to cover its cost. The fare in this case amounts to $c_p/N - \alpha^W \cdot N/(2q)$.[13] The fare includes the term c_p/N, because now the agency does have to increase its bus service to accommodate a new passenger; but the fare is then discounted below that amount because the increased service reduces waiting costs to other passengers.

So whether or not the constraint is binding, there are economies of density because either operating costs or waiting costs grow less than proportionally as output expands.

Analogous models can be constructed to show how the transit operator could respond by increasing route density instead of, or in addition to, increasing frequency along a route.[14] In this case it is savings in walking time as well as waiting time that account for increasing returns. Because there are now two ways the agency can save user cost by offering more service, optimal vehicle-miles offered grow more rapidly with passenger density – specifically, with its two-thirds power. As vehicle-miles are expanded, half of the increased service is configured so as to reduce waiting costs and the other half to reduce walking costs.

There are many ways in which we can make this model more realistic. We could consider off-peak travel as a separate output. We could consider the width of the peak period to be variable, and take into account the effect that peak broadening would have on parameter c_p. We could take into account the effect on average speed of additional passengers boarding or leaving the vehicle, thereby obtaining a positive optimal fare even when buses are not full. Mohring (1972) and Kraus (1991) show that this last effect can be quite important. We could recognize that bus capacity is not an absolute limit, but rather influences the degree of crowding and the probability that the first bus to arrive will be too crowded to enter.

We could also allow bus capacity to be endogenous, chosen as part of overall cost minimization, and thereby estimate optimal bus size. This approach is adopted by Jansson

(1980), Glaister (1986), and Nash (1988), who conclude that optimal bus size is much smaller than actual size in typical situations in Sweden and in the UK. There is some evidence from partial bus deregulation in the UK that small firms using small buses do, in fact, find a niche when allowed to do so.

The fact that economies of density result from treating waiting time as a cost provides a fundamental insight into public transportation modes. These modes depend on matching a set of desired trips, each at a particular time and place, to available vehicles. Similar results hold for airlines (Douglas and Miller 1974) and taxicabs (Frankena and Pautler 1986). The insight does not depend upon a literal view of waiting time, but applies to any disutility created by infrequent service; for example, deviations from most desired arrival times or the increased necessity to consult timetables when frequencies are lower. Any such disutility can be expected to diminish in service frequency which, in turn, typically increases with aggregate demand. The average user is then better off when ridership increases, provided, of course, there is no overriding negative impact on comfort. The practical consequences of this insight depend on the precise service arrangements. If intermingling of services by more than one firm causes the user to care only about the firms' combined service frequency, the economies of density are industry-wide and firms confer externalities on one another. If, on the other hand, the user has to pre-commit to one firm, the economies are firm-specific.

3.3 Highway travel: congestion technology

The importance of the automobile in urban travel patterns has created great interest in how best to cope with the various costs that it imposes. This question can be addressed by defining and measuring cost functions for motor vehicles on highways. Doing so facilitates pricing and investment analyses, which are the central contributions of economics to public policy in this area. For example, questions about optimal pricing or privately owned highways can be addressed by applying standard economic tools to carefully defined cost functions. The use of cost functions also makes precise what it really costs society to undertake a particular kind of trip by motor vehicle.

We therefore analyze the costs of highway travel in this and the next two sections. This section presents the pure technology of highway congestion, a subject brought squarely into transportation analysis by Beckmann, McGuire and Winsten (1956). Because it is so crucial to urgent policy questions, we provide considerable detail. We also argue that the static model used in the standard economic analysis of congestion is not fully satisfactory, and present a dynamic model that is tractable for the analyses of the following sections. Section 3.4 then derives short-run cost functions, *i.e.*, those for fixed road capacity, and confronts them with demand functions to characterize short-run equilibrium. The approach in that section is to incorporate user time directly as a cost, thereby making the congestion technology an integral part of the cost function; it also reviews empirical evidence on the magnitudes of short-run variable costs. Section 3.5 adds information about infrastructure costs in order to compute long-run cost functions.

3.3.1 *Fundamentals of congestion*

A rather general economic definition of congestion is that it occurs when the quality of service of a facility depends on the intensity of use. For transportation, important aspects of quality include expected travel time, expected arrival time, reliability, and convenience of travel.

Highway congestion arises from many causes. Traffic forms queues at signals. Cars entering from side streets wait for gaps in traffic on a main highway. Cars traveling behind slower vehicles on two-lane roads must wait for gaps in oncoming traffic before passing. Consequently, many types of congestion and modeling approaches can be distinguished. One distinction is between *link* and *nodal* congestion. The former involves slowing down of traffic when the traffic density increases, independent of upstream or downstream bottlenecks; the latter refers to intersections (or, in the case of other modes, to stations, harbors, and airports). When congestion at nodes or other bottlenecks take the form of queuing before entering, it can be characterized as *stock* congestion, as opposed to *flow* congestion that can be identified independent of prior traffic conditions. Another, related, distinction is between *static* or *stationary-state* congestion versus *dynamic* congestion, the latter involving changes in traffic conditions over time and often interdependencies across different points in time.

Distinctions like these are often clearer and more absolute when referring to different types of models than when used for characterizing congestion in reality – which often involves mixtures of these "ideal" types. Congestion models can furthermore be distinguished between models for *single links* (isolated from other links) versus *networks*; models with *homogeneous* versus *heterogeneous* travelers; and *deterministic* versus *stochastic* models. The choice of model type of course depends on the question under consideration.

We begin with what is probably the simplest case: uniform, stationary-state congestion on a homogeneous highway without traffic signals, used by homogeneous travelers. When many vehicles try to use the highway simultaneously, the resulting high *density D* (number of vehicles per unit of distance) forces them to slow down for safety reasons, thereby reducing average vehicle *speed S*. One way to depict congestion, then, is as a functional relationship $S(D)$. An example is shown in quadrant *a* of Figure 3.1, in mirror-image form in which D increases toward the left.

We are also interested in traffic *flow* or *volume V*, defined as the number of vehicles passing a given point per unit time. Traffic flow is identically equal to the product of speed and density:

$$V \equiv SD, \tag{3.7}$$

which is consistent with its units of measure: vehicles/hour $\equiv$ (vehicles/mile) $\cdot$ (miles/hour). Unless stated otherwise, we normalize V and D with respect to road width, so that "vehicles" becomes a shorthand for "vehicles/lane" in these definitions.[15]

Given identity (3.7), the congestion technology can be expressed equivalently as a functional relationship between *any* two of the variables V, D, and S. One is the *speed-flow relationship* $S(V)$ shown in quadrant *b*; it is defined over the region $V \in [0, V_K]$, where V_K is the per-lane *capacity* of the highway: the maximum flow it can carry. As seen in the figure, the relation is double-valued; we refer to the upper branch as *congested* or *normally congested* and the lower branch as *hypercongested*.[16] The third possible relationship, that between V and D, is called by Haight (1963, pp. 69–73) the *fundamental diagram of traffic flow*; it is shown (rotated clockwise by 90 degrees) in quadrant *c* of Figure 3.1. Haight shows that flow first rises and later falls as density increases from zero, as depicted in the diagram.

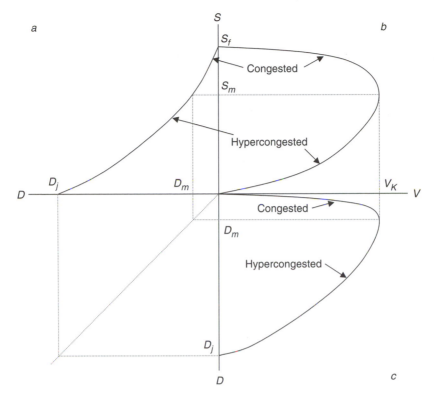

Figure 3.1 The fundamental diagram of traffic congestion in three forms.

Figure 3.1 shows diagrammatically how one can derive any of these three relationships from any of the others. The unused quadrant, in the lower left, is simply a diagonal line to equate values of density on the left horizontal axis and the lower vertical axis. The figure also shows the density D_m and speed S_m that correspond to maximum flow V_K. All other allowed flow levels can result from either a congested or a hypercongested speed and density. For example, a zero flow prevails when there are no vehicles on the road ($D = 0$), allowing the free-flow speed S_f; or when density reaches the value, known as the *jam density* D_j, that reduces speed to zero – this situation is shown at the origin of quadrant *b* and at the points marked D_j in quadrants *a* and *c*.

If these variables are defined over a very small region of time and space, the relationships shown in Figure 3.1 are instantaneous ones. Aggregate relationships can be built from them by relating the variables at neighboring times and places. This approach is used to build detailed computer models of a real facility (Coombe 1989). However, much of the economic literature has used the instantaneous speed–flow relationship to analyze aggregate performance of an entire highway. This may work well for situations where conditions change only slowly over time and space, but in other situations the instantaneous flow past a single point may be quite different from the economic demand for travel on the highway as reflected in the number of vehicles attempting to enter it. We discuss this problem more completely in Section 3.4.

3.3.2 Empirical speed–flow relationships

We begin with some empirical evidence concerning the fundamental diagram, and some extensions of it that have been found necessary to portray observed data.

Instantaneous relationships

There is uncertainty about the true shapes of the curves in Figure 3.1 in the neighborhood of maximum flow V_K and density D_m. Figure 3.2 illustrates why. Figure 3.2a plots observations of flow versus occupancy, a measure of density, for the Queen Elizabeth Way in Toronto, Canada. (Thus it is depicting the curve in Figure 3.1c after rotation by 90 degrees.) Although the two branches of the flow–density curve are reasonably well defined, the middle portion connecting them is obscured by scatter; and it is not clear whether the branches meet, *i.e.*, that the relationship is continuous.

Similarly, the speed-density data plotted in Figure 3.2b, from the Santa Monica Freeway in Los Angeles, California, appear to reflect two distinct regimes that are connected, not by a continuous curve, but by a region where the relationship is only vaguely defined.

At least two explanations have been put forth for the dispersion of observations where flow is close to capacity. Both posit two distinct flow regimes, one congested and the other hypercongested. One explanation is a measurement problem: since speed, flow, and density are in practice measured over a finite span of space and time, a given observation may inadvertently average two points from the two different regimes. Another explanation is that many intermediate-density observations correspond to disequilibrium conditions during transition between the congested and hypercongested regimes (Hall, Allen and Gunter 1986). Compounding matters is that in many data sets there is a paucity of observations at flows near capacity. This is presumably due to bottlenecks upstream or downstream from the point in question. Indeed, empirical estimates of speed-flow relationships are strongly influenced by nearby bottlenecks (Branston 1976; Hall and Hall 1990).

Despite these difficulties, many empirical estimates are reported in the literature; Hall (2002) provides a review. Some illustrative examples are described here.

Of historical interest is Greenshields' (1935) linear speed–density relationship, estimated on a two-lane, two-way road:

$$S = S_f \cdot (1 - D/D_j).$$

Applying identity (3.7) yields a parabolic speed–flow relationship. Later studies revealed that this parabolic shape is less accurate for larger highways, where instead speeds often remain constant, or nearly so, over a substantial range of flow levels.

Not surprisingly, the functional form used in the estimation may strongly affect the shape of the estimated function, even when the same data are used. For example, two separate research groups have fit speed–flow curves like that in Figure 3.1c to the same data from a four-lane section of the Washington (DC) Beltway. Boardman and Lave (1977) get the following result:[17]

$$V = 2490 - 0.523 \cdot (S - 35.34)^2,$$

where V is in vehicles per hour per lane. The two solutions to this quadratic equation in S represent congestion and hypercongestion. Inman (1978) obtains:[18]

$$V^{(2.95)} = 3.351 \cdot 10^9 - 231.4 \cdot (S - 7.2)^{(4.06)},$$

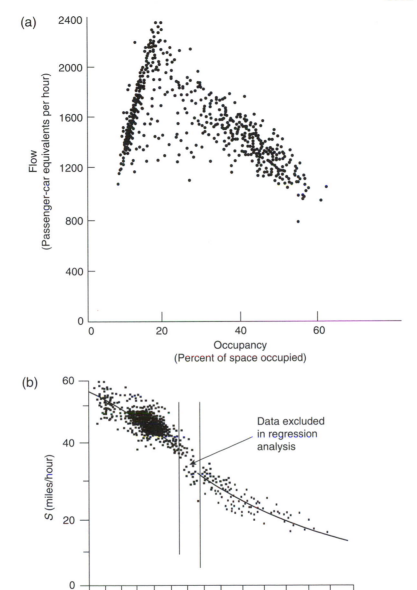

Figure 3.2 Flow-density and speed-density scatter plots.
      (a) Queen Elizabeth Way (Toronto). Adapted with permission from Hall *et al.* (1986, p. 204), copyright 1986, Pergamon Journals Ltd.
      (b) Santa Monica Freeway (Los Angeles). Adapted from Payne (1984, p. 145), with permission from Transportation Research Board, National Research Council, Washington, DC.

where, for any quantity X, $X^{(a)}$ denotes the Box–Cox transformation of X, defined as $(X^a - 1)/a$. The Boardman–Lave and Inman curves are both plotted in Figure 3.3, along with the scatter of data points. It appears that the Boardman–Lave curve represents the data more faithfully; but neither curve captures well the previously mentioned tendency, obvious from the raw data, for expressway speed in the region of normal congestion to remain nearly constant throughout most of the range of volume–capacity ratios.[19]

Figure 3.4 shows two more recent "official" speed–flow relations, which do account for this phenomenon: the COBA11 and Highway Capacity Manual (HCM2000) formulations in the UK and US, respectively.[20] Both portray normal congestion, not hypercongestion, and do so with two joined segments. HCM2000 joins a completely flat segment with a segment defined by a power function, with a continuous derivative; whereas COBA11 joins two linear segments with a discontinuous slope. The parameters depend on highway geometry, the share of heavy vehicles, and other factors. Also shown in the figure are dotted lines representing two other regimes posited by Hall, Hurdle and Banks (1992). One represents queue discharge within a bottleneck, and the other flow within a queue behind the bottleneck. In Section 3.4, we shall see that these regimes and their descriptions are consistent with emerging views on the hypercongested branch of the speed–flow relationship.

Space-averaged relationships

The relationship holding at a single time and place is not by itself useful for economic analysis of congestion, because it does not relate service quality for entire trips to the number of people attempting to travel. On real highways, queues form behind bottlenecks and traffic

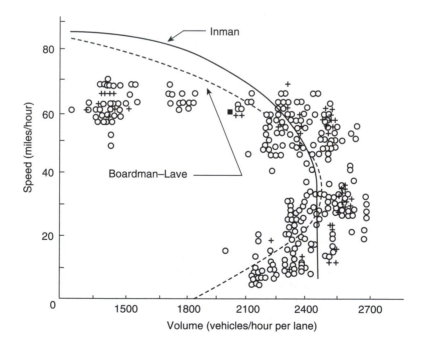

Figure 3.3 Washington, D.C. Beltway. Adapted with permission from Boardman and Lave (1977, p. 346), copyright 1977, Academic Press, Inc.

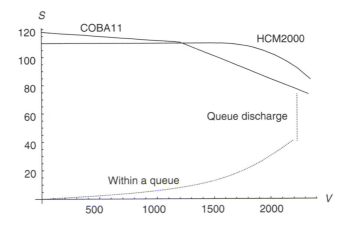

Figure 3.4 Sample speed–flow curves for US and UK government analyses.
Notes: S in km/h, V in veh/l/h. HCM2000 and COBA11 curves assume an expressway with no hills, bends, or heavy vehicles. Capacities under these idealized conditions are $V_K=2330$ (COBA) and $V_K=2350$ (HCM), and the break points V_B are 1200 (COBA) and 1450 (HCM). The two COBA segments are given by $S = 118 - 0.006 \cdot V$ for $V \leq V_B$ and $S = 110.8 - (33/1000) \cdot (V - V_B)$ for $V_B < V \leq V_K$. The two HCM segments are given by $S = 110$ for $V \leq V_B$ and $S = 110 - [(730/28) \cdot ((V-1450)/900)^{2.6}]$ for $V_B < V \leq V_K$. The two additional (dotted) segments proposed by Hall, Hurdle and Banks (1992) are hand-drawn.

volumes vary over time and place. One way to take such features into account is through formal network models, in which a speed–flow relationship applies to each link and users choose the resulting quickest routes (Marcotte and Nguyen 1998). Here we consider simpler approaches, namely averaging over space or time.

Keeler and Small (1977) use observations on three expressways in the San Francisco Bay area to estimate quadratic functions (like Boardman and Lave 1977) relating speed and volume–capacity ratio V/V_k, each averaged over a long stretch of highway. One resulting equation is:[21]

$$\frac{V}{V_K} = 0.8603 - 0.001923 \cdot \left(S - 45.68\right)^2.$$

In contrast to the instantaneous speed–flow curves, Keeler and Small's averaged curves show, on the upper (congested) branch, a substantial negative slope over the entire range of average vehicle flow. This reflects the fact that as traffic is added to a real highway, non-uniformities in the highway design or in demand patterns cause minor slowdowns even when the average volume–capacity ratio is well below one.

Clearly, the exact nature of an aggregate speed–flow relationship depends on the extent and nature of heterogeneity, so a curve fitted for one highway is unlikely to generalize. This is all the more true for streets and arterial highways subject to congestion at signalized intersections, whose technology is entirely different from that of an unobstructed highway. Here there are even more sources of heterogeneity including signal timing, turn lanes, intersection geometry, and on-street parking. Smeed (1968, p. 34) reports the following relationship, attributed to Wardrop, for city streets in London:

$$\frac{V}{w} = 68 - 0.13 \cdot S^2,$$

where w is width of road in feet. This relationship does not have a hypercongested branch, but rather approaches zero speed, implying infinite density, as $V \to 68w$.

For some purposes, it may be more useful to model speeds and flows over areas rather than along a single roadway. Ardekani and Herman (1987) use time-lapse aerial photography, combined with ground measurement of volumes, to estimate the following relationship between averaged values within the central area of Austin, Texas:[22]

$$S = 18.38 \cdot \left[1 - \left(0.01D \right)^{1.239} \right]^{2.58}, \tag{3.8}$$

where D is vehicle density per lane. They verify separately that (3.7) holds, to a good approximation, for their space-averaged quantities; this enables (3.8) to be converted into a speed–flow curve, for which maximum flow occurs at 9.1 miles per hour and which does include a hypercongested branch.

Time-averaged relationships

The space-averaged relationships just described cannot tell us what happens when demand exceeds the maximum flow. In such situations, speed depends not only on contemporaneous flow but also on past flows, usually via queuing. Time-averaged speed–flow functions incorporate such time dependence by relating average speed over a specified period to the average vehicle inflow over that period.

Two functional forms that allow for traffic flow above capacity are in common use. The first specifies travel delay as a power function of the volume–capacity ratio:

$$T = T_f \cdot \left[1 + a \cdot (V / V_K)^b \right], \tag{3.9}$$

where T denotes travel time per mile (the inverse of speed). This function has been used in many economic models of congestion such as Vickrey (1963), with parameter b typically assumed to be between 2.5 and 5.0. With parameter values $a=0.15$ and $b=4$, it is known as the Bureau of Public Roads (BPR) function, used widely in US transportation planning.[23] With values $a=0.2$ (freeways) or 0.05 (arterials), and $b=10$, it is known as the "updated BPR function" (denoted BPR-U below), derived by Skabardonis and Dowling (1996) to approximate the speed–flow functions in the 1994 Highway Capacity Manual, a predecessor to HCM2000 discussed above. While the potentially unlimited flow permitted by (3.9) might seem unrealistic, if it is used sensibly the traffic will be limited by other factors such as total demand or upstream bottlenecks.

One drawback of (3.9) is that it does not account for how long traffic exceeds capacity. This disadvantage is remedied in a duration-dependent function derived by Small (1983) to express the average travel time over a peak period of fixed duration P, when peak-period inflow V is at a uniform rate and delay results from queuing behind a single bottleneck with a constant capacity V_K. It yields a piecewise-linear relationship:[24]

$$T = \begin{cases} T_f & \text{if } V \leq V_K \\ T_f + \frac{1}{2} P \cdot (V / V_K - 1) & \text{if } V > V_K. \end{cases} \tag{3.10}$$

Both equations (3.9) and (3.10), when estimated using non-linear least-squares with simulation-based data points reported by Dewees (1978), fit these data surprisingly well.[25] Similarly, Small (1983, pp. 32–33) finds that (3.10) approximates the pattern of travel times during the afternoon peak period on an 11-mile stretch of freeway in the San Francisco Bay area.

Akçelik (1991) develops a travel-time function that is smooth, like (3.9), and that also approaches linearity for very high flows, like (3.10). It introduces a "delay parameter" J_a that is motivated by stochastic queuing models with random arrivals. The function is:

$$T = T_f + 0.25P \cdot \left[\left(\frac{V}{V_K} - 1 \right) + \sqrt{\left(\frac{V}{V_K} - 1 \right)^2 + \frac{8J_a V/V_K}{V_K P}} \right],$$

(3.11)

which has (3.10) as a special case when $J_a = 0$.[26] Akçelik's function seems to produce reasonable results when used in network models (Dowling, Singh and Cheng 1998).

Figure 3.5 compares the relationships depicted by (3.9), (3.10), and (3.11) by plotting normalized average speed (relative to S_f) versus normalized inflow (relative to V_K) for $P = 1$ hour, $V_K = 2000$ veh/hr, $J_A = 0.1$, and two different values of T_f, one corresponding to a one-mile-long road with top speed 75 mi/hr and the other to a 75-mile-long road with the same top speed. The curves labeled BPR, BPR-U, and PL represent BPR, updated BPR, and piecewise-linear functions, respectively, the latter from (3.10).

For the shorter road, the speed–flow curves derived from Small's and Akçelik's models are similar over most of the range considered, but diverge for inflows near V_K. For the longer road, the two functions become graphically indistinguishable; this is because the absolute travel delay in these functions, arising from bottleneck queuing, is unaffected by the length of the road and thus is diluted when averaging over the longer road. The BPR speed–flow functions, by contrast, do not depend on road length. The BPR functions are less steep than the two time-dependent functions for the short road, but steeper for the long road. These differences reflect the focus of the BPR functions on flow congestion along the entire length of the roadway.

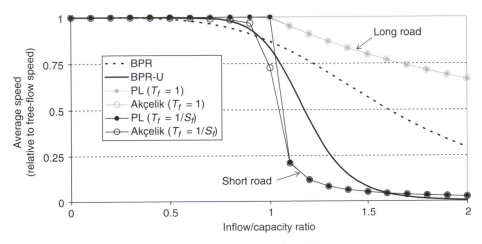

Figure 3.5 Inflow rates and travel times in time-averaged models.

Can such formulations be generalized to a dense street network, such as the downtown of a large city? Olszewski and Suchorzewski (1987) discuss ways to define the capacity of a downtown street network in Warsaw, Poland. May, Shepherd and Bates (2000) go further by defining a matrix of origin–destination demands on a simulated network and multiplying it by a series of scalars to represent increasing demand. They find that in terms of averaged flow and speed on the network itself, a backward-bending speed–flow relation as depicted in Figure 3.1*b* still applies, suggesting the existence of hypercongestion for the area as a whole. But if they account also for queuing times on approaches to the network, they find that trip travel times increase monotonically with demand, yielding average speeds like the curves in Figure 3.5. This could suggest a modeling approach for downtown areas in which flow greater than capacity creates both hypercongestion and bottleneck queuing, an approach developed by Small and Chu (2003) as discussed later.

3.3.3 Dynamic congestion models

Queuing at a bottleneck

Although the functions just discussed explicitly incorporate queuing, they take demanded flow as given and as constant over the period of interest. A dynamic formulation with queuing behind a bottleneck can deal better with extreme congestion. Furthermore, we can safely restrict attention to deterministic queuing – the kind we have been discussing – because stochastic queuing, which arises due to random fluctuations in the traffic stream, accounts for only a small fraction of travel delays (Newell 1971, p. 125).

Let $V_a(t)$ be the volume of traffic arriving at time t at a point bottleneck of capacity V_K, or at the queue behind it if there is one. Let $V_b(t)$ be the volume passing through the bottleneck. Flows V_a and V_b are often called "arrivals" and "departures" (at and from the queue), respectively, in the queuing literature; but *vice versa* in the bottleneck congestion literature, where V_a is often referred to as "departures from home" and V_b as "arrivals at work" (both on the assumption that travel times upstream and downstream of the bottleneck are zero). To avoid confusion, we call V_a *queue entries* and V_b *queue exits* – even when the queue is of zero length.

Let $N(t)$ be the number of vehicles stored in the queue. It is common to ignore the physical length of highway required to store them or, equivalently, to consider the queue to be "vertical" rather than horizontal. Suppose we can ignore the reduction of speed from congestion so long as inflow is less than capacity V_K. Then the following kinked performance function relates queue-exits to queue-entries:

$$V_b(t) = \begin{cases} V_a(t) & \text{if } V_a(t) \leq V_K \text{ and } N(t) = 0 \\ V_K & \text{otherwise.} \end{cases} \tag{3.12}$$

The number of vehicles N in the queue, if any, changes depending on the difference between inflow and outflow:

$$\dot{N}(t) = V_a(t) - V_b(t), \tag{3.13}$$

where the dot denotes a time derivative (possibly one-sided).

Consider the typical case where the entry rate starts low, builds, then decreases, always remaining finite. Let t_q be the time when $V_a(t)$ first equals capacity V_K. Then $N(t) = 0$ for $t \le t_q$ and has a right derivative at t_q given by $V_a(t_q) - V_K$; the queue builds, then shrinks, changing at rate $V_a(t) - V_K$ until it finally disperses at some time $t_{q'}$ defined by:

$$N(t_{q'}) \equiv \int_{t_q}^{t_{q'}} (V_a(t) - V_K)\, \mathrm{d}t = 0.$$

With a first-in, first-out queuing discipline, each vehicle entering the back of the queue at time t must wait for $N(t)$ vehicles to pass through the bottleneck before it can pass through. This causes a *queuing delay* T_D which, for a driver entering the queue at t, is equal to:

$$T_D(t) = \frac{N(t)}{V_K} = \int_{t_q}^{t} \left(\frac{V_a(z)}{V_K} - 1 \right) \mathrm{d}z, \quad t_q \le t \le t_{q'}, \tag{3.14}$$

where z is a variable of integration. We shall also refer to T_D as *travel-time delay* or simply *travel delay*.

An example, taken from Newell (1987), is shown in Figure 3.6. The two curves show cumulative queue-entries and queue-exits as functions of time, so that their slopes represent entry and exit flows V_a and V_b. When V_a exceeds V_K, a queue develops, and $N(t)$ can be found as the vertical distance between cumulative entries and exits. The queuing delay $T_D(t)$, for

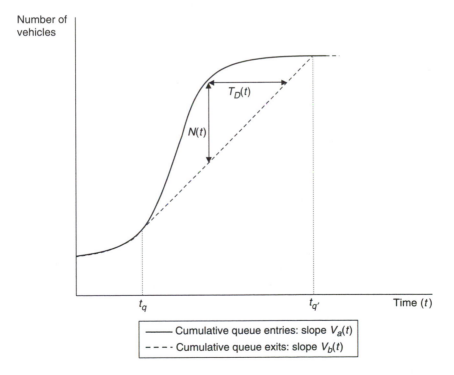

Figure 3.6 Deterministic queuing.

the driver entering the queue at t, is given by the horizontal difference between cumulative entries and exits.

Consider the special case of a fixed peak period for input flows, with incoming traffic constant at V_a during the time interval $[t_p, t_{p'}]$ and zero outside it. If a queue forms, it begins at time $t_q = t_p$. These equations then yield the following queuing delay, for $t \in [t_p, t_{p'}]$:

$$T_D(t) = \begin{cases} 0 & \text{if } V_a \leq V_K \\ \left[(V_a / V_K) - 1 \right] \cdot (t - t_p) & \text{if } V_a > V_K. \end{cases}$$

(3.15)

The average travel delay is:

$$\overline{T}_D = \frac{1}{(t_{p'} - t_p)} \int_{t_p}^{t_{p'}} T_D(t) dt$$

$$= \begin{cases} 0 & \text{if } V_a \leq V_K \\ \tfrac{1}{2}(t_{p'} - t_p) \cdot \left[(V_a / V_K) - 1 \right] & \text{if } V_a > V_K. \end{cases}$$

Adding a free-flow travel time T_f per unit distance for the journey yields equation (3.10) for $P = (t_{p'} - t_p)$. Note that the period of outflows lasts longer than the period of inflows P, and extends from t_p to $t_p + P \cdot (V_a / V_K)$.

We shall refer to this congestion technology, where travel delays result exclusively from vertical queuing at a bottleneck, as "pure" bottleneck congestion. Its consequences for equilibrium queues and optimal pricing are considered in Section 3.4 and Chapter 4.

Analysis of shock waves

While much of the dynamic congestion modeling done in economics has considered pure bottleneck congestion as just described, some has begun to take advantage of more sophisticated dynamic models. We provide here a brief survey based in part on Lindsey and Verhoef (2000).

Probably the most famous dynamic model is the *hydrodynamic* or *kinematic* model, developed by Lighthill and Whitham (1955) and Richards (1956) and therefore known as the LWR model; see Daganzo (1997) for a review. It is a *continuum* model in that traffic characteristics V, D, and S are assumed to be continuous functions of location x and time t, in a manner similar to physical models of fluids (*i.e.*, liquids and gases). Three essential assumptions are the following. First, a relationship $S(D)$ holds between speed and density, as shown in Figure 3.1a, even under non-stationary conditions. Second, identity (3.7) holds everywhere, thus defining functions $V(D)$ and $V(S)$. And third, vehicles are neither created nor destroyed along the road, resulting in the following *conservation* or *continuity equation*: [27]

$$\frac{\partial V(t, x)}{\partial x} + \frac{\partial D(t, x)}{\partial t} = 0.$$

(3.16)

The resulting dynamics can be described in terms of *shock waves*, which are disturbances to traffic caused by traffic lights, accidents, lane reductions, or other discrete variations. Specifically, a shock wave is the moving boundary between two stationary states, *i.e.*, it is the moving point at which vehicles leave one state and enter another. Consider a discrete example, with an upstream steady state with $V_u = S_u \cdot D_u$, and a downstream steady state with $V_d = S_d \cdot D_d$. The location dividing these two states will propagate along the highway at some speed S_w, the value of which is to be determined. Upstream traffic catches up with the boundary at relative speed $S_u - S_w$, and hence enters the shock wave at rate $D_u \cdot (S_u - S_w)$. Similarly, downstream traffic leaves the boundary at relative speed $S_d - S_w$, and hence exits the wave at rate $D_d \cdot (S_d - S_w)$. Conservation of vehicles requires these rates to be equal, implying:

$$S_w = \frac{V_u - V_d}{D_u - D_d}.$$

(3.17)

It can be shown that a forward-moving shock wave can never travel faster than the traffic that carries it, provided the function $V(D)$ is concave and crosses the origin.[28]

Finding a solution for the LWR model is tedious when traffic inflow varies continuously over time (Newell 1988). Therefore a number of simplified models have been formulated. Indeed, the model of pure bottleneck congestion can be regarded as one of these, in which the shock wave, defined as the back of the queue, travels at speed $S_w = 0$ (since the queue is assumed to have no spatial extent). Equivalently, according to (3.17), the queue density D_d is infinite.

Agnew (1977) and Mahmassani and Herman (1984) propose a simplification involving *instantaneous propagation*, by which changes in a road's inflow rate V_i immediately affect its outflow rate V_o. With N denoting the number of vehicles on a finite stretch of road, Agnew's model is summarized by the differential equation of state:

$$\dot{N} = V_i - V_o(N),$$

where the function $V_o(N)$ has the same general shape as $V(D)$ in Figure 3.1c. This model is usually interpreted as implying that density is uniform along the entire road at every instant, so that shock waves propagate at an infinite speed. This has the unrealistic implication that drivers adjust speeds in response to changes in upstream traffic conditions.

A different simplification, by Henderson (1974) and Chu (1995), adopts the opposite assumption of *no propagation*: a vehicle's speed – assumed constant during the trip – is determined as a function only of the flow at one point in space and time. That point is either the entry of the vehicle onto the road (Henderson) or the exit of the vehicle from the road (Chu). This formulation therefore does not consider possible interactions between adjacent vehicles whose departure times are different, despite the fact that the distance between them may be changing during the trip because they travel at different speeds. Hence, there is no propagation of shock waves.

Mun (2002) uses the LWR model to examine the total travel time for traffic entering an otherwise uniform road with a bottleneck at its exit; *i.e.*, the exit has a lower capacity than the rest of the road and therefore a different speed–density function $S(D)$. When traffic exceeds the bottleneck capacity, a "horizontal" queue builds up, which occupies an endogenous and time-varying part of the road's length at the downstream end, and exits the bottleneck at a rate equal to bottleneck capacity. Mun assumes that traffic in the queue travels at the hyper-congested speed, with flow equal to the bottleneck's capacity. Given an exogenous inflow $V_a(t)$ upstream of the bottleneck, volumes and densities can then be found both upstream of the queue and within it; (3.17) determines the rate at which the back of the queue moves, allowing one to compute the queue length at every instant of time. Total trip time is the sum of time traversing the distance to the back of the queue at the speed determined by the inflow rate, plus the time spent in the queue itself. The model reduces to the Henderson model when inflow never exceeds the bottleneck's capacity, and to the deterministic queuing model of (3.14) – augmented by a constant free-flow travel time over the entire length of the road – when the upstream section has sufficient capacity so that its speed–flow curve can be approximated by a constant free-flow speed.

Car-following models

Another approach is to allow for continuous-time and continuous-space traffic dynamics, like LWR, but to treat traffic itself as consisting of discrete vehicles whose behavior is speci-fied. A car-following equation stipulates how the motion of vehicle $n+1$ (the "follower") depends on the motion of vehicle n (the "leader"). The dependent variable is usually accel-eration, and it depends on the distance between the leader and follower and on their speed difference, as in the General Motors model described by May (1990):

$$\ddot{x}_{n+1}(t+\delta) = \frac{a \cdot \left[\dot{x}_{n+1}(t+\delta) \right]^m}{\left[x_n(t) - x_{n+1}(t) \right]^l} \cdot \left[\dot{x}_n(t) - \dot{x}_{n+1}(t) \right], \tag{3.18}$$

where x denotes location, $\dot{x}$ is speed, $\ddot{x}$ is acceleration, δ is a reaction time, and a, l, and m are non-negative parameters.

Under stationary traffic conditions, car-following models imply a relationship between speed and density (the inverse of vehicle spacing) that is consistent with the relationships we have considered above. For example, May (1990) shows that if $m = 0$ and $l = 1$, integrat-ing (3.18) over t yields:

$$\dot{x}_{n+1} = a \cdot \log(x_n - x_{n+1}) + C_0,$$

with C_0 denoting a constant of integration. Equivalently,

$$S = a \cdot \log(D_j/D), \tag{3.19}$$

where density $D = 1/(x_n - x_{n+1})$ is the inverse of vehicle spacing, and $D_j = \exp(C_0/a)$ is the jam density, at which $S = 0$. This equation reproduces a speed–density relationship that was proposed by Greenberg (1959); it suffers from the disadvantage that free-flow speed is infinite. Other parameter values for (3.18) have been found to correspond to other macro-scopic models (Hall and Hall 1990).

Verhoef (2001, 2003) proposes a simpler car-following model which is even more obviously a dynamic extension of a steady-state model. Verhoef postulates a function

$S(D)$ to represent the behavior of the follower, where again D is the inverse of vehicle spacing:

$$\dot{x}_{n+1}(t) = S(D); \quad D = \left[x_n(t) - x_{n+1}(t) \right]^{-1}. \tag{3.20}$$

With $S(D)$ a non-decreasing function, this model reproduces the basic behavioral assumption in the more complex model of (3.18), namely that driver $n+1$ accelerates when driving slower than driver n. Verhoef finds the model to be quite tractable and useful for examining the stability of steady-state equilibria under conditions of hypercongestion.

Surprisingly, economists have rarely considered the behavioral motivations behind the relationship between density and speed that underlies most congestion models. If high density causes traffic to slow down, this must somehow reflect decisions by individual drivers, presumably decisions that trade off speed against safety. Rotemberg (1985) proposed precisely such a tradeoff within a steady-state car-following framework. Verhoef and Rouwendal (2004) show that such a model can produce a locus of equilibrium outcomes that forms a backward-bending speed–flow relation just like the one in Figure 3.1*b*. With this economic tradeoff identified, it is now possible to examine the desirability of regulation that might change individual driver behavior. In fact, both of these papers find that, for any given flow level, economic efficiency (taking into account the drivers' own evaluations of accident costs) could be improved by inducing drivers to voluntarily go faster than the equilibrium level. This is because an individual driver, considering his or her own optimal speed and vehicle spacing, ignores the effect this has on the accident risks (directly) and travel times (indirectly, after adjustments) experienced by other drivers. Interestingly enough, these two considerations both work in the same direction: for a given flow, an increase in speed implies a decrease in density, as shown by (3.7), which in turn reduces accident risks for other drivers.

3.3.4 Congestion modeling: a conclusion

Our review, even though selective, reveals a varied menu of approaches to modeling congestion.[29] Most economic analysis has used just two of these: the static speed–flow curve and the dynamic deterministic bottleneck model. Furthermore, researchers have barely begun to describe the behavior that underlies congestion technology or to identify externalities in that behavior.

Researchers face a difficult tradeoff between tractability and realism. The economic literature has mostly sided with tractability, producing many valuable insights but also many results that are not directly applicable in practice. There could be a considerable payoff from incorporating more realistic engineering models into economic analysis. Examples will be encountered later as we discuss dynamic congestion tolls and hypercongestion.

3.4 Highway travel: short-run cost functions and equilibrium

The congestion models we have described can be used to formulate cost functions for highway travel. In this section we deal with short-run models, which we define as describing a highway with fixed capacity (certain other types of capital, such as vehicles and parking facilities, may be variable). Section 3.5 considers long-run cost functions.

In order to simplify the exposition, we assume that everyone has an identical value of time, denoted in this chapter by α. The average cost c on a defined length of road then consists of monetary expenses c_{00} (like fuel consumption and maintenance), the cost of free-flow travel time $\alpha \cdot T_f$, the cost of travel delays $\alpha \cdot (T - T_f)$, and, in some models, the cost of undesirable schedules c_S (to be defined). The first two cost components make up the travel cost in absence of congestion, c_0; the latter two give the congestion-related cost c_g. Thus:

$$c = c_0 + c_g = [c_{00} + \alpha \cdot T_f] + [\alpha \cdot (T - T_f) + c_s]. \tag{3.21}$$

We ignore for simplicity any dependence of money costs on congestion.

We assume that average cost c is borne entirely by the user; it is sometimes called the *generalized cost* because it indicates the monetary value of the resources supplied by an individual taking a trip. The related concept of *generalized price*, denoted by p, adds to c any applicable tolls and taxes.

3.4.1 Stationary-state congestion on a homogeneous road

We begin with stationary-state congestion on a single homogeneous road with identical users. Simple as this set-up may seem, the resulting model has proven capable of creating great confusion. We therefore provide a detailed discussion.

We define a stationary state as a situation where traffic flow V is constant over time and space and is equal to the rates at which trips are started and ended. Thus the situation could in principle last indefinitely. In reality, of course, traffic congestion undergoes rapid changes; stationary-state models abstract from such changes, and their practical usefulness is limited for this reason. Their advantage is that they are basically static and therefore relatively simple.

The key simplification is to recognize that with V constant and equal to the inflow and outflow rates, it can represent both the per-unit-of-time quantity demanded (by users), and the per-unit-of-time quantity supplied (according to the congestion technology) at a given average cost c. Following Walters (1961), we might picture the situation as resulting from the interaction of a demand curve $V = V_D(c)$ or its inverse, $d(V)$, and a supply curve $c(V)$. When congestion is described by a speed–flow function $S(V)$ on a road of length L, and there are no scheduling costs, this supply curve takes the form

$$c(V) = c_{00} + \alpha \cdot T(V) = c_{00} + \alpha \cdot L / S(V). \tag{3.22}$$

So long as we stay on the normally congested portion of $S(V)$, this supply curve is rising and leads to conventional equilibrium results. We will need to keep in mind, however, that although the user is assumed to be a price-taker, and thus to perceive c as both average and marginal private cost, marginal social cost will be different unless $c(V)$ is constant. This is because $c(V)$ incorporates a *technological externality*: a direct technological dependence of one person's average travel cost on the travel decisions of others. We describe the consequences of this in the pricing analysis of the next chapter.

When we examine the hypercongested portion of $S(V)$, we run into trouble with Walters' interpretation. For one thing, the existence of hypercongestion implies that the average cost depicted by (3.22) is not single-valued – in fact, it does not fit the formal definition of a cost function, which is the *minimum* cost of producing a given output. Furthermore, when we confront it with the inverse demand function $d(V)$, as in Figure 3.7, we can get as many as three different candidate equilibria, whose properties have engendered considerable controversy (Verhoef 1999; Small and Chu 2003). The normally congested equilibrium, denoted x in the figure, resembles a standard economic market equilibrium with downward-sloping

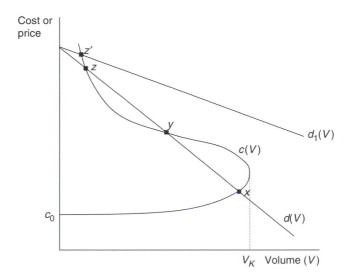

Figure 3.7 The conventional stationary-state average cost curve.

demand and upward-sloping supply. But for the two hypercongested equilibria, y and z, the "supply curve" slopes downward. Intuition warns that there is something peculiar here. How should one interpret a situation where an increase in traffic inflow produces faster travel and thus a lower average cost?

Conventional stability analysis of the candidate equilibria is inconclusive: x is stable for both price and flow perturbations, y for flow perturbations only, and z for price perturbations only.[30] Thus whichever type of perturbation is taken as the criterion for stability, the model produces two candidate equilibria in the case of the demand curve shown. If we insist that an equilibrium should be stable against both types of perturbations, we would reject both hypercongested candidate equilibria; but then we must acknowledge that for a higher demand curve like $d_1(V)$, there is no stable equilibrium.

One difficulty with conventional stability analysis is that the perturbations considered involve simultaneous changes in the flow rates *into* and *along* the road, which is physically impossible. It therefore seems more appropriate to consider perturbations of the inflow rate, treating flow levels along the road as endogenous. Doing so introduces the concept of dynamic stability: can a given stationary state arise as the end state following some transitional phase initiated by a change in the inflow rate?

Verhoef (2001) examines dynamic stability using the car-following model (3.20), allowing for vertical queuing before the entrance when inflows cannot be physically accommodated on the road. He finds that the entire hypercongested branch of the $c(V)$ curve in Figure 3.7 is dynamically unstable.[31] The locus of dynamically stable stationary states turns out to be the curve shown as $c_{stat}(V)$ in Figure 3.8; it follows the normally congested part of $c(V)$ and rises vertically once volume reaches capacity, just as with deterministic queuing. This generates a new stationary state, x', which is dynamically stable. This state involves a maximum flow on the road, a constant-length queue before its entrance with cost c'_q, and rates of queue-entries and queue-exits both equal to the capacity of the road. It does not involve hypercongestion on the road itself; rather, hypercongestion exists only within the entrance queue when it is modeled horizontally, as in Verhoef (2003). This is consistent with the terminology of Figure 3.4 as well as with empirical observations by Daganzo, Cassidy and Bertini (1999) who state that "evidence suggests that downstream bottlenecks cause these transitions [to hypercongested speeds] in a predictable way" (p. 365). Note that the flow rate and speed inside the queue are irrelevant to total trip time, making the economic properties of the model independent of the shape of the hypercongested portion of the speed–flow curve, even though traffic in the queue travels at a hypercongested speed.

Thus the true supply curve for stationary-state traffic, $c_{stat}(V)$, is rising everywhere and intersects any downward-sloping demand curve exactly once. It has two distinct regimes, one of them vertical; but it is smooth and may sometimes be approximated by a power function based on (3.9) (which we originally described as a time-averaged relationship):

$$c(V) = c_{00} + \alpha T_f \cdot \left[1 + a \cdot \left(V / V_K \right)^b \right]. \tag{3.23}$$

Our views on the dynamic instability of hypercongestion are not undisputed. McDonald, d'Ouville and Liu (1999) provide empirical results that appear to involve hypercongestion for sustained periods of time in the absence of a downstream bottleneck. Furthermore, alternative solutions to the questions raised by the conventional diagram of Figure 3.7 have been proposed. Else (1981), Hills (1993), and Ohta (2001) try to solve the problem by using traffic density, number of travelers on the road, or the total number of trips (not expressed per unit of time) as the relevant argument in static inverse demand and average cost functions. In our view, these non-flow-based quantities do not give a meaningful economic measure of aggregate stationary-state output. The total number of trips is not even defined for stationary state traffic until a time period for measurement is specified – in which case the measure becomes flow-based after all. Furthermore, traffic density is an aggregate measure of the proportion of road space occupied at a given point in time, not of the number of trips taken over an interval of time. A demand function defined over density would therefore assume that the good demanded is not the completion of trips but rather the occupation of road space. (Tell that to your average harried commuter!) We conclude that traffic flow is the appropriate output measure for stationary-state analyses, while the total number of trips is appropriate for time-averaged or dynamic models that specify, possibly endogenously, an applicable time period.

3.4.2 Time-averaged models

Cost models using the time-averaged congestion functions described earlier avoid these problems. They can accommodate temporary inflows greater than capacity, yet are single-valued and look much like the cost function of Figure 3.8. For fixed time period P, the time-averaged inflow volume V has a simple interpretation as quantity demanded: namely, it is the number of trips divided by P.

Figure 3.9 compares the cost functions derived from two different time-averaged speed–flow relationships, (3.10) and (3.11). The stationary-state average cost function $c_{stat}(V)$ of Figure 3.8 is shown for comparison. Both of the time-averaged functions become steeper for higher P; and both functions approach a vertical line at V_K as $P \to \infty$. This increasing similarity between time-averaged cost functions and the stationary-state function, as the time period becomes indefinitely large, makes intuitive sense. Yet the correspondence is imperfect in both cases: at flows below capacity, the piecewise-linear function allows for no congestion,

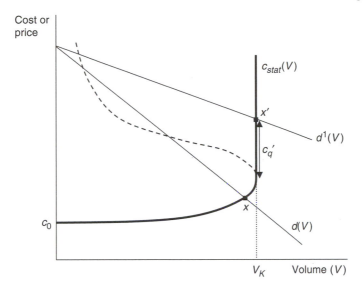

Figure 3.8 Stability of stationary-state equilibria and the stationary-state average cost function.

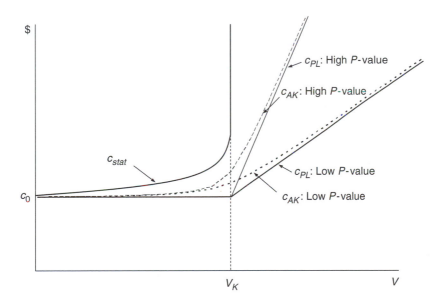

Figure 3.9 Short-run variable cost in stationary-state model (c_{stat}) and two time-averaged models: piecewise linear (c_{PL}) and Akçelik (c_{AK}).

while the Akçelik function c_{AK} may allow for too much since, for high enough values of P, it will cross the c_{stat} curve and exhibit arbitrarily high travel times even when $V < V_K$.

Furthermore, the time-averaged static models have some inherent weaknesses. First, it is not clear how to measure P from observed traffic patterns, which fail to adhere to the assumption of a constant flow occurring only over a well-defined period.[32] Second, P is set exogenously, but in reality will vary with traffic conditions and policies. Third, the assumed exogenous inflow rate is unlikely to be consistent with any rational demand behavior. All three problems are solved by formulating dynamic models that endogenize departure times, to which we turn in the next subsection.

3.4.3 Dynamic models with endogenous scheduling

The dynamic congestion technologies discussed in Section 3.3 allow construction of dynamic equilibrium models, in which departure times (and therefore peak duration) are endogenous and travel delays vary continuously over time. A common assumption in such models is that travelers choose an optimal schedule for their trip by trading off travel-time cost against schedule-delay cost, as in the demand model of Section 2.3.2. Average cost, as defined in (3.21), then includes a part c_S due to schedule delay. It could also include a part due to unreliability, but current theoretical models have not incorporated that separately.

We treat here the case where scheduling costs arise from deviations between an individual's actual and desired arrival time at work, following the notation of equation (2.58) with $\theta = 0$. (This case applies best to the morning peak period; modeling the afternoon peak would presumably require assuming a desired departure time from work – a case that has received far less analysis.) Recall that the per-minute costs of early and late arrival are β and γ, respectively. Then the travel cost for an individual departing from home at time t is:

$$c(t) = c_{00} + \alpha \cdot T(t) + c_S(t); \quad c_S(t) = \begin{cases} \beta \cdot \left(t_d - t - T(t)\right) & \text{if } t + T(t) \le t_d \\ \gamma \cdot \left(t + T(t) - t_d\right) & \text{if } t + T(t) > t_d, \end{cases} \tag{3.24}$$

where t_d is the desired arrival time at work and $T(t)$ the travel time incurred when departing at t. Of course, $T(t)$ and therefore $c(t)$ depend also on capacity and perhaps on past, current, or even future traffic levels (the latter possibility arising with instantaneous propagation).

We take the simplest dynamic congestion technology discussed in Section 3.3.3, namely pure bottleneck congestion, where congestion occurs solely through vertical queuing behind a bottleneck. It is convenient to assume one traveler per vehicle and to define *average congestion cost* by subtracting the constant $c_{00} + \alpha T_f$, i.e.,

$$c_g(t) \equiv c(t) - c_{00} - \alpha \cdot T_f.$$

For convenience, and without loss of generality when there is no route choice, we set free-flow travel time T_f to zero. Then $T(t)$ is equal to the travel delay $T_D(t)$ defined in (3.15), except that the time t_p when congestion begins is now endogenous and denoted by t_q.

Because desired schedules are defined in terms of arrival time at work, it is convenient to focus on the time t' when a traveler exits the queue. Given that $T_f = 0$, this is also that traveler's arrival time at work. If there were no congestion, the rate at which travelers depart from the queue would be simply the distribution of desired work-arrival times, which we denote by $V_d(t')$. We can now work backward to find the equilibrium queue-entry rate $V_a(t)$ (*i.e.*, the rate of arrivals at the vertical queue, or equivalently the rate of departures from home) that is consistent with travelers' uncoordinated scheduling decisions.

If $V_d(t') \le V_K$ for all t' there is no queuing or schedule delay, and the entry and exit rates are both equal to the desired rate: $V_a(t) = V_d(t') = V_b(t)$ for $t = t'$. If capacity is insufficient, however, people must trade off queuing delay against schedule delay in choosing their queue-entry times, which will imply a certain aggregate dynamic equilibrium queue-entry time pattern $V_a(t)$, for which no traveler has an incentive to reschedule the trip. The resulting equilibrium, analyzed by Hendrickson and Kocur (1981) and Newell (1987), can be quite complex. However, the following special case, first analyzed by Vickrey (1969, 1973) and further elaborated by Fargier (1983), is tractable and leads to surprisingly elegant and insightful results.

Suppose, then, that $V_d(t)$ is constant at V_d during the interval $[t_p, t_{p'}]$ and zero outside that interval. Hence there are a total of $Q \equiv V_d \cdot q$ travelers when demand is inelastic, where $q = t_{p'} - t_p$ denotes how long the peak period would last if capacity were unrestricted. Assume $\beta < \alpha$, which is supported by the empirical evidence of Section 2.3.2 and which is necessary to achieve an equilibrium without massed departures at a single instant in time. Consider the case $V_d > V_K$, so that the desired exit rate cannot be achieved and thus queuing and/or schedule delay must occur. Our analysis follows the logic and much of the notation of Arnott, de Palma and Lindsey (1990b).[33]

For a commuter exiting the queue before the desired time t_d, equilibrium requires that the chosen queue-entry time minimizes the combined costs for early exits in (3.24): $\alpha \cdot T_D(t) + \beta \cdot [t_d - t - T_D(t)]$. This requires that $T_D(t)$ change at rate $\beta/(\alpha - \beta)$ so long as anyone entering the queue at time t is exiting early. Similarly, so long as anyone entering at t is exiting late, $\alpha \cdot T_D(t) + \gamma \cdot [t + T_D(t) - t_d]$ must be minimized, so $T_D(t)$ must change at rate $-\gamma/(\alpha + \gamma)$.[34] The first and last commuters exiting must face a zero queue length in equilibrium, because otherwise a discretely lower travel cost could be realized by departing just before t_q or after $t_{q'}$.

Comparing these equilibrium rates of change in T_D to that implied by equation (3.15), namely $[(V/V_K) - 1]$, we see that vehicles must be entering the queue at rates

$$V_a^{early} = V_K \cdot \frac{\alpha}{\alpha - \beta}; \quad V_a^{late} = V_K \cdot \frac{\alpha}{\alpha + \gamma} \tag{3.25}$$

during the early and late parts of the peak period, respectively. The resulting pattern is shown in Figure 3.10, in which $N(t)$ is the number of vehicles in the queue, $\tilde{t}$ is the entry time for the commuter incurring maximum queuing delay T_{Dm}, and this commuter's exit time is:

$$t^* \equiv \tilde{t} + T_D(\tilde{t}) \equiv \tilde{t} + T_{Dm}. \tag{3.26}$$

Commuters with $t_d < t^*$ enter the queue before (or possibly at) $\tilde{t}$, and those with $t_d > t^*$ enter after (or possibly at) $\tilde{t}$. (Due to linearity in the cost function, each commuter is in fact indifferent among departure times $[t_q, \tilde{t})$ or else among departure times $[\tilde{t}, t_{q'}]$; however, we can remove this indeterminacy by making the quite natural assumption that commuters exit the queue in the same order as their desired queue-exit times.)

It remains to determine $\tilde{t}$. We accomplish this by equating the total numbers of travelers entering and exiting. The exit rate is constant at V_K during some interval $[t_q, t_{q'}]$ which, in order to accommodate the total of Q vehicles, must be of duration

$$t_{q'} - t_q = Q/V_K = q \cdot V_d / V_K > q. \tag{3.27}$$

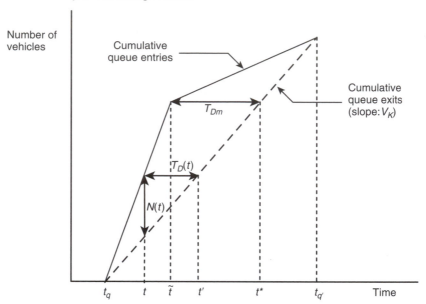

Figure 3.10 Dynamic queuing equilibrium. Adapted with permission from Arnott *et al.* (1990b, p. 117), copyright 1990, Academic Press, Inc.

This peak travel period encompasses but exceeds the desired peak [t_p, $t_{p'}$], whose duration is q; congestion begins prior to the earliest desired queue-exit and lasts beyond the latest desired queue-exit. Furthermore, the duration of this interval depends inversely on V_K, showing that expanding capacity narrows the peak period – as postulated, for example, by Downs (1962).

In order to solve for the entire equilibrium configuration, define

$$\sigma = \frac{t^* - t_p}{q} = \frac{t^* - t_p}{t_{p'} - t_p} \tag{3.28}$$

as the proportion of commuters who exit the queue before t^* (equivalently, the proportion who enter the queue before $\tilde{t}$). They enter at rate V_a^{early}, so their number must be:

$$\sigma \cdot Q = V_a^{early} \cdot \left(\tilde{t} - t_q\right). \tag{3.29}$$

Similarly, the proportion $(1 - \sigma)$ who enter after $\tilde{t}$ do so at rate V_a^{late}, so

$$\left(1 - \sigma\right) \cdot Q = V_a^{late} \cdot \left(t_{q'} - \tilde{t}\right). \tag{3.30}$$

Equations (3.25) through (3.30) can be solved for:

$$\sigma = \gamma / (\beta + \gamma) \tag{3.31}$$

$$t_q = t_p - \sigma \cdot q \cdot \left[(V_d / V_K) - 1 \right] \tag{3.32}$$

$$t_{q'} = t_{p'} + (1 - \sigma) \cdot q \cdot \left[(V_d / V_K) - 1 \right] \tag{3.33}$$

$$t^* = t_p + \sigma \cdot q$$

$$\tilde{t} = t_p + \sigma \cdot q - T_{Dm}$$

$$T_{Dm} = \delta \cdot Q / (\alpha \cdot V_K), \tag{3.34}$$

where

$$\delta \equiv \beta \gamma / (\beta + \gamma) = \beta \sigma. \tag{3.35}$$

The maximum delay (3.34) corresponds to a maximum travel-delay cost $\delta \cdot Q/V_K$.

Figure 3.11 shows how costs vary as a function of exit time. Travel-delay cost per traveler, $c_T(t')$, rises linearly from zero to $\alpha \cdot T_{Dm}$ (reached at time t^*) and falls linearly back to zero. Schedule-delay cost per traveler, $c_S(t')$, falls linearly from a maximum of $\beta \cdot (t_p - t_q)$ for the earliest traveler to zero (at t^*), then rises linearly to a maximum of $\gamma \cdot (t_{q'} - t_{p'})$; computing these maxima from (3.31)–(3.33), we find they are both equal to $(\delta \cdot Q/V_K) \cdot (1 - V_K/V_d)$. Note that their sum $c_g(t')$ need not be constant in equilibrium because each consumer has a different desired schedule t_d. (This differs from the Arnott, de Palma and Lindsey model.)

From the piecewise-linear cost patterns just described, we see easily that the time-averaged cost components, c_T and c_S, are just half their maximum values. Thus time-averaged travel-delay cost per traveler is:

$$\overline{c}_T = \frac{1}{2} \cdot \frac{\delta \cdot Q}{V_K} \equiv \frac{\delta \cdot q}{2} \cdot \frac{V_d}{V_K}. \tag{3.36}$$

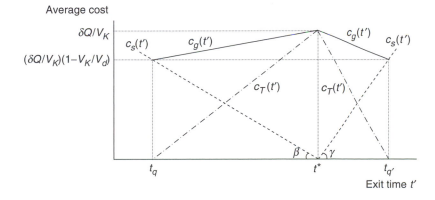

Figure 3.11 Equilibrium average costs of time delay (c_T), schedule delay (c_S), and their sum (c_g), under linear schedule delay cost functions and with a dispersion of desired queue–exit times.

The middle expression is the same formula as that derived by Fargier (1983, p. 246) and Arnott, de Palma and Lindsey (1990b, p. 116) for the special case $q=0$. Surprisingly, it depends only on the total number of travelers Q, not on the distribution of their desired queue-exit times. Similarly, the time-averaged schedule-delay cost per traveler is:

$$\bar{c}_S = \tfrac{1}{2} \cdot \frac{\delta \cdot Q}{V_K} \cdot \left(1 - \frac{V_K}{V_d}\right) \equiv \frac{\delta \cdot q}{2} \cdot \left(\frac{V_d}{V_K} - 1\right). \tag{3.37}$$

This does depend on the distribution of desired exit times; for a given number of travelers $Q \equiv V_d \cdot q$, distributing the desired exit times over a shorter interval q raises V_d and thereby raises average schedule delay cost. In the extreme case when $q = 0$ while $V_d = \infty$ (with Q finite), $\bar{c}_S$ becomes equal to $\bar{c}_T$, as derived by Arnott, de Palma and Lindsey (1990b).

Adding $\bar{c}_T$ and $\bar{c}_S$ and including the possibility of $V_d \leq V_K$ with its lack of queuing, we can write the time-averaged congestion cost as:

$$\bar{c}_g(V_d, q; V_K) = \begin{cases} 0 & \text{if } V_d \leq V_K \\ \dfrac{\delta \cdot Q}{V_K} \cdot \left(1 - \dfrac{V_K}{2V_d}\right) \equiv \delta \cdot q \cdot \left(\dfrac{V_d}{V_K} - \dfrac{1}{2}\right) & \text{otherwise.} \end{cases} \tag{3.38}$$

Equation (3.38) is the average congestion cost given the constraint that people are free to adjust their schedules according to their tradeoff between queuing delay and schedule delay. It should be viewed as part of a second-best aggregate cost function, in which the entry pattern $V_a(t)$ is determined suboptimally (namely such that there is a dynamic equilibrium, rather than that costs are minimized given q and V_d). This is why it is discontinuous at $V_d = V_K$: as soon as there is any congestion, the average queuing delay (3.36) jumps from zero to $\tfrac{1}{2} \cdot \delta \cdot q$. As we shall see in Chapter 4, a different queue-entry pattern would eliminate queuing delay and thereby reduce $\bar{c}_g$ to $\bar{c}_S$, making it the congestion cost for a first-best cost function and also making it continuous in V_d.

These costs have the remarkable feature of being independent of the value of travel time, α. So long as α remains greater than β so that the analysis applies, increasing the value of time causes no change in the duration or timing of the peak interval $[t_q, t_{q'}]$, nor in the proportion of travelers who exit early; instead, it causes the queuing delay to decrease just enough to hold queuing cost constant, while schedule delay remains unchanged. This point was first noted, for a closely related model, by de Palma and Arnott (1986).

Equally remarkable is that the entire pattern of queue-entries and queue-exits shown in Figure 3.10 is unaffected by how demand Q is factored into q and V_d, so long as t^* is unchanged and V_d is greater than capacity. This again results from the perverse private incentives that cause a substantial queue to form even if V_d exceeds capacity by only a tiny amount. Spreading Q over a wider interval does, however, reduce scheduling costs because the pattern in Figure 3.10 imposes fewer costs when some people already prefer to arrive at some time other than close to t^*.

In the special case where all users are identical and have the same desired arrival time t^*, there is always congestion for any non-zero Q and (3.38) simplifies to a linear average cost function (since $V_d = \infty$):

$$\bar{c}_g(Q; V_K) = \frac{\delta \cdot Q}{V_K}. \qquad (3.39)$$

The lack of heterogeneity across commuters now causes equilibrium travel cost to be constant over time. This model has the advantage that demand is summarized by a single quantity, Q, rather than two quantities (q and V_d) as in (3.38). It is therefore very easy to interact it with an inverse demand function to derive the equilibrium. Indeed, this is one of the advantages noted by Arnott, de Palma and Lindsey (1993): once the model is solved in this form, as a function of Q, average cost looks exactly like that of the stationary-state model (3.22) with travel-delay cost proportional to Q. We will, in what follows, use the term "basic bottleneck model" to refer to this widely used version of the model with identical desired arrival times, a linear schedule delay cost function, and pure bottleneck congestion.

The derivation of dynamic equilibrium for other dynamic congestion technologies involves roughly the same steps as for the bottleneck model. Because most dynamic congestion technologies are non-linear, the analytics become more cumbersome and typically no closed-form analytical solutions can be obtained. Other demand structures can also be assumed: for example, Ben-Akiva, Cyna and de Palma (1984) analyze a model incorporating a probabilistic demand similar to that of Section 2.3.2.

Summary

We have considered three types of models to study short-run variable cost: stationary-state, time-averaged, and dynamic. Each leads to a tractable formula for short-run variable cost under certain assumptions. Stationary-state and time-averaged models are both characterized by a rising average cost function (in one case with a vertical asymptote), so conceptual analyses are often similar for both models; when this is the case in later chapters, we will treat the two models jointly and refer to them as "static models." Dynamic models show how scheduling flexibility reduces or eliminates the time variation in costs that underlie time-averaged models. Dynamic models permit internally consistent analyses of staggered and flexible work schedules as well as the "shifting-peak phenomenon" discussed in the next chapter. Furthermore, as we have seen, a conventional static model can be derived from a dynamic model as a reduced-form relationship among time averages or cumulative quantities.

3.4.4 Network equilibrium

Up to this point we have ignored the fact that traffic usually operates on a network. Accounting for this requires us to recognize that the cost of a trip depends on flows on one or more links, each of which may be serving several trip types. Furthermore, users will seek out the best routes for their trips, and the resulting cost will depend on the allocation of traffic to links that results from this process. Typically we assume that the search for routes settles down rather quickly to an equilibrium characterized by each user choosing the route that minimizes cost for that particular trip. Such a situation is called a *user equilibrium* (UE) because it results from individual optimization by each user, as opposed to any collaborative procedure. [35]

To analyze such problems, we define a network structure consisting of M origin–destination pairs or "markets" (denoted $m = 1, \ldots , M$), R routes (denoted $r = 1, \ldots , R$), and L directed links (denoted $l = 1, \ldots , L$). "Directed" means that a two-way roadway is represented by two links carrying traffic in opposite directions. A single origin–destination (OD) pair may be served by multiple routes; each route may comprise multiple links; and any link may be part of more than one route. As a result, traffic serving different origin–destination pairs is likely to interact on certain links, and of course this affects how congestion forms. We define a set of dummy indicators δ_{rm} to denote whether route r serves market m (in which case $\delta_{rm} = 1$), and another set δ_{lr} to denote whether link l is part of route r.

The simplest case is when all users are identical, alternative routes are perfect substitutes, and congestion on a link depends only on the flow on that link (as opposed to, say, an intersection). An appropriate concept for the user equilibrium is then *Wardrop's first principle* (Wardrop 1952): for a given OD pair, all used routes (those with positive flows) should have equal average cost, and there should be no unused routes with lower costs. So long as users take aggregate traffic conditions as given, this principle is consistent with the standard game-theoretic concept of Nash equilibrium: no user can reduce cost by unilaterally changing route. When demand for trips between an OD pair is elastic, an additional equilibrium condition is that the equalized average cost for used routes be equal to the marginal willingness to pay for trips between that origin and destination.

These conditions can be expressed mathematically in terms of route flows V_r as follows, where the first statement signifies that it applies only for every $\{m,r\}$ for which $\delta_{rm} = 1$:

$$\forall \, \delta_{rm} = 1 : \begin{cases} \sum_{l=1}^{L} \delta_{lr} \cdot c_l(V_l) - d_m(V_m) \geq 0 \\[2mm] V_r \geq 0 \\[2mm] V_r \cdot \left[\sum_{l=1}^{L} \delta_{lr} \cdot c_l(V_l) - d_m(V_m) \right] = 0, \end{cases} \tag{3.40}$$

where

$$V_l = \sum_{\rho=1}^{R} \delta_{l\rho} \cdot V_\rho \quad \text{and} \quad V_m = \sum_{\rho=1}^{R} \delta_{\rho m} \cdot V_\rho$$

are the link and market flows, respectively, and where ρ denotes a route. The inverse demand functions d_m are defined at the level of OD pairs, rather than having separate functions for distinct routes, because of the assumed perfect substitutability: people do not care about any characteristics of routes except their costs.

Beckmann, McGuire and Winsten (1956) have shown that the equilibrium problem (3.40) can be formulated and solved as an equivalent convex optimization problem, meaning that there exists an optimization problem that has the equilibrium equations of (3.40) as its optimality conditions. This remains true even when direct link interactions are present, provided they are symmetric (Sheffi 1985). Such a formulation facilitates analyzing the existence and uniqueness of equilibria as well as finding them numerically. (Equilibria are typically unique in terms of link flows and OD flows but not in terms of route flows.) The objective to be minimized in this equivalent optimization problem involves integrals of average cost functions $c_l(\cdot)$ between 0 and V_l, summed over all links, minus the integrals of marginal benefits $d_m(\cdot)$ between 0 and V_m, summed over all OD pairs. This objective has no meaningful economic interpretation, and is best viewed as an artificial mathematical construct that produces the equilibrium conditions (3.40) as the necessary first-order conditions. The classic algorithm to solve this minimization problem numerically is that of Frank and Wolfe (1956); improved algorithms are also available (Sheffi 1985; Patriksson 2004).

Network equilibrium may sometimes lead to surprising and counterintuitive implications for public policy. A famous example is the so-called *Braess paradox* (Braess 1968): adding a new link to a congested network may cause equilibrium travel times to increase! Intuitively, this can happen if using a newly available route results in a lower average time but a higher marginal contribution to congestion than using competing routes.[36] Formally, it is possible because the objective function whose minimization yields the UE conditions, described above, is different from the negative of social surplus (benefits minus costs); therefore users may use the new link even if, due to congestion, using it lowers social surplus. Another paradox, known as the Downs-Thomson paradox, occurs in a simple two-link, two-mode network in which one mode (public transport) operates with scale economies. When the capacity of the other mode (a road) is increased, the average cost of both modes can go up!

Such paradoxes are extreme examples of "induced demand," which is simply a consequence of downward-sloping demand curves as discussed in Section 5.1.3. They occur because user prices are not set optimally. We show in Chapter 4 that optimal pricing for a network involves link-based tolls that bridge the gap between average and marginal cost. Including these in the user equilibrium conditions (3.40) would makes those conditions correspond to the necessary first-order conditions for maximizing social surplus; the paradoxes could then no longer occur.

Sometimes route choice is stochastic – for example, because travel times are uncertain and people have different expectations, or because people have idiosyncratic preferences over different routes. The UE concept then extends to the *stochastic user equilibrium* (Daganzo and Sheffi 1977), in which no traveler can reduce *expected* travel cost (sometimes referred to as "*perceived*" travel cost) by unilaterally changing route. Route choice probabilities are then modeled using the same discrete-choice models (notably logit and probit) as discussed in Chapter 2 (Sheffi 1985).

More recent advances have shown how the existence and uniqueness of a solution to Wardrop's equilibrium conditions can be guaranteed even when asymmetric link interactions are present. The conditions can be interpreted as the solution to a mathematical optimization problem known as *variational inequality* (Dafermos 1980). Doing so permits some far-reaching generalizations by means of a trick: a larger network is defined as multiple copies of the original one with certain links interacting with the corresponding links in a copy. Two examples illustrate the usefulness of this approach.

The first example is to model networks dynamically by creating "time-space networks," in which each copy of a physical link corresponds to a different time period. Link interactions then arise because the travel time on the physical link during a certain period depends on past and current flows. (These interactions are asymmetric because travel time does not depend on future flows.) An example of such a model is METROPOLIS (de Palma and Marchal 2002).

A second example treats multiple user classes that differ with respect to value of time or other preferences (Dafermos 1972; Boyce and Bar-Gera 2004). Each user class occupies its own copy of the network; cost interactions between links in the extended network then capture congestion arising from more than one class using the same physical link of the original network. Link interactions could then be asymmetric when, for example, values of time or vehicle types differ. These two examples, and other aspects of network models, are reviewed in several recent works, including Ran and Boyce (1996), Nagurney (1999), and Patriksson (2004).

3.4.5 *Parking search*

In many urban locations, parking is sufficiently scarce that drivers spend a substantial amount of time searching for an empty space, an activity known as *cruising*. Shoup (2005, Chapter 11) lists studies estimating that in various cities, 8% to 74% of cars in downtown traffic at any moment are cruising, for an average time of 3.5 to 14 minutes per trip. If parking spaces are underpriced, then anyone occupying one of them imposes a mis-priced externality on others by making it harder for them to locate a vacant space.

This is a kind of crowding externality that shares certain features with congestion. Both are examples in which common property resources are overused. Some of these resources are more valuable than others – for example, the most popular routes in the case of congestion and the best-located spaces in the case of parking. Thus the problem has two features: there is too much use overall, and the use is inefficiently distributed across locations, with the more desirable locations being more overused.

Some interesting models capture one or the other of these features. Arnott and Rowse (1999) focus on the first. All spaces are equally desirable because they are located evenly around a circular city, as are destinations. People can choose either a mode that uses parking spaces (auto) or one that doesn't (walking). All residents considering a potential destination of interest will walk if it is close, drive if it is somewhat more distant, and forgo the trip if it is more distant still, these reservation distances all being determined endogenously within the model. If they drive, they also choose another reservation distance, that at which they will accept a vacant space if they see one. The model *may* generate multiple equilibria, including a desirable one in which most people drive and easily find a place, walk quickly to their destination, transact their business, and leave, keeping parking-space occupancy low. But it *always* generates at least one undesirable equilibrium, in which people who drive must park far from their destination, thus keeping their space occupied while they walk a long distance, which in turn maintains a high occupancy rate of parking spaces causing long search times.

Anderson and de Palma (2004) focus on the second feature mentioned earlier: the relative overuse of parking at the most desirable locations. In their model, total demand for parking is fixed, and spaces are ranked according to their distance x from a common destination (*e.g.*, a central business district). Each traveler must choose x and commit to searching for a space there – for example, by entering a side street or an off-street parking lot. The time required for that search depends on the proportion of spaces that are occupied. Just as with congestion, users ignore an external cost that is greater the more desirable the location. The result is that too many people park close to the CBD and have to spend too much time finding a parking space.

Parking is also linked to congestion because vehicles engaged in entering, exiting, or looking for a parking space slow down other vehicles.[37] Anderson and de Palma (2004) allow for this factor by postulating that vehicles parking at location x slow down those drivers wishing to park closer to the CBD than x (since they must pass location x to do so). This sets up another externality, which tends to offset the first because the effect of cruising is to discourage people from seeking the best located parking spaces.

A more elaborate model by Arnott and Inci (2006) considers travel to the destination and cruising for parking as two parts of a trip, the demand for which depends on the time spent in both parts. They obtain stable equilibria that they refer to as "hypercongested," in which cruising actually declines, while total time traveled increases, as demand shifts outward. They show further that the second-best optimal number of parking spaces provided, given inefficiently low parking prices, is greater than the first-best optimal number, even though these spaces remove some capacity from the streets that could otherwise be used to improve traffic flow.

As we will see in the next subsection, urban parking is often supplied in such abundance that search costs are negligible. The Arnott–Inci result just cited might justify such a situation if one accepts that parking fees are impossible to enact. But other cities use parking scarcity to limit downtown traffic, a policy with considerable intuitive appeal but largely ignored within the types of model just described. Thus we anticipate a continuation of the tentative steps taken so far to model parking search and its contribution to street congestion. What is clear so far is that the results of such models are sensitive to fine details of the situation.

3.4.6 Empirical evidence on short-run variable costs

In this section we compile estimates of short-run average variable costs of urban automobile travel.[38] Our purpose is to illustrate how one can use existing research, including many far more exhaustive studies, to glean the most relevant information for use in policy analysis. Such information includes the overall size of such costs in typical urban areas, the relative sizes of their constituent categories, and the factors that determine which costs are external to the user. A subsidiary purpose is to immunize the reader against some of the more extreme claims that are sometimes made by advocates of particular approaches to urban transportation policy.

In the interest of simplicity and comparability, we focus on US urban commuters and present estimates in US dollars per vehicle-mile, at 2005 prices, for a medium-size car. Due to the prevalence of ample parking at US workplaces, we do not include parking search costs. In converting between distance- and time-related costs, we assume that trip distance and time are those for the average US urban commute using private modes, namely 12.1 miles and 22.5 minutes (implying average speed of 32.3 mi/hr).[39]

We distinguish between private and social average cost. The former includes fuel taxes as well as the user's own congestion costs, while the latter excludes taxes but adds external costs imposed by highway users on non-users. In the case of social cost, we also distinguish between average and marginal cost. Average social cost is the total cost borne by society, including all users, divided by total vehicle-miles. Marginal social cost is the corresponding incremental social cost due to one additional vehicle-mile of travel; it thus includes the external component of costs imposed by congestion.

For convenience, we divide variable costs into the two categories shown in Table 3.3: those borne directly by highway users as a group (so that private and social average costs are equal) and those borne partly by non-users. Fixed costs are treated in Section 3.5.3.

Variable costs borne primarily by users

(1) OPERATING AND MAINTENANCE

The costs of fuel, maintenance, and tires are usually assumed to be proportional to distance traveled, and are typically estimated from such data as fuel consumption, tire wear, maintenance experience, and prices. The American Automobile Association estimates these expenses in 2005 to be US$0.141 per mile, of which 58% is for fuel and oil.[40] About $0.016 of this is for fuel taxes, which we subtract here but add later as a private payment toward fixed roadway costs, which is how they are normally viewed in the US.[41] Barnes and

Table 3.3 Some typical short-run costs of automobile travel: US urban commuters

Type of cost	Private	Social	
	Average[a]	Average	Marginal
Variable costs			
Costs borne mainly by highway users in aggregate			
(1) Operating and maintenance	0.141	0.141	0.141
(2) Vehicle capital	0.170	0.170	0.170
(3) Travel time	0.303	0.303	0.388
(4) Schedule delay and unreliability	0.093	0.093	0.172
Costs borne substantially by non-users			
(5) Accidents	0.117	0.140	0.178
(6) Government services	0.005	0.019	0.019
(7) Environmental externalities	0	0.016	0.016
Short-run variable costs	0.829	0.882	1.084
Fixed costs			
(8) Roadway	0.016	0.056	
(9) Parking	0.007	0.281	
Short-run fixed costs	0.023	0.337	
Total costs	0.852	1.219	1.084

Notes: All costs in US$ per vehicle-mile at 2005 prices.

a   If increased vehicle travel requires a proportionate expansion of the car fleet, then private marginal cost is approximately the same as private average cost (including average fixed cost). In the opposite case where increased travel occurs solely in the form of longer trips, then the following items should be excluded from private marginal cost because they are fixed in the short run: 60% of (2), and all of (6) and (9). The intermediate case, where increased travel occurs using the same vehicle fleet but in the form of more rather than longer trips, is like this second extreme except some private parking costs in (9) become variable to the extent that the additional trips are to locations with parking fees. We arbitrarily allocate user fees among private cost categories as follows: vehicle and license fees count toward government services, and fuel taxes toward roadway capital; hence for private average cost, item (8) is actually variable rather than fixed.

Langworthy (2003) show that maintenance cost rises dramatically with age, a fact that comes as no surprise to anyone who has owned an automobile more than a few years old.

(2) VEHICLE CAPITAL

Motor-vehicle ownership costs are sometimes treated in ways that to an economist seem astonishingly naïve, including confusion between fixed and variable cost and between economic and accounting cost. They can be analyzed using standard discounting techniques for capital assets (Nash 1974). As a starting point, we can approximate the combined interest and depreciation costs, averaged over the life of the car, by applying the *capital recovery factor* to the price of a new car.[42] In the US, that price was on average $22,013 in 2005, cars were driven 12,375 miles per year, and the median lifetime was approximately 16.9 years.[43] Using the continuous-time capital recovery factor to annualize at an interest rate of 6%, the average ownership cost comes to $0.170 per mile, a potentially important cost component.

Vehicle capital cost varies considerably by age of the vehicle. This is determined by examining the shape of depreciation: *i.e.*, how the loss in value each year varies over the life of the vehicle. Using international data, Storchmann (2004) finds that the market price of an automobile largely follows a declining exponential pattern by age, declining on average by 31% and 15% per year in OECD countries and developing countries, respectively. It can be shown that such a depreciation pattern, in which the absolute depreciation cost is greater for a newer than an older car, implies that the value of the car to the user is also declining, presumably because of rising maintenance costs and technological obsolescence. This means that the use of a capital recovery factor, which implicitly assumes a constant value, is at best an approximation to the annualized cost averaged over all vehicles.

This average ownership cost does not tell us the marginal depreciation cost of operating a car conditional on owning it. Barnes and Langworthy (2003) analyze data from the *Official Used Car Guide* of the National Association of Automobile Dealers to determine the effect of increased mileage on a given vehicle's market price. They conclude that marginal depreciation cost is \$0.068/mile (in 2005 prices), or 40% of the average ownership cost just computed (not shown in the table).[44]

In asking about the cost of driving, do we want only this incremental depreciation, or should we include the much larger time-related depreciation as well? That is, should we consider most capital cost as fixed? It depends on how output (vehicle-miles per year) is expanded for the question being asked. Consider two policies that increase the aggregate number of vehicle-miles traveled on commuting trips (to and from work), one by affecting commute length and the other by affecting commute mode. The first does not affect the size of the vehicle fleet, so the applicable marginal ownership cost includes only distance-related depreciation. The other causes some workers to increase their auto ownership and still others to impose inconvenience on family members by tying up the family vehicle for part of each week. In this latter case, some or all of interest and time-related depreciation cost is variable as well. In the table, we show the case where it is all variable: *i.e.*, the vehicle fleet expands proportionally to vehicle-miles.

(3) TRAVEL TIME

Our review in Section 2.6.5 suggests that a typical value of time for work trips is 50% of the wage, or approximately \$9.69/hr for US metropolitan areas in 2005.[45] This amounts to \$0.303/mi for a single-occupant automobile moving at 32 mi/hr, the average speed for US urban commuting trips as noted above. We use this figure for both average private and average social cost, since it is all borne by users as a group.

Our analysis of congestion shows that there is, in addition, an external social cost of driving in urban areas due to the contribution of a given vehicle to travel delays for others. This external cost varies greatly by time and location. Parry and Small (2005) review a number of studies and suggest that a nationwide average for 2000 might be \$0.035/mi in the US and twice that in the UK. Most of the costs are in urban areas, which account for 65% of vehicle travel (US FHWA 2006, Table VM-1), so we may assume the figures are about 40% higher in US urban areas, or \$0.056/mi after updating to 2005.[46] Because commuting is more heavily concentrated in peak periods, the external congestion cost of a commute trip is probably higher; we add 50% to the above figure to account for this, making it \$0.085. This external congestion cost is therefore added to the average social cost of travel time to obtain marginal social cost of \$0.388. As a point of reference, the ratio of marginal to average travel time just derived (1.28) would for the US Bureau of Public Roads (BPR) function of (3.9) occur at a volume-capacity ratio V/V_K of 0.84 (0.82 for the updated BPR for freeways).

Traffic congestion also imposes time costs on pedestrians, but we are aware of no estimates so do not include one here. We suspect that aside from accidents, which we treat below, the external cost of traffic to pedestrians is mostly aesthetic and depends strongly on the specifics of urban design.

We also omit the external time cost imposed on transit agencies and their riders due to buses and streetcars sharing streets with automobiles. To take an extreme example, the 15% reduction in automobile traffic within Central London during the daytime hours due to congestion charging is estimated by Transport for London to have speeded up bus travel in the area by 6%;[47] scaling the results of Small (2004) accordingly, this may have provided benefits of time savings to drivers and users together valued at nearly one-fourth of initial agency operating costs. [48] We also omit the additional costs to freight that may occur due to paid drivers' higher values of time and the inventory costs of delays to expensive vehicles and their loads.[49]

(4) SCHEDULE DELAY AND UNRELIABILITY

Just as the tradeoff between travel time and money implies a value of time, the tradeoff between non-ideal travel schedules and money defines the cost of putting up with those schedules. These are called *schedule-delay costs*. As in Section 3.4.3, we let β and γ be the marginal cost of making an early schedule earlier or making a late schedule later, respectively, assumed to be constant as in the model by Small (1982) described in Section 2.3.2.

Empirical estimates show schedule-delay costs, like travel-time costs, to be substantial. For example, the average commuter in the sample used by Small (1982) incurred an amount of schedule delay equivalent, given the estimated coefficients, to 7.0 minutes of in-vehicle travel time, or $1.13 at the value of time just given.[50] With the average urban commuting distance stated above, this cost is $0.093/mi. We assume this includes the cost of unreliability due to congestion.

Now consider the external component to be added to this for social marginal cost. The estimates above suggest that in the current situation, the ratio of schedule delay to time cost of congestion is 0.93.[51] Note that this is close to the ratio of 1 that applies in the unpriced equilibrium of the basic bottleneck model with identical desired arrival times, while this ratio decreases when introducing a dispersion in desired arrival times.[52] We assume that the *marginal external* costs (*mec's*) of schedule delay and travel time are in the same ratio as are their *average* costs (0.93). This implies a *mec* for schedule delay of $0.079/mi, which is added to the social average cost to get social marginal cost.

Variable costs borne substantially by non-users

(5) TRAFFIC ACCIDENTS

Accident costs affect such diverse policy issues as fuel taxes, drunk-driving laws, and fuel-efficiency standards. However, estimating them requires care and sophistication, and estimating their external components even more so because the responsibility for accident costs is shared in complex ways among victims, their relatives and friends, other parties to accidents, insurance companies, and government agencies.

A good starting point is the study by Blincoe *et al.* (2002), who estimate total tangible economic costs due to US motor vehicle accidents in 2000. Their result is $263.4 billion, or $0.096 per vehicle-mile, at 2005 prices.[53] The largest categories are productivity loss due to injury and death, property damage, travel delay, and insurance administration.

Productivity loss, however, is a poor measure of the value to an individual of avoiding a casualty or injury. A more theoretically justified measure is the individuals' willingness to pay for reducing the probability of such an event. Traffic hazards raise all drivers' risk of being hurt or killed; their willingness to pay for a reduction in that risk is the relevant measure of the cost those hazards impose. To take an example: suppose people are willing to pay $5000 each to reduce the risk of fatality from 0.001 to zero. The willingness to pay per unit of risk reduction is then $5000/0.001 = $5 million. Equivalently, 1000 such people would in aggregate pay $5 million and would reduce expected fatalities by one. As a shorthand, such willingness to pay is summarized as a *value of a statistical life* (VSL) of $5 million. Similarly, the magnitude of people's willingness to pay to reduce the risk of specific kinds of injuries may be expressed as the *value of a statistical injury*.[54]

There is considerable empirical evidence on the magnitude of these values.[55] For fatalities, most comes from observing wage premiums required by workers in competitive labor markets, a measurement with two advantages: risk levels tend to be stable, and people are likely to have some knowledge of them. Several reviews and meta-analyses are available to assess the large number of studies on this topic, especially prevalent for the US. The most significant unresolved issue is whether to account for variation in unmeasured working conditions across industries (Mrozek and Taylor 2002, p. 269). Because industry differentials constitute one of the main sources of variation in risk, using industry-specific dummy variables greatly reduces the remaining risk variation and so lowers statistical precision. But if high-risk industries also offer less attractive working conditions that require a compensating wage differential, then the wage premium attributable to that risk is overestimated unless such dummy variables are used.

Mrozek and Taylor (2002), advocating inclusion of industry dummy variables, find VSL from a meta-analysis to average $1.8–3.0 million from US studies (after updating to 2005 prices). Viscusi and Aldy (2003), arguing against such inclusion, find the predicted mean for US studies to be $6.3–8.7 million. Day (1999) obtains a "best" estimate of $7.3 million from a meta-analysis including studies both with and without industry dummies, but mostly without.[56] From this evidence, it seems reasonable to adopt a range for value of life of $2–8 million, with the most likely value $5.5 million.

For non-fatal injuries, Viscusi and Aldy (2003) review 39 studies from around the world, finding most estimates for developed nations in the range of $20,000–$70,000 per serious injury (sometimes defined as an injury resulting in at least one lost workday). Miller (1993) provides estimates disaggregated by type of injury.

It is well established that the average value of a statistical life or injury rises with income, as would be expected if safety is a normal good (*i.e.*, demand for safety exhibits positive income elasticity). However, the income elasticity appears to be considerably less than one, probably between 0.5 and 0.6 (Viscusi and Aldy 2003, pp. 36–42). This is relevant for transferring results from the US or Europe, where most studies have been undertaken, to developing nations. It is also relevant for updating figures measured in one year to price levels of later years.[57]

Just replacing the productivity costs of fatalities used by Blincoe *et al.* (2002) by a VSL of $5.5 million (in 2005 dollars) raises their total accident costs by more than 70%. A more detailed estimate is provided by Parry (2004), who analyzes 1998–2000 US accident data.[58] Parry applies a VSL of $3 million and, for other categories including non-fatal injuries, updates valuations by Miller (1993). Parry provides figures by type of cost and type of accident, the latter described by the worst injury sustained. In Table 3.4, we show his results at 2005 prices, recalculated using a VSL of $5.5 million. Average social cost is $0.140/veh-mi, a figure we adopt for our overall compilation of automobile costs. The table shows that costs are dominated by accidents involving death or injury and by the "intangible" willingness to pay to avoid such outcomes.

Table 3.4 Components of social average cost of accidents

By type of cost		By type of accident	
Type	Cost ($/veh-mi)	Type	Cost ($/veh-mi)
WTP of death, injury	0.103	Fatality	0.077
Productivity	0.013	Disabling injury	0.024
Medical expenses	0.008	Other injury	0.033
Property damage	0.007	Property damage only	0.004
Legal, police, fire	0.004	Unknown	0.002
Insurance admin.	0.003		
Traffic delay	0.002		
Total	**0.140**	**Total**	**0.140**

Source: Computed from Parry (2004, Tables 1, 2).

Notes: WTP = willingness to pay (for avoidance). All costs are for US, 1998–2000, stated in 2005 prices. Price levels are updated by multiplying the 1998–2000 costs by 1.181, the average between the growth factors of hourly earnings and of the Consumer Price Index for all urban consumers, all items (US CEA 2006, Tables B-47, B-60).

How much of these costs are external to the individual user? To fully address this question would require models of driver behavior, insurance, tort and criminal law, and the effects of congestion on accident rates. The literature is only beginning to produce such models, despite early discussions by Vickrey (1968). To give an idea of the difficulties, consider the simple question of whether adding more vehicles to the road raises accident costs for existing drivers – if so, this would be an inter-user externality just like congestion, and could be analyzed similarly. Empirical evidence suggests that more congestion causes a higher rate of accidents but that they are less severe, probably due to lower speeds.[59] The resulting effect on average accident costs is ambiguous, and for this reason it is sometimes assumed to be zero.[60]

Parry (2004) allocates various costs of single- and multiple-vehicle accidents in plausible but largely heuristic ways to determine how much is external. For example, 85% of medical and emergency-service costs are assumed external in his "medium" scenario, as is 50% of property damage.[61] More important, half the cost of injuries or fatalities to occupants of a given vehicle involved in a two-vehicle crash is assumed to be caused by the other vehicle, hence external. All these external costs cause social marginal cost to exceed private cost; those imposed on non-users also cause social average cost to exceed private cost. We allocate the external costs computed by Parry assuming that those based on willingness to pay for risk reduction are inter-user externalities while all others are imposed on non-users.

The resulting estimates are shown in Table 3.3. The average costs include all costs associated with accidents, including those parts that are covered by insurance payments; by placing them under "variable costs" we are assuming that even private insurance payments are at least roughly proportional to the amount of driving, because there are various mechanisms that tend to raise insurance rates for high-mileage drivers (including the greater likelihood that they will acquire driving records regarded by insurance companies as making them higher-risk). The accident externality (social *mc* minus private *ac*) is $0.061/mi or 52% of private *ac* – a serious impediment to efficient resource allocation. This percentage can be compared to the 74% figure implied by Lindberg (2001, Table 6) for urban car traffic in Sweden, using a very different procedure.[62]

The externality derived here assumes that all drivers are identical and so are all vehicles. Thus, it measures the over-incentive to drive if the external cost is not offset through other incentives. When one considers more specific decisions, such as driver behavior or vehicle choice, the problem of external costs may be even greater. Two prominent issues involving such decisions are alcohol consumption and vehicle size. Levitt and Porter (2001) estimate that drivers who have been drinking impose more than seven times the external accident risk of other drivers.[63] This kind of finding is one justification for the considerable attention devoted to policies toward drunk driving.

As for vehicle size, White (2004) finds that the probability of an automobile driver or passenger being killed in a two-vehicle crash is 61% higher if the other vehicle is a "light truck" (van, pickup truck, or sport utility vehicle) than if it is another car. For a pedestrian, the risk is 82% higher if hit by a light truck versus being hit by a car; for a motorcyclist the figure is 125%. White also calculates that replacing a million light trucks by automobiles in the US would eliminate 30 to 81 fatalities annually.[64]

The incentive problem is highlighted by another of White's findings: the larger vehicle is safer for its own occupants in a given two-car crash.[65] So long as the vehicle stock is diverse, so that many accidents involve vehicles of different sizes, White's findings suggest that the greater use of light trucks as passenger vehicles in the US may be imposing very large accident costs. White also notes several reasons why such external costs are not likely to be eliminated by insurance or tort law.

Current laws in most nations address accident externalities in various ways: for example through tort law, criminal law, and insurance regulation. Boyer and Dionne (1987) and White (2004) provide helpful analyses. Whether such arrangements provide efficient incentives to avoid causing accidents depends to a large extent on how they affect the marginal decisions of those potentially causing an accident, prior to its realization. (This is an important reason why per-mile insurance premiums, also known as "pay-as-you-drive" schemes, have gained interest as a substitute for fixed, yearly premiums.) Infrastructure investments and mandated safety features on vehicles are often justified on grounds of reducing accident costs, and indeed they may do so. However, consumers are likely to partly offset such benefits by choosing more dangerous driving habits and by simply driving more, since the risks associated with more and/or more aggressive driving have been reduced.[66]

(6) GOVERNMENT SERVICES

Governments provide many services to highway users, from pavement maintenance to police patrols. We estimate this as the sum of three components of disbursements identified by the US Federal Highway Administration (US FHWA 2006, Table HF-10): (a) maintenance and traffic service, (b) administration and research (after subtracting a portion that we prorate to capital outlays), and (c) highway law enforcement and safety. These total $55.7 billion or $0.019/veh-mi, of which the majority is for highway maintenance. Most is covered by state and local governments, in about equal proportions. We somewhat arbitrarily take the private portion of these costs to be represented by state-imposed fees for vehicle licenses, vehicle title certificates, and drivers' licenses, which we estimate at $0.005/mi.[67] States also use fuel taxes for these costs, but we allocate fuel taxes later as payments toward road capital costs. The local portion of government services is largely covered by general tax revenues, so may be considered a subsidy to motor-vehicle operations. This subsidy is quite large in aggregate, but a very small portion of average costs of travel.

(7) ENVIRONMENTAL EXTERNALITIES

Extensive studies have been carried out of the health costs of major air pollutants in the lower atmosphere – particulate matter, nitrogen oxides, volatile organic compounds, sulfur oxides, carbon monoxide, and ozone (a product of atmospheric reactions involving other primary pollutants). To form such estimates, one must know emission rates, how emissions determine ambient air concentrations, how ambient concentrations damage people's health, and the costs of that damage including people's willingness to pay to avoid it. There are uncertainties in each of these steps, leading to a range of estimates; yet a reasonable consensus has emerged on the order of magnitude of the costs.

Even more striking is the agreement on the main components of these costs. Numerically, health costs of air pollution are overwhelmingly dominated by mortality, which in turn is dominated by the effects of particulate matter. Some of the particulate matter is emitted directly, but a substantial portion is formed in the atmosphere from nitrogen oxides, sulfur oxides, and hydrocarbons. Ozone also has important health effects but has generally not been linked to long-term mortality.[68]

With mortality dominating air-pollution costs, VSL is even more important for them than for accident costs. Furthermore, fatalities from air pollution usually occur many years after the time of exposure and among elderly people, which raises two additional analytical issues. First, because VSL is measured from the relationship between *current* willingness to pay and *current* fatality risk (as in labor-market studies), the willingness to pay for changes in fatality risk that take place far in the future should be discounted to the present time just like any other expenditure. This is widely accepted among analysts, although some people mistakenly think of it as "discounting lives" and therefore objectionable. Second, an individual's VSL may depend on that person's remaining expected life span. Here the evidence is equivocal. Alberini *et al.* (2004) "find weak support for the notion that [VSL] declines with age, and then, only for the oldest respondents (aged 70 or above)" (p. 769). By contrast, Viscusi and Aldy (2003, pp. 50–53) conclude that VSL does decline with age.[69] Considerations of discounting and possible age dependence together make it reasonable to assume a lower VSL in evaluating environmental mortality than accident mortality. In what follows, we accept for air pollution the VSL used by the US Department of Transportation, which updated to 2005 is $4.15 million, or 78.3% of the VSL we use for traffic accidents.[70]

Using the principles just outlined, US FHWA (2000) estimates the average pollution cost of an automobile in the US in 2000 at $0.017/mi (in 2005 prices).[71] We note that 99.8% of this cost is due to particulate matter (both directly emitted and produced through atmospheric reactions), and 77% is due to fatalities. We adjust their estimate upward to reflect urban emissions, but downward to reflect reduced emissions rates between 2000 and 2005, for a result of $0.013/mi.[72] A similar number can be derived from a somewhat older study by McCubbin and Delucchi (1999).[73]

While we restrict our scope to automobiles, pollution from trucks is often several times larger per vehicle-mile than from automobiles – and increasingly so as trucks have lagged behind cars in the strictness of control measures. Trucks contribute heavily to mortality due not only to direct particulate emissions, but also to heavy emissions of nitrogen oxides and sulfur oxides, which form particulates in the atmosphere (Small and Kazimi 1995). This situation is changing rapidly as greater controls on trucks and on the sulfur content of diesel fuel are phased in. Motorcycles and other small vehicles are also heavy emitters of particulates, especially in developing nations where they are numerous – for example, two- and three-wheeled vehicles in New Delhi, India, are said to have accounted for 45% of particulate emissions in the mid-1990s (Gwilliam 2003).

Conventional lower-atmospheric pollution has many well-documented effects besides those on human health, including soiling of materials, reduced visibility, and damage to crops, materials, and ecosystems. However, attempts to measure the costs of these effects are virtually unanimous in yielding far smaller estimates than for human health effects (see, *e.g.*, Delucchi 2000). The same is true for water pollution and noise, at least from automobiles.[74] We therefore omit such costs.

Motor vehicles are also a major contributor to global warming through the "greenhouse effect," due to their emissions of carbon dioxide. Precise prediction of effects of carbon dioxide on climate is impossible. Furthermore, most of the effects occur many decades after the emission, making it highly speculative to forecast what economic impacts those changes will produce – especially in light of the ability of individuals and societies to take counter-measures, perhaps using technologies that are currently unknown. Nevertheless, a number of studies have estimated the present value of projected costs of current emissions. Tol *et al.* (2000, p. 199) conclude that the marginal damage cost is very likely less than $50/tC (metric ton carbon), a bound that in fact substantially exceeds most of the estimates. Indeed, more recent studies that incorporate standard discounting techniques (essential to any intelligible interpretation of future costs) and account for adaptation obtain results well below this bound. Based on this evidence, we follow Parry and Small (2005) in adopting a value of $25/tC, which for our US commuter converts to $0.061/gal or $0.003/mi.[75] Even this is probably on the high side, and the real cost could be much smaller. Nevertheless, this estimate is less than one-fourth our estimate of cost from conventional air pollutants; the two combined are $0.016/mi, the figure entered in Table 3.3.

The upshot is that the environmental costs of motor vehicles are large in aggregate, justifying substantial expenditures on control measures, but far smaller than other costs of driving. Consequently, internalizing them on a per-mile basis would make little difference to people's travel decisions. It follows that optimal policy toward environmental externalities from automobiles would focus on specific measures to reduce the externalities rather than general measures to reduce automobile travel.

Summary

The upper panel of Table 3.3 summarizes the figures just presented for variable costs of automobile travel. These costs are very large and give some idea of the importance of policy decisions affecting use of motor vehicles. Their relative size, and especially the size of the gaps between private and social marginal cost, highlight the importance of certain categories – especially travel time, travel scheduling, and motor vehicle accidents – in such policy decisions.

3.5 Highway travel: long-run cost functions

In order to complete the cost analysis for highway travel, we need to include the capital cost of building roads, converted to an annual or daily flow. Defining this cost as a function of capacity and adding it to a short-run cost function enables us to derive a long-run cost function by choosing, for each output, the size of highway that minimizes the two costs combined. Such a function provides a comprehensive summary of what it costs society to undertake different amounts of motor-vehicle travel in a corridor. This is important, for example, in evaluating policies designed to influence the total amount of highway travel.

The long-run cost function may be derived under the assumption that capacity is continuously variable, or that it can be built only in discrete units such as lanes. In the latter case, the resulting function is not smooth but rather is the lower envelope of several distinct short-run curves. The actual possibilities for capacity, however, are probably continuous, despite the fact that *changes* in road capacity are usually made in discrete units. The design capacity of a lane can vary widely depending on lane width, shoulders, curves, median, exits and entrances, intersections, and traffic signals. Hence it is possible to design a highway with virtually any capacity, and the question really becomes whether the cost function exhibits small or large bumps. Choice among continuous highway capacities can be formulated analytically in an illuminating manner, as we illustrate in this section.

We first derive analytic long-run cost functions for some common situations. We then consider the impact of capacity-augmenting information technologies. Finally, we provide some empirical evidence on capital costs.

3.5.1 Analytic long-run cost functions

As shown in Section 3.1, an analytic long-run cost function can be derived by combining a short-run cost function with information about the cost of capacity. To simplify, we begin with several assumptions. First, we assume a single uniform output, measured as vehicle trips or flow on a road of unit length.[76] Second, we assume that capital investment serves solely to expand road capacity; we therefore ignore parking requirements as well as any auxiliary benefits of road investment such as higher free-flow speeds, lower operating costs, and greater safety.[77] Third, capital cost is linear in capacity:

$$K(V_K) = K_0 + K_1 \cdot V_K, \tag{3.41}$$

with $K_1 > 0$. Fourth, interest and depreciation on capital can be written as $\rho \cdot K(V_K)$ per day, where ρ is the annual capital recovery factor[78] divided by the number of days per year during which the travel conditions under consideration apply.

We specify the average short-run variable cost (3.21) to be a function of volume-capacity ratio V/V_K during that period, as it is in every example considered in Section 3.4:

$$c(V) = c_0 + c_g\left(V / V_K\right), \tag{3.42}$$

where $c_g(\cdot)$ describes congestion-related average user cost and $c_g(0) = 0$. Depending on the model, V may represent static flow, time-averaged flow, or desired arrival rate, each measured over a given time period of duration q; thus short-run total variable cost over that period is $q \cdot V \cdot c(V)$. Several such periods h may be considered, in which case a function like (3.42) applies in each one; if so, we assume for simplicity that each has the same value of c_0.

Multiplying (3.41) by ρ and adding it to (3.42), short-run total cost may be written as:

$$C(V, q; V_K) = \rho K_0 + c_0 Q + C_g(V, q; V_K),$$

where V is the vector of flows V_h, q that of durations q_h, $Q = V'q$ is total vehicle-trips, and C_g includes all the parts of (3.41) and (3.42) involving V_K. The first two terms of this equation are unaffected by capacity, so we can ignore them in deriving investment criteria. We thus focus on the tradeoff between the costs of capacity and congestion in the third, congestion-related, term. We consider two alternate congestion models: a static (stationary-state) model and the dynamic bottleneck model with endogenous scheduling.

Static congestion model

Suppose the typical weekday is divided into distinct periods $h = 1, \ldots, H$, each with constant flow V_h for a duration q_h. With short-run variable cost given by (3.42) in each period, the resulting congestion-related part of the long-run total cost function (cost per day) is:

$$\tilde{C}_g(V, q) = \min_{V_K} C_g(V, q; V_K) = \min_{V_K} \left\{ \sum_h q_h \cdot V_h \cdot c_g(V_h/V_K) + \rho K_1 V_K \right\}. \tag{3.43}$$

The first-order condition for minimization in (3.43) leads to the following investment rule:

$$\rho K_1 = -\sum_h q_h \cdot V_h \cdot \frac{\partial c_g(\cdot)}{\partial V_K} = \sum_h q_h \cdot \left(V_h / V_K \right)^2 \cdot c_g'(\cdot), \tag{3.44}$$

where c_g' denotes the derivative of c_g with respect to the ratio V_h/V_K. The marginal capital cost of expanding the highway is equated to marginal travel-cost savings. Solving this for V_K as a function of the vector V and substituting into the minimand in (3.43) gives the long-run cost function, individual terms of which give the congestion cost in each time period and the capital cost.

Kraus, Mohring and Pinfold (1976) and Keeler and Small (1977) estimate such a cost function, using expressway data from the Minneapolis-St. Paul, Minnesota, and San Francisco, California, regions, respectively. Kraus, Mohring and Pinfold use two time periods and Keeler and Small use five. Both assume that the ratios of volumes in different periods remain constant as traffic expands, thereby reducing output to just one dimension. Both assume the function $K(V_K)$ to be continuous and linear, as here, with a positive intercept K_0 in Kraus, Mohring and Pinfold and a zero intercept in Keeler and Small. Kraus, Mohring and Pinfold find that optimal capacity produces a peak-period speed between 32 and 56 miles per hour, depending on parameters.[79] Keeler and Small find optimal peak speed between 47 and 56 miles per hour, depending on capital cost, interest rate, and value of time.[80] Starrs and Starkie (1986) apply the Keeler-Small model, with a locally estimated speed-flow curve, to urban arterials in Adelaide, South Australia, finding optimal peak speeds of about 24 miles per hour. These results illustrate the point that peak-period congestion would not be eliminated by socially optimal investment in capacity.

It is illuminating to write the long-run cost function analytically for the special case of just one time period. Dropping the time subscripts, the total number of vehicle-trips served is $Q \equiv V \cdot q$; but as discussed earlier, V and q are really distinct outputs. This is because the cost of providing for Q differs depending on whether it results from a very high volume for a short duration, or from a lower volume for a long duration, the latter being cheaper to accommodate. The failure of most literature in transportation economics to distinguish between these two outputs has limited its ability to analyze policies that affect the duration of the peak period. We illustrate here for the case where $c_g(\cdot)$ is the power function $\alpha \cdot T_f \cdot a \cdot (V/V_K)^b$ as in (3.23). Applying (3.44) and solving for V_K, we obtain:

$$\rho K_1 = q \cdot \left(\frac{V}{V_K}\right)^2 \cdot \alpha T_f ab \cdot \left(\frac{V}{V_K}\right)^{b-1} \Rightarrow V_K^* = V \cdot \left(\frac{q\alpha T_f ab}{\rho K_1}\right)^{1/(b+1)}.$$

The capacity chosen is proportional to traffic volume V, with proportionality constant depending on duration of the congested period, value of time, parameters of the congestion function, and capacity cost. Substituting V_K^* into the total cost function, we obtain after some calculations:

$$\tilde{C}_g(V,q) = c_{bpr} \cdot V \cdot q^{1/(b+1)} \quad \text{with: } c_{bpr} = \left(\rho K_1\right)^{b/(b+1)} \cdot \left(\alpha T_f ab\right)^{1/(b+1)} \cdot \left(1+b^{-1}\right).$$

We see that the congestion-related part of the long-run cost function exhibits no scale economies or diseconomies with respect to V; but it exhibits scale economies with respect to q because the same investment in capacity can accommodate more people at a given level of service if the time period is longer. This, of course, is the basis for attempts to spread traffic peaks, for example by staggering work hours. These scale economies in q are greater the more sharply curved is the congestion function, *i.e.*, the greater is the exponent b. In the special case $b = 1$, congestion-related costs are proportional to $V \cdot q^{1/2}$.

Dynamic congestion model with endogenous scheduling

We now turn to dynamic bottleneck congestion. We have already seen that the average variable congestion-related cost is $\bar{c}_g$ as given by (3.38), in which demand is represented by volume V_d with duration q (of desired queue-exits). This equation again conforms to the restriction in (3.42) that congestion depends on volume only through the volume-capacity ratio V_d/V_K. Thus daily congestion-related total cost is in the form (3.43) with just one time period, but now with V_d replacing V_h, q replacing q_h, and $\bar{c}_g$ replacing c_g where

$$\bar{c}_g(V_d/V_K) = \begin{cases} 0 & \text{if } V_d \leq V_K \\ \delta \cdot q \cdot \left(\dfrac{V_d}{V_K} - \dfrac{1}{2}\right) & \text{otherwise.} \end{cases}$$

There are two possible solution regimes. If ρK_1 is small, it will be cheaper to provide enough capacity so that no queuing occurs; *i.e.*, $V_K^* = V_d$. Capacity is then proportional to V_d and is independent of q. If ρK_1 is larger, it will be cheaper to allow some queuing, in which case (3.44) applies with $c_g'(\cdot) = \delta \cdot q$; this yields the investment rule $\rho K_1 = q \cdot (V_d/V_K)^2 \cdot \delta \cdot q$, whose solution is:

$$V_K^* = \left(\frac{\delta}{\rho K_1}\right)^{1/2} \cdot V_d \cdot q.$$

In this regime, optimal capacity is proportional to $Q \equiv V_d \cdot q$; the proportionality constant is greater if the composite scheduling-cost parameter δ is large or if the capacity-expansion cost ρK_1 is small.

The total congestion-related cost in the first regime is simply $\tilde{C}_g = \rho K_1 V_d$, and in the second it can be written as:

$$\tilde{C}_g (V_d, q) = V_d \cdot q \cdot \left(c_{bot} - \frac{\delta \cdot q}{2} \right) \quad \text{with: } c_{bot} = 2 \left(\rho K_1 \delta \right)^{1/2} .$$

In both regimes, total congestion-related costs show scale economies with respect to duration q: average long-run congestion-related cost $\tilde{C}_g / (V_d \cdot q)$ is equal to $\rho K_1 / q$ in the first regime and $(c_{bot} - \delta \cdot q / 2)$ in the second, in both cases declining with q. This is again because if demand is spread out more, it takes less capacity to keep congestion to a reasonable level.[81] Note that there are still neutral scale economies with respect to the *level* of peak demand, V_d.

Thus if there are no scale economies or diseconomies in capital cost (*i.e.*, $K_0 = 0$), total long-run cost is proportional to the peak volume of desired trip completions, but less than proportional to the duration of this demand – just as we found for the static model with congestion given by a power function. In both models, then, it is important to distinguish flow from duration in considering the properties of long-run costs.

As with the short-run function on which it is based, this long-run cost function is second-best because it is constrained by the requirement that users time their trips according to their own individual interests, which does not yield the lowest possible total cost.

3.5.2 The role of information technology

There has been a growing interest in the role of various information and communication technologies in the functioning of congested roads and networks. These technologies may offer other ways besides physical road expansion to increase road capacity. Two main types of information technology are discussed here: automated highway systems and advanced traveler information systems.

Automated highway systems

Automated highway systems (AHS) use information and control technologies that allow "hands-off and feet-off" driving. With vehicles' speeds controlled electronically, eliminating fluctuations due to human factors, safety may increase substantially: crashes could be reduced by 26% to 85% on urban highways according to the Transportation Research Board (1998). Because smaller vehicle spacings can be allowed, highway capacity may also rise considerably, with lane capacities potentially ranging from one to five times those for driver-controlled traffic. There is a tradeoff between capacity and safety, just as with driver-controlled traffic. Due to frequent on-and-off ramps, the potential of AHS may be smaller in urbanized areas – precisely where capacity augmentation is most important due to high construction costs; but capacity may still nearly be double that of a conventional highway (Hall and Caliskan 1999).

Despite the potential of AHS, various considerations warn against too much optimism. First, improved highway capacity is of limited use when bottlenecks remain. For example, if AHS technology is applied on highways leading into a city where the urban street network has limited capacity, it may merely shift congestion from highways to city streets. Second, mixed use of automated and manually operated vehicles may pose particularly high demands on the technical performance of the AHS, while at the same time yielding limited improvements in flow. Third, a single AHS highway in a network of conventional highways would induce route shifts, which could be counterproductive if Braess-type effects occur. Fourth, legal considerations and driver resistance to relinquishing control may be barriers to implementation. Other factors include costs, the need to standardize equipment across locations, and vulnerability to sabotage. It therefore remains to be seen whether or not AHS can play a major role.

Advanced traveler information systems

Advanced traveler information systems (ATIS) use information and telecommunication technologies targeted to road users. Emmerink and Nijkamp (1999) provide an overview. A major purpose is to reduce the effects of unexpected incidents on travel times, thereby improving both expected travel time and reliability. Schrank and Lomax (2005, p. 58) suggest that slightly over half of total congestion delay across major US metropolitan areas is attributable to non-recurring incidents.

There is little doubt that information could lead to a more efficient use of an otherwise optimized road network – specifically, if the externalities in the user equilibrium of Section 3.4.4 were all eliminated (de Palma and Lindsey 1998). However, a network with a user equilibrium need not necessarily be improved by information – yet another paradox analogous to the Braess paradox mentioned earlier. Ben-Akiva, de Palma and Kaysi (1991) provide examples where information provision is welfare-reducing.

Figure 3.12, based on Verhoef *et al.* (1996), shows why this can happen. Suppose capacity is stochastic, with a high-capacity state (subscript 0) and low-capacity state (subscript 1) occurring with equal probability. Therefore either of two average cost curves, shown as c_s, $s = 0, 1$, may apply. Since each is rising, there is an associated (social) marginal cost curve mc_s above it. Expected average cost $E(c)$ and inverse demand d are also shown, all as functions of flow V. If drivers have no information about the actual state and they are

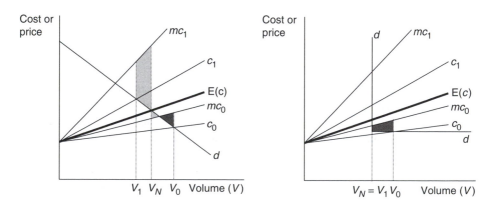

Figure 3.12 Stochastic road capacity and information provision: welfare gains (light shading) and welfare losses (dark shading).

risk-neutral, equilibrium road use occurs at the intersection of d and $E(c)$, at volume V_N. With perfect information, the equilibrium depends on which state occurs: for each state s it is at V_s, at the intersection of d and c_s. (The optima in both states, not indicated in the diagrams, are at the intersections of d and mc_s; see Chapter 4.)

Let us define expected social surplus as expected total benefits minus expected total cost. Its change due to perfect information is measured by determining in each state the change in area under the demand function minus the change in total cost (which is the area under the marginal cost function). Averaging the results for the two states gives the change in expected social surplus. With net benefits shaded lightly and net costs shaded darkly, the left panel shows that expected social surplus increases. It can be shown that this result always holds for linear demand and cost functions, under relatively mild conditions.[82] It often holds in more general settings as well, for example when two parallel roads are available (Emmerink 1998). The basic reason is that although information produces a net loss in state 0 (because it increases use of the road, which is already more than optimal), it produces a bigger net gain in state 1 (because the extreme losses due to congestion are ameliorated by a reduction in demand).

However, the right panel shows that the result is not generally true if the inverse demand function is convex, here represented in an extreme way as a kinked demand function. In this case, the net benefits in state 1 disappear because demand is unaffected, and only the net loss in state 0 remains. Thus, providing information causes the congested road to be even more overused in the good state, with no compensating reduction of use in the bad state, resulting in a net loss of expected social surplus.

Arnott, de Palma and Lindsey (1991a) similarly examine information provision in the bottleneck model with stochastic capacity. They find that *perfect* information increases social surplus, but information subject to some uncertainty may reduce social surplus. So not only is there a paradox in which information can be harmful, but the results are not even monotonic with respect to how accurate the information is.

These insights suggest that the value of information may be enhanced when pricing is also in place to control congestion externalities, a question we will return to in Chapter 4.

3.5.3 Empirical evidence on capital costs

In this section we address the two most important capital costs that are fixed in what we have defined as the short run, but are variable in the long run. These are the costs of building roads and parking spaces.

Roads

Capital costs vary greatly with terrain – e.g., flat, rolling, or mountainous – and with the degree of urbanization. Both affect such factors as the number and types of structures required (e.g., bridges, overpasses, intersections, drainage facilities, retaining walls, sound walls), ease of access to construction sites, difficulty of grading, extent of demolition, and of course land prices.

Scale economies with respect to capacity, s_K, may be defined analogously to equation (3.3) as the ratio of average to marginal cost of capacity. Scale economies might arise from fixed costs of administration, better equipment utilization, fixed land requirements such as shoulders and medians, and efficiencies of multi-lane traffic flows (Mohring 1976, pp. 140–45). Scale diseconomies could result from the increased cost of building more or bigger intersections, especially when they require complex signals or overpasses (Kraus 1981).[83] If we generalize from a cost function (with fixed factor prices) to a general-equilibrium supply function (with variable factor prices), as defined in Section 3.1, then scale diseconomies could also arise from a rising supply price of urban land, especially in large cities where urban land is scarce and roads use a substantial fraction of it (Small 1999a).

Several empirical studies have examined scale economies and the magnitude of highway capital costs. Meyer, Kain and Wohl (1965) estimate a cost function like (3.41) based on engineering standards, assuming scale economies due to fixed costs of administration and fixed land requirements. For a six-lane expressway in a typical suburban area, their results imply scale economies, with $s_K = 1.74$ (Meyer, Kain and Wohl 1965, p. 207). However, there is reason to doubt their assumption that the right of way needed for median and shoulders is independent of the number of traffic lanes; physical separation of traffic and provision for stopped vehicles are often used to maintain safety in the face of high total traffic levels.

Keeler and Small (1977) estimate construction and land costs statistically from a sample of 57 highway segments in the San Francisco Bay area, based on construction data for the years 1947–72. Urbanization is represented by three categories: central city (Oakland or San Francisco), urban (other incorporated cities), and rural (unincorporated areas). Highway type is expressway or other arterial. Construction cost for any of these categories is assumed to be proportional to the number of lanes raised to the power $1/s_K$. They estimate scale economies $s_K = 1.03$ (standard error 0.39), which may be taken as weak evidence for neutral scale economies.[84] Land costs are estimated as fractions of construction costs, the fractions ranging from 26.7% to 36.7%. Starrs and Starkie (1986) similarly estimate a power function, using data from 27 projects involving urban arterials in South Australia; omitting land, they estimate scale economies $s_K = 1.28$ (standard error 0.22).[85]

Kraus (1981) estimates the degree of scale economies on urban road networks while explicitly accounting for the costs of intersections, which he finds to be quite large. Using UK data on costs and design standards, he estimates overall scale economies at $s = 1.19$ for a circular urban area of 10-mile radius containing a specified highway network.[86] This value reflects substantial scale *economies* in constructing individual road segments, significantly offset by scale *diseconomies* of intersections (the latter due to the fact that their size tends to be proportional to the square of the width of the highways being connected). This offset, seen only at the network level, is ignored by the other studies just mentioned. Those studies (and Kraus as well) may furthermore overestimate scale economies by taking land prices as fixed.

Altogether, the evidence supports the likelihood of mild scale economies for the overall highway network in major cities. Scale economies are probably substantial in smaller cities in which one or two major expressways are important, and may disappear altogether in very large cities where expanding expressways is extraordinarily expensive due to high urban density.

What can we say about the average capital cost per vehicle-mile? The US Department of Commerce (2005, Table 11B) estimates the depreciated value of the entire US highway capital stock, excluding land, at $1688 billion in 2004. Annualizing at a 7% real interest rate and a 20-year average remaining life, and updating to 2005 prices, this implies an annual cost of $166 billion.[87] Following the cost-responsibility allocations for year 2000 projected in US FHWA (1997, Table V-21), we assume that 71% of this cost is attributable to passenger vehicles. The result is $0.043 per passenger-vehicle-mile for the entire US.[88] Given the evidence that scale economies, if any, are small, this figure is a reasonable estimate of the average cost of physical capital for urban areas as well. We add 30% for the cost of urban land, based on Keeler and Small (1977, p. 9), bringing the average capital cost to $0.056/veh-mi. Because the size of the capital stock is not necessarily optimized, this figure is listed as a "short-run fixed cost" at the bottom of Table 3.3.

Passenger vehicles contribute toward paying roadway costs in the US mainly through fuel taxes, which we estimated above at $0.016/mi and list in the table as a private average cost for roadways.

Parking

Providing parking spaces is costly wherever land is expensive. As emphasized by Shoup (2005), there are three to four parking spaces for every registered vehicle in cities. If we consider just commuting trips, and allow for a 20% vacancy rate, we could assume that adding a trip by car requires $1/0.8 = 1.25$ parking spaces (at the workplace) if the vehicle fleet is not expanded, and 2.25 (including one at the residence) if it is.

Willson (1995, p. 39) and Shoup (2005, Chapter 6) present evidence on costs from southern California. In suburban office parks, Willson finds the average cost per space to be $7870 for surface lots and $17,550 for structures, both restated at 2005 prices.[89] In urban westside Los Angeles, specifically the University of California, Los Angeles (UCLA) campus, where surface lots are uneconomic, Shoup measures the incremental cost per space in parking structures, relative to surface lots, obtaining $33,190. The latter figure is calculated by dividing the construction cost of the structure (without land) by the number of additional spaces it holds beyond what a surface lot would hold; it thus has the advantage of being independent of land cost except insofar as optimal structure height depends on land costs.[90] These figures are easily within the national ranges suggested by Cambridge Systematics *et al.* (1998, p. 9–18).

Annualizing with a 40-year lifetime and 7% real interest rate and adding an estimate of annual operating cost,[91] these figures imply an annual fixed cost per parking space at a workplace of $889, $1835, and $3008 for suburban surface lot, suburban structure, and urban structure, respectively. Assuming 250 round trips per year and a 20% vacancy rate,[92] the corresponding average capital cost for parking at the workplace adds $4.44, $9.18, or $15.04 per day to the average cost of a commute trip.[93] For the short-run fixed cost of parking in Table 3.3, we use the average of the two suburban figures, divided by round-trip distance of 24.2 miles, yielding $0.281/mi. It may seem anomalous that parking costs are more than three times roadway costs; but this reflects our focus on an urban commuting trip, whose parking space typically has a high opportunity cost and is not shared by any other trips, whereas the roads used for commuting trips are used also at other times of the day and so have their costs averaged over more users.

For private cost, we hazard the guess that US urban commuters pay for at most 2.5% of workplace parking cost on average, or $0.007/mi.[94] We have listed average private parking cost as fixed in the short run: *i.e.*, independent of short-run variations in vehicle-miles traveled. This is the appropriate assumption if expanding vehicle travel is in the form of longer trips to the same destinations. If instead people take more trips to destinations that charge for parking, then this cost would be partly or fully variable. (Similarly, the question of whether the social costs of parking are variable in the long run would depend on the extent to which more vehicle travel involves people spending more time parked at destinations requiring expensive parking facilities.)

Urban parking costs are clearly a significant portion of the cost of automobile travel, and are all the more remarkable because they are fully absorbed by the vast majority of US employers rather than being charged to the commuter.

3.5.4 Is highway travel subsidized?

Calculations such as those shown in Table 3.3 are often used to debate whether automobile travel, or highway travel more broadly, is subsidized. Such debates can be confusing because "subsidy" has several different meanings, and for each there are conceptual issues in how to measure costs and user payments that cannot necessarily be resolved in a scientific manner.

We can discern at least four meanings for "subsidy," which are not mutually exclusive. The first is *fiscal*: is a particular set of government accounts in balance? We might seek such balance as a way of facilitating public scrutiny of financial decisions in order to encourage honest and competent management; we might also care about budgetary imbalances because raising public funds to cover deficits generally has some economic cost (the so-called "excess burden"). These concerns are reflected in the frequent use of ear-marking, or hypothecation, of highway-based revenues to be spent only on highway-related purposes.

A second meaning is *distributional*: does the system of highway finance benefit certain groups at the expense of others? Here the motivation might be understanding the political economy of decision-making, or simply the desire to promote a broad trust in the fairness of the system. These concerns, as well as fiscal ones, are prominent in the highway cost allocation studies that have been done periodically at both the federal and state levels in the US.

A third meaning involves *long-run allocation*: does the gap, if any, between social costs and revenues from highway transportation indicate likely misallocations of investment? Some discussions, especially in the literature on privatization, appear to take the position that allocation of investment across sectors of the economy are best made as in unregulated private markets, by allowing investment funds to flow out of sectors that make losses into sectors that make profits. This could be justified, for example, if the industry exhibits neutral scale economies and minimal external costs, so that average total cost approximates long-run marginal cost.

A fourth meaning is *efficiency*: is there a discrepancy between social and private marginal cost that will cause market failures? This question is the basis for most economic analysis of optimal pricing and investment, which we describe in subsequent chapters. It has been prominent in many research projects on cost measurement sponsored by the European Union, as suggested by such project titles as "**UNI**fication of Accounts and Marginal Costs for **T**ransport **E**fficiency" (UNITE) (Nash *et al.* 2003). Such questions also influenced, although incompletely, the most recent US federal highway cost allocation study (US FHWA 1997, 2000). In contrast to the first three meanings of "subsidy," this one has more of a short-run focus because of the prominence of short-run marginal cost in economic pricing theory; it is also more focused on the marginal decision-making of a single user, as opposed to a policy maker who can influence many users simultaneously.

Conceptual difficulties abound. In assessing fiscal balance, which taxes should be considered to be user taxes? For example, what about the portion of a normal sales or value-added tax that falls on fuel? Or what about a specific exemption of fuel from such taxes? Similarly, which expenditures are undertaken primarily for the benefit of highway users, especially when they are part of broader efforts to promote public safety (as with police, emergency response, and alcohol-abuse prevention)? The same problems afflict attempts to assess distributional impacts, hence all the more so the formulation of a concept of fairness. The third and fourth meanings are somewhat more amenable to precise definitions because they can be used to address precise questions, such as what would happen if a particular suite of policies was introduced to restrain downtown road traffic; but then the most direct approach is to model the policies explicitly and forgo the step of measuring the long-run average or marginal cost of expanding road traffic.

Even in addressing efficiency, the most valuable lessons from computing social and private costs most likely come from the individual components. For example, the bottom row of Table 3.3 could be used to argue that in the short run, private decision-makers are "subsidized" at the margin by US$0.232 per vehicle-mile if they choose to travel by car. Given the capital decisions that have been made with respect to provision of roads and parking spaces, this measures the extent of the distortion in the average incentive facing car users. But more striking is that most of this discrepancy arises from the congestion externality, and most of the rest arises from inter-user externalities connected with accidents. These externalities are well understood to vary greatly by circumstance. So from an efficiency point of view, the table is most useful by pointing to congestion and accidents as two places to look for big savings from more efficient policies. Similarly, looking at long-run policies, we see that parking is supplied with an enormous subsidy – to such an extent, in fact, that we deemed the short-run costs of searching for parking spaces too small to bother to quantify for the US. So very likely there are big savings to be reaped from policies that reduce provision of parking spaces, especially if some of the fixed costs can be recovered by converting parking lots to other uses or by arranging for existing parking structures to be shared with nearby new users.

We therefore see little value in arguing over the extent of aggregate subsidies to road users, but much value in examining specific cost components and how decisions affecting them are made.

3.6 Intermodal cost comparisons

One way to use cost functions such as those developed in this chapter is to compare them for different modes. This is not as easy as it might seem, because of the many required assumptions regarding demand, geography, land use, and other factors. Inevitably, some of the cost categories discussed earlier are omitted for simplicity. Furthermore, because a cost comparison does not incorporate an explicit demand model, it cannot take into account preferences of users for service characteristics other than those quantified in the study, nor can it predict the mix of modal choices that would be efficient. Nevertheless, it is a conceptually transparent way to summarize the advantages and disadvantages of alternate modes for producing a carefully specified type of service.

The pioneering study is by Meyer, Kain and Wohl (1965). Their costs exclude the value of user-supplied inputs like time, but they compensate for this by constraining the various modes to provide comparable levels of service. Several later studies incorporate the value of user-supplied time explicitly, while still others discuss differences in service quality but do not incorporate them formally.[95]

Figure 3.13, adapted from Meyer, Kain and Wohl, shows a typical result for commuting trips along a corridor connecting residential areas to a high-density business district. All results are for a 10-mile limited-access line-haul facility (auto-only expressway, exclusive busway, or rapid-rail line), combined with a two-mile downtown distribution route. Bus service is integrated, meaning that collection, line haul, and distribution are all done by a single vehicle. Downtown distribution for rail and for one of the bus systems is accomplished using exclusive underground right of way; for the other bus system and for auto, it is accomplished using city streets.

Costs for all transit modes decline as a function of hourly passenger volume along the corridor (shown in 1000's), reflecting scale economies in vehicle size. At the lowest volumes, automobile travel is cheapest. At somewhat higher volumes (above approximately

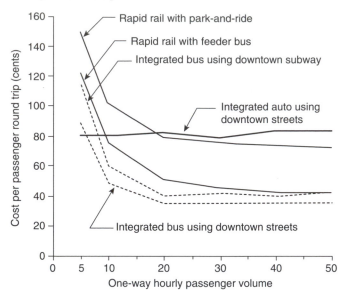

Figure 3.13 Results of intermodal cost comparisons. Adapted with permission from Meyer, Kain and Wohl (1965, p. 300), copyright RAND Corporation 1965.

5000 passengers per hour in this example), the bus becomes more economical. At still higher volumes, rail transit may become the cheapest, although not for this particular set of parameters.

These results help delineate the natural markets for each of these modes. One of the problems with transit subsidies is that they have encouraged expansion of transit services beyond where they are most suitable. Rail systems are built in small cities which are more economically served by bus; bus systems are extended to low-density suburbs where auto is cheapest. Meyer and Gómez-Ibàñez (1981, pp. 51–55) identify the primary markets for bus transit in the US as high-income radial commuters and low-income central-city residents. Research suggests that service has been expanded beyond these markets at least in part because of federal subsidies (Pucher and Markstedt 1983).

Meyer, Kain and Wohl (1965) do find that rail transit can be cheaper than bus above 30,000 passengers per hour if residential densities are higher than those applicable to Figure 3.13. The findings of some other studies are even less optimistic for rail. Neither Keeler *et al.* (1975) nor Boyd *et al.* (1973, 1978) find any situation where rail is cheaper than bus. The study by Keeler *et al.* estimates rail costs using the San Francisco area's Bay Area Rapid Transit (BART) system, which may be an atypically high-cost system (Viton 1980); while Boyd *et al.* use several North American rail systems built since 1945. In contrast, Allport (1981), with the cheaper Rotterdam rail system as his model, finds that elevated rail transit is cheaper than bus for corridor volumes above 10,000 per hour. Allport also analyzes a light-rail system, which dominates both bus and rapid rail for peak-direction passenger volumes in the range of 8400 to 13,100 per hour[96] – in contrast to the results of Wunsch (1996), described earlier, for a broad cross-section of European cities.

The biggest factor accounting for these differences is the capital cost of infrastructure. Kain (1999) focuses on this item, comparing more recent evidence for four types of express

Table 3.5 Construction costs of North American transit systems

	Construction cost (2005 US dollars)[a]	
	Per route mile ($ millions)	Per daily trip[b] ($ thousands)
Heavy rail (average of four systems)	201.9	34.73
Light rail (average of four systems)	62.7	33.66
Exclusive busway:		
Ottawa	53.3	3.41
Pittsburgh	28.1	6.44
Shared carpool lane:		
El Monte Busway, Los Angeles	17.0	4.31
Shirley Hwy, northern Virginia	18.0	3.39
I-66, northern Virginia	31.6	9.73
Houston transitways (average)[c]	7.5	6.50

Source: Kain (1999, Table 11-3); original sources are Pickrell (1989) and Kain *et al.* (1992).

Notes

a   Updated from 1989 to 2002 prices using the ENR (formerly *Engineering News-Record*) construction cost index (rose 41.7%); and from 2002 to 2005 using the US Census Bureau index for houses under construction (excluding land) (rose 19.4%). The figures are from US Census Bureau (1992, Table 1203; 2004, Table 921; 2006).

b   Includes trips in carpools for shared carpool lane. Cost per daily trip by transit is two to nine times greater.

c   Average of four new "transitways" operational in 1989: Katy, Gulf, North, and Northwest.

transit in North American cities: rapid rail, light rail, bus on exclusive busway, and bus on shared carpool lanes. Some of Kain's results are shown in Table 3.5. It is evident that at the ridership levels achieved by these systems, both heavy and light rail are many times more expensive than express bus, even before accounting for their higher operating costs as documented in Section 3.2.

Comparisons such as these have led to widespread skepticism among economists toward new rail systems. The evidence is strong that in all but very dense cities, equivalent transportation can be provided far more cheaply by a good bus system, using exclusive right of way where necessary to bypass congestion. Recent attention has been focused on designing bus systems that more closely match the quality of service offered by rail. This concept, known as "bus rapid transit," has been successfully implemented in a number of cities – most famously Curitiba, Brazil.[97]

3.7 Conclusions

Cost models may be simple or excruciatingly complex, depending on their purpose. But to be useful they must at least be rigorous. That means carefully distinguishing what is an output, what is a parameter, and what is being held constant. By doing this, the researcher can summarize a host of information in useful ways, such as average costs, marginal costs, and economies of scale and scope. Carefully distinguishing between long-run and short-run variations, and rigorously defining the associated cost functions, help to clarify what costs need to be considered in particular policy decisions.

Such summary measures and their underlying components can, in turn, be used to understand significant features affecting how transportation services are, or could be, supplied. As just one example, recognizing that the time supplied by users is a necessary input into the production of trips leads to a recognition of scale economies for producing scheduled services such as public transit, which in turn implies that marginal-cost pricing, often recommended on efficiency grounds, will produce revenue shortfalls.

Turning to congested highways, it is possible to use cost functions to understand the outcome of allowing many users to choose trip frequencies, routes, and possibly travel schedules endogenously, even as their choices in aggregate determine the pattern of travel times they each face. The relatively simple static model of congestion provides a valuable insight about the inefficiencies of such situations and (as we shall see in the next chapter) about the possibilities of pricing to alleviate them. When applied to an artificial network of two or three competing routes, the static model shows that unexpectedly perverse results can occasionally occur from widening a highway or from adding a new highway link; when applied to a realistic network, it enables planners to estimate the effects of changes in transportation demand or infrastructure, so long as these changes are modest enough that the model's assumptions continue to be valid approximations. Dynamic models provide further insights: for example, that the total congestion cost may be dominated by how strongly people care about their preferred schedules rather than how much they value the time lost in delays. We have argued that further progress in refining our understanding of policies on the public agenda today will require researchers to combine economic analysis with increasingly detailed engineering models of dynamic congestion formation and evolution.

The most important components of transportation costs have been studied so extensively that reasonable empirical estimates of them can be compiled and compared. We have done this for urban commuting by automobile in the US. The results suggest that the costs are dominated by congestion, accidents, and parking – all areas where charging users for these costs is not straightforward. There are considerable differences between marginal social costs and average private costs, suggesting the likelihood of overuse. We will have more to say about this in the next chapter when we consider the implications of different ways to price automobile users.

4   Pricing

Having described demand and cost structures, we can now ask what happens when the two operate simultaneously: that is, when economic actors constrained by these two structures interact in markets. Our analysis of short-run equilibria in the previous chapter provided some first insights. But to obtain a more complete picture, we must also specify how suppliers take into account demand and cost structures in formulating pricing, investment, or other policies.

There are many ways to do this, each leading to an equilibrium analysis that answers a different question. For example, if we specify that firms maximize profits, we determine equilibrium in an unregulated environment. If we specify that highway capacity is fixed and there is no charge for using it, as in Chapter 3, we determine road use in short-run unpriced equilibrium. If we specify that prices are set to maximize some social objective function, we determine a short-run optimum. These and other possibilities are considered in this and the following two chapters.

Our discussion is organized around policy questions. This chapter describes first-best and second-best optimal short-run pricing, aimed at maximizing social welfare. Chapter 5 discusses investments and how their financing relates to revenues from pricing, including a brief discussion of cost–benefit analysis. Chapter 6 considers institutional arrangements and how they facilitate or hinder the achievement of efficient pricing and investment. These institutions include public or private ownership of highways, public or private provision of public transit, regulation, and freedom of entry by firms into established markets.

The present chapter exemplifies the ramifications of a standard argument in economics: that efficiency is achieved in many situations by marginal-cost pricing. This means that each economic agent, in deciding whether to undertake an activity, faces a perceived price for doing so equal to that activity's social marginal cost. Landmark works applying this principle to transportation include Dupuit (1844, 1849), Hotelling (1938), and Walters (1968). Doing so in practice, however, is often impossible so we must also consider various constraints on what prices can be charged. We then enter the world of "second-best" as exposited for general situations by Lipsey and Lancaster (1956), Baumol and Bradford (1970), and others. The occurrence of such constraints is the rule rather than the exception in applied transportation pricing, and we therefore discuss in considerable detail and for various situations how one can determine second-best prices that optimize welfare given some constraints on policies. Of course, actual pricing policy often does not follow any optimization rule but rather responds to political considerations. To examine those considerations thoroughly would take us well outside our scope, but we do provide a few insights regarding public transit subsidies in Section 4.5.

Section 4.1 sets the scene by discussing first-best pricing in the context of congested highway traffic. Section 4.2 then moves on to consider second-best road pricing with such examples as the inability to price all links on a network, the inability to distinguish between classes of users, the inability to vary tolls continuously over time, imperfect information by users, and distortions outside the transportation market. Section 4.3 discusses some practical applications of congestion pricing, all of which involve second-best pricing. Section 4.4 considers a very common applied pricing problem: parking. Section 4.5 discusses the pricing of public transportation.

4.1 First-best congestion pricing of highways

Economists have long recognized that the principle of marginal-cost pricing applies to peak-load problems in general (Bye 1926; Boiteux 1949; Steiner 1957) and to roads in particular (Pigou 1920; Knight 1924). These authors' basic concepts have been elaborated and extended by many, including Walters (1961), Mohring and Harwitz (1962), Vickrey (1963, 1969), and Strotz (1965). The resulting models have been applied empirically to cities around the world.[1]

This section presents the basic economic motivation for congestion pricing. To that end, we abstract from various complications and consider a world in which traffic congestion is the sole distortion in the economy, and where fully flexible road pricing is possible. Thus, for example, we assume for now that any other externalities associated with travel are priced, *e.g.,* by a fuel tax; and we exclude so-called "external benefits" that may occur if the marginal social benefit of a trip exceeds the benefit to the traveler.

The basic idea is easily stated within the framework of highway costs developed in Chapter 3. Recall that congestion technology and the costs of travel have been placed directly into the average cost function. All congestion functions considered in Chapter 3 have an important feature in common: short-run average variable cost $c(\cdot)$ increases with the level of road use, be it expressed in traffic flow (V) as in static models, or in the total number of travelers over the peak (Q) as in dynamic models. This implies that short-run marginal cost exceeds short-run average variable cost. Intuitively, this is because short-run marginal social cost mc includes not only the cost incurred by the traveler herself but also the additional cost she imposes on all other travelers by adding to the congestion they encounter.[2] This additional cost is known as the *marginal external congestion cost*, here denoted *mecc*.

An efficient level of road use is obtained when each trip that is made provides benefits as least as great as its social cost, *mc*, and when no trip meeting this condition is suppressed. To obtain this situation through pricing, each traveler should face the marginal social cost of her trip. This requires a charge equal to the difference between the marginal cost and the cost already borne by the traveler, which is short-run average variable cost, *c*. This charge, known as the optimal *congestion fee* or *congestion toll*, is therefore $\tau = mc - c = mecc$.

These arguments can be formalized by determining a *Pareto-optimal* distribution of traffic, defined as one that maximizes any one person's utility while holding all others' utilities constant and meeting aggregate resource and technological constraints. Equivalently, we find the allocation of road space to users that maximizes *net welfare*, defined as the difference between aggregate consumer benefit and total cost. (We can ignore fixed cost because it does not affect the solution.) For first-best pricing, total cost embodies all relevant resource and technological constraints; when we consider second-best pricing, we will add feasibility constraints explicitly when maximizing net welfare. Here we consider first-best pricing with static congestion (Section 4.1.1), then with dynamic congestion (Section 4.1.2).

4.1.1 Static congestion

Static models are the easiest way to understand the underlying principles of congestion pricing. They are appropriate when traffic conditions do not change too quickly or when it is thought sufficient to focus policy attention on average traffic levels over extended periods rather than engaging in fine-tuned attempts to influence the time pattern of trips. Chapter 3 distinguished between two types of static models of traffic congestion: those assuming that traffic is in a stationary state and those dealing with time averages. The analytical derivation of optimal road prices does not differ fundamentally between these models, provided the inflow period P is kept fixed in time-averaged models. We will therefore treat them together.

Our exposition proceeds from the simplest to the more complex versions, all using the same basic principles, followed by a discussion of distributional implications.

Single road, single time period

Consider first the case of a single road and a single time period. As before, let $d(V)$ denote the inverse demand function and $c(V)$ the average variable cost function. In equilibrium, individuals equate their marginal willingness-to-pay $d(V)$ to generalized price, p, which is defined as average cost $c(V)$ plus toll τ:

$$d(V) = p \equiv c(V) + \tau. \tag{4.1}$$

The aggregate benefit from road use, B, is the value of travel to users, as measured by the area under the demand curve up to the equilibrium travel flow:

$$B = \int_0^V d(v)\mathrm{d}v. \tag{4.2}$$

Total cost, holding capacity fixed in the short run, is:

$$C = V \cdot c(V) + \rho K, \tag{4.3}$$

where, as before, ρK is the annualized cost of capital expenditures K.

An appropriate measure of aggregate welfare in this setting is social surplus W, defined as total benefit minus total cost. Maximizing $W = B - C$ with respect to V yields the necessary first-order condition:

$$d(V) - c(V) - V \cdot \frac{\partial c}{\partial V} = 0 \Rightarrow d(V) = mc(V). \tag{4.4}$$

This implies, using (4.1), that the optimal price is:

$$p = mc(V) = c(V) + V \cdot \frac{\partial c}{\partial V}, \tag{4.5}$$

thus yielding the usual marginal-cost pricing rule. Equivalently, the optimal toll is:

$$\tau = mc(V) - c(V) = V \cdot \frac{\partial c}{\partial V} = mecc. \tag{4.6}$$

The optimal congestion toll is thus the difference between short-run marginal and average variable cost. It is often referred to as a "Pigouvian toll," named after Arthur Pigou (1920).

Figure 4.1 provides a graphical illustration. The left panel shows the conventional diagram of optimal congestion pricing. The unpriced equilibrium occurs at the intersection of $d(V)$ and $c(V)$; it involves traffic flow V^0 and cost c^0. The optimal flow V^1 occurs at the intersection of $d(V)$ and $mc(V)$, according to (4.4); it can be achieved by imposing the optimal fee τ shown in the diagram. The average cost c falls from c^0 to c^1, but the generalized price rises from $p^0 = c^0$ to $p^1 = c^1 + \tau$. The quantity $(c^0 - c_0) \cdot V^0$ can be interpreted as the total cost of congestion in the unpriced equilibrium; but the total cost of *inefficient* congestion, $(c^0 - c^1) \cdot V^1 + (c^0 - c_0) \cdot (V^0 - V^1)$, is smaller because some congestion is optimal in this example. The gain in social surplus is depicted by the shaded "Harberger" triangle, which gives the difference between social cost saved (the area below mc) and benefit forgone (the area below d) when reducing traffic flow from V^0 to V^1.

In many cases the Pigouvian toll takes an intuitive form mathematically. Using the Bureau of Public Roads (BPR) congestion function of equation (3.9), average cost is given by (3.23), which we can write as:

$$c = c_0 + \alpha T_f a \cdot \left(\frac{V}{V_k}\right)^b, \tag{4.7}$$

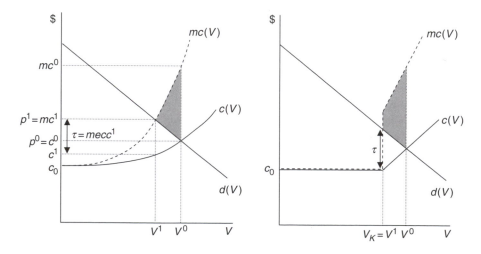

Figure 4.1 Optimal tolls in static models: smooth average cost (left panel) and piecewise linear average cost (right panel).

where again α is the value of time, $c_0 \equiv c_{00} + \alpha T_f$ includes the value of free-flow travel time T_f, and a and b are parameters. Then:

$$mc \equiv \frac{\partial (V \cdot c)}{\partial V} = c_0 + \alpha T_f a \cdot (b+1) \cdot \left(\frac{V}{V_k}\right)^b \qquad (4.8)$$

and

$$\tau = mecc \equiv mc - c = \alpha T_f ab \cdot \left(\frac{V}{V_k}\right)^b. \qquad (4.9)$$

In this case, the optimal congestion fee is just b times the average congestion cost c_g in the optimum, a result derived by Vickrey (1965). To determine τ numerically, one must still solve (4.6) simultaneously with the equilibrium condition (4.1), which can be written as $\tau = d(V) - c$, yielding the condition $d(V) = mc$, as also can be seen in the figure. Depending on the form of $d(V)$, this may or may not have an analytical solution.

Using instead a piecewise-linear cost function based on congestion function (3.10), a corner solution is possible as illustrated in the right panel of Figure 4.1. The optimal volume is where the demand curve crosses the mc curve, namely V_K. The optimal congestion fee is the fee that keeps demand at that level; in this case, it completely eliminates congestion. Because the cost function is kinked there, marginal cost mc is formally undefined; but conceptually it can be interpreted as the value of the marginal trip displaced by the last traveler using the available capacity. For other demand curves, a corner solution need not obtain. If the demand curve were lower, so as to intersect the average cost function on its flat segment, then the optimal toll would be zero and the optimum would coincide with the unpriced equilibrium. If instead the demand curve were higher, so as to intersect $mc(V)$ on its rising segment, the optimal volume would entail some congestion, just as in the left panel. In this case, the relevant part of the cost function is:

$$c = c_0 + \tfrac{1}{2}\alpha P \cdot \left(\frac{V}{V_k} - 1\right), \qquad (4.10)$$

where P denotes the exogenous inflow period; the optimal toll is then:

$$\tau = mecc \equiv mc - c = \frac{\partial (V \cdot c)}{\partial V} - c = \tfrac{1}{2}\alpha P \cdot \left(\frac{V}{V_k}\right). \qquad (4.11)$$

Again, to determine a numerical value for the toll, this equation must be solved simultaneously with condition (4.4) for user equilibrium.

A cost function that becomes vertical, like c_{stat} in Figure 3.8, also implies a section where mc is vertical. If the marginal-cost toll occurs on that section, it has an interpretation like that just described for the piecewise-linear congestion function.

Single road, multiple time periods

The above model is easily extended to multiple periods of stationary-state congestion. Consider, as before, a highway of capacity V_K serving H distinct daily time periods, each of exogenous duration q_h with endogenous flow V_h under stationary traffic conditions. Then the $q_h V_h$ users of the highway during period h incur short-run total variable cost $q_h V_h c_h$; the short-run marginal cost of adding another user is therefore:

$$mc_h \equiv \frac{\partial\left(q_h V_h c_h\right)}{\partial\left(q_h V_h\right)} = \frac{\partial\left(V_h \cdot c_h\right)}{\partial V_h} = c_h + V_h \cdot \frac{\partial c_h}{\partial V_h}. \tag{4.12}$$

With independent inverse demand functions $d_h(V_h)$ applying for each period, social surplus W is:

$$W = \sum_h q_h \int_0^{V_h} d_h(v)\mathrm{d}v - \sum_h q_h V_h \cdot c_h(V_h) - \rho K. \tag{4.13}$$

The first-order conditions to maximize W produce optimal tolls just like (4.6):

$$\tau_h = mc_h(V_h) - c_h(V_h) = V_h \cdot \frac{\partial c_h}{\partial V_h}. \tag{4.14}$$

This toll is typically higher in those periods when equilibrium demand V_h is higher, and is guaranteed to be so if $c_h''(V_h) \geq 0$ as is usual; hence it is an example of peak-load pricing.

Network optimum, single time period

A second extension of interest concerns optimal congestion pricing on a network. Equation (3.40) in Section 3.4.4 presented the *user equilibrium* conditions for an unpriced network, also referred to as *Wardrop's first principle* (Wardrop 1952). Recall that subscripts l denote links, r and ρ routes, and m markets or OD-pairs. When link-based tolls τ_l are in place, these equilibrium conditions continue to hold with $c_l(V_l)$ replaced by $c_l(V_l) + \tau_l$:

$$\forall \, \delta_{rm} = 1 : \begin{cases} \sum_{l=1}^{L} \delta_{lr} \cdot \left(c_l(V_l) + \tau_l\right) - d_m(V_m) \geq 0 \\ V_r \geq 0 \\ V_r \cdot \left[\sum_{l=1}^{L} \delta_{lr} \cdot \left(c_l(V_l) + \tau_l\right) - d_m(V_m)\right] = 0, \end{cases} \tag{4.15}$$

where again $\delta_{rm} = 1$ for any route r that serves market m, $\delta_{lr} = 1$ for any link l that is part of route r, and

$$V_l = \sum_{\rho=1}^{R} \delta_{l\rho} \cdot V_\rho, \quad V_m = \sum_{\rho=1}^{R} \delta_{\rho m} \cdot V_\rho.$$

The interpretation is that in a user equilibrium, all used routes for an OD-pair should have equal generalized prices, all equal to marginal benefits $d_m(V_m)$ for that OD-pair; and that there are no unused routes with lower generalized prices.

The optimal flow pattern, often referred to as the *system optimum* in the engineering literature, can be found by maximizing social surplus (W), now defined as the benefits in (4.2) summed over OD-pairs minus the costs in (4.3) summed over links. Including non-negativity constraints for route flows, the optimization problem becomes:

$$\operatorname*{Max}_{V_{r=1\ldots R}} W = \sum_m \int_0^{V_m} d_m(v)\,\mathrm{d}v - \sum_l V_l \cdot c_l(V_l; V_{K,l}) - \sum_l \rho \cdot K_l(V_{K,l})$$

$$\text{with: } V_l = \sum_{r=1}^{R} \delta_{lr} \cdot V_r \quad \text{and} \quad V_m = \sum_{r=1}^{R} \delta_{rm} \cdot V_r \tag{4.16}$$

$$\text{subject to: } V_r \geq 0 \quad \text{for all } r.$$

Taking derivatives with respect to all possible route flows V_r, we obtain Kuhn–Tucker first-order conditions that are identical to (4.15) except that τ_l is replaced by $V_l \cdot (\partial c_l / \partial V_l)$. These conditions express *Wardrop's second principle*: in a system optimum, all used routes for an OD-pair have identical marginal costs equal to the marginal benefits for that OD-pair, and there are no unused routes with marginal costs lower than this. Comparing the first-order conditions of (4.16) to the equilibrium conditions (4.15), it is easy to see that the following pricing rule guarantees satisfaction of those first-order conditions:

$$\tau_l = V_l \cdot \frac{\partial c_l}{\partial V_l} \quad \text{for all } l. \tag{4.17}$$

The single-road toll in (4.6) is therefore just a special case of the optimal link tolls for a full network, shown in (4.17). Link-based marginal cost pricing throughout the network ensures that on all "active" routes (*i.e.*, with $V_r > 0$), users will enter up to the point where marginal benefits are equal to marginal cost, while a route remains "passive" (*i.e.*, $V_r = 0$) when marginal benefits on the OD-pair it serves are below the marginal cost of using the route.

The tolls in (4.17) need not be the unique set of tolls achieving the optimum. The comparison between the equilibrium conditions (4.15) and the optimality conditions only tells us that the sum of link tolls over each route should be equal to the sum of marginal external costs on all the route's links. This may give some freedom in setting link-based tolls. The simplest example is when two serial links are always used together if used at all: what affects the flow pattern is not the individual link tolls but their sum, so all combinations of tolls with a given sum are equivalent. A further degree of freedom arises when demand is perfectly inelastic for all OD-pairs: adding a constant to all the link-based tolls of (4.17) would then leave route choices unaltered, allowing one to choose them to meet a secondary objective (Hearn and Ramana 1998).

The practical challenge of setting optimal link-based tolls is daunting given that neither the demand functions nor the link-specific speed-flow curves can be known precisely. This has raised interest in trial-and-error approaches, in which tolls are set and then adapted based on observed results. Li (2002) and Yang, Meng and Lee (2004) develop strategies for doing this.

Heterogeneity of users

When users are heterogeneous, should tolls be differentiated across users? If so, the practical problems of toll collection are exacerbated; if not, we say the tolls can be *anonymous*.

The principle that the toll should equal marginal external congestion cost (*mecc*) does not change. The value of *mecc* for different users may differ, however, for two possible reasons. First, their vehicles (*e.g.*, truck versus car) may contribute differently to congestion; in that case, optimal tolls are not anonymous. Second, they may self-sort into different parts of the network with different values of *mecc* in equilibrium. In that case, the toll can still be anonymous, but must be differentiated across links as in (4.17). For example, Verhoef and Small (2004) consider differentiated first-best tolls for a simple parallel-route network with dispersion in values of time. The route with the higher toll is faster and therefore attracts drivers with higher values of time. The higher optimal toll on this route reflects a higher *mecc*, despite the fact that congestion is lower than on the other route; but the *mecc* imposed by a given user is not high because of that user's own value of time, but rather because of the value of time of her co-travelers, on whom she imposes a congestion externality.

Distributional impacts and acceptability of road pricing

Although imposition of the optimal toll generates a net welfare gain, the social and political acceptability of road pricing has proven to be very limited. The left panel in Figure 4.1 shows an important reason why. Users between 0 and V^1 on the horizontal axis experience an increase in generalized price from p^0 to p^1 and therefore are worse off unless they receive benefits from the use of toll revenues. The users between V^1 and V^0 have shifted from the untolled road to some less-preferred alternative (such as public transportation or not traveling at all), and are therefore also worse off.

It is interesting to compare these two groups in terms of how much worse off they are. The shifters' losses range from zero for the driver at V^0 to $p^1 - p^0$ for the driver at V^1, with the others somewhere between. Thus their average loss in surplus is smaller than that for drivers who remain using the road (for example, with a linear demand curve, it is just half). The intuition is that, by changing behavior, drivers can avoid incurring the full loss $p^1 - p^0$, and will only choose to do so when changing is more attractive than staying on the road.

Ignoring revenue allocation, then, all the initial travelers lose from the policy (assuming no heterogeneity). The only gain is to the public sector, in the form of toll revenues. Whether this gain is recognized by citizens in the political process depends on how revenues are used and on whether the authorities are able to effectively and credibly commit to these uses and communicate them to the public. One consequence is that various allocation schemes have been proposed in attempts to leave major user groups better off (Goodwin 1989; Small 1992b).

Another consequence is that revenue allocation has been identified as a key determinant of the political acceptability of congestion pricing. In a Dutch survey by Verhoef, Nijkamp and Rietveld (1997), road users expressed the following preference (in decreasing order) for the use of toll revenues: investment in new roads, reduction in vehicle ownership taxes, reduction in fuel taxes, investment in public transportation, subsidies for public transportation, investment in carpool facilities, general tax cuts, and expansion of other public expenditures. Evidence suggests that the British have a greater preference for public transportation, while residents of the US prefer road construction or tax reduction. Interestingly, the largest of all congestion pricing schemes implemented in practice, namely in Central London starting in 2003, included a very explicit and well-publicized component of investing revenues in London's transit system. In North America and Norway, by contrast, nearly all pricing schemes that exist or are close to implementation have a direct connection to road infrastructure finance.

Revenue use can also affect the geographical distribution of benefits and costs. Many observers, especially those with financial interests in central cities, fear that the inner city will suffer economic decline if city streets or arterials leading downtown are priced. Small (1992b) and Levine and Garb (2002) give this potentially adverse effect as a reason to target some revenue toward improving inner-city public amenities.

When there is heterogeneity of travelers, some initial road users may be better off after imposition of optimal pricing, even before accounting for the use of revenues. This can happen because for an individual whose value of travel time is sufficiently high, the value of travel-time gains may exceed the toll. Aggregate demand by such users may then increase due to the implementation of congestion pricing. Aggregate demand added over *all* users' groups would of course still decrease; otherwise the travel-time gains would not occur.

Since high-value-of-time travelers benefit more, or lose less, from road pricing, it is likely to be regressive (not counting the use of toll revenues) because the value of time is positively correlated with income. This tendency is mitigated by the tendency of overall travel to increase with income (Foster 1974). With toll cordons, higher-income groups face more tolls than others if they live more predominantly outside the cordon. The ultimate net distributional effect of congestion pricing also depends on how the revenues are used and how the burdens are shifted through markets for land, labor, and commercial space.

Finally, public attitudes towards road pricing may differ before and after implementation. Tretvik (2003) reports how local support for Norwegian toll rings, defined as the percentage of respondents who judged the scheme positively, increased dramatically after implementation, from 19% to 58% in Bergen, from 30% to 41% in Oslo, and from 9% to 47% in Trondheim. Transport for London (2004) reports an increase from 39% support (average over three waves) to 54% (average over four waves). Such increases may reflect initial skepticism about the scheme's potential effectiveness.

4.1.2 Dynamic congestion

We now discuss congestion pricing from a dynamic perspective. This enables us to develop some important principles by which pricing can cause people to make substantial changes in the time pattern of their trips. These changes, as we shall see, can produce significant benefits going beyond those produced by prices that are constant over a lengthy time period.

To this end, we focus on dynamic-equilibrium models that endogenize departure-time decisions. We begin with the "basic bottleneck model" of Section 3.4.3, which allows for a particularly transparent analytical treatment and is currently, at least among economists, the most widely used conceptual model of dynamic congestion pricing. We then turn to two extensions of it that we considered before – heterogeneous users and networks – and show how the insights of the basic model are modified in these more realistic situations. Finally, we describe pricing results from other types of dynamic congestion models, which open the path to still greater realism in designing pricing strategies.

First-best pricing in the basic bottleneck model

Recall that the "basic bottleneck model" considers a single "pure bottleneck," *i.e.*, one for which there are no delays if inflow is below capacity V_K, and for which the rate of queue exits is equal to capacity when a queue exists. The basic bottleneck model further simplifies by setting free-flow travel time equal to zero and by assuming that cost parameters are identical for all users: namely, the value of travel time α, the shadow prices of early and late arrivals β and γ, and the desired arrival time t^*. Total demand for passages Q is inelastic.

For ease of reference, we summarize the equilibrium conditions for this model, as derived in Section 3.4.3 in the limit where duration q of the desired queue-exit-time interval approaches zero while the total number of travelers, qV_d, remains finite at value Q. The peak starts and ends at times:

$$t_q = t^* - \frac{\gamma}{\beta+\gamma} \cdot \frac{Q}{V_K} \tag{4.18}$$

$$t_{q'} = t^* + \frac{\beta}{\beta+\gamma} \cdot \frac{Q}{V_K}. \tag{4.19}$$

The queue-entry rates for early and late arrivals are given by (3.25), which ensures that the average congestion cost $\bar{c}_g$ remains constant over all queue-entry times. Adding superscripts 0 to denote the unpriced equilibrium, its equilibrium value $\bar{c}_g^0$ and its two components, average travel delay cost $\bar{c}_T^0$ and average schedule delay cost $\bar{c}_S^0$, are:

$$\bar{c}_g^0 \equiv p^0 = \delta \cdot \frac{Q}{V_K}; \quad \bar{c}_T^0 = \bar{c}_S^0 = \tfrac{1}{2} \cdot \bar{c}_g^0, \tag{4.20}$$

where $\delta = \beta\gamma/(\beta + \gamma)$. Total equilibrium costs are consequently:

$$\bar{C}_g^0 = \delta \cdot \frac{Q^2}{V_K}, \tag{4.21}$$

implying marginal cost equal to:

$$\overline{mc}_g^0 = 2\delta \cdot \frac{Q}{V_K} = 2\bar{c}_g^0. \tag{4.22}$$

Figure 4.2 depicts this unpriced equilibrium graphically, by showing schedule-delay cost $c_S(t')$ and travel-delay cost $c_T^0(t')$ as functions of arrival time t'. Because the queue-exit rate V_b is constant over time, the time-averaged value of per-user schedule-delay cost is given by the two triangular areas under $c_S(t')$ (between t_q and $t_{q'}$), divided by $(t_{q'} - t_q)$; while for travel-delay cost it is the inverted triangle between $c_S(t')$ and the horizontal line at p^0, again divided by $(t_{q'} - t_q)$. The equality between these two averages, stated in (4.20), is therefore visible geometrically from the diagram.

Now let's consider what an optimal travel pattern must look like. The optimum can be identified by intuitive reasoning. First, as long as exits occur, the exit rate should not be below V_K, as otherwise the period of exits could be shortened and hence total schedule-delay

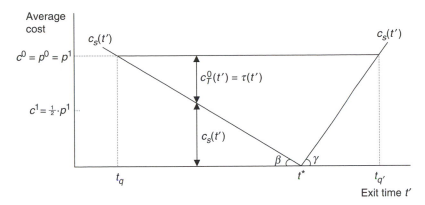

Figure 4.2 Average cost components and optimal tolls by queue–exit time in the basic bottleneck model for the unpriced equilibrium and under first-best tolling.

cost could be reduced without increasing travel delay. Second, no queue should exist in the optimum, as otherwise total travel-delay cost could be reduced without increasing schedule delay. These two observations together mean that the entry and exit rates should both be equal to V_K throughout the peak. Third, the timing of the period of exits should be such that the schedule-delay costs of the first and last drivers are equal, as otherwise total schedule-delay cost could be reduced by shifting the entire pattern of exits over time. This means that exits should occur between the same instants t_q and $t_{q'}$ as in the unpriced equilibrium.

The optimum just described thus involves the same pattern of *exits* from the bottleneck as the unpriced equilibrium, but it has a different pattern of *entries*. It can be decentralized by a triangular toll schedule $\tau(t')$, with two linear segments, that replicates the pattern of travel delay costs in the unpriced equilibrium, $c_T^0(t')$:[3]

$$\tau(t') = \begin{cases} 0 & \text{if } t' < t_q \\ \beta \cdot (t' - t_q) = \delta \cdot \dfrac{Q}{V_K} - \beta \cdot (t^* - t') & \text{if } t_q \leq t' < t^* \\ \gamma \cdot (t_{q'} - t') = \delta \cdot \dfrac{Q}{V_K} - \gamma \cdot (t' - t^*) & \text{if } t^* \leq t' \leq t_{q'} \\ 0 & \text{if } t' > t_{q'}. \end{cases}$$ (4.23)

This toll schedule is shown in the diagram as $\tau(t')$. It results in the same constant generalized price $p^1 = p^0$ (where superscript 1 denotes the first-best tolled equilibrium) and the same pattern of schedule-delay cost as in the user equilibrium, but it produces zero travel delay cost. The resulting tolled-equilibrium queue-entry pattern therefore satisfies:

$$V_a^1 = V_K.$$ (4.24)

From the figure, we find the following price and average costs levels:

$$p^1 = \delta \cdot \frac{Q}{V_K}$$

$$\bar{c}_g^1 = \tfrac{1}{2} \cdot \delta \cdot \frac{Q}{V_K}; \quad \bar{c}_T^1 = 0; \quad \bar{c}_S^1 = \bar{c}_g^1. \tag{4.25}$$

Total cost is therefore half as large as in the unpriced equilibrium:

$$\bar{C}_g^1 = \tfrac{1}{2} \cdot \bar{C}_g^0 = \tfrac{1}{2} \cdot \delta \cdot \frac{Q^2}{V_K}. \tag{4.26}$$

The net welfare gain from optimal pricing is equal to the value of travel time savings, and therefore also to the total toll revenues generated. Neither equality is generally true in the static model of Figure 4.1.

Several points deserve emphasis. First, in contrast to most static models, no travel delays exist in the optimum. Second, the generalized price remains unchanged after imposition of the optimal toll schedule, because tolls exactly replace travel time delays; this suggests that social acceptability should be less of a problem than is predicted by the static model. Third, exit times and hence arrival times at the destination need not change between the unpriced equilibrium and the optimum, and no alternative to (solo) car use is required for the elimination of queues. In the context of the morning commute, only departure times from home have to be adjusted for queues to disappear. Moreover, if commuters retain their order of departure and their arrival times, everybody (except the very first and last driver) should depart later than in the unpriced equilibrium. This gives room for optimism about the possibility of achieving a significant reduction in queues in reality under optimal pricing. Note that these results are due to the kinked performance function for a pure bottleneck, and will at best only approximately apply for models with different performance functions.

We have assumed thus far that total demand Q over the peak is fixed, which leaves an ambiguity in the optimal toll: any constant could be added to the toll schedule of (4.23) and still support the optimal pattern. What if, instead, total demand has non-zero elasticity with respect to generalized price? We have seen that toll schedule (4.23) produces the same constant generalized price as the user equilibrium, $p^1 = p^0$. Therefore the two policies also produce identical total quantities demanded (Q), even if demand has some elasticity. Surprisingly, this implies that total demand Q^0 in the user equilibrium, which is inefficiently high in that situation, is just right when an optimal toll is in place.[4] One way to think about this puzzling result is that dynamic tolling so substantially reduces the adverse consequences of adding to total traffic that there is no longer a reason to curtail traffic, as there is in the unpriced equilibrium.

More formally, observe from (4.26) that in the optimal pattern, the marginal cost of increasing Q is:

$$\overline{mc}_g^1 = \delta \cdot \frac{Q}{V_K}, \tag{4.27}$$

which is the same as the generalized price p^1. Thus marginal cost equals marginal benefit with the toll schedule (4.23) in place, and no additional constant needs to be added to it even though it has failed to reduce Q from its no-toll value. The toll schedule (4.23) can also be interpreted as the marginal external cost of a traveler arriving at t', defined as the difference between the (time-independent) marginal social cost (4.27) and the (time-dependent) private cost $c_g(t')$.

Yet another way to look at these results is that imposing optimal time-varying tolls causes the average and marginal cost curves to rotate downwards by a factor of $\frac{1}{2}$, as seen by comparing (4.21) to (4.26) and (4.22) to (4.27). The cost curves in the static models of Section 4.1.1, in contrast, do not change when pricing is imposed.

Heterogeneous users

The logic of optimal pricing in the basic bottleneck model carries over even if users are not identical, which of course is a more realistic assumption. Newell (1987) provides a general analysis of equilibrium at a pure bottleneck with heterogeneous commuters, each of whom minimizes a deterministic cost function belonging to a specified parametric family. He provides diagrammatic and algorithmic solutions for determining the equilibrium queuing-delay function $T_D(t)$ (and, from that, the queue-entry times and resulting schedule delays for all commuters), given two cumulative distribution functions: that of desired queue-exit times, $F(t)$, and that of the cost-function parameters. (The desired queue-exit rate $V_d(t)$ in the previous chapter is just $F'(t)$ in this notation.)

A few very general features can be derived from minimal assumptions on these functions. Figure 4.3 shows cumulative counts $A(t)$ of queue-entry times, $B(t)$ of queue-exit times, and

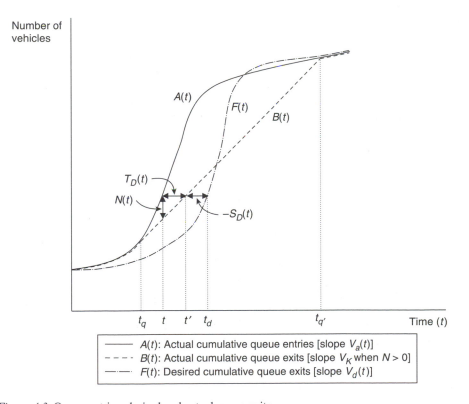

Figure 4.3 Queue entries, desired and actual queue exits.

$F(t)$ of desired queue-exit times. At any given queue-entry time t and desired queue-exit time t_d, queuing delay $T_D(t)$ and schedule delay $S_D(t) \equiv t' - t_d \equiv t + T_D(t) - t_d$ are the horizontal distances shown in the figure. (S_D is negative at the time t shown, indicating a queue-exit earlier than desired.) Denote the cost of queuing delay by $c_T(T_D)$, the cost of schedule delay by $c_S(S_D)$, and the derivatives of these functions with primes.[5] Each commuter chooses t to minimize $c_T(t) + c_S(t)$, leading to the following first-order condition, which must make the sum constant over the time interval when users with the corresponding particular set of cost parameters depart:

$$c'_T \cdot T'_D(t) + c'_S \cdot \left(1 + T'_D(t)\right) = 0, \tag{4.28}$$

or:

$$\frac{c'_S}{c'_T} = -\frac{T'_D(t)}{1 + T'_D(t)}, \tag{4.29}$$

assuming the derivatives exist.[6] Note that the assumed first-in, first-out queue discipline implies that $T'_D(t) > -1$.

Several qualitative results follow. First, the queue grows while early travelers (those who will exit before their desired arrival times) are arriving, and it shrinks while late travelers are arriving.[7] Second, a person exiting the queue exactly at his desired time must incur the maximum travel time incurred by users with the same characteristics.[8] Third, under certain circumstances, Newell obtains for this more general model a key pricing result of the basic bottleneck model: if users have identical values of time, a time-varying toll can be defined which has no allocative effects on the number of travelers or their time of passage through the bottleneck. Such a toll collects revenues equal to the entire cost of queuing delay in the unpriced equilibrium, and it leaves each commuter exactly as well off (before redistribution of toll revenues) as in the no-toll equilibrium. This last-mentioned result illustrates a point that emerges from simulation exercises by Arnott, de Palma and Lindsey (1993): the reallocation of departure times may be a greater source of benefit from time-of-day pricing than the reduction in total trips.

Now suppose heterogeneity is more limited: the desired queue-exit time t_d varies across travelers, but the per-unit costs of travel and schedule delay do not. (One example is our treatment of the bottleneck model in Chapter 3.) Hendrickson and Kocur (1981) provide an elegant and general analysis. Within limits, the heterogeneity in desired queue-exit times affects only schedule-delay costs, not travel-delay costs or the time pattern of queuing in the unpriced equilibrium. This is true so long as the cumulative desired exits, $F(t)$ in Figure 4.3, intersects the cumulative exits $B(t)$ only once. The optimal time-varying toll is then the same as for the basic bottleneck model, and will again eliminate all travel delay costs and leave schedule delay costs unaffected. Optimal tolling now reduces generalized cost by more than half (instead of exactly half as in the basic bottleneck model) because in this case total schedule delay cost is smaller than total travel delay cost in the unpriced equilibrium – as can be seen, for example, in Figure 3.11 and equations (3.36)–(3.37).

If there are multiple intersections of $F(t)$ and $B(t)$ in Figure 4.3, the queue will wax and wane more than once over the peak in the unpriced equilibrium (but not necessarily disappear completely in between). Then both schedule-delay costs and travel-delay costs are lower than in the basic bottleneck model. Arnott, de Palma and Lindsey (1988) show that in such equilibria, the queue-entry rates of (3.25) remain valid. Likewise, the optimal toll schedule has slopes β and $-\gamma$ just like that for the basic bottleneck model, and it again eliminates all travel delay costs and leaves schedule delay costs unaffected.

Arnott, de Palma and Lindsey also consider the contrasting case, in which distinct groups of travelers have identical desired schedules $t_d = t^*$ but different relative costs of schedule delay versus travel delay, as measured by the ratios β/α and γ/α. This model is interesting because it shows how marginal external costs may differ between seemingly identical vehicles, and also because it illustrates that in the unpriced equilibrium, the ordering of travelers as well as their departure rates may be non-optimal.

Figure 4.4 illustrates this case for a simple symmetric example with two groups of users, denoted A and B. For graphical convenience we assume that the groups are equal in size. The parameters α, β, and γ are all lower for group A; the ratios β/γ are the same for both groups; but the ratios β/α and γ/α are higher for group A. Group A could be blue-collar workers, for whom all shadow prices are lower due to a lower income, but for whom scheduling is relatively more important than delays because they work in shifts.

The solid line in the upper panel shows travel delay $T_D(t')$ in the unpriced equilibrium, which is a piecewise linear function with slopes equal to β_G/α_G and $-\gamma_G/\alpha_G$ during the intervals when people from group G arrive early or late (G = A, B). Equilibrium entails temporal separation, with group A arriving closest to t^*. Both types of drivers would lose

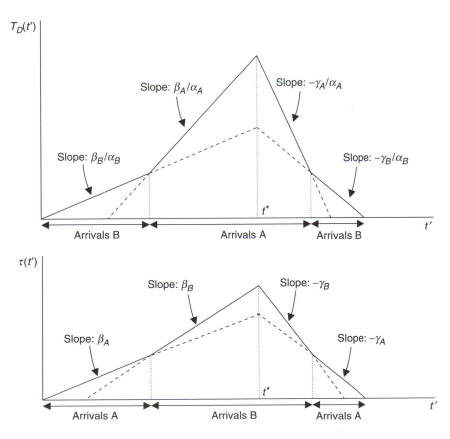

Figure 4.4 Optimal tolling in the bottleneck model with heterogeneous users.

individually if either were to reschedule to an arrival time occupied by the other group. The dashed lines extrapolate a group's experienced travel delay function into the other group's arrival intervals, thus showing the required travel delays to make an arrival with these other group's drivers equally attractive as in their own interval(s). These extrapolations are always below equilibrium travel delays, confirming that there is no incentive to mix with drivers from the other group.

Drivers in group A benefit from heterogeneity, in the sense that they would be worse off if a type B driver changed and became type A. This is because type B drivers spread out their departure times more widely and therefore cause less travel delay. The marginal external cost is therefore higher for type A drivers than for type B drivers: the identity of an extra driver is immaterial to group B, but group A prefers an additional driver to be of type B (see Arnott and Kraus 1998a). As we will see later, the second-best "flat" (time-independent) tolls would therefore differ between the two groups, making these tolls non-anonymous.

The optimal time-varying toll schedule, shown in the lower panel of Figure 4.4, eliminates all travel delay and therefore requires the slope of the toll schedule $\tau(t')$ to be equal to β_G and $-\gamma_G$ during group G's arrivals. It induces a voluntary reversal in arrival times: group B now arrives closest to t^*. Again, the dashed lines show for each group the hypothetical toll schedule that would make its members willing to switch to the other group's arrival interval; it is below the actual toll schedule so they do not switch. The toll eliminates all travel delays, as in the basic bottleneck model, and also produces another efficiency gain: it reduces aggregate schedule-delay cost because drivers in group B, with the higher β and γ, now exit the queue closer to the desired time t^*. Therefore, this example shows that additional gains may arise when users are heterogeneous due to arrival-time adjustments, which do not occur with homogeneous users.

Another interesting reversal occurs: it is now group B that benefits from heterogeneity, while group A does not. This is consistent with another property: it can be shown (by comparing generalized trip prices as implied by the intersections with the horizontal axes in Figure 4.4) that before redistribution of toll revenues, group A suffers from the imposition of tolling while group B benefits. The finding that high-value-of-time users can benefit from imposition of optimal pricing, while low-value-of-time users lose, also occurs with the static model.

Networks of bottlenecks

In reality, most pricing applications involve more than a single road. It is not necessarily straightforward to generalize from a single bottleneck to a network of bottlenecks. Arnott, de Palma and Lindsey (1998) provide an insightful discussion. They show that interactions between different bottlenecks may be either simpler or more complicated than between links in a conventional static network.

For example, a particularly simple result appears in the case of two bottlenecks in series, with different capacities and with no active origin or destination in between. The unpriced equilibrium, the optimum, and the optimal time-varying toll are all the same as in absence of the higher-capacity bottleneck – regardless of which of the two bottlenecks is upstream of the other. The higher-capacity bottleneck can therefore be entirely ignored in the analysis.[9]

A more complex case is two bottlenecks in parallel. Arnott, de Palma and Lindsey (1990a) consider this situation with homogeneous users. The free-flow travel times T_f can then no longer be set arbitrarily to zero unless they are equal between the two roads. Again, all travel-delay costs are eliminated in the optimum. The time-varying tolls are analogous to those for a single bottleneck, and the timing of exits and the route split are identical between the unpriced equilibrium and the optimum.

One might be tempted to conclude from these examples that queuing can never be socially optimal on a network of pure bottlenecks. However, de Palma and Jehiel (1995) show that some queuing may be optimal when drivers are heterogeneous. It seems hard to identify precisely the characteristics of a network that would make this happen. Nevertheless, a naïve rule that sets tolls so as to eliminate all queues, even if not optimal, will typically produce substantial efficiency gains (de Palma, Kilani and Lindsey 2005). The same is not necessarily true for other types of congested networks, where substantial delays may occur at the short-run optimum even in simple models.

For all but very simple networks, one must turn to numerical methods to find equilibria. Ben-Akiva, de Palma and Kanaroglou (1986) provide a computer simulation model that includes both mode and route choice. Rather than model equilibrium directly, they consider traveler behavior that responds to conditions on previous days, and simulate the approach to a stable pattern. The METROPOLIS model mentioned in Chapter 3 also uses this technique while simulating individual traveler decisions about trip schedule, route, and mode. Congestion in METROPOLIS consists of queuing on each link, and scheduling decisions incorporate a preferred time-of-arrival window, schedule-delay costs from arrival outside this window, and logit choice between automobile and public transit.

To determine the optimal time-varying fee in such models, one must know all the parameters and be able to solve the entire model. In practice, one needs a way to use observed data to adjust the fee in response to changed conditions. In at least one very stylized case with perfect advance information, setting a fee that varies instantaneously with queue length approximately accomplishes this (de Palma and Arnott 1986). Without advance information, the behavioral response to instantaneous toll adjustments is limited to route choice; while pre-trip decisions, such as departure time and mode choice, are based on *expected* rather than on *actual* toll and queue patterns and are therefore unaffected by instantaneous toll adjustments. Such toll adjustments may then frustrate drivers when an unexpectedly long queue is matched with an unexpectedly high toll, presumably limiting social acceptability without strongly benefiting efficiency.

Alternative dynamic congestion technologies

As we indicated in Chapter 3, the bottleneck model uses a description of traffic flow that omits many details arising on real roads. More sophisticated traffic-flow models are available, as described in Chapter 3, but the difficulty of combining them with endogenous scheduling has deterred most researchers. Nevertheless we can describe two studies that have done so, focusing on how well the insights from the basic bottleneck model hold up when extended to these more realistic settings.[10]

Chu (1995) investigates optimal pricing for a road that is characterized by no-propagation flow congestion as presented in Section 3.3.3, where the travel time depends solely on the flow at the road's exit at the instant that the trip is completed, $V_o(t')$. The demand side of his model is the same as for the basic bottleneck model discussed above. The optimal time-varying toll turns out to be a straightforward dynamic generalization of the standard toll for static congestion in (4.6):

$$\tau(t') = \alpha \cdot V_o(t') \cdot \frac{dT(V_o(t'))}{dV_o(t')}. \tag{4.30}$$

This expression follows from the optimality condition that the marginal social cost of an arrival at t' should be constant throughout the period during which arrivals occur.[11]

Chu provides an interesting comparison between his model and the basic bottleneck model. Several qualitative differences are worth emphasizing. First, total schedule delay cost is smaller than total travel delay cost in the unpriced equilibrium. This is because to keep the generalized price p^0 constant over time, the exit rate must be higher the closer to t^* one completes the trip. Many drivers therefore have relatively high travel delay costs and relatively low schedule delay costs. The simple geometry of Figure 4.2, which was due to the constancy of the queue-exit rate, breaks down. Second, the optimal toll does not eliminate all travel delays in Chu's model, and raises total schedule delay cost. Third, applying the optimal toll lengthens the duration of the peak because it reduces the rate at which trips near the desired arrival time are completed. Fourth, applying the optimal toll raises the generalized price of traveling, because of the increased peak duration.[12] Finally, the total variable cost in Chu's model depends on the value of travel delay, α.

An interesting question is whether these results are due to the difference between flow congestion and bottleneck congestion or to the absence of hypercongestion in the unpriced equilibrium in Chu's model. (Recall that queue density in the basic bottleneck model is infinite, which can be seen as an extreme form of hypercongestion.) Some insight can be obtained from numerical analyses by Verhoef (2003), which can be compared to numerical results provided by Chu. Verhoef uses the car-following model of (3.20) to investigate optimal time-varying tolls on a road with a sudden reduction in the number of lanes by half. This model does produce hypercongestion with real effects in the unpriced equilibrium, in the form of a queue immediately upstream of the bottleneck. Optimal tolling eliminates queuing, but increases the duration of the peak and therefore also raises the generalized price. Qualitatively, the differences with the basic bottleneck model are therefore similar to those found in Chu's model.

Thus, it appears that the basic bottleneck model overestimates the benefits from optimal tolling, and underestimates the resulting increase in generalized price, by exaggerating the extent to which travel delays can be eliminated without increasing scheduling costs. But opposite biases may exist in flow-based dynamic models, especially when they ignore the waste of hypercongested queuing. The simulation results of Mun (2002) support similar conclusions.

Verhoef's study also provides a potentially useful computational device for approximating the optimal toll schedule. Although no analytical solution for it is found, more than 99% of the possible welfare gains from tolling appear to be captured by adopting a time- and location-specific version of (4.30). Specifically, the toll for traversing a link is calculated as the integral over distance of:

$$\tau(t,x) = \alpha \cdot V(t,x) \cdot \frac{d[1/S(V)]}{dV}\bigg|_{V(t,x)}, \tag{4.31}$$

where $S(V)$ is the stationary-state speed flow function from which the first-order car-following equation is derived, and the combinations of times t and locations x to be considered should, of course, be mutually consistent. In other words, the logic of the basic Pigouvian toll in (4.6) not only extends to a dynamic setting with flow congestion, as shown by (4.30), but apparently also to more realistic cases where congestion varies both temporally and spatially in a continuous manner. The shape of this link toll as a function of time is approximately triangular, similar to that in the basic bottleneck model, but although it eliminates hypercongestion it does not fully eliminate travel delays: in fact, eliminating all travel delays by naïvely copying the triangular toll schedule from the basic bottleneck model is a disastrous policy in Verhoef's numerical simulations, as it produces a welfare loss (compared to the unpriced equilibrium).

A practical advantage of a toll based on (4.31) would be that it can in principle be set adaptively, based on local and instantaneous traffic conditions. This allows a regulator to iterate toward the desired toll by trying a toll structure, observing $V(t, x)$, and calculating (4.31) from a previously measured speed-flow relationship.

Discussion

Dynamic models suggest that a main source of efficiency gains from optimal pricing would be the rescheduling of departure times from the trip origin. With heterogeneous users, additional gains may also result from changing the order of arrivals at the trip destination. Despite severe practical limitations, the basic bottleneck model and its generalizations have proven useful in generating understanding of these features.

4.2 Second-best pricing

The rules for marginal-cost pricing discussed in the previous section are often referred to as "first-best" because there are no constraints on the pricing instrument and there are no market distortions other than the congestion externality. Although extremely useful as a theoretical benchmark, first-best pricing is increasingly recognized to be of limited practical relevance. We therefore need to consider explicitly how such constraints and distortions alter the properties of tolls.

Because lump-sum taxes do not exist in reality and governments need budgets to pursue redistributional policy objectives or to supply public goods, any modern economy operates under second-best conditions because distortive taxes are in place, especially those on labor but also those on a variety of goods and services. As a consequence, marginal social benefits and marginal social costs are not equalized in most markets. Any transportation policy that directly or indirectly affects equilibrium quantities in these markets will therefore create non-zero net social costs or benefits in them, which should be accounted for in the economic evaluation and design of the policy. A policy that does so in the most efficient way possible is called the second-best policy.

A policy can also be second-best when the tools for implementing it are not as flexible as assumed in the theory generating first-best rules. For example, perfect price or toll differentiation may not be possible. It is instructive to consider a simple graphical example of second-best pricing of this type, which allows us to make some basic but important points about second-best pricing before moving to more elaborate cases.

In our example, we ignore congestion but consider a pollution externality. Suppose that there are two types of cars: "clean" cars (type A) and "dirty" cars (type B), so that $mec_B > mec_A$. If we assume that the cars are otherwise identical and have equal user costs c, then total marginal costs (including the external costs) also differ: $mc_B > mc_A$. If we also assume that the two inverse demand functions d are the same, then with no government pricing the vehicle flows of the two types, V_A^0 and V_B^0, would be identical. These flows are shown in the two panels of Figure 4.5.

First-best pricing in this case would involve group-specific tolls (not shown in the diagrams), each equal to that group's *mec*. The result would be flows V_A^1 and V_B^1, producing

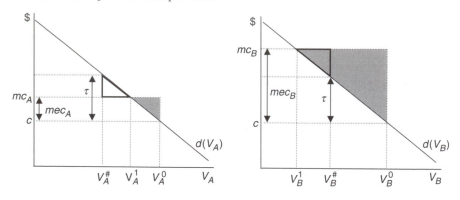

Figure 4.5 Second-best pricing for an environmental externality when tolls cannot be differentiated.

social surplus gains as given by the areas of the shaded triangles. When tolls cannot be differentiated, however, a second-best identical toll can be determined that optimally compromises between the two first-best tolls (Verhoef, Nijkamp and Rietveld 1995a). In the case sketched, with identical linear demand functions, it is exactly equal to the average of the *mec*'s. The welfare losses from overpricing group A and underpricing group B, compared to first-best pricing, are given by the two bold triangles. We discuss this example further, in a more general setting, in Section 4.2.3.

This simple example already illustrates some important aspects of second-best pricing. First, tautologically, the welfare gains cannot exceed those from first-best pricing, and are usually smaller (unless the constraint does not bind). Second, although tolls are not equal to marginal external costs, they are of course still related to them; in this simple example, the toll is the average of the *mec*'s. And third, the key to determining the second-best toll is the tradeoff between welfare losses from non-optimal pricing in the various (sub)markets involved. In this example, because equal demand sensitivities are assumed, it is optimal to have the vertical sides of the bold triangles equally long (because the toll is the average of the *mec*'s), so that a marginal change in the toll would create a surplus loss in the one market that is exactly compensated for by a surplus gain in the other market. In diagrammatic terms, when characterizing the welfare-loss triangles from non-optimal pricing, one could say that "two small Harberger triangles are better than one large one" (Arnott and Yan 2000, p. 171).

Because second-best problems come in so many variants, it is not instructive to combine all possible sources of second-best constraints into one grand exposition, even if it were possible. Rather, more insight is gained from considering different sources of second-best distortions in isolation, *i.e.*, in an otherwise first-best world. The insights will remain relevant in explaining what is going on in more realistic but complex cases, where various distortions occur simultaneously. This section considers five cases: when not every link in a network can feasibly be priced; when tolls cannot be varied smoothly over time; when tolls cannot be differentiated among different classes of users; when tolls must be set before knowing what the actual demand and/or capacity will be; and when pricing affects labor supply which is already discouraged due to income or other taxes. Much of our discussion follows Lindsey and Verhoef (2001).

4.2.1 Network aspects

Probably the earliest example of second-best road pricing considered in the literature concerns the case where not every congested link in a network is tolled. Reasons for this might include excessive cost for charging each link, political constraints requiring that road charging be implemented gradually, or an acceptability constraint that a toll-free alternative should always be available. Lévy-Lambert (1968) and Marchand (1968) were the first to address this type of problem, using a simple network featuring a toll road and a parallel untolled road between a common origin and destination.[13] This setting is still relevant today, as it describes the main constraint faced when setting a congestion toll on an express lane with parallel untolled lanes.

But the general problem of untolled links encompasses a much wider set of practical congestion-charging mechanisms. A toll cordon as used in various Norwegian cities corresponds to a situation in which tolls are in place only on the links that define the cordon. An area charge as applied in Central London can be viewed as a priced "virtual" link that is added, for modeling purposes, to all routes that pass through the charging area, with all other routes unpriced. Parking charges can be modeled by adding a tolled virtual link to all routes that end within the area in which the parking charge applies.

We start our discussion with the static two-route problem just mentioned, and provide the full derivation of the second-best optimal toll for this case. This model provides fundamental insights which, as we will see later, also help us understand how to price public transit when it competes with automobiles for passengers. We then go on to other second-best problems, which can be solved using similar Lagrangian approaches.

Static congestion: two routes in parallel

The classic two-route problem considers static congestion on two parallel roads connecting a single OD-pair. A congestion toll can be applied on one of the two roads (route T), while the other (route U) must remain untolled. Total traffic V is equal to the sum of traffic on the two roads, V_T and V_U, and average user cost on road R is $c_R(V_R)$.[14] Users consider the roads as pure substitutes, so Wardrop's first principle applies. Users are homogeneous in all respects except that willingness to pay for trips differs across users, so that overall inverse demand $d(V)$ is elastic, where $d(\cdot)$ is the generalized price including user cost and toll.

The optimal toll on route T, τ_T, can be found by maximizing the following Lagrangian function:

$$\Lambda = \int_0^{V_T+V_U} d(v)\mathrm{d}v - V_T \cdot c_T(V_T) - V_U \cdot c_U(V_U)$$
$$+ \lambda_T \cdot \left[c_T(V_T) + \tau_T - d(V_T + V_U) \right] + \lambda_U \cdot \left[c_U(V_U) - d(V_T + V_U) \right], \qquad (4.32)$$

where the first three terms form the social objective of social surplus, the variables λ_R give the shadow price of the equilibrium constraint for route R, and capacities are suppressed as arguments in cost functions because we consider only the short run.

The equilibrium value of a Lagrange multiplier reflects the marginal impact of a relaxation of the associated constraint upon the optimized value of the objective. For the Lagrangian (4.32) this means that the equilibrium value of λ_R should give the impact on social surplus of a marginal increase in the toll on route R. We therefore expect to find $\lambda_T = 0$ in the second-best optimum (τ_T should be set optimally), and $\lambda_U > 0$ when route U is congested (since surplus would be increased if a positive toll could be included in the second constraint). The first-order conditions to (4.32) confirm this:

$$\frac{\partial \Lambda}{\partial V_T} = d - c_T - V_T \cdot c_T' + \lambda_T \cdot (c_T' - d') - \lambda_U \cdot d' = 0$$

$$\frac{\partial \Lambda}{\partial V_U} = d - c_U - V_U \cdot c_U' - \lambda_T \cdot d' + \lambda_U \cdot (c_U' - d') = 0$$

$$\frac{\partial \Lambda}{\partial \tau_T} = \lambda_T = 0 \qquad\qquad (4.33)$$

$$\frac{\partial \Lambda}{\partial \lambda_T} = c_T + \tau_T - d = 0$$

$$\frac{\partial \Lambda}{\partial \lambda_U} = c_U - d = 0,$$

where primes denote derivatives. These first-order conditions can be solved to yield:

$$\lambda_U = \frac{V_U \cdot c_U'}{c_U' - d'}, \qquad\qquad (4.34)$$

which is positive as expected (recall that d', the slope of the inverse demand function, is non-positive). Furthermore, λ_U increases in the congestion externality on route U (the numerator) and in the sensitivity of equilibrium demand to price changes on route U (which decreases the denominator). Both factors would indeed boost the welfare gains from introducing a marginally positive toll on route U.

Starting with the first-order condition for V_T in (4.33), we first substitute the solutions for the two Lagrange multipliers, namely (4.34) and $\lambda_T = 0$. Next, using Wardrop's condition for route T (*i.e.*, the first-order condition for λ_T), we replace $d - c_T$ by τ_T, and obtain the following second-best toll τ_T:

$$\tau_T = V_T c_T' - V_U c_U' \cdot \frac{-d'}{c_U' - d'}. \qquad\qquad (4.35)$$

The toll is equal to the marginal external congestion cost on route T, minus a certain fraction of the marginal external congestion cost on route U. The first term reflects the direct beneficial impacts of the toll upon congestion on route T. The second term, which is negative, captures the toll's indirect spillovers on route U through induced route diversion. The fraction in that term gives the number of trips added to route U per trip removed from route T: it is less than one (provided demand is not perfectly inelastic) because some of the trips removed from T are no longer made on either route.[15] Under perfectly inelastic demand ($d' \to -\infty$), the fraction becomes unity and the two effects are equally important: only route choice matters for overall efficiency with inelastic demand, and it is optimized by setting the toll on route T equal to the difference between marginal external costs on the two routes. In contrast, when demand is perfectly elastic ($d' = 0$), the second term vanishes: V_U cannot be

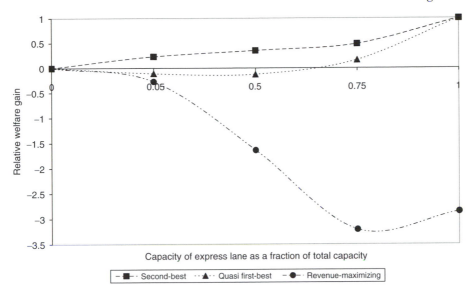

Figure 4.6 Relative efficiency of three express-lane pricing regimes.
Source: Computed using the base-case numerical model of Verhoef and Small (2004). The "quasi first-best" case presents previously unpublished calculations.

affected by τ_T because it is fully determined by Wardrop's condition $d = c_U(V_U)$, with d constant. The best thing the regulator can then do is to ignore route U altogether and optimize the use of route T by perfectly internalizing the congestion externality.

This example illustrates two lessons that turn out to be more general. A first is that the difference between welfare gains from first-best and second-best pricing can typically be determined only when detailed information is available. The upper curve in Figure 4.6 illustrates this point by plotting, for the simulation model of Verhoef and Small (2004), the relative efficiency of second-best pricing – *i.e.*, its welfare gain (compared to no pricing) as a fraction of the welfare gain from first-best pricing. This relative efficiency (the top line in the figure) rises from 0 to 1 as the relative size of priced capacity increases from 0 to 1. The sigmoid shape of the curve underlines that unless a significant portion of capacity is priced, the welfare losses from spillovers on unpriced capacity, reflected in the second term of (4.35), are substantial. The relative efficiency at one-third of capacity in Figure 4.6, approximately 0.3, is higher than the corresponding estimate by Liu and McDonald (1998) for the express lanes on the SR-91, which is about 0.1. The reason is probably that Verhoef and Small allow for heterogeneity in values of time; the relative efficiency increases with heterogeneity because the travel time gains on the tolled lane are enjoyed by higher-value-of-time users, whereas the travel time losses on the free lane are incurred by lower-value-of-time users (see also Small and Yan 2001). Both with and without heterogeneity, however, the gains from express-lane pricing are disappointingly small in static models. As we will see, more optimistic conclusions are derived from dynamic models.

A second lesson from the example leading to (4.35) is that second-best pricing rules are usually more complex than first-best; compare equation (4.6). The reason is that second-best rules account for the indirect effects of the price.[16] Because the rules are more complex, the chance of making mistakes in setting second-best optimal tolls is also greater; accounting for this would further diminish the expected welfare gains from pricing. Moreover, more information is required: one needs to know not only marginal external costs but also demand and cost elasticities.

One might think a safer course is to use first-best reasoning, ignoring the constraints that apply, and hope it is close enough to a true second-best solution. We call such a prescription *quasi first-best* tolls, defined in the current example as toll $V_T \cdot c'_T$ on route T and no toll on route U. However, this is not an attractive option either because it is often far inferior to the second-best toll. It may even lead to a welfare loss compared to no pricing, as shown by the middle line in Figure 4.6: in this example, unless at least 65% of capacity is priced, the quasi first-best toll is worse than no toll.

The third curve in Figure 4.6 shows the relative efficiency from a private (revenue-maximizing) express lane, which will be discussed in Section 6.1.

Dynamic congestion: two bottlenecks in parallel

By allowing for gains that arise from departure-time adjustments, dynamic models of the two-route problem tend to give more optimistic indications of the relative welfare gains from second-best pricing (Braid 1996; de Palma and Lindsey 2000). Consider two bottlenecks of equal capacity V_K in parallel, in a setting that is otherwise identical to the basic bottleneck model. Now suppose one can implement a time-varying toll on one of the two bottlenecks, but no toll on the other. In this case the quasi first-best toll, as given by (4.23) with Q taken to be only those people using the tolled road, will eliminate all travel delays for this bottleneck. Because the equilibrium price on the tolled bottleneck remains unaffected by the toll, it induces no route shift and therefore produces no spillover of congestion onto the unpriced road. As a result, the relative welfare gain of this policy is exactly 50%.

Even higher welfare gains occur using a true second-best toll on the priced link (Braid 1996). This toll takes into account the fact that with equal traffic, the marginal cost on the tolled route (where only schedule delay cost is incurred) is lower than on the untolled route (where both schedule delay cost and travel delay cost are incurred) – in this example it is only half as large, as can be seen by comparing equations (4.22) and (4.27) with equal values of Q. To equalize them, the tolled alternative should carry two-thirds of all traffic and the untolled alternative one-third. This requires a time-independent subsidy to users of the tolled route, added to the time-dependent toll, such that exactly half the users of the tolled bottleneck receive a net subsidy while the other half pay a net tax. This second-best equilibrium achieves two-thirds of the welfare gain from first-best pricing.[17]

Other networks

The case of two parallel routes, discussed above, is just one of many where second-best congestion pricing is relevant. A similar case arises when travelers face a mode choice between driving and using public transportation (Tabuchi 1993) where public transportation is obliged to be self-financing for political or other reasons. Average-cost pricing of transit causes the generalized price of a transit trip to exceed its marginal social cost, due to scale economies as argued in Section 3.2.4. The second-best toll on the road then exceeds marginal external cost in order to boost demand for public transportation. This can also be viewed as an example of a distortion in the economy outside the road sector, in this case making it desirable to charge road prices higher than the Pigouvian values.

Verhoef (2002a, 2002b) derives second-best optimal tolls for any subset of tolled links on a network of arbitrary size and shape.[18] The toll formulas are complex; (4.35) is a special case.

Verhoef shows how, in larger networks, the Lagrange multipliers reflecting zero-pricing constraints may be useful in computational algorithms for finding second-best optima. A complication in such algorithms is that the interior second-best optimum need not be unique nor even exist – especially if there are untolled links with relatively high marginal external costs. If an interior solution does not exist, then the global optimum is a corner solution in which tolls are set so that for at least one OD-pair, one or more links (and hence routes) are exactly balanced in their attractiveness between being used or not being used.

Second-best questions can be explored by trial and error rather than by formal optimization. A typical starting point is one of several well-developed applied network models, in which route choices are determined as a user equilibrium using either Wardrop's first principle or some stochastic route-choice mechanism. The model is then applied to pricing schemes that incorporate the researcher's view of technical, political, acceptability, equity-based, or other practical considerations. In some cases a search is carried out over various parameters such as toll levels and number and locations of toll charging points.

The trial-and-error approach has been applied quite successfully to at least two questions. The first question is how to introduce pricing incrementally by applying it to just a subset of the network, perhaps in conjunction with other policies such as free passage to high-occupancy vehicles. Safirova *et al.* (2004) provide a good example, analyzing policies for the Washington metropolitan area using a model known as START that was developed in the UK. As a general rule, such studies have found that the best candidates for road pricing are expressways and major urban arterial roads, because of their high traffic volumes, high speeds, and lack of close substitutes (Lindsey and Verhoef 2001).

The other question is toll-cordon design: where to place the cordon, how high to set the toll, and how to improve incrementally over a pure cordon. (We define a pure toll cordon as one where a single charge is applied to anyone crossing a well-defined boundary enclosing a highly congested area.) We give just a few examples of such studies here. Santos, Newbery and Rojey (2001) apply the SATURN network model to eight small English cities, finding that pure cordon tolls produce large reductions in cordon crossings with only small impacts on overall quantity of vehicle travel. They also find that the cordons can produce substantial welfare gains, but that those gains are easily lost if the toll is too high. Researchers from Leeds have applied the SATURN model to road networks depicting Cambridge (UK), Edinburgh, and other cities.[19] Their results suggest that even simplified analytical rules for choosing the tolled links produce great improvements over cordons selected by expert judgment. These and other studies show that substantial further welfare gains can be achieved by allowing toll levels to differ at different charging points or by using two cordons, one inside the other, with different charge levels. Yet other studies incorporate land-use effects by considering cordon tolls within broader models of urban structure.[20]

4.2.2 Time-of-day aspects

A second type of constraint on congestion tolls is when they cannot be varied freely over time. The simplest but most instructive examples again involve the basic bottleneck model.

Flat pricing of a bottleneck

Assume first that only a single fixed ("flat") toll can be charged throughout the peak period. This toll can affect the overall use Q, provided demand is not completely inelastic, but it does not affect queue-entry rates. Therefore the reduced-form average, total, and marginal cost functions for an unpriced equilibrium, (4.20)–(4.22), remain valid. The second-best optimal flat toll τ_F is therefore:

$$\tau_F = \overline{mc}_g^0 - \overline{c}_g^0 = \delta \cdot \frac{Q}{V_K}. \tag{4.36}$$

The optimal time-invariant charge (4.36) is exactly twice the time-average of the optimal time-varying toll (4.23); intuitively, this is because adding a new traveler to the system imposes both schedule-delay and travel-time costs, instead of just the former. The relative efficiency of this second-best charge depends strongly on the elasticity of demand.

The results are a little more complex if we allow for dispersion in desired queue-exit times, as in the model of Section 3.4.3. Let V_d and q again denote the height and width of the density function describing desired queue-exits (*i.e.*, people would like to exit at rate V_d over time interval q). Hence $Q = q \cdot V_d$. The relevant average cost function is that in (3.38):

$$\overline{c}_g^0 = \delta \cdot \frac{qV_d}{V_K} \cdot \left(1 - \tfrac{1}{2} \cdot \frac{V_K}{V_d} \right). \tag{4.37}$$

The marginal cost now depends on whether a marginal increase in use would *intensify* the period of desired queue-exits by increasing V_d, or *extend* it by increasing q.

To fix ideas, suppose one wishes to influence the decisions of developers whose buildings generate traffic according to some known process, by charging them with the marginal external cost of new traffic generated assuming that tolls cannot be differentiated by time of day. The new development might then *intensify* desired queue-exits if work-start times are the same everywhere and buildings are all about the same distance from the bottleneck's exit. In this case the marginal cost of one unit of traffic (an increase in Q holding q constant) is $(1/q) \cdot \partial \left(qV_d \overline{c}_g^0 \right) / \partial V_d$; subtracting average cost (4.37) yields the following optimal flat toll (where superscript I denotes *intensify*):

$$\tau_F^I = \delta \cdot q \cdot \frac{V_d}{V_K}, \tag{4.38}$$

which is identical to (4.36).

The new development might *extend* desired queue-exits (raise q but not V_d) if firms practice staggered work-hours or if the development is at the edge of an already developed area. The marginal cost of one unit of traffic (an increase in Q holding V_d constant) is now $(1/V_d) \cdot \partial \left(qV_d \overline{c}_g^0 \right) / \partial q$; subtracting average cost (4.37) yields the following optimal flat toll (with superscript E designating *extend*):

$$\tau_F^E = \delta \cdot q \cdot \left(\frac{V_d}{V_K} - \tfrac{1}{2} \right), \tag{4.39}$$

which is smaller than (4.36). One would therefore charge a developer (or the drivers using the new development) less for extending demand than for intensifying it, because extending demand has less impact on other users.

Coarse tolls

A more sophisticated variant of the flat toll is a coarse or "step" toll, defined as one that allows one or more non-zero toll values, each applying during a specific time interval that can be chosen to maximize welfare (Arnott, de Palma and Lindsey 1990b, 1993). The simplest has a single step: the toll is zero except for a time interval (presumably a subset of the peak period) when it is a positive constant. Analytical derivations for this case are cumbersome, even for the basic bottleneck model. Using numerical simulation, Arnott, de Palma and Lindsey find that the second-best single-step toll produces relative efficiency gains of just over one-half. This performance compares favorably to the flat toll, whose relative efficiency is less than one-third even under fairly generous assumptions about the elasticity of demand for peak-period travel. Chu (1999) also compares coarse and flat tolls, finding relative efficiencies of 38%–79% for the coarse toll and 27%–66% for the flat toll, depending on parameters.

Network and time-of-day aspects combined: an application

A recent study by de Palma, Kilani and Lindsey (2005) uses the dynamic queue-based METROPOLIS model, described in Section 4.1.2, to simulate a number of second-best policies on a stylized circular network with eight radial roads connecting four concentric ring roads to a central point. Origin-destination demands are distributed around the network. They find that welfare gains are substantially higher with step tolls (in half-hour steps) than with flat tolls, and also higher with area pricing (*i.e.*, pricing all trips within a cordon) than with cordon pricing. Step tolls also have a more favorable acceptability impact than flat tolls, in that they have a higher proportion of travelers whose consumer surplus change is positive (without considering use of revenues). However, area tolls have a lower acceptability impact than cordon tolls. Thus area pricing with step tolls achieves the highest welfare gain (61% of the first-best gain); while cordon pricing with step tolls achieves the highest proportion of positive consumer-surplus changes (41%), along with a substantial relative welfare gain (44%). These results further support the cordon studies described earlier in suggesting that pure cordons can be greatly improved by allowing even modest flexibility in the locations and toll levels of charge points.

4.2.3 *User heterogeneity*

Another second-best problem arises when the price cannot differ by user group. In this case, the second-best toll is a weighted average of the marginal external costs for the different groups, at least within a static model (Verhoef, Nijkamp and Rietveld 1995a). A group's weight depends positively on its price-sensitivity of demand. The welfare losses from undifferentiated prices generally increase in the price-sensitivity of demand of those user groups whose marginal external costs differ the most from the weighted average.

Undifferentiated tolls give up two advantages of optimally differentiated tolls: they fail to secure optimal use levels by all groups of travelers, and also to provide optimal incentives for choice among groups. For example, tolls differentiated by pollution emissions would encourage owners of dirty cars to curtail their use (securing optimal use levels across groups), and would also encourage them to buy clean cars instead (choice among groups). Without the ability to differentiate charges, supplementary policies may become desirable. In the pollution example, such inability might justify setting technological standards for emissions control. As another example, the inability to differentiate tolls by distance traveled might justify land-use controls or spatial planning. Doing this in a second-best optimal manner requires the regulator to possess much more information than just the marginal external costs that are required for short-run optimal pricing. The risk of mistakes in second-best policies is therefore again larger than for first-best policies.

4.2.4 Stochastic congestion and information

Uncertainty about actual traffic conditions may also affect the optimality of pricing rules. It is useful to distinguish between two types of uncertainty: idiosyncratic and objective.

Idiosyncratic uncertainty exists when traffic conditions are predictable, but individual travelers do not know them precisely and instead form idiosyncratic perceptions of their own travel times. The standard approach to describing behavior in this case is the Stochastic User Equilibrium (SUE), discussed in Section 3.4.4. Smith, Eriksson and Lindberg (1995) and Yang (1999a) investigate the conditions under which a system optimum (in which total travel time is minimized) can be supported as a stochastic user equilibrium with non-negative tolls. Under certain conditions, tolls equal to marginal external cost will accomplish this.

Objective uncertainty exists when traffic conditions vary unpredictably due to accidents, bad weather, demand shocks, or other factors. Chapter 3 already discussed some aspects of this: for example, that providing real-time travel information is guaranteed to increase welfare only when optimal pricing is in place. Recent research has elaborated on such potential synergies between information and road pricing.

In many situations, the benefits from pricing and information provision seem to be approximately additive – *i.e.*, equal to the sum of benefits of each instrument in isolation. Furthermore, they tend to be complementary: that is, under conditions when one instrument does not yield much benefit, the other does particularly well.[21] But other results can arise. Benefits are super-additive beyond a certain level of market penetration in the model of Yang (1999b). Benefits from providing information can be negative if pricing is *non-responsive*; that is, if the toll varies according to a preset schedule instead of according to conditions as they are realized (de Palma and Lindsey 1998). (Note that non-responsive pricing is different from flat pricing: in non-responsive pricing the toll can vary dramatically over time, but in a predictable fashion.)

Nevertheless, at least two studies find that if second-best non-responsive pricing is in place and *perfect* information is provided, benefits are often almost as great as those from first-best responsive pricing.[22] This suggests an attractive combination in practice. Information provision makes travelers feel that they have some control over their trip, if only in planning for unexpected delays. And non-responsive pricing avoids a psychologically treacherous feature of first-best pricing, namely that the toll is unexpectedly high just when the conditions encountered are unexpectedly bad.

4.2.5 Interactions with other distorted markets

The imposition of prices in transportation, as well as the use of the revenues, may have non-marginal welfare effects in other markets when these markets do not function efficiently. Such distortions can be considered constraints, from the point of view of transportation pricing, in the sense that they could be eliminated with appropriate instruments but such instruments are assumed unavailable.

An important example is labor markets. Income taxes lower the nominal wage paid to labor, while indirect taxes (*e.g.*, sales or value-added taxes) tend to increase the price level and thereby to reduce the real wage. In both cases, the taxes create an incentive against work that will reduce labor supply below its efficient level unless the incentive is offset in other ways; the resulting cost to the economy is called the *deadweight loss* of the existing tax system.

A congestion toll, or indeed any Pigouvian tax, will tend to discourage labor supply even if there is no direct connection with commuting, because it raises the average cost of living faced by workers and therefore lowers the real wage rate earned by those workers. Therefore it will aggravate the deadweight loss of labor taxation, just as do other indirect taxes. That aggravation may be partially mitigated if toll revenues are used to reduce the original distorting labor tax; if revenues are spent in some other way, for example as lump-sum compensations to groups thought to be hurt by the tolls, the aggravation may instead be enhanced (because a higher non-wage income discourages labor supply) and become quite severe. Thus, revenue uses have implications for efficiency as well as for equity and political feasibility.[23]

Mayeres and Proost (2001) evaluate the efficiency effects of transportation charges in Belgium by using a general-equilibrium model. They consider a social welfare function that incorporates a certain degree of aversion to income inequality, through a parameter that can be varied parametrically. They find that a marginal increase in peak-period road prices yields the highest benefit when revenue is spent on road capacity expansion. But it yields a *negative* benefit when it is spent on public transportation, unless the degree of social inequality aversion is very high. This latter result is mainly because public transportation is already heavily subsidized, and it illustrates a critical point about congestion pricing: because the revenues are typically large compared to the value of the time savings, inefficient spending of those revenues can completely undo the net benefits of the policy.

Parry and Bento (2001) also find general-equilibrium effects of road pricing that are large and sensitive to the allocation of revenues. Specifically, the interaction with a tax-distorted labor market can cause road pricing to be welfare-reducing if revenues are distributed in a lump-sum manner, because doing so discourages labor supply. On the other hand, when revenues are used to reduce the distorting labor taxes, the usual efficiency advantage of such tax reductions is magnified by the same complementarity. In that case welfare gains are twice as large as would be predicted by the standard partial-equilibrium analysis and the optimal tax is set to the Pigouvian level. Van Dender (2003) generalizes the Parry–Bento model, obtaining similar but less extreme results using more realistic assumptions.

4.2.6 Second-best pricing: a conclusion

First-best analysis of congestion pricing provides important insights; but, because constraints and distorted markets abound in reality, second-best analysis is the only way to translate those insights into practical advice in policy design. The resulting pricing rules are more complex, because they reflect indirect effects, and they require more information. This increases the chance of making mistakes in setting prices. Yet ignoring indirect effects can result in much smaller efficiency gains or even losses.

Happily, second-best models do provide some general guidance as to which factors are most important to consider. For example, toll cordons can be designed that achieve a high proportion of theoretically possible benefits, but they do not necessarily look much like what an expert would intuitively draw on a map. Relaxing typical constraints, such as that all cordon crossings must be tolled at the same amount or that the toll must be flat over the entire peak period, can significantly improve results. Providing information on traffic conditions may sometimes be harmful if tolls are absent or set *ex ante* based on expected traffic conditions. Finally, taxes affecting labor supply can greatly influence the welfare effects of congestion tolls, and accounting for them introduces an important efficiency factor in choosing how to use toll revenues – generally favoring using them to offset those taxes creating the distortion.

Most of the constraints we have considered are really "soft," reflecting judgment about how to account for the regulatory costs (*i.e.*, technical, bureaucratic, or political implementation costs) of toll collection. If those costs could be incorporated into the objective function, then maximizing it would achieve what we might call *broadly first-best* pricing. By contrast, the conventional definition of first-best ignores those so is only *narrowly first-best* (Milne, Niskanen and Verhoef 2000). We cannot formulate the broadly first-best pricing problem because we cannot quantify the relevant costs. But in many cases, a second-best analysis (one assuming hard constraints) may be a good approximation; if so, we can say that it is broadly first-best to apply second-best pricing. This, of course, leaves open the possibility that future developments could change regulatory costs and thus make certain constraints obsolete.

4.3 Congestion pricing in practice

Even ignoring the ancient world, road pricing has a long history, with turnpikes dating back at least to the seventeenth century in Great Britain and the eighteenth century in the US (Levinson 1998). Road pricing for congestion management is more recent. The earliest modern application is Singapore's Area License Scheme, established in 1975. Since then, other applications have appeared, varying from single facilities such as bridges or toll roads to tolled express lanes as in the US, toll cordons as in Norway, and area-wide pricing as in London. We describe here selected applications where managing congestion is explicitly or potentially a significant goal in the design of the pricing scheme. Small and Gómez-Ibáñez (1998) provide a more extended review of the earlier applications.

4.3.1 Singapore

In 1975, Singapore implemented the first operational congestion pricing scheme in the world, the Area License Scheme (ALS). A license had to be purchased and displayed at the windscreen before entering the central 'Restricted Zone' (RZ) during designated peak hours; compliance was monitored manually at control points. Peak hours and tolls were adjusted a number of times. An afternoon peak charge was implemented in 1989, and in 1994 an access fee for inter-peak day-time passages was introduced. When first implemented, the number of vehicles entering the RZ fell by an amazing 44%. While speeds rose dramatically in the zone itself, displaced traffic caused increased traffic outside the zone, and average commuting times to jobs inside the zone even increased (Small and Gómez-Ibáñez 1998). If this increase in travel times was entirely due to the toll system, it would provide a good example of how second-best distortions and spillovers, if not properly accounted for when setting tolls, may undermine the efficiency gains from road pricing. The fee may have been (far) above the second-best optimal level, as argued for example by Watson and Holland (1978) and McCarthy and Tay (1993).

In 1995, Singapore extended the ALS with a Road Pricing Scheme, which added some pricing of expressways. Although traffic volumes on tolled expressways dropped by 17%, 40% of these drivers switched to major by-pass roads (Goh 2002), underlining the second-best character of the policy and the empirical relevance of the two-route problem of Section 4.2.1.

Singapore switched to a scheme known as Electronic Road Pricing (ERP) in 1998. Since then, charges are deducted from a smart card when passing through an ERP gantry using microwave technology. The scheme features 28 gantries that form a daytime toll cordon around the central area and 14 tolled expressways and arterial roads further out during morning peak hours only. There are no tolls on weekends. Charges vary by time of day in 30-minute steps and are adjusted quarterly, depending on average speeds measured in the previous quarter. Despite the fact that the average charge for ERP is lower than it was for ALS, traffic into the CBD decreased by another 10%–15% compared to the ALS scheme (Keong 2002). One reason might be that every entry by a given car is charged under ERP, whereas ALS allowed for unlimited access throughout the day with a single permit.

4.3.2 Norwegian toll rings

Four toll cordons operated in Norway for some time: Bergen (initiated in 1986), Oslo (1990), Trondheim (1991), and Stavanger (2001). These toll rings were designed to raise revenue, not to manage congestion. Nevertheless we discuss them here because cordon pricing is often considered as a possible form of congestion pricing, and this possibility has been extensively discussed in Norway. In addition, the Trondheim scheme, which evolved from a ring into a multi-zonal scheme, incorporated some time-of-day differentiation into its pricing structure; however it was discontinued in 2007.

In the Norwegian toll rings, tolls are relatively low and seasonal passesø further reduce the marginal charge. Not surprisingly, the impact on traffic has been modest, with vehicle crossings reduced by only 5%–10% (Tretvik 2003; Ramjerdi, Minken and Østmoe 2004). Time-differentiated charging in Trondheim nevertheless caused substantial shifts in timing for car trips: a decrease by 10% for charged periods and an increase by 8%–9% for uncharged periods (Meland 1995).

4.3.3 Value pricing in the US

Congestion pricing has gained momentum in the US since federal legislation began funding congestion pricing pilot projects under the so-called Value Pricing Program, and allowing limited pricing on Interstate highways.[24] By the end of 2004, the US Federal Highway Administration (FHWA) listed 39 projects, divided into various categories and further subdivided into operational projects and projects under development.[25]

One type of project introduces congestion pricing on existing, previously untolled infrastructure. The conversion of high-occupancy vehicle (HOV) lanes into high-occupancy/toll (HOT) lanes is an example. HOT lanes are free of charge for high-occupancy vehicles, and allow other vehicles to use the lane by paying a toll. Two examples are San Diego, California's *FasTrak* scheme, implemented in 1999 on Interstate 15 (I-15), and Houston, Texas's *QuickRide* scheme on the Katy Freeway and on US290, starting 1998 and 2000, respectively. In the San Diego scheme, the toll is responsive (in the terminology of Section 4.2.4): it is varied in real time, depending on congestion, in order to maintain a target speed. (This procedure is also called "dynamic pricing" although it has little to do with the dynamic models discussed in this chapter.) The San Diego toll is usually between US$0.50 and US$4.00 but can be as high as US$8.00. Half the revenues are used to support transit services. Brownstone *et al.* (2003) analyze users' responses, finding among other things that HOT-lane use is higher for commuters, higher-income people, women, people between 35 and 45 years of age, highly educated people, and homeowners.

Another form of tolling existing infrastructure, cordon tolls, is under consideration in Lee County (Florida) and central New York City.

Somewhat more popular in the US is the idea of using tolls to finance new infrastructure. Most such cases are conventional toll roads, with no time differentiation for user charges. But one relatively early and well-studied example was initiated in 1995 as a time-varying toll on a new set of express lanes added to the Riverside Freeway (State Route 91, known as SR-91). This is a heavily-peaked commuter route in Orange County, California, leading to employment centers in Orange and Los Angeles Counties. By the middle of 2007, the preset tolls varied hourly and by day of the week, with tolls reaching a maximum of US$9.50 for an outbound afternoon trip from 5:00 p.m.– 6:00 p.m. on Fridays. Apart from travel-time savings, users perceive greater comfort and safety from using the Express Lanes (Sullivan *et al.* 2000).

Initiated as a private undertaking, the so-called "91 Express Lanes" reverted to public ownership and control in 2003. The main reason was a non-compete clause in the original contract that precluded expansion of competing capacity on parallel untolled routes, including the untolled lanes of SR-91 itself. This clause became problematic after congestion had grown worse on the untolled lanes, presumably much sooner than the government had envisaged when signing the original contract. This experience emphasizes the differences in interest between public and private road operators (see also Chapter 6): whereas heavy congestion on parallel connections is good news for a private operator because it improves profits, it is generally bad news from the public perspective. Such fundamental conflicts in interests pose great challenges for policies aimed at facilitating private road investments for congestion relief.

A third category of value-pricing projects involves introducing time-of-day variation to tolls on existing toll facilities. Examples of such variable tolls include two bridges in Lee County, Florida (introduced in 1998), bridges and tunnels crossing the Hudson River between New York and New Jersey (2001), the New Jersey Turnpike (2000), and the San Joaquin Hills Toll Road in Orange County, California (2002). In many of these cases the variation in rates is small. Such policies appear to be successful in encouraging the rescheduling of trips (DeCorla-Souza 2004). For example, surveys indicate that over 71% of motorists with an electronic toll-collection transponder have shifted their travel time at least once a week in the Lee County project in response to a toll difference of just US$0.25. In the case of the Hudson River crossings, one year after giving off-peak toll discounts of 20%, morning peak traffic had fallen by 7% and evening peak traffic by 4%, with overall traffic stable.

The impacts of value pricing depend, of course, on local circumstances and project design. But the applications are generally believed to have demonstrated that variable pricing can have substantial impacts on trip timing, vehicle occupancy, and modal choice. For recent reviews, see Supernak *et al.* (2001) and DeCorla-Souza (2004).

4.3.4 London congestion charging

In 2003, London introduced a congestion charging scheme in its central area covering 22 square kilometers. A charge of £5, later raised to £8, applies to all vehicles driving or parking on public roads in the area between 7:00 a.m. and 6:30 p.m. on working days. Vehicles are identified by number plates using video cameras, an expensive technology but one that could be implemented quickly with existing technology.

In terms of congestion reduction, the scheme appears to have been a success. After a year, traffic circulating within the zone had decreased by 15%, and traffic entering the zone by 18%, during charging hours (Transport for London 2004). Congestion, measured as the actual minus free-flow travel time per kilometer, decreased by 30% within the zone, leading also to an improvement in travel-time reliability. Travelers primarily switched to public transportation (50%–60%), but also changed routes to bypass the cordoned area (20%–30%) or made other adaptations including carpooling, destination changes, and trip-timing adjustments. The surprisingly large mode-switching effect was presumably caused by the good initial coverage of London's public transportation network and by further improvements financed, in part, by congestion charge revenues. The scheme's initial effectiveness was at the high end of the original projections, but was financially less successful due to an unexpectedly large reduction in traffic and the high cost of collecting the congestion charge.

The politics behind the London scheme, described in detail by Richards (2006), are quite unusual. As of this writing, attempts to implement similar schemes elsewhere in the UK have not been successful. In 2007, the London scheme was expanded westward, nearly doubling the size of the initially charged area.

4.3.5 Other applications

Additional examples of congestion pricing are also in place. These include projects on Highway 407 north of Toronto, Canada, introduced in 1997; and the M6 motorway in Birmingham, UK, introduced in 2003. These projects have only minimal time-of-day differentiation. Another example is the introduction of time-varying pricing on Sundays on Route A1 near Paris (Small and Gómez-Ibáñez 1998). Area-wide schemes were considered several times in Stockholm, Sweden, and in the Netherlands, with Stockholm undertaking an eight-month trial in January 2006. The results were again encouraging, with a 22% drop in cordon crossings and an associated projected annual cost–benefit surplus of about SEK 760 million (around US$114 million) (Stockholmsförsöket 2006). A referendum resulted in approval of the scheme (with, as one might expect, majorities of "yes"-voters inside the cordon area, and of "no"-voters outside it). The Swedish government declared it will implement the congestion tax permanently in 2007.

4.3.6 Technology of road pricing

Decisions on what kind of pricing to adopt are strongly influenced by the capabilities of technologies available for charging motorists. This is a field that is changing very rapidly. Here, we give a brief history of some of the main developments, followed by an analysis of the key tradeoffs facing system designers.[26]

Brief history

As already mentioned, Singapore's original Area Licensing Scheme began in 1975 with paper stickers mounted on vehicles' windshields. Soon after, existing toll roads began introducing electronic transponders mounted in the vehicle and read by roadside equipment. Singapore's current Electronic Road Pricing (ERP) system also uses such transponders, as do most of the pricing implementations discussed above. Communication between transponder and roadside reader is by dedicated short-range communications (DSRC), *i.e.*, radio-frequency signals whose sole purpose is toll charging.

Enforcement of DSRC systems is usually done by taking video images of license plates. Usually these images are processed automatically using character-recognition software, a technology known as automated number plate recognition (ANPR). At least two pricing systems – on Highway 407 in Toronto, Canada, and in Central London – apply ANPR to all vehicles, rather than just those with missing or invalid transponder signals. However, accuracy remains a problem, causing high costs for follow-up enforcement and/or significant loss of revenues from unreadable plates.

As authorities have become more interested in charges that vary by location and distance traveled, they have turned to global positioning systems (GPS). Using GPS allows a vehicle to determine its location using satellite signals, and this information can be recorded or sent to a central processor. GPS is already being introduced by vehicle manufacturers to provide travel information, route guidance, or logistics control for fleets. Germany installed a GPS system to charge trucks on its motorways starting in 2005, and the UK is studying GPS as part of a future system of distance-based charges on motorways throughout the country (UK Department for Transport 2004). Proposals for more widespread GPS-based charging schemes have raised vigorous debate about the potential for government surveillance of individual travel patterns.

Another system, not widely implemented, uses a mobile telephone network to handle communications between the vehicle and the charging system, thereby obviating the need to locate expensive roadside communication devices wherever charging is to take place.

Any of these systems may use a plastic card with a magnetic stripe or embedded computer chip, in conjunction with an on-board card reader and transponder, to store charging information anonymously. Such a card is called a "smart card" if it has sufficient "brain" power.

Issues and tradeoffs

A partial list of significant issues that affect technology choice, and hence the degree of potential flexibility in pricing, is as follows.

- *Cost and lifetime of on-board devices*: Because there are so many vehicles, it is very expensive to install and maintain high-priced in-vehicle devices. This factor favors the use of relatively simple transponders (unit cost as low as US$8 in 2006)[27] and is creating interest in using even cheaper radio-frequency identification (RFID) tags. Of course, these advantages foreclose capabilities that might be useful to meet other objectives. Cheap in-vehicle equipment for automated number plate recognition (ANPR) also increases the market penetration of electronic tolling and thus reduces the expense of providing toll booths and coin machines.
- *Required vehicle speed and location*: Many older devices require vehicles to slow down and stay in a well-defined channel while being charged. Roadside readers have improved so that it is routine to read transponders at highway speeds, but doing so during lane-change maneuvers in normal traffic has proven a challenge and requires more costly and visually intrusive roadside readers. A charging system that requires neither speed reduction nor limitations on lane movements is known as open-road tolling.
- *Location of account information*: Information about stored or available funds may be stored cheaply in a central system, or more expensively in an on-board magnetic or

smart card. This affects the user's privacy and flexibility in shifting funds from one vehicle or user to another.

- *Interoperability*: Most users would like to have a single device work for any toll collection point they may cross. The market, however, has produced a variety of incompatible technologies. In many areas agencies within a region have coordinated to adopt the same technology, but this limits their flexibility to innovate. One solution being developed commercially is transponders that are compatible with two or more systems.
- *Integration with other services*: Some users and planners would like to use a single device, such as a smart card, to pay for parking, transit, and even retail transactions. This rules out the least sophisticated devices and requires coordination among agencies.
- *Original equipment on new vehicles*: Road-charging capability would be cheaper and easier to disseminate widely if manufacturers built in devices at the time of manufacture. Of course, this requires foresight as to what capabilities will be desired throughout the vehicle's life. Such equipment is already sometimes provided for other purposes: for example, a GPS for navigation. This could encourage toll authorities to opt for GPS-based charging systems.
- *Point versus distance-based charging*: As noted, there is interest in pricing schemes that are proportional to distance traveled, sometimes called "variabilization" (*e.g.*, Proost and Van Dender 1998). It is motivated by several factors, including a desire to promote economic efficiency, a desire to reduce vehicle use, and dissatisfaction with fuel taxes as a financing mechanism. GPS and mobile-telephone networks are amenable to distance-based charging, and many dedicated short-range communications (DSRC) systems can already track individual vehicles as they pass through the network.
- *Automated vehicle classification and occupancy measurement*: Pricing schemes may vary the charge by type of vehicle, occupancy, or vehicle emissions characteristics. Enforcement of these distinctions is difficult, and development is under way to use on-board or roadside devices to record these characteristics automatically.

Obviously decisions about these tradeoffs are sensitive to local conditions and objectives. This makes it likely that no one technology will emerge as the best, and that interoperability will be incomplete. We suspect that just as technological progress has made the toll booth nearly obsolete, it will overcome many limits to interoperability, allowing agencies to meet more of their goals while maintaining transparency to the user. We also believe that even though any given implementation of pricing is constrained by available technology, a far-sighted approach will design the pricing regime to evolve along with technology. The more important constraint is not technology, but rather the kind of complexity that users and political representatives will tolerate.

4.4 Pricing of parking

As shown in Chapter 3, parking accounts for a major part of the social costs of automobile trips to central cities. Furthermore, parking is heavily subsidized by many governments, employers, and businesses. One might suspect, then, that pricing it at either marginal or average cost would make a substantial difference in travel behavior. This suspicion is confirmed by many demand studies and by direct comparisons of the commuting choices of people with and without free parking at work. Eliminating free parking reduced the number of solo drivers by 19% to 81% in four sites in Los Angeles, and by 20% in Ottawa. In eight California case studies, the number of solo commuters fell by 17% for employers affected by a 1992 law requiring them to "cash out" employer-paid parking by offering an allowance in cash as an alternative.[28]

All this provides ample evidence to support Shoup's (1982) claim that free parking is one of the major factors distorting mode choices in high-density urban core areas. This distortion is especially perverse because subsidized employee parking not only misallocates resources by creating too many parking facilities; it also exacerbates the congestion externality caused by underpricing peak-hour highways. Furthermore, cities that insist on free downtown parking may undermine the ability of the downtown area to fully capture the advantages of agglomeration because the land needed to produce a high density of activities is instead used for parking (Shoup 2005, Chapter 5). Shoup notes that parking subsidies are encouraged by US municipal zoning ordinances, which typically require builders to provide enough parking to satisfy the demand expected at zero price, and by the greater deductibility of employer-paid parking costs relative to other transportation subsidies under US tax laws governing employer-provided benefits.

The situation for parking at shops is more complex, making it especially important to consider spillover effects before advocating pricing reform. Low parking prices encourage shoppers to drive rather than use transit, but by reducing turnover (because vehicles will remain parked for a longer time) can actually reduce the total number of auto trips (Glazer and Niskanen 1992). Street parking also interacts with traffic flow in complex ways (Arnott, Rave and Schöb 2005). Generally, parking charges may reduce congestion but do not discourage through trips and do not differentiate by how much a given driver adds to congestion.[29]

Parking charges may also help to internalize other social costs besides the resource value of the parking spaces themselves. Examples include visual intrusion of parked cars, search externalities in finding parking places, congestion cost imposed by parked cars upon moving traffic, and externalities imposed during the trips made before and after parking.

The parking models considered in Section 3.4.5 have various pricing implications. Arnott, de Palma and Lindsey (1991b) find that a spatially differentiated parking fee is necessary to induce the optimal parking pattern, in which parking spaces furthest from the CBD are taken first instead of last. Anderson and de Palma (2004) similarly find that the optimum in their model can be achieved using a spatially differentiated parking charge, which falls by distance from the city center (as in Verhoef, Nijkamp and Rietveld 1995b). Provided searching causes no road congestion, this charge could be achieved through private ownership of parking spaces in a monopolistically competitive market. In the model of Arnott and Rowse (1999), the existence of multiple equilibria implies that a marginal-cost tax on the parking externality cannot guarantee an optimum. Arnott, Rave and Schöb (2005, Chapter 2) identify a potential triple dividend to be reaped from the pricing of parking: reduced search, reduced traffic congestion, and use of parking revenues to lower other taxes.

Calthrop and Proost (2006) consider the interaction between publicly provided on-street parking and privately provided off-street parking. In their model, wasteful searching for on-street parking occurs when it is cheaper than private parking, to the point where the generalized prices in the two parking markets are equalized. The optimal on-street parking charge is equal to the off-street charge if off-street parking is supplied competitively, and somewhat lower if its suppliers have market power.

Given the cost figures in Section 3.5.3, it seems clear that eliminating subsidized parking for employees in high-density business districts is a high priority for improved efficiency in urban transportation. Doing so would reduce expenditures on parking facilities, free up land for other uses, and favorably alter the modal mix on congested roads. Charging more for on-street parking would have similar advantages and would in addition reduce congestion from cruising. Fears that such charges would undermine the economic vitality of business districts do not seem to be supported by the available empirical evidence (Marsden 2006).

4.5 Pricing of public transit

We now turn to pricing for public transit. While the technologies and institutions are very different from those dealt with so far in this chapter, and the specific analytical techniques have been developed in a somewhat separate literature, the basic principle of marginal-cost pricing is the same. As a result, the pricing rules and their derivations bear surprising similarities, and indeed can sometimes be viewed as extensions of the models already discussed in which public transit is viewed as an additional set of links on a network.

Setting prices for transit service involves at least three issues: the average fare level, the fare structure, and the incentive effects of transit subsidy programs. We treat each in turn, and then briefly consider the political considerations governing subsidies.

4.5.1 Fare level

We noted in Section 3.2.4 that optimal transit fares might not fully cover average costs because of increasing returns to scale when the value of user inputs is taken into account. In fact, in the simple model presented there, the optimal fare is zero whenever there are empty seats. This can be viewed as an example of public-goods pricing: once it is decided to offer a public good with high enough quality (*i.e.*, frequent enough service that there are empty seats), it costs nothing to serve an extra passenger. This, of course, abstracts from costs the passenger may impose by slowing the bus, and from adverse effects of taxes that finance the service.

The problem is more complex if a competing mode is not priced optimally. The case most often considered is underpricing of peak-hour automobile travel. Using straightforward models, Glaister (1974) and Henderson (1977, Chapter 7) derive the second-best solution and confirm our intuition that such underpricing justifies a higher subsidy of transit service, especially if the cross-elasticity of demand between transit and auto is high relative to transit's own-price elasticity. Dodgson and Topham (1987) add several features, including distributional preferences, distorting taxes, and cost-sharing by higher levels of government.

We can understand these two arguments for transit subsidies – scale economies and underpriced automobile travel – through a concrete model that generalizes the two-route problem of Section 4.2.1. The generalization is in two directions. First, the two competing alternatives are no longer required to be perfect substitutes. Second, one of them (representing public transit) has scale economies based on user-supplied inputs, as in Section 3.2.4. As with the two-route problem we take a second-best approach, where one of the competing alternatives (now representing automobile travel) is underpriced. The result is a second-best optimal transit fare that is similar to the second-best road toll (4.35) in the two-route problem, but modified in two ways corresponding to the two directions of generalization.

For simplicity, we consider rail transit only, assuming it does not interact with automobiles on the roads, and we assume automobile occupancy to be 1.0. Let q_A and q_R be the numbers of automobile and rail trips per unit of time, with vehicle flow rate $V_A = q_A$. Under the reasonable assumption that income effects in demand are negligible (see Section 2.2.5), the joint demand for these two types of travel can be derived from a benefit function $B(q_A, q_R)$, which expresses the consumer benefits from these amounts of travel as their total willingness to pay for the particular combination $\{q_A, q_R\}$.[30] $B(\cdot)$ is therefore a generalization of the area under the inverse demand curve, equation (4.2), to the case of more than one good. An important property is that the inverse demand for either type of travel, given the amount consumed of the other type, is given by the corresponding partial derivative of the benefit function, just as it is in our earlier models of multiple time periods and multiple roads:[31]

$$d_k(q_A, q_R) = \frac{\partial B(q_A, q_R)}{\partial q_k}, \quad k = A, R. \tag{4.40}$$

Let $C_A(\cdot)$ and $C_R(\cdot)$ be the total cost functions for auto and rail, including user costs for auto and both user and agency costs for rail:

$$C_A = C_{A\text{-}users} = q_A \cdot c_A(q_A)$$

$$C_R = C_{R\text{-}agency} + C_{R\text{-}users} = q_R \cdot c_{R\text{-}agency}(q_R) + q_R \cdot c_{R\text{-}users}(q_R). \tag{4.41}$$

Note that the average agency and user costs, $c_{R\text{-}agency}$ and $c_{R\text{-}users}$, play important roles in transit finance and in user satisfaction, respectively. Both may be decreasing functions of q_R due to scale economies, as derived in Chapter 3. The costs on the two modes are independent of each other. Recall that the generalized price of mode k ($k = A, R$) is defined as the average user cost c_k plus toll or fare payment τ_k, and the user equilibrium conditions are such that marginal benefits are equalized to this price for each transportation good:

$$\partial B / \partial q_A = c_A(q_A) + \tau_A$$
$$\partial B / \partial q_R = c_{R\text{-}users}(q_R) + \tau_R. \tag{4.42}$$

Social surplus can be defined as benefits minus cost:

$$W = B(q_A, q_R) - C_A(q_A) - C_R(q_R). \tag{4.43}$$

First, we can check that the first-best solution gives the expected marginal-cost prices for each mode. The first-order conditions for maximizing (4.43), after substituting (4.42), produce the following first-best prices:

$$\tau_A = q_A c_A'$$
$$\tau_R = q_R c_{R\text{-}users}' + c_{R\text{-}agency} + q_R c_{R\text{-}agency}' \equiv \chi_R, \tag{4.44}$$

which indeed confirm our expectations. The optimal road tax is the familiar Pigouvian toll. The optimal transit fare is the average agency cost with downward adjustments for any scale economies there might be in user costs (first term) and agency costs (last term). For later reference we introduce the short-hand χ_R for the sum of these three rail-cost terms, even when we depart from first-best conditions; thus χ_R can be thought of as the quasi-first-best toll, *i.e.*, the toll calculated from the first-best formula but perhaps at other values of the quantity variables.

Now consider the second-best solution, where the auto toll is fixed at zero. We set up a Lagrangian that closely resembles (4.32):

$$\Lambda = B(q_A, q_R) - C_A(q_A) - C_R(q_R)$$
$$+ \lambda_A \cdot \left[c_A(q_A) - \partial B/\partial q_A \right] + \lambda_R \cdot \left[c_{R\text{-users}}(q_R) + \tau_R - \partial B/\partial q_R \right]. \tag{4.45}$$

The solution to maximizing this Lagrangian also closely resembles that of (4.32). We find that $\lambda_R = 0$ and, substituting this and the constraints into the first-order conditions with respect to q_A and q_R, we obtain the following optimality conditions:

$$\tau_R - \chi_R + \lambda_A B''_{AR} = 0$$
$$-q_A c'_A + \lambda_A \left(c'_A - B''_{AA} \right) = 0, \tag{4.46}$$

where B''_{AR} and B''_{AA} are second derivatives of $B(q_A, q_R)$. The second-best transit fare is therefore:

$$\tau_R = \chi_R - q_A c'_A \cdot \frac{-B''_{AR}}{c'_A - B''_{AA}}. \tag{4.47}$$

This fare, also derived independently by Ahn (2007), equals the non-internalized marginal cost of transit χ_R, less a term that multiplies the marginal congestion externality on the road ($q_A c'_A$) by a weight depending on demand sensitivities and marginal congestion cost. So far this sounds just like our description of the optimal second-best fare in the two-route problem (4.35). However, the weight is somewhat different, depending this time not only on the slope B''_{AA} of the auto inverse demand curve, but also on the cross-effect B''_{AR}. This weight is equal to the number of new road travelers per rider deterred from rail.[32]

We can understand (4.47) better by considering some special cases. In the case of perfect substitutes, $B''_{AR} = B''_{AA} < 0$ and both are equal to d', the slope of the combined inverse demand curve for auto and rail trips together; in that case (4.47) becomes the same as (4.35) except that (4.47) contains the quasi first-best rail fare χ_R where (4.35) has the quasi first-best road toll. When the two types of travel are imperfect substitutes, the fraction in (4.47) remains positive (so that the entire second term is negative) but it is smaller in absolute value than for the case of perfect substitutes. This is because the cross-derivative in the numerator is smaller in absolute value than the second derivative in the denominator – reflecting the fact that auto and rail trips substitute imperfectly for each other, which also makes it less attractive from an efficiency perspective to lower the rail fare in order to reduce auto congestion. When the cross-elasticity of demand is zero, the fraction in (4.47) becomes zero: quasi first-best pricing of rail transit ($\tau_R = \chi_R$) is then optimal, because automobile use cannot be affected anyway. Finally, when the two goods are complements, so that B''_{AR} reverses sign and becomes positive, the fraction in (4.47) becomes negative and the entire correction term becomes positive: we then raise the rail fare beyond marginal cost in the transit market alone because doing so reduces automobile traffic. (An example of complementarity would be if most auto traffic consisted of people traveling to a subway station.)

It is easy to show that if some non-zero price τ_A is being charged for autos, equation (4.47) still holds with $q_A c'_A$ replaced by $q_A c'_A - \tau_A$. We can also rewrite χ_R in terms of average and marginal rail costs, based on cost function (4.41), and put the result in terms of the per-user transit subsidy σ_R required to cover deficits from second-best pricing. Doing so yields:

$$\sigma_R \equiv c_{R\text{-}agency} - \tau_R = \left(ac_R - mc_R\right) + \left(q_A c_A' - \tau_A\right) \cdot \frac{-B_{AR}''}{c_A' - B_{AA}''}. \qquad (4.48)$$

Note that offering this per-unit subsidy to a profit-maximizing rail operator would not necessarily be second-best nor induce the operator to charge the fare calculated in (4.47), due to the additional constraint that the operator follow its first-order conditions for maximizing profits.

Equation (4.48) clearly shows the two sources of second-best transit subsidies in our model. The first is scale economies: if average cost exceeds marginal cost (for agency and user costs combined), it is desirable to subsidize the difference. The second is automobile congestion: insofar as lowering transit price is effective in reducing congestion costs by drawing away automobile users, it is desirable to use subsidies to encourage that result. The second effect is likely to be large in magnitude in many situations, which leads to an important observation. The size of this component of the optimal transit subsidy depends directly on the degree of underpricing of automobile traffic. If optimal congestion pricing were in place, so that $\tau_A = mec_A$, that term would disappear and the efficient subsidy would be much smaller, thereby greatly ameliorating the incentive problems associated with subsidies. Thus, congestion pricing of automobiles can be viewed as a solution not only to problems of traffic congestion and road finance but also to problems of transit finance, at least if transit is priced according to second-best principles.

This argument could raise the objection that we have ignored the deadweight loss of the taxes required to finance transit subsidies – that is, their adverse effects on economic output over and above the actual revenue raised. This is true, but we have also ignored a less obvious factor that tends to offset such deadweight loss. It is the same phenomenon as discussed in Section 4.2.5, only working in reverse. There, we noted that a Pigouvian *tax*, even though implemented for efficiency reasons, raises the cost of living and thereby lowers the real wage, thus aggravating any deadweight loss caused by using labor taxes to finance public expenditures. By the same reasoning, a *subsidy* that is implemented for efficiency reasons, as described here, reduces the cost of living and thereby tends to ameliorate the deadweight loss from labor taxes. This advantage of subsidies may in large part offset the deadweight loss of financing them – all the more so if transit use is complementary with labor supply so that transit subsidies directly lower the ancillary costs of being employed.

The type of model given here is presented more fully by Glaister (1974), who also considers two time periods with cross-period demand substitutability. Glaister finds that under plausible conditions the automobile externality may be so strong as to warrant reverse peak-load pricing on transit: *i.e.*, setting the fare lower during peak times despite the prevalence during those times of capacity constraints and higher agency expenses.

This and other models of second-best transit pricing have been used to investigate optimal transit subsidies for specific cities. They typically encompass some but not all pertinent factors such as variation in conditions over times and locations, substitutability of demand across times and locations, transit-agency operating policies, externalities from transit vehicles, and crowding on transit vehicles. Consequently, results vary greatly. For example, Glaister and Lewis (1978) estimate optimal rail and bus fares for London at about 50%–60% of marginal operating costs.[33] Viton (1983) finds optimal fares for the San Francisco Bay Area and for Pittsburgh, Pennsylvania, to be virtually zero. Winston and Shirley (1998) find quite the opposite for the US as a whole, with optimal bus and rail fares covering 84% and 97% of marginal operating costs, respectively. For Brussels and London, Van Dender and Proost (2004) estimate optimal transit fares to be nearly zero in peak periods, yet double the current fares in off-peak periods. These conflicting results will probably be resolved only by building a model that incorporates all the factors considered separately in the various studies, and by applying it consistently to several cities.

4.5.2 Fare structure

A complete schedule of marginal-cost prices would distinguish many trip characteristics, including distance, time of day, direction, and density of loadings and boardings. Mohring (1972) provides a comprehensive analysis. In practice, only time of day and trip distance are normally considered as potential bases for price differentials, and even they are often ignored for simplicity. Cervero (1986) claims that the handful of US transit operators that charge peak-hour premia, in order to reflect the higher vehicle and operator costs attributable to peak operations, reap substantial efficiency and financial benefits from doing so.

The fare structure may also be designed to pursue distributional goals, with narrowly defined population subgroups often receiving discounts. As argued by Starrs and Perrins (1989), this is a better approach to distribution than subsidizing transit fares across the board, since many transit users are well-off financially – especially users of high-quality radial commuting services.

4.5.3 Incentive effects of subsidies

In practice, most transit systems in the world are subsidized, whether for reasons discussed here or for other reasons.[34] However, subsidy programs inevitably have rules that distort the decisions of the transit operators.

One such distortion occurs in programs that subsidize capital but not operating costs. Not surprisingly, recipients tend to use a higher ratio of capital to other inputs than would be cost-minimizing. For example, Armour (1980) calculates that an 80% federal capital subsidy cuts in half the bus retirement age that minimizes local costs in Seattle, Washington. Frankena (1987) verifies the same effect empirically for municipal bus systems in Ontario, Canada, by observing the effect of a province-wide capital-subsidy program on scrappage rates. He also finds that an accompanying monitoring program, designed to prevent this result, was ineffective.

Another form of capital bias can occur in the choice among types of transit. It is widely believed that in the US, at least, capital subsidies have encouraged local authorities to build rail systems, which are very capital-intensive, in locations where corridor volumes do not justify them. Interest in these systems persists, even for small metropolitan areas, despite evidence of extremely high costs compared to buses and a record of severely overpredicting demand and underpredicting cost (Pickrell 1989; Flyvbjerg, Skamris Holm and Buhl 2003, 2006).

The capital bias could be reduced by subsidizing operating costs as well. But increasing the total subsidy has its own incentive problems. Several studies have found that subsidies cause costs to increase, for example Savage (2004) – even after controlling for the possible reverse causation (*i.e.*, that high costs require more subsidies). This appears to be largely due to labor costs, including both higher wages and lower productivity. The evidence of other studies, as reviewed by De Borger and Kerstens (2000), suggests that the adverse effect of subsidies is worse when the source of the funds is a level of government remote from the operator, but can be ameliorated by designing incentives into subsidy formulas or contracts. In the US, another effect of subsidy programs has been to encourage inefficient expansion of service to low-density suburbs, a problem exacerbated by the consolidation of transit systems across large parts of metropolitan areas.[35]

These results are discouraging for the prospects of achieving optimal pricing of public transit. We can offer two responses. First, subsidy programs can be designed to minimize adverse incentives, for example by making subsidies a fixed proportion of fare revenues (restricting fare levels) or by basing them on ridership. The use of concession schemes for transit operations might provide an alternative way to reduce the extent and adverse impacts of subsidies, because subsidies that are too large or operations that are too inefficient (in terms of both cost-efficiency and pricing) should reduce the probability of winning the concession. Still, it does so at the expense of other disadvantages, including transaction costs and reduced incentives to invest in technologies that pay off only over a time span exceeding the duration of the concession. Second, the low price-elasticity of transit use (typically measured at −0.3 to −0.4) mitigates the force of our first argument for subsidies, that of scale economies. Indeed, evidence on privately provided transit service suggests that unsubsidized transit is already viable in many markets. Simulation studies suggest it would become much more so if congestion and parking were priced anywhere near their marginal cost, and in that case the other argument for subsidies (to relieve traffic congestion) would also be diminished or eliminated. Thus the solution to institutional difficulties with transit subsidies may be to let prices rise for both transit and competing forms of urban transportation.

4.5.4 Political considerations

We have tried to present the main economic advantages and disadvantages of transit subsidies. But two questions remain. What actually determines the shape of subsidy programs within a democratic political system? And why do these programs persist despite what many observers see as extreme inefficiencies?

Borck (2007) offers several possible answers. The traditional answer is the capture theory: participants in the industry succeed in lobbying legislative, administrative, and regulatory bodies for subsidies in a form that they can partly turn into higher economic returns for themselves. Those participants include construction companies, public employees, engineering firms, consultants, and labor-union leaders. Support for this theory includes the high percentage of subsidies that, as we have noted, is captured by workers in the form of higher wage rates (Winston 2000).

Borck offers two other explanations that depend on differences between the average effects of subsidies and their effect on the median voter, the latter being assumed crucial to political viability. First, suppose demand for public transit is less elastic with respect to income than are tax payments. (For example, demand might be relatively income-inelastic while tax payments might be proportional to income.) Then, because the income distribution is skewed to the right (*i.e.*, more people are far above the median than far below it), the average citizen wants less transit than the median citizen. This could cause the democratic system to provide more transit than is economically justified by conventional criteria (Corneo 1997).

Borck's other explanation is more speculative, but interesting. Urban land markets tend to separate richer and poorer citizens geographically, leading under some conditions to an equilibrium where richer citizens live further from the central part of a city – even in the absence of housing discrimination, crime, or differences in public services. In that case, poorer people pay high land rents in return for accessibility to central city jobs. Those high rents are partly maintained by the strong potential demand from richer people, who would happily move closer to the city center if given the right financial incentives. In these circumstances, any innovation that discourages richer people from coveting central locations would lower central land rents, and thereby benefit poorer residents who are renters (at the expense of their landlords, who in this argument are presumed to have higher incomes). One such innovation could be transit subsidies, which make commuting from a distance relatively more attractive. Borck and Wrede (2005) therefore propose that the median voter is willing to help subsidize transit, even if it is used mainly by richer people, in order to reduce demand for central city housing and thereby reduce central city land rents.

4.6 Conclusions

How important is it to "get the prices right"? And what does it mean? Two recent policy statements offer perspectives on what we can learn from the concepts reviewed in this chapter. Both define "right" as reflecting marginal social costs.

The European Commission's transportation research program (EXTRA 2001) suggests that the concept of marginal social cost (msc) pricing can be translated into practical pricing or taxation measures using existing technology, and that simple second-best approaches such as cordon tolls can achieve most of the benefits of a theoretically optimal solution. It also concludes that pricing measures are effective in changing people's travel behavior.

Delucchi (2000) argues, by contrast, that msc pricing is good for economic efficiency, but that its effects would be too modest to solve pressing problems of traffic congestion and ballooning transit deficits. Furthermore, other important social concerns may alter the prescription – for example, distributional equity, uncertainty, and concerns for the environment, future generations, and quality of life. He also regards certain second-best constraints as barriers to implementation of msc pricing.

We think that both these views are extreme. The constraints that operate in real-world applications will inevitably lower the benefits to be reaped from pricing, more so if one settles for "simple" approaches as suggested by EXTRA. But Delucchi is too pessimistic about our ability to analytically account for many of the social concerns that he fears are being neglected. For example, it is by now well accepted that social costs formerly thought to be unquantifiable, such as pollution and safety externalities, can be incorporated. We have shown here that many feasibility constraints can also be explicitly modeled and taken into account in choosing prices, albeit at some cost in complexity and data requirements. An important benefit of such explicit modeling has been to demonstrate how certain practical limitations posed for simplicity, such as equal tolls at all entry points through a cordon, can be relaxed slightly with major resulting welfare gains – even if perhaps not quite as large as those suggested by EXTRA. Furthermore, tractable models can be built that account for decisions, such as trip scheduling, that have often been taken as given; and doing so considerably changes the nature of optimal pricing.

Does pricing change people's behavior? We agree with Delucchi that under currently foreseeable constraints, marginal-cost pricing will not eliminate congestion and transit deficits. And we certainly agree that it will not, nor should it, reverse the long-standing trend of growing reliance on automobile travel. However, we believe pricing can substantially tame the many problems now associated with both transit and automobile transportation by reducing trip times, increasing their reliability, reducing air pollution and traffic accidents, reducing transit deficits, and facilitating targeted improvements to transit service. The problems are significant, so the potential role of pricing is important.

Our views are well within the range of the professional opinion of economists. However, it would be a mistake to view such opinion as monolithic. Consider, for example, congestion pricing. Nearly all economists would argue that some type of congestion pricing would be good policy. But there is a wide range of opinion about specific features: how complex to make it, how politically feasible it is, how well it would guide investment, whether it should be accompanied by privatization, its distributional effect, and how revenues should be spent (Lindsey 2006). In our view, such diversity is a healthy sign that economics does not neglect practical considerations but rather is struggling with the best way to rigorously account for them.

5   Investment

While pricing as discussed in the previous chapter may be the economist's knee-jerk reflex to transportation problems, most policy makers appear to consider capital investment as a more natural response. From the economic perspective, pricing and investment are both important instruments in managing transportation. We can ask: What are the consequences of optimizing investment, with or without pricing in place?

This chapter adds choice of capital stock to our analytical framework. In the terminology introduced in Chapter 3, this means moving from a short-run to a long-run analysis. Section 5.1 discusses capacity choice for highways. We focus on the interactions and interrelations between pricing and capacity choice, and between toll revenues and capacity cost, under first-best and second-best conditions. We also address the perennial question: Is it possible to build our way out of congestion? Section 5.2 extends the framework to lumpy investments or other discrete policy changes, introducing a very general technique known as cost–benefit analysis.

5.1 Capacity choice for highways

We return to the framework of Section 4.1, in which we sought to maximize the difference between benefits and cost, and now apply it to the choice of highway capacity as well as short-run usage. In this way we can generalize the capacity results of Section 3.5, obtained as part of finding long-run cost functions, to more complex situations. Treating optimal pricing and capacity within the same framework also makes transparent the close relationship between revenues and capacity costs, a relationship of great importance for financing capacity. It also reflects that from the economic perspective, pricing decisions and capacity choices can be evaluated in essentially the same way, namely in terms of their contributions to social welfare.

We first re-derive the rule for determining first-best optimal highway capacity under optimal road pricing, and discuss the relationship between capacity cost and the revenues from optimal pricing – first within a basic model and then considering more complex settings. Next we turn to second-best capacity choice when pricing is constrained to be suboptimal. We will see, for example, that with underpricing, the threat of "induced traffic" causes a downward adjustment of second-best capacity. We also consider the impacts of unpriced congestion elsewhere in a network upon second-best capacity choice for a priced link. We conclude this section by discussing the potential effects of using "naïve" investment rules that ignore behavioral responses to capacity expansion.

5.1.1 Basic results: capacity choice with first-best pricing and static congestion

A basic difference between pricing and capacity choice is that road capacity cannot be varied over the day. We therefore consider the multi-period static model of Section 4.1.1 as our starting point.

Optimizing capacity

We earlier defined social welfare $W = B - C$ for this model as equation (4.13), which we now rewrite making explicit its dependence on road capacity V_K:

$$W = \sum_h q_h \int_0^{V_h} d_h(v)\mathrm{d}v - \sum_h q_h V_h \cdot c_h(V_h; V_K) - \rho \cdot K(V_K). \tag{5.1}$$

Earlier, we maximized W with respect to the vehicle flows V_h and obtained the marginal-cost pricing rule (4.14) for each time period:

$$\tau_h = V_h \cdot \frac{\partial c_h}{\partial V_h}. \tag{5.2}$$

Now, we also maximize W with respect to capacity V_K to obtain an investment rule. Doing so is identical to minimizing C, since B (the first term in W above) does not depend on V_K. This is therefore the case already considered when deriving the long-run cost function of Section 3.5, except that here we do not limit $K(V_K)$ to be linear. The first-order condition for maximizing W therefore yields the same optimal investment rule derived before as equation (3.44):

$$\rho \cdot K'(V_K) = -\sum_h q_h V_h \cdot \frac{\partial c_h(\cdot)}{\partial V_K}. \tag{5.3}$$

The marginal cost of adding capacity is equated to the resulting marginal user-cost savings from lower congestion. These cost savings are calculated holding flows V_h constant: the envelope theorem assures this is correct because we are dealing with a marginal change from a first-best optimal starting point. That is, because marginal benefits and marginal social costs of flows are equalized through optimal pricing according to (5.2), any indirect marginal benefits or costs of capacity changes via traffic flows have zero net welfare effects. We will see later, in Section 5.1.3, that such indirect effects do have to be taken into account when first-best pricing is not in place.

Self-financing of capital cost

The congestion fees derived in Section 4.1 may be viewed as charges for the use of capacity, which is scarce because it is expensive. It is natural, then, to ask whether the fees will bring in enough revenue to cover the cost of capacity.

By combining investment rule (5.3) with pricing rule (5.2), we can relate total revenue to total cost. To do so, we need first to relate $\partial c_h / \partial V_h$ to $\partial c_h / \partial V_K$. This is easy for any model in which c_h depends only on the volume–capacity ratio V_h/V_K, a condition interpretable as *constant returns to scale in congestion technology*. Under this assumption we can use the quotient rule and chain rule of differentiation to show that:

$$V_K \cdot \frac{\partial c_h(\cdot)}{\partial V_K} = -V_h \cdot \frac{\partial c_h(\cdot)}{\partial V_h},$$

which is an example of Euler's theorem.[1] Under optimal pricing and capacity choice as defined by equations (5.2) and (5.3), we get the following equation for total revenue R:

$$R \equiv \sum_h q_h V_h \tau_h = -\sum_h q_h V_h V_K \cdot \frac{\partial c_h}{\partial V_K} = V_K \rho \cdot K'(V_K). \tag{5.4}$$

This can be simplified by using the economies-of-scale indicator s_K introduced in Section 3.5.3, which was defined as the ratio of average to marginal capacity cost:

$$s_K = \frac{K(V_K)}{V_K \cdot K'(V_K)}. \tag{5.5}$$

Using (5.5), we find that (5.4) implies the following "degree of self-financing":

$$\frac{R}{\rho \cdot K(V_K)} = \frac{1}{s_K}. \tag{5.6}$$

The ratio of total revenue to total capacity cost is equal to $1/s_K$, which is also the elasticity of capacity cost with respect to capacity. We refer to this as the *self-financing result*.

Optimal fees therefore exactly cover the cost of providing capacity if there are *neutral scale economies in capacity provision* ($s_K = 1$); we call this equality *exact self-financing*. A deficit arises under economies of scale ($s_K > 1$), and a surplus under diseconomies of scale ($s_K < 1$). This was demonstrated for transportation by Mohring and Harwitz (1962), and is simply an extension of the result in equation (3.4) to this more complex formulation of capacity costs and (congestion) pricing. Note that the self-financing result applies no matter how $K(V_K)$ is constructed, so long as s_K is defined as above. For example, $K(V_K)$ may or may not entail constant input prices. Of course, for the result to represent actual financial balance for a highway provider, $K(V_K)$ must reflect the provider's actual costs.

The benchmark result of exact self-financing when $s_K = 1$ thus requires three technical assumptions to be fulfilled: (I) constants returns to scale in the congestion technology; (II) neutral scale economies in capacity provision; and (III) perfect divisibility of capacity. How likely are these assumptions to be satisfied? As far as assumptions I and II are concerned, one can freely choose the units of capacity to satisfy II, which means that what eventually matters is only the combined effect of the two assumptions. Our earlier discussion in Section 3.5.3 suggests that, overall, there are probably mild economies of scale in major cities, which may disappear altogether in very large cities. Thus the degree of self-financing in (5.6) may be close to one.

Condition III seems unrealistic on the face of it, given that the number of lanes of a road must be an integer. But, as noted in Section 3.5, capacity can be fine-tuned in various ways such as widening lanes, adding shoulders, or straightening the road, so it is less discrete than might first appear. Nevertheless, indivisibility of capacity is likely to be important for sub-urban streets and rural roads. As we shall see shortly, the exact results of this section break down when capacity is imperfectly divisible, although the amount of deviation from exact self-financing is not necessarily very large as long as conditions I and II remain fulfilled.

Implications of the self-financing result

It is useful to note some policy implications of the self-financing result, before we describe how it holds up under various generalizations of the model. Our discussion focuses on situations where assumptions I–III are reasonable approximations so that exact self-financing nearly applies.

First, when applicable, the exact self-financing results provide a necessary condition for optimal capacities and prices – namely, financial balance when capital costs are properly accounted for – that is more readily observable than variables entering the first-order conditions for optimal capacities and prices. Thus it provides a practical check on whether the road system is efficient. Note, though, that there will be many possible combinations of capacity and toll that produce the same (zero) profit for the operator, only one of which is efficient. Financial balance is therefore no guarantee of efficiency. Second, the self-financing result implies that other taxes are not needed to sustain the road sector, which is good for economy-wide efficiency because other taxes are likely to cause distortions. Third, it promotes public acceptability of road pricing because road finance can be perceived as fair (since roads are paid for by users) and transparent (since it depends on observable money flows). Finally, under certain conditions, the exact self-financing result provides an iterative way for a road authority (or private providers) to achieve first-best optimal capacity: namely, by expanding road capacity whenever short-run optimal congestion pricing yields revenues that exceed the incremental capital cost of capacity.[2] The market thus indicates whether expansion is socially warranted, just as in competitive private markets. The proviso of optimal pricing is an important one, however; unless there is perfect competition among road operators, an unlikely scenario, private operators would have incentives to price according to other objectives, which destroys the equality between optimal revenues and capacity cost.

We warn against the erroneous conclusion that when assumptions I–III are fulfilled, all revenues from optimal congestion tolling should be used to finance further capacity expansions. This interpretation of the self-financing result confuses current investment expenditures with the annualized cost of capital. Furthermore, the annualized cost of capital coincides with financial outlays only if the financing mechanisms for capital recovery exactly reproduce social costs, which is typically not the case due to taxes on capital, explicit or hidden capital subsidies, financial mechanisms for risk-sharing, inadequate accounting standards, separation of ownership and control of private corporations, and even financial fraud.

Highway improvements designed to increase free-flow speeds or to improve safety, independent of capacity, do not engender congestion fees under optimal pricing and therefore are not included in the self-financing result. (Equivalently, one could say that they are a source of fixed cost in the function relating capital cost to capacity, therefore creating economies of scale in capacity.) But many such improvements simultaneously increase capacity. It is possible that a substantial portion of highway investments in rural or even suburban areas falls into this category, and hence need to be subsidized (Larsen 1993). Unfortunately, this question has received little attention. Jansson (1984, Chapter 10) models it as a type of scale economy, while Larsen treats it as a quality variable that is produced jointly along with capacity. To better understand this issue, we need empirically estimated models in which safety and free-flow speed, as well as capacity, are affected by capital investment. Such models might reveal that uniform design standards, such as characterize the US Interstate Highway System, result in excessive free-flow speeds in urban areas where their production is presumably more expensive.

5.1.2 Self-financing in more complex settings

This section considers a number of complications in which the self-financing result carries over in some form, either exactly or as an approximation under certain conditions. Our discussion follows and sometimes draws from earlier reviews such as Lindsey and Verhoef (2000), de Palma and Lindsey (2005), and Verhoef (2005).

Discrete capacity

Especially for smaller roads, assumption III involving continuous capacity will often be unrealistic. Discreteness of capacity generally causes the self-financing result to break down. This is most easily seen for a road for which demand is so small that it will never be congested once constructed at minimum feasible capacity. The revenues from optimal road pricing are then zero, and the road cannot be self-financing.

Figure 5.1 illustrates the problem more generally. The heavy solid line marked *lratc* shows the long-run average total cost, where the "total" means that it includes both average user cost c and per-user capacity cost $\rho \cdot K / V$ (with K optimized, in a discrete fashion, with respect to V). This *lratc* curve is the lower envelope of many U-shaped short-run average total cost $atc(l)$ curves, each valid for a different discrete number of lanes (denoted l). A different short-run marginal cost function $srmc(l)$ applies for every segment of the *lratc* curve, and each $srmc(l)$ curve cuts the *lratc* curve through its relevant local minimum. In any short-run optimum, the optimal toll is the difference between $srmc$ and c (with c not drawn in the figure), and the per-user capacity cost is the difference between atc and c. Thus, if V is such that $srmc < atc$ at the optimum, a deficit occurs; if $srmc > atc$, there is a surplus. Only by coincidence would the inverse demand function (also not drawn in the figure) cut the

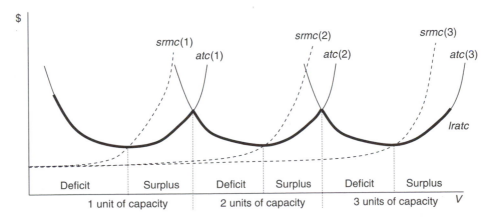

Figure 5.1 Surpluses and deficits with discrete capacity.

relevant *srmc* curve at its intersection with the associated *atc*, so that exact self-financing would apply.

Nevertheless, if the general trend of *lratc* is neither up nor down, we have a discrete analog of neutral scale economies and it is more or less equally probable to have a deficit or surplus with optimal pricing and capacity. In that case, the self-financing result will approximately hold under certain conditions likely to prevail in practice. First, if the number of possible capacity values is large and the difference between them small, then *lratc* will approach a horizontal line and self-financing will approximately apply. Second, if demand grows steadily over time, periods of deficit and surplus will tend to alternate, causing the discounted net deficit or surplus to be small. Third, on a network of many roads, deficits and surpluses on individual roads can be pooled, causing most of them to cancel. These considerations make the discreteness issue less important in practice than would appear from Figure 5.1.

Short-run dynamics

We next consider dynamic congestion. Does the self-financing result of equation (5.6) remain intact? Arnott and Kraus (1998a) have shown that this is indeed the case under rather general conditions.

The basic bottleneck model for a single period, extended to incorporate elastic demand, can illustrate this. Recall from equation (4.25) that the average user cost under optimal pricing for this model amounts to $\bar{c}_g^1 = \bar{c}_S^1 = \frac{1}{2}\delta \cdot Q / V_K$. This equation is proportional to the total number of trips Q and to the inverse of capacity V_K, implying that the congestion technology exhibits constant returns to scale. The appropriate social objective can next be written as a single-period variant of (5.1), with q_h normalized to 1 and Q replacing V_h. Because the average optimal time-varying toll $\bar{\tau}$ is equal to $\bar{c}_g^1$, it is also equal to $Q \cdot \partial \bar{c}_g^1 / \partial Q$. Equation (5.2) therefore remains valid (with adapted notation). Because (5.3) also remains valid (again with adapted notation), the self-financing result of equation (5.6) again applies.

Surprisingly, the result goes through even if the time pattern of tolls is not optimal, so long as the toll level is optimized subject to whatever constraint on the time pattern applies. Recall from equation (4.36) that second-best optimal flat pricing for the basic bottleneck model with elastic demand can be determined by solving its reduced-form time-independent representation as if it were a static model with an average user-cost function $\bar{c}_g^0 = \delta \cdot Q / V_K$. Again this function exhibits constant returns to scale in the congestion technology, and the result is derived just as for the case of an optimal time-varying toll. The same is true for coarse tolls. We see, then, that the essential aspect of a pricing scheme that makes the self-financing result applicable is not that prices be first-best, but rather that prices equal marginal costs. As explained in Chapter 4, flat pricing of a bottleneck involves a toll equal to the marginal external cost given that departure times are not affected by the toll. It thus qualifies as marginal cost pricing, although it is second-best in nature, and it leads to self-financing under conditions I–III.

Long-run dynamics

Arnott and Kraus (1998b) consider a variety of situations when capacity need not be fixed over the period of analysis, accounting for depreciation, maintenance, adjustment costs, and irreversibility of investments. They find that the self-financing theorem remains valid in present-value terms, provided that the size of capacity additions is optimized conditional on the timing of investments. This holds irrespective of whether capacity is added continuously or in discrete units, and whether or not the timing of investments is optimal.

Networks

Yang and Meng (2002) demonstrate that if the self-financing result holds for every individual link in an optimally priced network, it holds also for the network as a whole, despite the demand interdependencies across links that result from user equilibrium. This is another example of the envelope theorem at work: we can ignore the indirect effects of policy variables (link tolls, link capacities) upon other markets (other links) in welfare analysis provided optimality conditions on these other markets are fulfilled. In other words, one can then analyze each link individually, and derive (5.6) for it, without worrying about network spillovers.[3] Section 5.1.3 will show that this is no longer true when some links are not optimally priced.

Heterogeneity

Arnott and Kraus (1998a) address heterogeneity across users and find that it does not undermine the self-financing theorem as long as marginal cost pricing applies to all users. But if practical considerations prevent tolls from being differentiated optimally among users, for example with flat pricing in the model of Figure 4.4, the self-financing result generally breaks down.

User heterogeneity in relation to capacity choice also raises the question of whether segregation of traffic onto different roads or lanes is desirable. Such segregation generally becomes more attractive as cross-congestion effects (congestion that one group inflicts on another) become stronger relative to own-congestion effects (congestion inflicted on members of one's own group). If cross-effects are high in both directions for all pairs of groups, appropriate segregation can arise spontaneously; but if they predominate in only certain directions, regulation or pricing may be required to bring about an optimal degree of segregation. Consider, for example, the case where cars travel faster than trucks, due for example to safety regulations or vehicle capabilities. Separation may then be desirable, depending on discreteness of capacity and any resulting cost premium. But these cross-effects are asymmetric, since passenger cars prefer to avoid sharing lanes with trucks but not vice versa. Thus lane restrictions for trucks, truck-only roads, or lane-specific truck tolls may be desirable in order to enforce separation.

Another possibility is to segregate users by value of time, enabling the planner to optimize toll and capacity separately for two substitute facilities. Simulations by Verhoef and Small (2004) and Small, Winston and Yan (2006) suggest that the benefits of such segregation are negligible if first-best pricing can be practiced, but can be substantial if one is restricted to no pricing or to second-best pricing of just one roadway (*i.e.*, priced express lanes). Small, Winston and Yan also find that segregation permits a compromise pricing scheme, involving differentiated tolls on both roadways, that achieves higher welfare than second-best pricing of an express lane, with much lower direct impacts on users (measured as consumer surplus loss before accounting for revenue uses). All these results depend critically on the existence of substantial differences among users in value of time, differences which seem to exist empirically both in the Netherlands and in southern California according to empirical evidence presented in the above-mentioned papers.

Yet another possibility is to segregate vehicles with different numbers of passengers by reserving certain lanes for high-occupancy vehicles (HOVs). These lanes may be on the highway itself or on metered entry ramps. Mohring (1979) and Small (1983) estimate the welfare gains from such restricted lanes on city streets and on expressways, respectively, finding substantial welfare gains under somewhat ideal conditions. Dahlgren (1998), however, finds that only in rather exceptional circumstances does an HOV lane outperform a general-purpose lane: namely, when there is high initial congestion and when the initial proportion of vehicles that are HOVs falls within a rather narrow range. Small, Winston and Yan (2006) get more favorable results for HOV lanes, but they also depend strongly on the factors identified by Dahlgren and on relatively highly elastic demand. The results stated above assume no pricing is possible; if instead marginal-cost pricing is in effect, then the welfare gain from segregating HOVs is essentially negligible (Small 1983; Yang and Huang 1999).

Road maintenance

So far, we have ignored road damage, road maintenance cost, and the choice of durability (*e.g.*, thickness of the pavement) in construction. These questions are treated in some detail by Small, Winston and Evans (1989) and de Palma and Lindsey (2005). Here we focus on implications for self-financing.

Newbery (1989) considers whether the combination of optimized congestion charges and road-damage charges would cover the cost of constructing and maintaining roads, taking into account maintenance costs due to pavement damage and the extra construction costs undertaken to limit such damage. Newbery shows that self-financing holds in this broader sense, provided that heavy vehicles uniformly affect user and maintenance costs on the entire width of the road. (This extra condition may be thought of as an extension of neutral scale economies of road use.) Under these circumstances, capital costs, even those incurred to make the road stronger, are proportional to capacity and so are recovered through congestion charges just as in the basic self-financing theorem.[4] Maintenance costs incurred due to heavy vehicles (*e.g.*, periodic repaving) are recovered through road-damage charges, following the same logic – road strength is optimized by balancing the extra capital cost with the maintenance-cost savings. User costs due to road damage (*e.g.*, damage to vehicle tires) do not create an additional externality on average over a network, given certain rather strong technical assumptions about traffic growth and the criteria for undertaking maintenance; therefore they create no additional charges or revenues under optimal pricing (Newbery 1988).

Small, Winston and Evans (1989) reach a similar conclusion empirically, without adopting Newbery's assumptions. They treat congestion and road damage in a multi-product framework, where the products are number of trips and the total weight of their loads (more precisely, the number of standardized units of road damage done by the heavy loads). Even though they find substantial economies of scale in providing for each product separately, this is balanced by diseconomies of scope in that the presence of heavy trucks makes it more expensive to handle large volumes of passenger cars. (Diseconomies of scope imply that if there were no indivisibilities, it would be cheaper to segregate trucks and cars.) Overall, neutral scale economies approximately hold.

Variable input prices

Contrary to the conventional assumptions, in urban areas the supply function of land for roads (*i.e.*, its price as a function of amount purchased) is likely to be upward-sloping, since taking more land for roads drives up its scarcity value for other uses. The distinction between returns to scale (a property of production functions) and economies of scale (a property of cost functions) then becomes important. A general-equilibrium analysis by Berechman and Pines (1991) demonstrates that constant returns to scale in the production function for roads implies that optimal revenues equal imputed costs, which include the amount of land multiplied by its equilibrium price (once road capacity is optimized). For a road authority that has to take prices as given, imputed land costs would coincide with actual land costs. But a road authority with market power in the land market will account for the rising supply function in its cost function, which will then show a degree of scale economies, s_K, that is less than the degree of returns to scale in production. Small (1999a) shows that optimal revenues are then determined by degree of scale economies, s_K, of the actual cost function, just as in equation (5.6). Thus self-financing still applies: if $s_K = 1$, revenues equal costs when prices and capacity are optimal.

This point has practical relevance. As discussed in Section 3.5.3, many studies ignoring the rising supply price of land find economies of scale in road building. To the extent that these economies are offset by the rising supply price of land, the end result is closer to one where self-financing applies.

Other externalities

The self-financing result equates revenues from congestion charges to capacity costs. That equality remains even if other road charges are levied to cover externalities affecting non-users, such as pedestrian injuries, noise, and air pollution. These charges do not change the user-cost or capacity-cost functions, so the relationships already established for congestion remain valid although they will now describe equilibrium at a different (lower) traffic volume. Thus if conditions I–III hold, optimal congestion charges exactly cover capacity costs and the revenues from charges for externalities affecting others create a financial surplus. If externalities other than congestion also affect average user cost (*e.g.*, accidents), and if those externalities are included in marginal-cost prices, then self-financing still holds provided technical conditions analogous to I–III hold for these other externalities as well.

Demand uncertainty

How are capacity rules affected if the demand for travel that will apply is not known with certainty? Such uncertainty can take various forms. Suppose the inverse demand function in period h can take on different positions on different days, with known probabilities – as in the model of Section 3.5.2. The self-financing result then continues to hold, both in expected value terms and asymptotically over a sufficiently long planning period, under responsive pricing and perfect information. The proof in Section 5.1.1 applies with h reinterpreted as an index also indicating states of nature in a certain time period, so that q_h indicates the duration of the period multiplied by the probability of the state.

Alternatively, future demand conditions may depend on exogenous developments that are still uncertain at the time of investment. Again, the road operator may have expectations that take the form of a set of demand functions with associated probabilities, but now not all of them will become real at some moment in the future. First-best pricing now depends on which demand function(s) materialize; it will lead to a deficit if demands are below expectations (since both the tolls and the use levels are lower than expected), and to a surplus in the opposite case. The *expected* surplus, however, is still zero, because the interpretation of

q_h remains as just given. An operator that faces this type of uncertainty, who holds unbiased expectations, and who can pool uncorrelated risks of many roads may thus expect a zero budget over the entire network provided $s_K = 1$.

5.1.3 Second-best highway capacity

Capacity choice under first-best pricing provides an important benchmark, but in practice investment decisions are made under more constrained conditions. We now ask how this affects capacity choice and the degree of self-financing. We first consider suboptimal pricing on the road whose capacity is being chosen, and then on other roads within a network. Finally, we address the case where public funds can be raised only at some efficiency cost to the economy.

Capacity choice with suboptimal pricing

Several authors consider capacity choice in a second-best world where the optimal congestion fee cannot be charged.[5] The problem can be analyzed within the multi-period static model by fixing arbitrarily determined tolls τ_h^A for each period h. The objective function (5.1) is then augmented by adding a Lagrangian term for this constraint, becoming:

$$\Lambda = \sum_h q_h \cdot \int_0^{V_h} d_h(v)\,dv - \sum_h q_h V_h \cdot c_h(V_h; V_K) - \rho \cdot K(V_K)$$
$$+ \sum_h \lambda_h \cdot \left[c_h(V_h; V_K) + \tau_h^A - d_h(V_h) \right]. \tag{5.7}$$

The first-order conditions for maximizing (5.7) with respect to V_h, V_K and λ_h can be solved to yield the following second-best investment rule:

$$\rho \cdot K'(V_K) = -\sum_h (q_h V_h - \lambda_h) \cdot \frac{\partial c_h}{\partial V_K}, \quad h = 1, \ldots, H$$
$$\text{with: } \lambda_h = q_h \cdot \frac{V_h \cdot (\partial c_h / \partial V_h) - \tau_h^A}{(\partial c_h / \partial V_h) - d_h'(V_h)}. \tag{5.8}$$

The second-best policy rule deviates from the first-best rule unless the Lagrange multipliers are all zero. That would require, in each period h, that toll τ_h^A be set optimally or that demand be perfectly inelastic ($d_h' = -\infty$). We assume finite d_h' for purposes of discussion. Then if τ_h^A is below its optimal value, λ_h must be positive and the marginal benefits of capacity expansion are calculated as if fewer than $q_h V_h$ travelers benefit from the expansion. (With overcharging, the opposite occurs.) This reflects that with undercharging, the social benefit of an additional user is smaller than the private benefit because of the congestion externality. Limiting capacity is one way to discourage this additional user from entering the road.

While the Lagrangian multipliers in equations (5.8) reduce second-best capacity below its first-best value at any given value of flows V, those flows are of course different from their first-best values. Typically in the period of undercharging, the flow will be greater than the first-best value, which has the opposite effect on (5.8). Therefore, whether in the end second-best capacity is smaller or larger than first-best capacity depends on demand and cost elasticities and their impact on equilibrium use levels (d'Ouville and McDonald 1990). Still, Wheaton (1978) shows that if the toll starts at its first-best level and is reduced marginally, optimal capacity increases – at least in a single-period model. Wilson (1983) derives more general conditions, which he judges to be reasonable, under which second-best road capacity with underpricing exceeds the first-best level. Thus it seems likely that one should compensate for lack of pricing by building more and bigger roads. Or to put it another way: optimal pricing would probably allow us to get by with less pavement.

The self-financing result of equation (5.6) generally breaks down under arbitrary pricing and second-best capacity choice. This is of course obvious for the case where tolls are zero.

Induced traffic

Whether or not second-best capacity is greater than first-best, equation (5.8) shows clearly that a naïve application of cost–benefit analysis to an incremental capacity increase will mislead if there is underpricing (so that $\lambda_h > 0$). Capacity should then not be expanded just because travel-time savings to existing users would be valued at more than the cost of expansion. Rather, the marginal social benefit of such expansion is lowered by the fact that expansion reduces the equilibrium generalized price and therefore attracts new traffic, known as *induced traffic* or *induced demand*.[6]

The problem is especially acute if demand is highly elastic. To see why, consider again the left panel of Figure 4.1, illustrating equilibrium congestion in a simple static model. If the inverse demand curve were nearly flat, neither shifting it to the left (demand-limiting policies) nor shifting the cost curve to the right (capacity-augmenting policies) would make much difference to the equilibrium average cost. The second-best investment rule in (5.8) reflects this ineffectiveness as follows: with perfectly elastic demand and zero tolls, $\lambda_h = q_h V_h$ and the right-hand side of (5.8) – which expresses the marginal benefit of capacity expansion – is zero. The reason is that any expansion will be filled up with new traffic whose marginal benefit (height of the inverse demand curve) equals its average cost, so that the new traffic yields no net gain in social surplus. Furthermore, infra-marginal traffic does not benefit because, with perfectly elastic demand, equilibrium average cost does not change.

Even in less extreme situations, induced traffic in a situation like that of the left panel of Figure 4.1 represents the release of potential traffic that is deterred by congestion itself. Such potential traffic consists of people who, because of congestion, now choose an alternative route, mode, time of day, or home or workplace location, or do not travel at all. It is sometimes called *latent demand* because in the initial situation it is unobserved; yet, in a sense, it lies just beneath the surface. Unfortunately, latent demand is prevalent in just those areas where capacity expansion seems most needed – namely, in high-density urban areas during times when congestion is severe. Under such conditions, the release of latent demand is likely to undo much of the congestion relief that capacity expansion or demand reduction might otherwise bring about.

The undesirable filling up of new unpriced capacity by induced traffic is sometimes called the "law of highway congestion." It forms the basis for important debates concerning highway investment policy.[7] While not usually true in its extreme form (where new capacity is completely filled by induced traffic), it can come uncomfortably close to the truth

(Downs 1962; Thomson 1977). Smeed (1968) opines that in British cities, "the amount of traffic adjusts itself to a barely tolerable speed. [...] if it were not for the inhibiting effects of congestion, we might well have 4 to 5 times as much traffic in Central London as we have now" (pp. 41, 58). The Standing Advisory Committee on Trunk Road Assessment (SACTRA 1994) provided more systematic evidence, causing a major rethinking of road-expansion policies in the UK.

More formal empirical evidence for induced traffic is now available, most often expressed as the elasticity of traffic with respect to road capacity. (A positive elasticity indicates at least some induced traffic, while an elasticity of 1.0 would imply the fundamental law of highway congestion.) Naturally this elasticity depends on specifics: it is expected to be larger when initial congestion is high, when the facility is a small part of a larger network, and when measured over a long enough time period for many adjustments to take place. The best empirical studies account, among other things, for the possibility that road capacity is endogenous (with road authorities assumed to respond, logically enough, to actual or anti-cipated traffic); accounting for endogeneity somewhat reduces the measured elasticity, but still it seems to be quite high. Goodwin (1996) reviews several studies with estimates of short- and long-run elasticities averaging 0.20 and 0.77. Noland (2001) estimates short-run (five-year) and long-run elasticities of around 0.5 and 0.8, whereas Cervero and Hansen (2002) find an elasticity of 0.79 that applies over a six-year period.[8] Cervero (2003), using data that enable him to control for traffic increases from other causes, finds an elasticity of traffic with respect to capacity of 0.4 over a seven- to eight-year period, with one-fourth of that due to land-use shifts.

As already noted in connection with the left panel of Figure 4.1, the problem of releasing latent demand occurs not only with policies that shift the cost curve to the right, but also with those that shift the demand curve to the left. Thus demand management policies and improved transit, when implemented as measures to relieve congestion, are also vulnerable to induced traffic. Empirical evidence supports this conclusion. Sherret (1975) analyzes trip rates on the Bay Area Rapid Transit (BART) line between Oakland and San Francisco during the first few months after it opened, and on the parallel San Francisco–Oakland Bay Bridge; he finds that the diversion of 8,750 automobile trips to BART was soon followed by the generation of 7,000 new automobile trips, so that "traffic levels at the busiest hours showed only small reductions" (pp. xii–xiii).

One reason for high latent demand during peak periods is substitutability among travel at different times. For example, nearly half the latent demand reported by Kroes, Antonisse and Bexelius (1987) was from "travel taking place at times other than the desired time" (p. 237). Other evidence comes from before-and-after studies of major capacity changes. The opening of a section of the M25 London Orbital Motorway apparently caused peak narrowing at a main Thames River crossing (Mackie and Bonsall 1989, p. 415). By the same token, peak periods tend to spread when demand grows faster than road capacity. In London between 1962 and 1981, a time when downtown traffic increased dramatically with little new street capacity, midday speeds actually became slower than peak speeds (Mogridge *et al.* 1987, p. 297). A shifting peak is, of course, precisely what is predicted by equilibrium models with endogenous scheduling such as we reviewed in Section 3.4.3. Obviously the phenomenon reduces the attraction of static models that assume predefined periods of fixed duration with constant demands.

In our example using the left panel of Figure 4.1 with a perfectly elastic demand curve, capacity expansion has no benefits. In more realistic cases, there are benefits from expansion because some of the induced traffic previously used other roads or time periods that were underpriced. Relieving conditions at those alternate locations or times may confer substantial benefits to other travelers. Thus, for example, if a road expansion causes the peak period to narrow, those who travel at adjacent times may see big reductions in travel times.

Some people think the "fundamental law of traffic congestion" negates all policies aimed at reducing traffic, including pricing. But this is not true even if the "fundamental law" is true, because pricing operates on the demand and supply curves differently than other policies. Again returning to the left panel of Figure 4.1, pricing does not shift the demand or cost curves to the right or left, but rather inserts a wedge between the cost curve and the generalized price perceived by users. Thus, it does not attract latent demand and it is able to reduce congestion and produce welfare gains. Furthermore, if pricing is in place, capacity expansion is no longer frustrated by latent demand, as can be seen from the investment rule in (5.8): the closer τ_h^A approaches its optimal value, the smaller is λ_h and therefore the higher are the marginal benefits from capacity expansion for given flows. Thus pricing is especially well suited to overcome the policy limitations imposed by induced traffic.

Does the existence of induced demand mean it is impossible to "build our way out of congestion"? Not really – with realistic demand elasticities there is some amount of capacity that will eliminate severe congestion. The relevant questions are whether that amount is affordable in practice, and whether capacity expansion is an efficient response to the problem. Affordability depends on the demand elasticity and the costs of expansion; we suspect that satisfactory congestion relief through capacity expansion may be practical in many smaller cities but is doubtful in large ones – although even in large cities some expansion may well have great benefits. As for efficiency, at current demands and capacities, pricing often seems a much more efficient solution to congestion than further capacity expansion; if pricing is ruled out politically, then some capacity expansion may be the next most efficient policy, but the optimal amount of such expansion may well leave a great deal of congestion in place.

Network spillovers

Another type of second-best situation occurs when it is not the toll on the road itself that is imperfect, but the tolls on other roads in the network. We consider the case where tolls on other roads are completely absent, and discuss how this affects a road's second-best optimal capacity, as well as the degree of self-financing. It turns out that the answer depends on whether the unpriced capacity is parallel to or in series with the road whose capacity is under consideration. (More generally, the question is whether travel on the unpriced links is a substitute or complement to that on the link in question.) We therefore consider two extreme cases, defining for each a simple two-link network in which both toll and capacity can be optimized for one link (*T*), while an unpriced link (*U*) of fixed capacity exists either parallel to or in series with link *T*. We simplify by considering a single period only, whose duration q_h is normalized to one.

Consider first the case where the links are parallel. We already treated pricing for this case using the Lagrangian function (4.32); we need only modify it to include capacities and their costs:

$$\Lambda = \int_0^{V_T+V_U} d(v)\,\mathrm{d}v - V_T \cdot c_T(V_T; V_{KT}) - V_U \cdot c_U(V_U; V_{KU}) - \rho \cdot K_T(V_{KT}) - \rho \cdot K_U(V_{KU})$$
$$+ \lambda_T \cdot \left[c_T(V_T; V_{KT}) + \tau_T - d(V_T+V_U) \right] + \lambda_U \cdot \left[c_U(V_U; V_{KU}) - d(V_T+V_U) \right], \qquad (5.9)$$

where V_{KT} and V_{KU} are the capacities of the two links (with V_{KU} fixed) and where $d(\cdot)$ is the inverse demand function for the entire corridor. The first-order conditions (with respect to V_T, V_U, V_{KT}, λ_U, and λ_T) can be solved to yield:

$$\tau_T = V_T \cdot \frac{\partial c_T}{\partial V_T} - V_U \cdot \frac{\partial c_U}{\partial V_U} \cdot \frac{-d'}{(\partial c_U / \partial V_U) - d'} \tag{5.10}$$

$$\rho \cdot K_T'(V_{KT}) = -V_T \cdot \frac{\partial c_T}{\partial V_{KT}}. \tag{5.11}$$

The second-best toll (5.10) is the same as second-best toll (4.35), while the second-best capacity rule (5.11) is identical to the first-best rule (5.3). Thus the toll on link T is set to account for the underpriced parallel link, while the capacity of link T is set to minimize the cost incurred by its users.

Because the investment rule for V_{KT} is the same as the first-best rule, we already know that revenues under a first-best toll would balance capacity cost under the conditions for the self-financing result. But revenues under the second-best toll (5.10) are smaller than this. Therefore the self-financing result breaks down. This is basically because the second-best distortion leads to a downward adjustment in pricing compared to marginal external cost pricing.

How does the second-best highway capacity compare to first-best capacity in this example? We are not aware of any systematic analyses of this question. We can say something about the case where capacities on both links can be optimized. Suppose users are homogeneous and the links are equally long; then the optimal capacity of the untolled link is zero so that, effectively, the link is eliminated while the tolled link is expanded to first-best tolled capacity. This result would change with sufficient dispersion in values of time, since it may then be desirable to leave an untolled link available for the lowest-value-of-time drivers. However, the relatively small numerical difference that Verhoef and Small (2004) find between optimal tolls on parallel links for heterogeneous drivers suggests that the second-best capacity for an untolled link would still be very small.

Now suppose the unpriced link U is in series with link T, with a single origin at one end and single destination at the other so that all traffic must use both links. The Lagrangian function is now:

$$\Lambda = \int_0^V d(v)\,dv - V \cdot \left[c_T(V, V_{KT}) + c_U(V, V_{KU}) \right] - \rho \cdot K_T(V_{KT}) - \rho \cdot K_U(V_{KU})$$
$$+ \lambda \cdot \left[c_T(V, V_{KT}) + c_U(V, V_{KU}) + \tau_T - d(V) \right]. \tag{5.12}$$

The first-order conditions with respect to V, V_{KT}, and λ imply:

$$\tau_T = V \cdot \left(\frac{\partial c_T}{\partial V} + \frac{\partial c_U}{\partial V} \right) \tag{5.13}$$

$$\rho \cdot K_T'(V_{KT}) = -V \cdot \frac{\partial c_T}{\partial V_{KT}}. \tag{5.14}$$

Not surprisingly, the toll rule (5.13) perfectly internalizes the congestion externalities on both links jointly, and therefore exceeds the first-best toll for link T whenever link U is congested. The investment rule again has the familiar first-best form. With a first-best investment rule and a toll higher than the first-best value, we can see that now a surplus occurs at link T, compared to the degree of self-financing as given in (5.6). As a matter of fact, in this simple example the toll would raise sufficient revenues to finance the entire network if both capacities are optimized with neutral scale economics.

Unpriced congestion elsewhere in the network therefore does not seem to affect the optimal investment rule for a tolled road. Of course, because flows will differ between first-best and second-best optima, the equilibrium *size* of the second-best capacity for link T is generally different from first-best. The self-financing result also breaks down. The two examples above suggest that, for links in larger networks, surpluses will result if the network contains mostly unpriced complements, and deficits will result if the network contains mostly unpriced substitutes.

Marginal cost of public funds

As a third source of second-best pricing and capacity choice, we consider the case, also discussed in Section 4.2.5, when it is costly to raise government funds because taxes are distortionary. This situation can be quantified in terms of the *marginal cost of public funds* (MCF), defined as the cost to society of raising one dollar of tax revenue. A value greater than one indicates an imperfect, distortionary tax system. In practice, the value need not be a constant but may depend on the specific taxes or expenditure categories affected by a proposed transportation investment (Mayeres and Proost 2001; Kleven and Kreiner 2006).

Intuition tells us that when the relevant MCFs exceed one, an optimal policy would try to increase revenues from congestion tolls as this could replace other distortionary taxes as a revenue-generating mechanism. But as noted in Section 4.2.5, this intuition is counteracted by the fact that congestion tolls themselves aggravate the distortion (insofar as it is caused by taxes on labor income) by raising the cost of living, thus making a dollar of earned income less valuable. Intuition also tells us that a high MCF would reduce the desirability of expanding road capacity at public expense; although again, this effect is at least partially offset by the fact that road capacity reduces congestion, which effectively reduces the cost of living. More in-depth analyses are provided by Mayeres and Proost (2001), Parry and Bento (2001), and Proost, De Borger and Koskenoja (2007).

We can extend our model to show how investment rules are affected. We allow the MCF to take one value $(1 + \lambda_\tau)$ for toll revenues, and another value $(1 + \lambda_K)$ for funds required for new capacity. In order to keep the analysis simple, we let λ_τ incorporate some of the general-equilibrium effects of prices just discussed; thus it is lower than would be measured by a partial-equilibrium analysis of the tax system, and can even be negative if a higher generalized price of travel is economically damaging (*e.g.*, by discouraging labor-force participation) and/or if the revenues are spent unwisely. In one particular case, where travel and work are perfectly complementary (commuting being the only travel motive) and revenues are spent reducing a distorting tax on labor, then the damage done by a higher generalized price of travel is exactly offset by the advantageous use of revenues (Parry and Bento 2001); here this would be represented by setting $\lambda_\tau = 0$.

With a single road, the objective then becomes:

$$\Lambda = \int_0^V d(v)\,\mathrm{d}v - V \cdot c(V, V_K) + \lambda_\tau V \cdot \left[d(V) - c(V, V_K) \right] - \left(1 + \lambda_K \right) \rho \cdot K(V_K), \tag{5.15}$$

where we have inserted the equilibrium condition $\tau = d - c$ in calculating toll revenues. (Note that toll revenues are a transfer so would not appear except for the fact that they have the extra welfare value λ_τ per dollar of revenue.) The first-order conditions with respect to V and V_K are:

$$\tau_T = V \cdot \frac{\partial c}{\partial V} - \frac{\lambda_\tau}{1 + \lambda_\tau} \cdot V \cdot d' \tag{5.16}$$

$$\left(1 + \lambda_K\right) \rho \cdot K'(V_K) = -\left(1 + \lambda_\tau\right) V \cdot \frac{\partial c}{\partial V_K}. \tag{5.17}$$

Note that each term in these equations is positive. When $\lambda_\tau > 0$, indicating that the value of revenue used exceeds any harm from raising the cost of travel, the optimal toll in (5.16) is above the conventional Pigouvian toll (*mecc*), confirming the intuition mentioned above.[9] When $\lambda_\tau = 0$ (5.16) reproduces the conventional Pigouvian toll (*mecc*), confirming the Parry-Bento result. When $\lambda_\tau < 0$, we obtain a result common in the literature on environmental externalities (*e.g.*, Bovenberg and de Mooij 1994): tax distortions cause the optimal toll to be smaller than the Pigouvian toll.

The investment rule (5.17) is somewhat more surprising. The prescription that marginal user benefits equal marginal investment cost is modified, in a direction that depends on the relative sizes of λ_τ and λ_K. If they are equal, the conventional investment rule of (5.3) re-emerges, even if each MCF exceeds 1; the reason is that user-cost reductions from capacity expansion can be fully captured by the operator through toll increases, so that the implicit desire to raise funds affects the tax rule (5.16) only.[10] If $\lambda_\tau = 0$, then (5.17) states that marginal user benefits are equated to marginal investment cost, but with the latter inflated by the relevant MCF.

It is difficult to recommend empirical values for MCF because its value varies greatly, not only by situation but also by the assumptions used in calculating it – including whether or not the public expenditures being financed will tend to reduce labor supply through income effects.[11] Some typical values for the US and UK, based on literature reviews, lie between 1.12 and 1.25.[12] One can make a case for using a smaller value if one believes that the tax distortions are offset by other factors, such as a tendency for public services to be spent in a way that favors those with higher incomes (Kaplow 1996); or that labor taxes partly or fully offset distortions in the opposite direction due to people's concern for relative status, which would cause them to overwork in a sort of arms race to outdo their neighbors in consumption ability.[13] On the other hand, several authors have argued that tax distortions are larger, for a variety of reasons including greater tax avoidance (Feldstein 1999) and non-marginal tax disincentives for labor-force participation (Kleven and Kreiner 2006). Kleven and Kreiner also find that most European nations have considerably higher MCFs than the UK due to higher marginal tax rates and higher transfers to people not working, obtaining values between 1.1 and 3.5 for five European nations under various labor-supply assumptions.[14]

5.1.4 Naïve investment rules

We finally address a question of considerable importance to the interpretation of conventional investment analysis, but rarely analyzed. This is the question of whether and how a planner's misperceptions of the true preference structure of travelers, or the true congestion technology, might lead to systematic biases in capacity choice. We discuss two examples. One involves the neglect of induced traffic, the second of rescheduling.

Ignoring induced traffic

Applied investment analysis often overlooks the problem of induced traffic. How this affects investment decisions depends on whether the neglect stems from a misperception of the actual demand elasticity or from the erroneous use of the conventional first-best investment rule (5.3) where the second-best rule (5.8) is appropriate.

Let us first consider, as a benchmark, the case with optimal pricing in place – admittedly irrelevant to current practice. In this case, an erroneous mixing up of the conventional investment rule (5.3) and the second-best rule (5.8) would be harmless because, with all $\lambda_h = 0$ in (5.8), the rules are identical. But if demand is erroneously assumed to be highly inelastic, optimal flow and capacity will be underpredicted, leading to an unpleasant surprise once the new capacity is opened. Even so, the mistake could be corrected iteratively by further adjusting capacity to the newly revealed level of traffic demanded, presuming such iterations would be convergent.

Now consider the more realistic case where no toll can be charged and the regulator is aware of the second-best rule (5.8) but erroneously assumes that demand is completely inelastic. Again there will be an unexpected increase in demand after an expansion. There are now two possibilities. The first is that the regulator learns from the previous experience, adjusts the estimate of demand elasticity to the correct value, and ends up in the second-best optimum. The second is that the regulator is unable or unwilling to learn, instead treating the newly observed flow V as an exogenous shock to an inelastic demand function. This regulator ends up in an equilibrium where (5.8) is satisfied under the incorrect assumption that $\partial d_h/\partial V_h = -\infty$, hence $\lambda_h = 0$ – that is, the regulator applies the first-best rule because, in the mistaken belief that demand is inelastic, the first-best and second-best rules would coincide. This equilibrium is the same as that attained in yet another case, where the regulator knows about induced traffic but mistakenly applies the conventional first-best rule (5.3) to analyze investment. This is perhaps the most common case, since the second-best investment rule is not widely known in practice.

To determine the impacts of mistakenly applying the first-best investment rule, let us define two alternate expressions for the marginal benefit of capacity expansion: the true value MB_K, equal to the right-hand side of (5.8), and the naïve value MB_K^n, equal to the right-hand side of (5.3). The regulator expands capacity until MB_K^n equals the marginal cost of capacity. But since $MB_K > MB_K^n$ at any given set of traffic volumes, this means the road will be overbuilt for the situation: the last increment of capacity was not worth its cost, given the restriction on tolling.

Ignoring rescheduling of trips

Another type of naïve cost–benefit analysis would ignore endogenous scheduling and the implied departure-time adjustments that a capacity expansion may induce. Intuitively, one may expect two errors in opposite directions from this mistake. On the one hand, capacity expansion leads to a stronger concentration of trip completion times (peak narrowing), causing aggregate scheduling cost to fall – a benefit that is ignored in the naïve analysis. On the other hand, peak narrowing limits the ability of the capacity expansion to reduce congestion, so savings in travel-delay cost are likely to be less than predicted in the naïve analysis.

To illustrate, suppose the world operates according to the bottleneck model of Section 3.4.3, with uniformly dispersed desired queue-exit times. What happens when the regulator is ignorant of scheduling costs and tries to optimize capacity subject to a static congestion model such one based on the US Bureau of Public Roads (BPR) congestion function of equation (3.9)?

To keep it simple, we assume that total demand Q is fixed and this is correctly perceived by the regulator. We observe the system in equilibrium when capacity is V_K^0 (assumed less than the desired queue-exit rate V_d), and we wish to assess the benefits of expanding it slightly to V_K. The true marginal benefit is then found by differentiating the average cost $\bar{c}_g$ of equation (3.38) and multiplying by Q:

$$MB_K = -Q \cdot \frac{\partial \bar{c}_g}{\partial V_K}\bigg|_{V_K=V_K^0} = \delta \cdot \left(\frac{Q}{V_K^0}\right)^2. \tag{5.18}$$

But under our assumptions, the regulator instead uses a naïve measure of marginal benefit, MB_K^n, computed under the following assumptions:

1 average congestion cost (call it c_g^n) consists only of travel-time cost;
2 for a given demand, c_g^n is inversely proportional to $(V_K)^b$;
3 the initial value of c_g^n is the observed average travel-delay cost, which we know from the true model is $\bar{c}_T = \frac{1}{2}\delta \cdot Q / V_k^0$ (equation (3.36)).

Thus the regulator uses the following naïve average cost as a function of V_K:

$$c_g^n = \left(\frac{1}{2}\delta \cdot \frac{Q}{V_K^0}\right) \cdot \left(\frac{V_K^0}{V_K}\right)^b. \tag{5.19}$$

Differentiating, evaluating the result at $V_K = V_K^0$, and multiplying by Q yields the naïve marginal benefit:

$$MB_K^n = -Q \cdot \frac{\partial c_g^n}{\partial V_K}\bigg|_{V_K=V_K^0} = \frac{1}{2}b\delta \cdot \left(\frac{Q}{V_K^0}\right)^2 = \frac{1}{2}b \cdot MB_K. \tag{5.20}$$

Comparing (5.18) with (5.20), we see that the naïve calculation underestimates true marginal benefits when $b < 2$ and overestimates them when $b > 2$. Which of the two mistakes dominates – ignoring scheduling benefits or overestimating travel time benefits – therefore depends on the curvature of the naïve cost function. This is because the convexity determines how seriously travel-delay savings are overestimated: with small b that error is small and overshadowed by the naïve neglect of scheduling-cost savings, but with large b the mistaken forecast of reduced congestion is the more serious mistake.

It seems quite likely that the error in computing marginal benefits could be large, in either direction. If the conventional BPR value of $b = 4$ is used, marginal benefits would be overestimated by 100%. But if the BPR function were fit using observed data generated by the bottleneck model (here assumed to be the true one), we know from equation (3.36) that it would appear linear, *i.e.*, $b=1$; then marginal benefits would be underestimated by 50%.

Other examples can be considered. What if the observed pattern of queue-exit times is thought to be fixed, when it really is determined by the bottleneck model? Small (1992a) finds in that case that $MB_K^n = \frac{1}{2}(\alpha/\delta) \cdot MB_K$. Using the empirical values $(\alpha/\beta)=1.631$ and $(\alpha/\gamma)=0.417$ from equation (2.24), $\frac{1}{2}(\alpha/\delta)=1.02$, so the marginal benefit is overestimated by just 2%. But Henderson (1992) considers the same question in the context of the no-propagation model already mentioned in Section 3.3.3. He finds that under a mild parameter restriction, the marginal benefit is always overestimated, causing the road to be overbuilt.

It appears, then, that ignoring trip scheduling in investment analysis can cause serious mistakes. But there seems no general rule as to which direction those mistakes will take.

5.2 Cost–benefit analysis

The investment analysis we have described thus far depends on the possibility of incremental investments whose purpose is to enlarge a well-defined measure of capital such as "capacity." It also assumes that the relevant benefits and costs can be described as continuous functions. Sometimes these conditions are not met. More generally, we often want to analyze policy initiatives that are arbitrarily defined and may have little to do with any describable optimality conditions. It then becomes useful to have a more general method for comparing benefits and costs of proposed projects.

Cost–benefit analysis is a set of tools for making such comparisons. As its name implies, it focuses on economic effects; thus it is not by itself a complete decision mechanism. Nevertheless it can incorporate many factors that are sometimes considered non-economic – just as we showed in Chapter 3 that cost functions can incorporate air pollution, noise, and risk of injury and death. Indeed, the way that was done illustrates a central principle of cost–benefit analysis: namely, that benefits can be measured as the willingness of individuals to pay for them.

We begin by explaining some basic principles embodied in cost–benefit analysis and why they provide a useful reference point for summarizing project impacts. We then consider just a few of the many measurement issues that afflict cost–benefit analysis. The topic is vast, but our goal is modest: to help the reader understand the implications of particular analytical choices that have been used in, or are suggested for, particular applications.[15]

Cost–benefit analysis need not be restricted to long-term investments. It can be applied to routine maintenance activities or to major rehabilitation projects, both of which have shown greater potential than new roads in many less-developed nations (Kerali 2003). It can be applied even to operational policies under consideration such as air-pollution standards, road pricing, or transit subsidies.

5.2.1 Willingness to pay

The starting point for measuring costs or benefits is *willingness to pay*: that amount of money that an individual or firm could pay after a proposed change and still be equally well off (by his or her own evaluation). This concept incorporates consumer sovereignty: *i.e.*, the belief that individuals are the best judge of the value to them of their consumption decisions. This does not mean that externalities are to be ignored – on the contrary, the willingness-to-pay principle allows one to assess how much people care about relieving the externality. The principle does, however, exclude analysts' or governments' beliefs about the inherent worth of activities unless those beliefs can be articulated in terms of benefits that people, as individuals, will appreciate. For example, fostering a healthy ecology is often thought to have its own moral value; cost–benefit analysis can account for this but only insofar as that value can be translated into privately valued improvements such as better health, more pleasant living conditions, or more reliable resource availability for current and future residents of the earth.

The willingness-to-pay principle has actually been present throughout the analysis of this book. For example, in Chapter 2 we measured the values of travel time and reliability from the way individuals trade them against price in travel-demand models; they are simply travelers' willingness to pay for time savings or reliability improvements. The costs defined in Chapter 3 measure the collective willingness to pay by individuals and transportation providers for any savings in their required inputs of time, fuel, labor, and other things. The area under a demand curve, introduced in Chapter 4 as a benefit measure, is an approximate indicator of travelers' collective willingness to pay for an increase in the quantity of travel.

Figure 5.2 illustrates the relationship between willingness to pay and the demand curve. The sloping line depicts the demand for bus trips by users with identical values of time (but who differ in other ways, causing some but not all to choose the bus at a given generalized price). Suppose a service improvement speeds up the buses and thereby lowers the full price from p^0 to p^1. There are Q^0 existing users, each willing to pay $(p^0 - p^1)$ for the improvement; their aggregate willingness to pay is therefore the rectangular area $p^0 A F p^1$. The improvement also attracts $Q^1 - Q^0$ new users; some (those most easily attracted) are willing to pay almost $(p^0 - p^1)$ for the improvement, while others (those just barely attracted) are willing to pay very little. Adding them together, aggregate willingness to pay for new users is the triangular area ABF. The total willingness to pay for the change, from both existing and new users, is therefore the trapezoid $p^0 A B p^1$. This area can also be expressed as the change in consumer surplus (*i.e.*, the change in the area under the demand curve and above the price).

Equivalently, we could express this area as the sum of two terms: (1) an increase in benefits from bus trips, $Q^0 A B Q^1$; and (2) the change in spending on other things, $p^0 A Q^0 0 - p^1 B Q^1 0$. The first component is just another application of viewing the area under

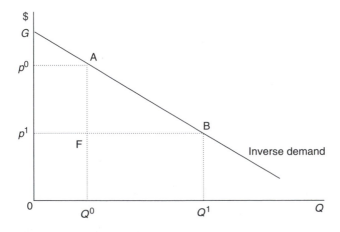

Figure 5.2 Benefits to existing and new users.

the demand curve as an indicator of the benefits to consumers of consumption represented by that demand curve. The second component is the negative of the change in "expenditures" on bus travel. Recalling that the vertical axis is generalized price, some of these "expenditures" are payments to the bus company and others are costs incurred by the users themselves; but in either case they represent consumers' increased ability to purchase other goods or to enjoy better service quality – as indicated in the terms entering generalized price as, for example, in equations (2.32) or (2.33). We note in passing that this decomposition makes clear that the change in spending on other things is already captured in the area representing the change in consumer surplus in the bus transit market; there is no need to consider the other markets that are affected. (This result changes if prices in those other markets do not reflect marginal costs, as we discuss in Section 5.2.5.)

Figure 5.2 also illustrates a useful "rule of thumb" for calculating the net benefits to new users of a decrease in generalized price. With a linear demand curve as drawn, area ABF is half the number of newly attracted users multiplied by the reduction in generalized price. If demand is not linear but the change in quantity is fairly small, this statement is still a reasonable approximation, known as the "rule of half." The rule of half remains valid for full networks and with interdependent demand functions, provided cross-demand effects are linear. (Such cross-demand effects, for example, occur when there are shifts in destination choice, and therewith in demand functions d_m, in response to the expansion of one link's capacity.) Denote the equilibrium flows on market m before and after the investment as V_m^0 and V_m^1, respectively; and the corresponding generalized prices as p_m^0 and p_m^1. The rule of half then states that the change in aggregate consumer surplus over the full network from an investment is given by:

$$\Delta W = \sum_{m=1}^{M} \tfrac{1}{2} \cdot \left(V_m^0 + V_m^1 \right) \cdot \left(p_m^0 - p_m^1 \right),$$

which is the sum (over markets) of the average use (before and after the investment) multiplied by the price reduction. (To determine the change in social surplus, changes in total toll revenues would have to be added to ΔW.) The rule clearly greatly simplifies the estimation of benefits to users because one need estimate only the initial and final quantities and the change in generalized price, rather than estimating all demand curves, including cross-demand relations.

Some inputs that are part of the users' price p are not freely traded in markets. We have already seen how to deal with these in the case of users' time, for which we imputed a value. But even money costs may not reflect free markets or, more generally, social values. For example, during the oil crises of 1973 and 1979, various price controls on gasoline were imposed in the US, resulting in informal fuel rationing. As a result, many consumers would have been willing to pay less for fuel than its resource cost. In such cases, the analyst may be able to calculate a *shadow price*, different from (in this case higher than) the market price, that reflects resource cost. As another example, a project may provide work for people who otherwise would be involuntarily unemployed; those people would have been willing to work for less than the actual wage, so the shadow wage to be applied in calculating the costs of that project would be lower than the actual wage. (A warning, however: this is valid only if the project truly causes a net change in employment, as opposed to a shift of employment from one sector to another.) Other sources of divergence between market and shadow prices are discussed by Willis (2005). Because they cannot be observed directly, shadow prices are often hard to measure, and may depend in subtle ways upon prevailing market conditions, including regulations such as taxes and quotas (*e.g.*, Johansson 1991).

Most projects have diverse effects that will benefit some people and harm others. Granted that we can measure each person's willingness to pay (negative if he or she is harmed), why should we be interested in the result of adding them all together? By doing so, cost–benefit analysis can identify projects that are *potential Pareto improvements: i.e.*, projects for which winners could compensate losers, leaving all better off. For example, a new highway interchange may save enough people time that they could compensate those harmed by extra noise and traffic. Mechanisms exist for such compensation but they are far from perfect; as a result, few if any projects can be strict Pareto improvements and thereby achieve unanimous support. Indeed, one can argue that it is precisely the absence of such unanimity that creates the need for cost–benefit analysis to aid public decision-making.

Nevertheless, if projects were consistently analyzed and undertaken only when they are potential Pareto improvements, one could expect that the losers from some projects would be winners from others. Given enough randomness in the effects of different projects, there would be "a strong probability that almost all would be better off" eventually (Hicks 1941, p. 111), so that the joint result of many potential Pareto improvements would be a strict Pareto improvement after all. Polinsky (1972) provides one attempt to formalize the kind of randomness required.

5.2.2 Demand and cost forecasts

The most critical component of a cost–benefit analysis is simply predicting what will happen. The desirability of a new or improved facility depends especially on how much it will cost and how many people will use it. Yet as already noted in Section 4.5.3, there are wide disparities between forecasted and realized results of transportation infrastructure projects, for both costs and demands. Furthermore, the discrepancies are generally not random or neutral in sign, but rather appear to be strategically related to their use, through cost–benefit or other types of analysis, in decision-making about the projects.

Flyvbjerg, Skamris Holm and Buhl (2004, 2006) analyze the factors determining the size and direction of forecasting errors based on worldwide samples of over 200 projects. For cost projections, they find that errors grow rapidly with the time it takes to build the project, and for bridges and tunnels they grow more than proportionally to the size of the project. Surprisingly, they find no evidence that errors are systematically worse with public than private projects; they do seem to be worse, however, for state-owned enterprises that lack financial transparency. For demand projections, they find forecast errors for roads that are significant but evenly balanced in sign; whereas for rail projects, the errors are enormous and positively biased, with 90% of projects overestimating demand by an average of 106%.

Various proposals have been made to reduce such discrepancies and especially to eliminate the biases that systematically result in poor investments being undertaken. These include performing sensitivity analysis, limiting the time span over which projections are made, and subjecting forecasting procedures to peer review (Pickrell 1989). Because the biases appear to be strategic, and the main use of cost–benefit analysis is to inform political decision-making, any remedies must be consistent with an overall plan to improve the political process for choosing investments. Indeed, there is ample evidence that politics plays a dominant role in infrastructure investment: for example, Cadot, Röller and Stephan (2006) find statistically that infrastructure investments in France's regions from 1985 to 1992 were strongly influenced by measures of political needs but not at all influenced by measures of productivity effects.

5.2.3 Discounting future costs and benefits

We already mentioned how costs or benefits incurred over time can be converted to an equivalent present value or an equivalent constant annualized flow (Section 3.4.6). The basic principle is that any expenditure C undertaken in year t could be funded by investing some smaller amount PV today (year 0) and regularly reinvesting its financial yield. Assuming a constant interest rate r, compounded annually, they are related by $PV \cdot (1 + r)^t = C$; *i.e.*, $PV = C/(1 + r)^t$. The quantity PV is called the *present value* of the future expenditure. More generally, a series of expenditures C_t in years $t = 1, \ldots, T$ has present value

$$PV = \sum_{t=1}^{T} \frac{C_t}{(1+r)^t}. \tag{5.21}$$

The same principle works for benefits if one assumes that people have access to capital markets at interest rate r. This is because if they were required to pay an amount PV in conjunction with receiving a stream of benefits $\{B_t\}$ over time, they could borrow or lend in the capital markets in order to be just as well off in each year as before, provided PV is given by (5.21) with C_t replaced by B_t.

However, capital markets are far from perfect and many transactions are carried out at interest rates different from the one observed in formal capital markets, which we have called r. On the one hand, consumers can usually receive only low rates on their savings and so they may be willing to trade money against time at that relatively low rate, called the *marginal rate of time preference*. This rate may therefore be appropriate for discounting costs that will be financed out of consumption or benefits that are in the form of consumption. On the other hand, businesses must pay taxes on their investment returns, causing them to undertake socially productive investment only when its rate considerably exceeds the rate at which they can raise capital through borrowing or equity. When a proposed investment displaces private investment subject to such taxes, the appropriate rate for cost–benefit analysis would then be the before-tax rate of return to private capital, sometimes called the *value of marginal product of capital*. Finally, when inflation is expected, the value of future consumption or cost savings brought about by investing capital today will be less than the nominal returns indicated by financial accounts; we account for this by defining a *real rate of interest* approximately equal to $r = n - \pi$, where n is any particular nominal rate of interest and π is the rate of inflation.[16]

Defining the interest rate or rates that should apply to the elements in a cost–benefit analysis therefore requires considerable sophistication. Unfortunately, the outcome of such an analysis is often very sensitive to the interest rate chosen, especially in the case of long-lived capital investments as are common in transportation. This sensitivity is even more pronounced if benefits are small at the beginning and grow over time, as is typical of new transportation facilities in areas undergoing population growth. Partly because of this, cost–benefit practitioners have often found it easy to manipulate the results to favor an outcome that they desire by altering their assumed interest rate. As a damper to such practices, government agencies sometimes promulgate rules, or at least guidelines, for how other agencies and private parties should choose interest rates and other key analytical elements when presenting cost–benefit analyses of government projects.[17]

Most commonly, the recommended real interest rate is a weighted average of the two rates just defined: the marginal rate of time preference in consumption and the pre-tax real value of marginal product of capital. Boardman *et al.* (2006) suggest that, as an approximation, the weight on the former be the proportion of financing of the project that will come from higher taxes (as opposed to displaced private investment). They take the two rates, stated in real terms (*i.e.*, after inflation), to be 1.5% and 4.5%, respectively.[18]

Most analysts recommend substantially higher rates – as indeed did Boardman *et al.* in a previous edition of their book where the rates were given as 1.5% and 9.6%.[19] US OMB (2003) instructs government agencies to use a rate of 7% unless there is compelling reason otherwise. Transport Canada (1994, p. 66) recommends 10%. A universal recommendation is that sensitivity analysis be undertaken by recomputing results at different interest rates.

Some additional considerations occur when the benefits of a project occur very far in the future. Conventional discounting, even at the low interest rates recommended by Boardman *et al.* (2006), usually makes such very-long-term benefits virtually irrelevant in a cost–benefit analysis. For example, the quantifiable benefits of measures taken now to reduce global warming are small for this reason. Many observers find this situation unpalatable, as it appears to ignore the welfare of future generations. Actually it does not, because today's tradeoffs between consumption and capital investment will probably affect future generations' production capacity. For example, if we forgo expensive development of hydrogen vehicles and instead invest in technology for climate manipulation or adaptation, we might be able to counteract or ameliorate the future effects of that portion of greenhouse-gas emissions that could have been eliminated – leaving future generations doing at least as well as they would if we had developed hydrogen vehicles.

But is it true that we create more capital for future generations by refraining from undertaking expensive regulatory measures today? One could argue that this is an overly optimistic view of how smoothly the world's economy works. Is it not equally likely that money saved today is squandered in consumption? Working against that more pessimistic view is the bequest motive, which appears to have remained strong over millennia. In a capitalist society, some of the money saved today is placed in financial vehicles for people's heirs, and those financial vehicles are sources of real capital to enhance future consumption.

These are difficult arguments to evaluate rigorously. However, even within the framework of standard economics, at least two arguments can be made for using a lower interest rate when discounting economic transactions far in the future than when discounting just over the life of a typical capital asset. One is that the rate of return on capital is likely to decrease in the future as cumulative investment makes capital less and less scarce; thus, we should use an interest rate that declines gradually over time (Dasgupta 1994). Working against this is a long history of technological progress that has continually widened the scope for productive capital investments; if that can be relied upon, then expected new technologies become yet another reason for not worrying too much about problems we are creating for the distant future.

The other argument for a lower interest rate is given by Weitzman (2001). Weitzman notes that even within conventional analysis, experts disagree on the interest rate appropriate for cost–benefit analysis, mainly due to differing views about the capital-market imperfections already discussed. Not only is expert opinion varied but it is skewed, with a long "right tail": that is, a few experts think the appropriate rate is quite large, but no one thinks it is less than zero. Weitzman estimates the distribution of expert opinion on the appropriate rate r for discounting effects of global climate change, based on a survey of economists. He uses the results to compute the expected value (across experts) of the discount factor, *i.e.*, the factor

$1/(1+r)^t$ in (5.21),[20] for each time horizon t. He finds that the result is the same as he would get using an interest rate that diminishes the farther in the future we look (and which is smaller, for any given time horizon, than the average value of r favored by experts). Thus, both Dasgupta and Weitzman, using quite different approaches, conclude that events in the very far future should be discounted using a lower interest rate than that prevailing today.

5.2.4 Shifting of costs and benefits

One appeal of cost–benefit analysis is that it can identify the economic actors affected by an improvement and measure the value to each of them, thereby permitting some description of the distribution of these benefits across various groups.

However, price changes in ancillary markets may drastically alter this distribution by shifting benefits or costs from one group to another. A classic example is that land rents and land prices in areas made more accessible will increase through the normal working of land markets, as these locations become more desirable compared to others. Thus a change that appears to create benefits for, say, transit users who can take advantage of a new transit station is more likely to end up as an advantage to landowners in the area. Boyd (1976) gives a cogent account including some specific examples for urban land markets. Other markets that may shift transportation benefits from one party to another are those for labor and for retail goods and services.

5.2.5 External benefits and network effects

Promoters of projects often like to highlight various benefits such as jobs created, real-estate development induced, economic activity attracted, or industrial activities made more efficient by a transportation improvement. Economic analysis has shown that most such benefits are either transfers from other locations (*e.g.*, economic activity moved from one location to another) or the conversion of transportation benefits, already measured in conventional cost–benefit analysis, to another form.

To understand such conversions, consider the benefits of "industrial reorganization," by which transportation improvements enable firms to create more efficient systems of distribution or production.[21] Mohring and Williamson (1969) show that these benefits, while quite possibly real, are already captured in the demand curve for transportation that is the basis for conventional benefit measurement. To illustrate, consider again Figure 5.2 and suppose it represents demand for urban freight travel by industrial firms. The ability to reorganize distribution or production through cheaper transportation is represented by the amount the firms are willing to pay for the $Q^1 - Q^0$ new trips that make this reorganization possible. Thus area ABF already captures their value to the firm. Even if the firms are competitive, so that all their savings are shifted to customers or suppliers, the ultimate benefits are still measured by the area under the demand curve for transportation (Jara-Díaz 1986).

Nevertheless, some benefits may be truly "external" in the sense that they accrue to people other than the decision maker responsible for them. Such *external benefits* are likely to be important in at least two situations.

First, transportation improvements may reduce the market power of firms by promoting trade among previously isolated locations. Jara-Díaz (1986) illustrates this process with a model of two firms, each initially a monopolist within its own region, when a transportation improvement lowers the cost of shipping the good from one location to the other. Because the initial monopoly power caused prices to be higher than optimal, thereby creating a deadweight loss to the economy, welfare is increased when that power declines. Neither firm can capture all this benefit in its own use of transportation, so the demand curve for transportation does not fully reflect it. Indeed, this example amplifies our comment made in opening this book, that transportation is central to economic activity because it permits trade; we now can say that this benefit of transportation is partly external and so may justify government intervention to promote transportation. We hasten to add, as does Jara-Díaz, that this point applies mainly to developing economies or isolated rural areas where such benefits have not already been exhausted.

Second, urban areas are thought to exist because they enable firms to take advantage of *economies of agglomeration*, which are cost reductions made possible when a large number of firms exist in proximity. When an additional firm locates in such an area, it reaps some of these advantages but creates others that are external to itself, by adding to the density experienced by other firms. This phenomenon involves a reciprocal externality, very much like congestion except it conveys positive rather than negative benefits. Thus, just like congestion, free markets will not produce an optimal amount of agglomeration–they will tend to produce too little. Any improvement in transportation enlarges the number of firms whose mutual interaction create these economies, so should increase their size. The upshot is that agglomeration economies create another external benefit of transportation improvements.

There is some empirical evidence on the size of economies of agglomeration, and it has been used (and augmented) in at least two studies of transportation improvements to estimate the resulting external benefits. Shefer and Aviram (2005) examine a light-rail line in terms of the additional people it will allow to work in the Tel Aviv central business district, applying empirical results from studies of agglomeration that measure productivity as a function of city size. Prud'homme and Lee (1999) examine labor productivity in 22 French cities as a function of the size of the labor market, defined as the number of workers who can commute to a given job location within a specified amount of time, averaged over all job locations (or alternatively, the number of jobs within a specified commuting time of a household, averaged over all household locations). They obtain elasticities that are somewhat larger than those measured elsewhere, which could mean that labor-market size is a better measure than population of the potential for agglomeration. Prud'homme and Lee then go on to show quantitatively how labor-market size depends on transportation parameters, such as average speed, and on measures of urban form, such as the distances separating households and work locations.

Again, we hasten to add that in well-developed urban areas, incremental transportation improvements are likely to have only small effects on urban efficiency. By way of analogy, Fernald (1999) finds evidence that the US Interstate Highway System created substantial productivity gains in its early years, but that more recent additions have had much smaller effects.

The arguments made in this subsection are applications of a more general principle: shifts in demand or supply curves in markets related to the one under investigation represent shifts in the benefits and costs, rather than new benefits and costs, as long as prices in those markets are set at marginal cost (for example, if those markets are perfectly competitive with no externalities). The same principle applies to shifts in the demand or supply curves for other links in a network, caused by changes in a particular link under investigation. If those other links are priced at marginal cost, then no new benefits or costs are generated and the consumer-surplus analysis of the initial link is sufficient. (See, for example, how the Lagrange multiplier for the untolled route vanishes in the two-route problem of (4.32) and (5.9).) However, in the common case where other links in the network are not priced at marginal cost, the effects on them must be taken into account. To take an obvious example, if expanding transit service draws traffic away from a congested highway, analyzing consumer surplus in the transit market alone is insufficient; one must also include the changes in costs and consumer surplus for the highway. (The argument here parallels that for transit pricing in Section 4.5.1 and for second-best road capacity with network spillovers in Section 5.1.3.) Kidokoro (2004) shows in a quite general way that the total benefits from a change in conditions on one link can be measured as the sum over all parts of the network of changes in consumer benefits less travel cost (or more generally, if some links are supplied by private industry and at least some are tolled, in consumer plus producer plus government surplus). The network-wide rule of half presented in Section 5.2.1 reflects this principle for the situation without tolling.

5.2.6 Conclusion: the use and misuse of cost–benefit analysis

In the end, cost–benefit analysis is undertaken to inform decision makers. One can hope that by making the impacts of a project transparent and by quantifying them in consistent ways, the decision-making process – which in most cases is political – can be guided toward decisions that are better for most people. Indeed, this is the main purpose of recent legislation in several nations that subjects new regulations to cost–benefit analysis: the presumption is that exposing any negative economic effects will force regulators to articulate what they are trying to achieve, and allow the public to decide whether it is worth those negative effects. Should this indeed result in more efficient public investment decisions, the resulting social welfare gains may be substantial.

As a political process, cost–benefit analysis will inevitably be subjected to pressures to misuse it for the benefit of particular interest groups. Professionals can reduce such strategic misuse by developing clear procedural guidelines and articulating them clearly to the public. Furthermore, the cost–benefit analyses themselves need to be transparent as well as technically sound so that such misuse can be identified.

Sensitivity analysis is one good way to be sure that users can understand the implication of particular assumptions made in a cost–benefit analysis. One type of sensitivity analysis, sometimes called *risk analysis*, postulates specific probability density functions for uncertain parameters, then uses Monte Carlo simulation to compute the corresponding frequency distribution of any particular result of interest. There is a danger in formalizing uncertainty in this way, however, because it may lead to a false sense of precision about how uncertainty can be characterized; in many cases, especially developing nations, the outcome may be more affected by administrative competence, sabotage, or breakdown of related markets than by the elements formalized in risk analysis (Jenkins 1997).

5.3 Conclusions

Long-lived transport investments can be analyzed either as a problem of optimizing over a continuously varying quantity representing capital stock, or as a problem of choice among well-defined discrete packages. If done the first way, the analysis completes the characterization of long-run cost functions. If done the second way, it becomes part of a more general technique, cost–benefit analysis, which can be used to analyze other proposals such as pricing or regulatory changes. Indeed, it has become common for governments to mandate such analyses of a wide range of government initiatives, in order to increase the burden of proof on proposed actions that might have adverse economic effects.

Like pricing, investment analysis can be considered under first- or second-best conditions. The latter are of course far more prevalent, and in several cases we can identify the way investment rules should be modified to account for constraints, especially constraints on pricing the facility in question or other facilities that interact with it. Furthermore, we can sometimes describe the potential misallocations due to applying first-best rules (which might be thought of as common-sense cost–benefit analysis) to what are really second-best situations.

Public investment decisions are heavily influenced by political considerations. The goal of cost–benefit analysis is not to create rigid criteria that must be followed to the exclusion of all others, but rather to inform decision makers about how a project looks when judged by one set of criteria that are intended to be consistent with widely accepted economic principles. To be useful, these criteria need to be defined by a transparent process; to this end, it is especially important that transportation professionals understand the technical implications of proposed cost–benefit techniques and have the skills needed to explain them to others in non-technical language.

6 Industrial organization of transportation providers

So far we have discussed desirable investment and pricing policies. We now turn to a discussion of the forms of institutional structure that can best bring them about. The dominant organizational form for providing urban transportation services to individual users, especially in developed nations, is public ownership. This is supplemented by regulation of those firms allowed to operate privately. Observers increasingly question the efficacy of these arrangements.

A fundamental problem with private transportation markets is their tendency toward scale economies. This tendency has long been recognized in inter-city transportation industries such as ocean shipping and railroads, whose fixed costs take tangible forms like terminals and rail track. But scale economies also affect industries, such as airlines and trucking, where users place a premium on fast and reliable transfers across various links in a large network, because then scale economies on individual links – which can exist due to efficiencies of operating large vehicles – become important as firms seek to use those links to provide convenient service for many origin–destination pairs.

Both urban roads and urban public transit services operate on networks that collect users with diverse origins and destinations onto high-capacity links in order to take advantage of link-specific scale economies. We saw in Section 3.2.4 that the nature of scheduled services creates a type of scale economy even on feeder links. Therefore, much urban transportation faces the same underlying cost condition as inter-city transportation. Scale economies mean that marginal-cost prices do not cover average costs. In order for private firms to operate in such markets, they must either receive subsidies or forgo marginal-cost pricing. If we choose to forgo marginal-cost pricing, then we must permit some degree of market power, which has its own problems that depend on the nature of markets and the more general state of public control of business practices (Button 2005).

Of course, transportation is only one of many industries for which the question of private versus public operation arises. Two valuable general assessments are those by Kay and Thompson (1986) and Vickers and Yarrow (1991). One conclusion of these assessments is that a lot depends on details of the industry. Analyses of transportation industries have been important in coming to the more general conclusions of this literature, as well as in applying more general results to specific cases with significant public-policy implications. For these reasons, the economic study of industrial organization in transportation continues to provide insights of widespread interest.

This chapter, then, reviews issues related to private operators in urban transportation. Section 6.1 discusses profit-maximizing price and capacity choice for private highway operators, and compares these to welfare-maximizing choices. Section 6.2 discusses regulation and franchising of private highways, while Section 6.3 does the same for transit services.

6.1 Private highways

Some observers, such as Roth (1996), suggest that many of the recent difficulties with financing and pricing publicly-owned highways could be overcome through a return to private ownership, which was common in past eras.[1] Given perfect competition among road suppliers, first-best congestion pricing would be the equilibrium outcome (DeVany and Saving 1980). Even under the more realistic conditions of monopoly or oligopoly, private ownership would provide a type of congestion pricing, as we shall see – although not at first-best price levels. Naturally, the outcomes and hence the desirability of private ownership depend critically on market structure, which includes the nature of the highway network and the relationship among suppliers. In this section, we examine how one can analytically predict such outcomes.

6.1.1 Single road with static congestion

We start with an unregulated private monopolist on a single road, using the multi-period set-up introduced in equation (4.13). We can analyze this case by modifying the benefit–cost framework developed in Chapter 5. Instead of choosing capacity and tolls so as to maximize $W = B - C$, as in equation (5.1), we assume the monopolist maximizes profit Π, equal to its revenues minus its own costs:

$$\Pi = \sum_h q_h \cdot V_h \cdot \tau_h - \rho \cdot K(V_K),\tag{6.1}$$

where again h denotes a time period of duration q_h. The user-equilibrium condition from equation (4.1), equating marginal benefit $d(V)$ to the generalized price $p \equiv c(V) + \tau$, of course remains valid for each period h. It is convenient to directly substitute this condition into the objective function:

$$\Pi = \sum_h q_h V_h \cdot \left[d_h(V) - c_h(V_h;\, V_K) \right] - \rho \cdot K(V_K).\tag{6.2}$$

We maximize (6.2) with respect to capacity V_K and flows V_h.

Maximizing with respect to capacity produces, perhaps surprisingly, the first-best condition already encountered in (5.3):

$$\rho \cdot K'(V_K) = -\sum_h q_h \cdot V_h \cdot \frac{\partial c_h(\cdot)}{\partial V_K}.\tag{6.3}$$

For given flows V_h, the monopolist chooses capacity to minimize total social cost, including user cost. This is important as it shows that the monopolist is cost-conscious, even with those resources supplied by its customers. The intuition is that for any given flows V_h resulting from some generalized prices $p_h = c_h + \tau_h$, the monopolist would like to minimize user cost c_h and therefore maximize toll τ_h, while maintaining that generalized price. Every dollar reduction in total user cost can be turned into an extra dollar of toll revenues for given flow levels. The monopolist therefore faces the optimal incentive to minimize the sum of user cost and capital cost, just as in welfare maximization.

Maximizing (6.2) with respect to traffic volume, however, does not yield the first-best rule derived previously. Instead, we obtain the following first-order condition:

$$\tau_h = V_h \cdot \frac{\partial c_h}{\partial V_h} - V_h \cdot \frac{\partial d_h}{\partial V_h} - \sum_{i \neq h} \frac{q_i}{q_h} \cdot V_i \cdot \frac{\partial d_i}{\partial V_h}. \tag{6.4}$$

The first term on the right-hand side is equal to the first-best toll in (4.14) and (5.2). Thus, the profit-maximizing toll does at least partly internalize the congestion externality. However, two extra terms are added that take into account demand elasticities. With downward-sloping demand functions and substitutability across time periods, both terms are positive, so the toll is higher than optimal – just what we would expect from a monopolist. When demands in different time periods are independent of each other, the last term disappears and (6.4) simplifies to:

$$\tau_h = V_h \cdot \frac{\partial c_h}{\partial V_h} - V_h \cdot \frac{\partial d_h}{\partial V_h} \iff p_h \cdot \left(1 - \frac{1}{|\varepsilon_h|}\right) = mc_h \iff \frac{p_h - mc_h}{p_h} = \frac{1}{|\varepsilon_h|}, \tag{6.5}$$

where ε_h is the own-period price-elasticity of demand w.r.t. generalized price (p_h) and mc_h is defined, as before, as $\partial(V_h c_h)/\partial V_h = c_h + \partial c_h/\partial V_h$: i.e., marginal social cost.[2] Equation (6.5) looks like the familiar monopoly rule equating marginal revenue to marginal cost; but here the price and marginal cost both include user costs c_h. As usual with monopoly solutions, it is valid only when demand is elastic ($|\varepsilon_h| > 1$).

The monopolist internalizes the congestion externality because it has an interest in making its service attractive, so that users will pay more for it. When choosing the toll, just as when choosing capacity, the monopolist would like to reduce user cost in order to charge a higher toll. In doing so, however, it is constrained both by congestion technology and by users' demand elasticities. In fact, as we can see from the first of equations (6.5), the upward slope of the average user-cost function (representing congestion) affects the toll in exactly the same way as the downward slope of the inverse demand function; indeed, the inverse demand function $\tau_h(V_h)$ for the monopolist is given by $d_h(V_h) - c_h(V_h; V_K)$.

Because the monopolist takes marginal social cost into account in setting price, it may be said to practice a form of congestion pricing – but it then adds a markup represented by the bracketed term in the second equation in (6.5). This term multiplies the entire user-perceived price p_h, not just the toll τ_h. As a result, a substantial fee may be charged even during time periods when the optimal congestion fee is zero. An example of this in practice is the fact that the private operator of the express lanes on State Route 91 in southern California between 1995 and 2002 (see Section 4.3.3), in setting its time-varying fee, chose a non-zero fee even during night-time hours.

In the special case of perfectly elastic demand ($|\varepsilon_h| = \infty$), the demand-related monopolistic mark-up disappears and the monopolist undertakes socially optimal pricing and investment. This is the case in the classic analyses by Pigou (1920) and Knight (1924). Although important as a benchmark, it is of limited use in practice.

Note also from (6.5) that the fractional mark-up on marginal social cost, as given by the "Lerner index" $(p_h - mc_h)/p_h$, is simply the inverse of the absolute value of the demand elasticity $|1/\varepsilon_h|$. Again this is consistent with conventional microeconomics. A similar relationship holds in Ramsey pricing, in which social welfare is maximized subject to a minimum-profit constraint (Ramsey 1927; Baumol and Bradford 1970). We can derive the Ramsey result in this case by maximizing $B - C$ subject to a minimum constraint $\Pi^\#$ on profit Π, the latter defined in (6.2). Thus we maximize the Lagrangian function:

$$\Lambda = \sum_h q_h \cdot \int_0^{V_h} d_h(v) \, dv - \sum_h q_h V_h \cdot c_h(V_h; V_K) - \rho \cdot K(V_K)$$

$$+ \lambda \cdot \left\{ \sum_h q_h V_h \cdot \left[d_h(V_h) - c_h(V_h; V_K) \right] - \rho \cdot K(V_K) - \Pi^\# \right\},$$

where λ is the Lagrange multiplier associated with the profit constraint. The first-order condition for capacity V_K is unchanged: once again, V_K is chosen to minimize total social cost. The first-order condition for volume V_h, however, changes. It may be solved to yield:

$$\tau_h = V_h \cdot \frac{\partial c_h}{\partial V_h} - \frac{\lambda}{1+\lambda} \cdot V_h \cdot \frac{\partial d_h}{\partial V_h} \Leftrightarrow p_h \cdot \left(1 - \frac{\lambda}{1+\lambda} \cdot \frac{1}{\varepsilon_h} \right) = mc_h$$

$$\Leftrightarrow \frac{p_h - mc_h}{p_h} = \frac{\lambda}{1+\lambda} \cdot \frac{1}{|\varepsilon_h|},$$

where again mc denotes marginal social congestion cost. This equation is a well-known result for Ramsey pricing, but adapted here to incorporate a mutual externality and user-supplied costs.[3] When the constraint is not binding, substitution of $\lambda = 0$ confirms that we are back at first-best pricing. When the constraint becomes increasingly hard to satisfy, so that $\lambda \to \infty$, the toll approaches the profit-maximizing one of (6.5). Likewise, note that the conditions for the profit-maximizing toll (6.5) and capacity (6.3) are indeed also the same as those for a public operator who faces an infinite marginal cost of public funds, given (for the case of a single time period of duration normalized to one) by (5.16) and (5.17) when $\lambda_\tau = \lambda_K \to \infty$.

6.1.2 Single road with dynamic congestion

In models with endogenous scheduling, demands at different times within the peak period are determined by individual travelers' tradeoffs between travel delay and schedule delay. Does this affect a monopolist differently from a welfare-maximizer?

Arnott, de Palma and Lindsey (1993) show that if the monopolist charges only a time-invariant fee, the problem is exactly like that just analyzed. However, if a time-varying fee is possible, one might wonder whether the travelers' tradeoffs across time periods set up varying time-specific elasticities to be exploited by a monopolistic road owner. If so, the monopolist would choose a *pattern* of time variation that differs from the optimal pattern.

We can solve the problem for the basic bottleneck model, defined in Chapter 3 and used in Section 4.1.2. We consider a downward-sloping inverse demand function $d(Q)$. For convenience, we follow de Palma and Lindsey (2002) and decompose the time-varying toll $\tau(t')$ (for an exit at time t') into a time-independent "base toll" τ_0 and a purely time-varying component $\tau_v(t')$ that is zero for the first and last users to travel. This enables us to distinguish between the monopolist's choice of toll level t_0 and toll pattern $\tau_v(t')$. What we find is that the toll *pattern* is unaffected by monopoly – i.e., it is the same as the optimal toll pattern;

whereas the toll *level* is higher for a monopolist by exactly the same amount (and for the same reasons) as in the static result (6.5).

The reasoning is as follows. First, consider the toll *pattern*. A revenue-maximizer would set the toll pattern so as to eliminate any queuing, because queuing time can be replaced by toll revenues without affecting the generalized price p – exactly as we argued in the previous subsection when considering profit-maximizing investment. The toll schedule must therefore be at least as steep as the optimal one. But given the absence of queuing, the revenue-maximizer would also not make the toll schedule steeper than the optimal one. If it did, this would create periods within the peak where the bottleneck remains idle; but then it would be possible to extract some revenue from the earliest or the latest driver by shifting that driver to an empty slot within the peak, for which this driver is willing to pay because of lower scheduling cost. The purely time-varying toll component will consequently follow the same pattern as the first-best time-varying toll of (4.23).

Now consider the toll *level*. To see how the base toll τ_0 is chosen, recall from (4.25) that with this time-varying toll pattern, users adjust so that their average congestion-related user cost is $\bar{c}_g^1 = \frac{1}{2}\delta \cdot Q/V_K$, where Q is the total number of trips over the rush-hour and δ is a composite measure of how costly it is to deviate from the desired schedule. They also pay an average of $\bar{c}_g^1$ in tolls. Thus we can write

$$\bar{c}_g^1(Q; V_K) = \bar{\tau}_v(Q; V_K) = \frac{1}{2}\delta \cdot \frac{Q}{V_K}. \tag{6.6}$$

With the additional base toll added, generalized price, which must be equalized across users for them to be in equilibrium, is:

$$d(Q) \equiv p = \tau_0 + \bar{\tau}_v(Q; V_K) + \bar{c}_g^1(Q; V_K)$$
$$= \tau_0 + \delta \cdot Q / V_K. \tag{6.7}$$

Profit is toll revenue less capital cost, or:

$$\Pi(Q, V_K) = Q \cdot \left[d(Q; V_K) - \bar{c}_g^1(Q; V_K) \right] - \rho \cdot K(V_K). \tag{6.8}$$

This equation is just like (6.2) with one time period h, with $q_h V_h$ replaced by Q, and with c_h replaced by $\bar{c}_g^1$. So it leads to first-order conditions with the same properties as (6.3) and (6.4): namely, capital is chosen efficiently (given Q), and the toll level is set to account for marginal congestion cost (through $\bar{\tau}_v$) but with a monopoly markup (through τ_0). Writing out explicitly the first-order condition with respect to Q (and suppressing V_K as an argument in the functions), we have:

$$d(Q) - \bar{c}_g^1(Q) + Q \cdot d'(Q) - Q \frac{\partial \bar{c}_g^1}{\partial Q} = 0,$$

where d' is the slope of the inverse demand curve. Equation (6.6) implies that the fourth term is equal to $-\bar{\tau}_v$. Because $d - \bar{c}_g^1 - \bar{\tau}_v = \tau_0$, we find:

$$\tau_0 = -Q \cdot d'(Q). \tag{6.9}$$

There are two ways that we can interpret the base toll in (6.9) as a markup over marginal cost. First, as argued in Section 4.1.2, the time-varying toll component $\tau_v(t')$ is equal to the time-varying marginal external congestion cost *mecc* for a user exiting at t'. With the base-toll τ_0 set according to (6.9), the total toll $\tau(t')$ is therefore equal to $mecc(t')$ plus a time-independent demand-related markup.

Alternatively, we can rewrite (6.9) in a form like (6.5) by defining the marginal cost of adding a new user, given the optimal toll pattern:

$$mc = \partial(Q \cdot \bar{c}_g^1)/\partial Q = \bar{c}_g^1 + Q \cdot \partial \bar{c}_g^1 / \partial Q = 2\bar{c}_g^1.$$

Then the generalized price is

$$p = \tau_0 + \bar{\tau}_v + \bar{c}_g^1 = \tau_0 + 2\bar{c}_g^1 = \tau_0 + mc$$

so that (6.9) becomes (6.5) with the *h* subscripts removed and $1/|\varepsilon|$ defined as $-(Q/p) \cdot d'(Q)$.

The main insights from the static model on profit-maximizing tolling and capacity choice therefore survive in the basic bottleneck model.

6.1.3 Heterogeneous users

When individuals' values of time differ, another deviation between conditions for optimality and those for profit maximization is created. This is because the non-discriminating monopolist considers the interests only of marginal travelers (those nearly indifferent to using the highway in question); whereas conditions for optimality include infra-marginal travelers as well (Edelson 1971).

We can elaborate using the analysis of David Mills (1981). Mills considers the situation when individuals with different reservation prices (hence accounting for different parts of the inverse demand curve) have different values of time. Then the monopolist may allow too much or too little congestion because revenues resulting from a marginal change in price depend on just the marginal user, ignoring the benefits or costs for others. For example, suppose users with relatively high reservation prices (*i.e.*, they are willing to pay a lot to travel) also have relatively high values of time. The existence of these users tends to increase the level of the first-best toll because they would benefit a lot from reduced congestion. But such users do not affect the marginal revenue of the operator – the left-hand side of the second of equations (6.5) – because they will take trips regardless of marginal changes in congestion. (Hence they are called infra-marginal users.)

If the monopolist could price-discriminate – *i.e.*, charge different prices to users with different values of time – then the profit-maximizing and first-best congestion levels would coincide. However, distributional outcomes would differ because the price-discriminating monopolist would be able to extract consumer surplus otherwise enjoyed by users, in contrast to the toll authority in first-best pricing.

6.1.4 Private toll lanes: the two-route problem revisited

One way to allow a private road operator to implement pricing while limiting its market power is to maintain a close substitute that is free. This is in fact an arrangement of increasing practical interest, although usually it is combined with discounted or free travel for carpools.

We analyzed a similar situation under the rubric of second-best pricing and investment in Sections 4.2.1 and 5.1.3, by positing two parallel links that are perfect substitutes for each other, one tolled (route T) and the other untolled (route U). There, we maximized welfare (benefits minus costs) subject to a user-equilibrium constraint on each link, as summarized in the Lagrangian problem of equation (5.9). Here, we assume that a private operator would maximize profit, subject to the same constraints. This means maximizing the Lagrangian function:

$$\Lambda = V_T \cdot \tau_T - \rho \cdot K_T(V_{KT})$$
$$+ \lambda_T \cdot \left[c_T(V_T; V_{KT}) + \tau_T - d(V_T + V_U) \right] + \lambda_U \cdot \left[c_U(V_U; V_{KU}) - d(V_T + V_U) \right], \qquad (6.10)$$

where $d(\cdot)$ is again the inverse demand curve for the entire corridor. The first-order conditions can be solved to yield:

$$\tau_T = V_T \cdot \frac{\partial c_T}{\partial V_T} - V_T \cdot d'(V) \cdot \left(\frac{\partial c_U / \partial V_U}{(\partial c_U / \partial V_U) - d'(V)} \right) \qquad (6.11)$$

$$\rho \cdot K'_T(V_{KT}) = -V_T \cdot \frac{\partial c_T}{\partial V_{KT}}, \qquad (6.12)$$

where d' and K' denote derivatives.[4] The investment rule (6.12) has the familiar first-best structure indicating that conditional on travel volumes, capacity is chosen to minimize total social cost.

The toll formula in (6.11), however, is not second-best or even quasi first-best, as can be seen by comparing it with (4.35) and (4.6). Its first term shows that the profit-maximizer internalizes the congestion externality on the road under its control. Its second term gives the demand-related markup, which depends on how demand for the tolled link is affected both by congestion (on the untolled link) and by the overall corridor demand elasticity. (The markup is positive because d' is negative.) This second term is a fraction, defined by the term in large brackets, of the markup that would apply if there were no free alternative – i.e., the markup that occurs in the profit-maximizing toll (6.5) for a single road. This fraction is zero when the competing route U is uncongested, since then demand for the toll road itself is perfectly elastic. The fraction rises to one as congestion on route U becomes highly sensitive to traffic ($\partial c_U / \partial V_U \to \infty$), since then traffic on the free route is effectively fixed and so inverse demand for the toll road has the same slope d' as total inverse demand.

It is illuminating to compare (6.11) term by term with the corresponding second-best toll of equation (4.35). In both cases, the congestion externality on the toll road itself is accounted for through the usual term reflecting marginal external congestion cost on the toll road, which we may denote $mecc_T$. Where they differ is in how they account for congestion on the competing road. In computing the second-best toll, a positive term is *subtracted* from $mecc_T$ to account for congestion spillover to route U. But in computing the profit-maximizing toll, a positive term is *added* to $mecc_T$ to account for the additional revenue that can be extracted when congestion on the free road is heavy. Thus the profit-maximizing toll is higher than the second-best toll. It is no surprise, then, that the welfare gains from applying a profit-maximizing toll are below the already small gains from second-best tolling. Indeed they may well be negative when compared to the unpriced situation for the same capacity; this situation is in fact illustrated by the lowest curve in Figure 4.5 in Chapter 4. This is why Liu and McDonald (1998), in their study of partial pricing on southern California's SR-91, find a substantial efficiency *loss* in moving from no pricing to revenue-maximizing pricing on the express lanes; whereas they find a small but positive welfare *gain* from second-best pricing.

Why, then, is private ownership of express lanes receiving such favorable attention as a policy option? There are several reasons why it might be desirable in practice despite these theoretical results. First, although we have compared alternative regimes for a given amount of capacity, private ownership may in fact be the key to providing new capacity – as was true for SR-91 in California. In that case the relevant comparison is between a single free road and the same road augmented by a privately-operated express road. Computing the welfare gain then involves knowing the capital cost of the new capacity. Nevertheless, if the private road is a financial success and there are no adverse spillovers elsewhere on the network, then the net benefits of adding and pricing the express road cannot be negative because the free road offers travel at least as fast as before, the toll road is used only voluntarily (hence its users must be at least as well off as they were on the free road), and the operator makes non-negative profits.

A second reason is user heterogeneity. Small and Yan (2001) and Verhoef and Small (2004) find that even holding total capacity fixed, the welfare losses from profit maximization (as compared to no pricing) become smaller, and may in some cases turn into gains, when users have heterogeneous values of time. The reason is the same as for public express-lane pricing, discussed in Section 4.2.1, and involves socially beneficial self-selection of users according to value of time.

A third reason could be favorable impacts of revenue-maximizing pricing on departure times. As we have seen using the basic bottleneck model, revenue-maximizing pricing leads to a toll pattern over time that eliminates queuing. This remains true when an unpriced alternative exists and represents a potentially huge welfare gain (de Palma and Lindsey 2000).

Finally, the two roads may be imperfect substitutes. An example is Route 407 in suburban Toronto, Canada, a privately operated road that parallels, several miles distant, the main east-west freeway through the city center. Imperfect substitutability could either increase or decrease the distortions from revenue-maximizing pricing, depending on whether it serves more strongly to undermine the operator's market power or to reduce the congestion spillovers. Viton (1995) analyzes such a model.

6.1.5 Competition in networks

Private ownership has also been analyzed in various network configurations other than the classic two-route problem with a single, unpriced substitute. De Palma and Lindsey (2000), for example, consider various ownership regimes for a network of parallel links characterized as interacting bottlenecks. One result is that a duopoly of two private operators of parallel links achieves most of the potential efficiency gains from first-best pricing (over 90% in their base case with time-varying tolling). A mixed duopoly, with one public and one private operator, is even more efficient – consistent with more general results from oligopoly theory. (These results assume Nash-Bertrand competition, meaning that each operator takes the other's toll as given in choosing its own profit-maximizing toll.)

De Borger, Proost and Van Dender (2005) also consider a network of parallel links, but with static congestion and with two types of traffic: "regional" (able to choose the more favorable link) and "local" (forced by circumstances to use a particular link only). They study how two governments, each controlling one link, may engage in "tax competition," meaning they each try to attract revenue-producing travelers from the other's facility. They consider cases where the governments can and cannot distinguish between the two types of traffic in setting tolls, and also where they cannot toll the regional traffic at all. It turns out that social welfare is substantially enhanced by the ability to toll regional traffic. The ability to distinguish between regional and local traffic, by contrast, does not matter much for social welfare.

A different type of tax competition is studied empirically by Levinson (2001). He presents evidence that states in the US are more likely to apply tolls to their major through roads when their traffic contains a higher share of non-residents.

For more general networks, we can appeal to more general results of Economides and Salop (1992) involving substitutes and complements. These results suggest that competition among producers of goods that are substitutes (*e.g.*, operators of competing parallel roads) leads to lower prices than a combined monopolistic producer. By contrast, competition among producers of complements (*e.g.*, operators of serial links) leads to higher prices (but lower total profits) than a single monopoly.[5] If each good is produced by a separate (but otherwise monopolistic) firm, then each firm applies a conventional demand-related markup. The consumer needs all goods when these are perfectly complementary, so the final combined good (the trip, in a roads context) gets multiple markups applied on top of each other. These results suggest that in a general network of roads with private ownership (or private franchised operation), the results of various degrees of competition depend on whether the private operators control parts of the network that are predominantly substitutable (parallel) or complementary (serial).

We can illustrate this idea formally by considering two extreme cases of dividing control of a single corridor with only regional traffic. We allow a number F of identical revenue-maximizing firms to control different parts of the corridor, with F varying between one (monopoly) and infinity (perfect competition). Each firm's capacity and costs are fixed. In one case, the corridor is divided into F equal-capacity parallel roads, each operated by a different (and otherwise unregulated) firm. Total corridor traffic V divides across the roads according to the Wardrop conditions, constrained by $\Sigma_f V_f = V$. In the other case, the corridor is divided serially into F segments, each controlled by a different firm. The total corridor traffic level V then applies to each firm. In both cases, because the firms are identical, we consider only symmetric equilibria – *i.e.*, outcomes for which all firms have identical tolls, traffic, and hence revenues.

First, we consider the case of parallel roads that are perfect substitutes, a case analyzed by Engel, Fischer and Galetovic (2004). The equilibrium toll for firm f can be derived by maximizing the following Lagrangian:

$$\Lambda_f = V_f \cdot \tau_f + \lambda_f \cdot \left[c_f(V_f) + \tau_f - d\left(V_f + \sum_{g \neq f} V_g\right)\right]$$

$$+ \sum_{g \neq f} \lambda_f^g \cdot \left[c_g(V_g) + \tau_g - d\left(V_f + \sum_{h \neq f} V_h\right)\right],$$

(6.13)

where $d(\cdot)$ is the inverse demand function for the entire corridor, and each term in square brackets represents a user-equilibrium constraint. The first-order conditions can be solved to yield the following toll formula:

$$\tau = \tau_f = V_f \cdot \left(c'_f - d'\right) + \frac{-d'(F-1)}{c'_{-f} - d'(F-1)} \cdot V_f d',$$ (6.14)

where τ is the toll that each user will pay for a trip; τ_f is the toll for a specific firm (these are identical across firms and equal to τ because of symmetry); c_f is the user cost for the road controlled by firm f; and c_{-f} is the user cost for any other road (symmetry of course implies that $c_f = c_{-f}$). Equation (6.14) shows how the toll is equal to the monopolistic toll of (6.5) when $F = 1$, while it approaches the first-best toll of (4.6) when $F \to \infty$. These results are intuitive, and suggest that the equilibrium toll level is closer to the first-best level when the number of firms is large so that each firm has little market power.

Now consider when individual firms occupy serial segments, each carrying the same traffic V as determined by the inverse demand curve.[6] The following Lagrangian applies to firm f:

$$\Lambda_f = V\tau_f + \lambda \cdot \left\{ c_f(V) + \tau_f + \sum_{g \neq f} \left[c_g(V) + \tau_g \right] - d(V) \right\},$$ (6.15)

where $c_g(V)$ is the average user cost incurred just on the segment operated by firm g, so that the user cost for the entire trip is $c = \Sigma_g c_g$. The first-order conditions yield the following firm-specific toll:

$$\tau_f = V \cdot \left(c'_f + \sum_{g \neq f} c'_g - d' \right).$$ (6.16)

This firm thus internalizes not only the congestion on its own road segment ($V \cdot c'_f$), but also that on each other firm's segment ($V \cdot c'_g$). The reason is that congestion on the other firm's segments affects the firm's marginal revenues in exactly the same way as congestion on its own segment. Since every firm internalizes the congestion on the entire road, the combined toll facing the traveler over-internalizes congestion if $F > 1$. Furthermore, each firm applies a demand-related markup ($-V \cdot d'$) that is identical to what a single monopolist would charge; thus this markup gets charged F times when considering the entire trip. Writing this formally, the total trip toll τ is:

$$\tau = \sum_f \tau_f = F \cdot V \cdot \left(c' - d' \right),$$ (6.17)

which is exactly F times the monopoly toll of (6.5) – which already exceeds the first-best toll. We therefore now find the opposite result to the parallel competition case: here, the lower the number of firms, the closer the overall toll approaches the efficient level – although even with one firm it will never reach that level unless demand is perfectly elastic, whereas a larger number of firms produces an ever-larger total trip toll and hence drives demand toward zero.[7]

These opposing results for the extreme cases are exactly in the direction predicted by the general analysis of Economides and Salop (1992), as just discussed. Thus, the desirability of private road ownership and the ideal number of competitors depend critically on the network configuration and the distribution of firms over that network. Generally, an increase in competition among substitute roads would bring equilibrium tolls closer to first-best levels, while the opposite applies for complementary roads. This suggests that private operators, if allowed on a network, should serve full-length corridors but should face competition when doing so.

Another option, of course, is to regulate the private firms, a topic to which we now turn.

6.2 Regulation and franchising of private roads

The local monopoly power of a private road operator provides a potentially strong economic rationale for regulation. Moreover, it is impractical to allow unrestricted free entry of private road operators given the physical nature of road investment, including its network aspects, lumpiness, irreversibility, right-of-way requirements, and land-use implications. Under what institutional set-up, then, can private roads contribute most to social welfare? The question gains relevance with the growing interest in and importance of private involvement in road operations throughout the world (Estache 2001; World Bank 2006). This section explores various dimensions of such institutional arrangements, which are generally known as public–private partnerships (PPPs). Many of these considerations are part of a more general analysis of privatization in transportation, which is discussed at greater length by Nash (2005). Many of them also can be fitted into broader theories of contract design with limited information.[8]

Private involvement is often motivated by the desire to bring in private capital when public budgets are tight. A second motivation is the hope that private management will be more efficient than public management. Another motivation might be that the public would more readily accept road pricing from a private than from a public entity.

There are few if any truly standardized formats for PPPs, but several categories are generally recognized. The most basic is build–operate–transfer (BOT). Under such a scheme, the concessionaire finances, builds, operates, and maintains the road – usually to predefined specifications – while collecting tolls for a certain period such as 30 years, after which control is transferred to the government. A variant is rehabilitate–operate–transfer (ROT), involving the rehabilitation of an existing road instead of the construction of a new one. The design–build–finance–operate (DBFO) or design–build–operate–transfer (DBOT) format is similar to BOT, but the private party is invited to propose how the road should be configured as well as how it will be built and operated. Another format is leasing, where the government sells to a private operator the right to operate and charge users for an existing road for a specified time period; prominent recent examples are the Chicago Skyway and the Indiana Toll Road, two adjacent portions of US Interstate Route 90 for which long-term leases were sold in 2005 and 2006, respectively.

As an alternative to actual tolls, systems of "shadow tolls" have also been used in certain countries including the UK, Finland, and the Netherlands. In this case, users do not pay actual tolls, but the authority remunerates the concessionaire depending on the degree of utilization. A shadow toll may be better or worse, from the point of view of social welfare, than an actual toll depending on all the considerations discussed in Section 6.1. Shadow tolls are often used in conjunction with a DBFO system of private operation.

Experience with highway franchising has not always been positive. Engel, Fisher and Galetovic (1997) highlight two pitfalls: the frequent use of government guarantees and renegotiations in the face of financial trouble. The first reduces the incentives to control construction costs, while the second encourages bidders to submit overoptimistic bids ("lowballing") on the assumption that discrepancies will be made up later. Engel, Fisher and Galetovic attribute these problems mainly to the fact that most franchises are awarded for a fixed period. They therefore propose to use a variable-term contract instead, in which the franchise is awarded to the bidder that requires the *least present value of revenue* (LPVR) from tolling. In an LPVR auction, each possible revenue stream is converted to a present value through procedures defined in advance as part of the request for bids.[9] The bidder then specifies an amount for this present value that, once reached through the accumulation of toll revenues, ends the term of the franchise. Assuming there are multiple bidders, the smallest such bid wins the franchise. Such an approach is likely to limit the need for guarantees and the scope for contract renegotiations, and therewith the distorting impacts that such practices exert on both the original franchise and the subsequent operations.

Alternative criteria for auctions that have been used in practice include the total capacity cost, duration of the construction period, the toll rate at opening, and the length of the concession (World Bank 2006). Verhoef (2007) finds that toll rates and capacities may in fact depend strongly upon which criterion is used. His analysis considers static congestion, homogeneous travelers, neutral scale economies, and competitive auctions, and allows for unpriced congestion elsewhere on the road network. Perhaps surprisingly, a criterion based on maximizing traffic flow is usually capable of reproducing the zero-profit second-best outcome. An exception is when the road would produce something akin to a Braess paradox, in which case this criterion could lead to a minimum social surplus; but presumably this situation represents a planning failure at the very start of the process.

A key element of franchising is how the risk of uncertain future demand is shared between the government and the private operator. The parties to the agreement (including financial institutions providing capital to the franchisee) vary in their costs of bearing risk, in their information about contingencies, and in their ability to influence these contingencies. It is important to take account of these variations, in particular to provide incentives against any misuse of private information, while still allowing enough flexibility in setting fares to enable pricing to achieve its welfare-improving allocative effects. As an illustration of how such considerations are sometimes ignored, Nash (2005) describes how the UK paid shadow tolls to private road franchisees. Ostensibly the purpose was to transfer the risk of inadequate traffic to the franchisees; yet at the same time, the government removed the franchisees' control over traffic by retaining the power to build competing roads and by restricting the franchisees' ability to develop new interchanges or to implement other traffic-generating measures.

Because of the difficulties of foreseeing all contingencies, the franchising agreement may include some form of price and/or capacity regulation. Otherwise, competition to win the franchise would push bidders towards a profit-maximizing combination of capacity and toll, which, as we have seen, may be far from socially optimal when the road is part of a network. But setting rigid toll rates in advance makes future changes highly political, and may discourage pricing policies that are in the public interest. One solution to this is regulations that limit the rate of return on the project, as specified for example in the franchise that enabled the express lanes to be built on California's State Route 91 as described earlier. Private financial and consulting firms contain personnel with experience in designing contracts under conditions of uncertainty, and for this reason government agencies have often engaged a private firm as a financial advisor early in the process. Still, there is a basic dilemma: having more conditions in the franchise increases the probability that it will better serve the public interest; but it also creates opportunities for incompetence, political manipulation, and corruption on the part of the public authority – all of which tend to defeat the purpose of privatization and to discourage bidders in numbers sufficient for real competition to emerge.

Another dilemma is the need for non-compete provisions that protect a private toll-road operator against competing free roads that might be built by the public sector. Naturally, no private investor will want to put money at risk without some assurance against such competition, especially given turnover among responsible public officials and political parties. At the same time, the public tends to resent agreements that foreclose public options to solve public problems, and this can undermine support for the franchising operation. An example is State Route 91 in Orange County, California, where the original private operator of the 91 Express Lanes (under a very long-term lease) retained veto power over any capacity improvements on the free portion of the road. After it exercised this power in court, the provision became so controversial that it was part of the motivation for a public buyout of the express lanes. Similarly, citizens of Sydney, Australia, became incensed when competing roads were closed as part of a franchise agreement with the builder of the Cross City Tunnel. This resulted in a decision to reverse some of the road closings, presumably with compensation to the tunnel operator, and a public commitment by the prime minister not to permit such provisions in the future.[10]

A skeptic might well argue that, given such complexities, public road provision and tolling should remain the preferred option. A more pragmatic viewpoint is that private road operation should not be a goal in itself, but should be an option when conditions warrant. Such conditions could include competition from substitute road links, a lack of privately controlled complementary road links, an inefficient public road supplier, political limitations on the public sector's ability to implement pricing or to undertake desirable price discrimination, disadvantages for the public sector in capital markets, public budgeting constraints that lead to insufficient funds for investment, relatively small external effects other than congestion, and the availability of an efficient and effective auction mechanism. But libertarians might argue that some of these conditions are universally present, so that private provision should be the norm and only if it involves demonstrable and insurmountable problems should public provision be substituted (*e.g.*, Foldvary 2006).

We conclude, then, that it is impossible to say in general whether private or public road provision is more desirable. The extent to which the conditions just described apply, and therewith the relative desirability for private road supply, can be expected to vary strongly across nations, regions, and over time. Fortunately, many degrees and forms of privatization are possible and understanding these conditions is the key to choosing among them.

6.3 Privately provided transit services

Following widespread socialization of public transit during the middle of the twentieth century, the world has witnessed since 1980 a wave of privatization and deregulation that has resulted in much experimentation in organizational forms for providing transit service. This has created opportunities for comparing results of alternatives ranging from public ownership and operation, through various public coordinating or regulatory roles, to fully-deregulated private provision. Nash (2005) provides an insightful review of issues and experience.

Dissatisfaction with public control has been fueled by huge budgetary commitments to urban public transit, which in many places grew enormously following consolidation of operators under public ownership. For example, Pickrell (1983) and Lave (1991) examine the sources of rising US transit operating deficits, tracing much of the cause to wage increases and inefficiently capital-intensive operations, which in turn were encouraged by incentives built into subsidy programs. Analysts distinguish several other possible disadvantages of public ownership including political interference and inability of the public sector to finance timely investments. As noted by Nash (2005), these differing motivations for turning to the private sector do not necessarily lead to compatible directions for change: for example, cost control may require competition whereas raising funds for investment may require some monopoly power.

This last point bears emphasis. As we have already seen in the case of road franchises, there is a tension between the desire to best serve the public, which requires limiting the markup that private operators would provide to their marginal-cost prices, and the desire to maximize the value of the government's asset. This tension is not unique to transportation industries. Societal goals for efficient pricing and output in the short run are generally well served by fostering competition, whereas innovation and technical change are likely to involve fixed costs and so may require market power to be profitable. Unfortunately, it is difficult to separate this rationale for market power from the simple desire to exploit a profit opportunity.

In this section, we review the main forms that private-sector involvement takes, followed by an analysis of the outcomes likely under some of these forms – particularly as influenced by the nature of competition or lack thereof. We then examine empirical evidence on the extent to which private operators display lower costs and/or higher labor productivity. Next, we review worldwide experience with privatization and deregulation of public transit, with special attention to the rich lessons revealed by the UK since 1985 and to special problems in developing nations. Finally we consider paratransit (a loose collection of transit-like services, often provided privately) and conventional taxi service.

6.3.1 Forms of privatization

We have already seen, in discussing private highways, that there are many intermediate positions between the extremes of full public operation and unregulated private ownership. With transit, there are even more dimensions along which such intermediate positions can be defined, since we must consider not only infrastructure provision but also ongoing operation.

The least drastic form of privatization is *tendering*, also called *contracting* or *contracting out*. In this arrangement, the public authority retains full control over network design and services offered, but contracts with private firms to carry out specific parts of this overall design such as operating prespecified bus runs or maintaining rolling stock (*i.e.*, vehicles). An example of tendering is the private bus operators with which London Transport contracted in the early phases of UK deregulation during the 1980s.

Going somewhat further, the public authority can *franchise* some of these services by licensing private firms to operate them under less specific guidelines.[11] The franchise is for a specified period of time, which in the case of regional rail services has ranged from as little as two or three years in Sweden to several decades in parts of South America (Nash 2005). Performance goals may be mandated or encouraged through incentives, including the prospect of favorable consideration for later renewal of the franchise. Desired investments whose useful lifetimes would exceed the length of the franchise can be encouraged by contractual terms, government investment subsidies, or co-ownership arrangements. Needless to say, each of these options opens the possibility of contract disputes, strategic renegotiations, and outright abandonment of obligations by a financially failing firm.

Going further still, the market to provide certain services may be simply turned over to one or more private firms, as is common for example with telecommunications and electricity in many nations. This could be a *regulated monopoly*, in which a single firm is allowed to provide services under tightly controlled terms of price and service quality. If freedom of entry is allowed, the regulations over price and service may be relaxed on the assumption that competition will produce a desirable result just as for other goods in a largely market economy. Depending on how completely such regulations are relaxed, the result is some degree of *privatization with deregulation*. In virtually all cases, government oversight is maintained over such things as safety, financial disclosure, and matters covered by general business policies.

Naturally, the relative advantages of different forms of privatization depend on the nature of the industry. A primary consideration is whether or not the market is a natural monopoly, meaning that costs display scale economies that are strong enough to make it unacceptably inefficient to have more than one producer. Natural monopoly is often thought to characterize infrastructure (*e.g.*, rail track, large bus terminals) but not operations. However, as we have seen, transit operations are also subject to scale economies when they require substantial access costs on the part of users and when the desire to reduce such access costs, by providing frequent and/or geographically dense service, is a limiting factor in choosing the size of transit vehicles. Thus, transit operations may also be a natural monopoly and it is no coincidence that free entry into privatized transit markets has often led to consolidation of the market by one or at most a very few firms.

6.3.2 Market structure and competitive practices

If markets are left partially or fully unregulated, what will happen? This question has been addressed specifically for public transport through theoretical, empirical, and simulation analysis.

A first question is whether private firms could operate profitably without subsidies. Several authors have found a range of conditions under which this is possible. Harker (1988) formulates a model in which several types of transit compete with each other and with (uncongested) auto and applies it to three Philadelphia-area corridors; he finds profitable bus service in one of them, which has relatively high density and low incomes. Cervero (1990), reviewing individual transit routes in 25 US cities, similarly finds that those operating at a profit serve mostly high-density areas with low-income people and short trip lengths. By contrast, case studies analyzed by Morlok and Viton (1980, 1985) find a niche for expensive, high-quality service by commuter rail (Chicago), rapid transit (Lindenwold line into Philadelphia), and bus (express service into Manhattan). It seems then that there are two potentially profitable markets for conventional urban transit: high-quality express service from affluent suburbs to large employment centers, and local bus service serving low-income people in high-density areas.

A second question is whether private operation produces desirable results. This is a much broader question; to analyze it, we have to consider the complexities of competition under various market conditions.

One line of inquiry is the nature of unregulated and imperfectly competitive equilibria in which two or more firms compete. Often these are modeled as some variation of a Bertrand equilibrium, in which each firm assumes that the price and quality of service offered by other firms are fixed. For example, Evans (1987) considers an unregulated non-cooperative oligopoly with free entry. The equilibrium exhibits higher fares and higher service frequency than would result either from unconstrained welfare maximization or from welfare maximization subject to a breakeven constraint. However, in Evans' simulations (p. 23), welfare in the oligopolistic case falls only slightly short of that resulting from constrained or unconstrained welfare maximization, whereas it far exceeds (at most demand levels) that resulting from monopoly. Hence, Evan's results are supportive of deregulation as a viable policy when the market is likely to accommodate two or more firms.

But will such an oligopolistic structure emerge in an unregulated market? Dodgson and Katsoulacos (1988b) examine entry conditions in order to address this question for local bus service. They find a wide range of market conditions under which just two firms share the market. However, the firms differentiate their products in order to increase their market power, so the results are not necessarily as desirable as in Evans' more symmetric solutions. Similarly, Viton (1981a) finds that two transit firms would significantly differentiate their products if they engaged in Cournot-like competition, in which each assumes the other will respond to its actions so as to maintain its customer base.

Despite the theoretical possibility of oligopoly, experience in the UK suggests that in most deregulated local bus markets, one firm becomes dominant through superior efficiency, predatory practices, mergers, or luck. Thus we need to ask whether it is necessary to regulate such a firm in order to prevent the high price and low ridership expected from a monopoly. A key question here is whether *potential* entry by competitors would serve to discipline a monopolist's decisions about price and service. At the extreme, we can ask whether the transit market is *contestable*: is the prospect of hit-and-run entry sufficiently threatening to force a monopolist to choose competitive fare and service policies? Contestability requires that the entrant have low barriers to entry and exit (the latter requiring an absence of sunk costs), and also that the incumbent be unable to change fares and service levels too quickly (Baumol, Panzar and Willig 1982).

Button (1988) argues that there is substantial though not perfect contestability in urban transit. Certain features favor low barriers to entry and exit: lack of significant economies of scale in providing vehicle-hours of service, low set-up costs, and a good market in used bus equipment. On the other hand, substantial investments may be required to establish a reputation, build terminal facilities, or achieve efficiency through learning-by-doing. These investments by an entrant cannot be retrieved if the monopolist responds to entry by quickly lowering fares or increasing service. If the monopolist can credibly threaten to do so temporarily, in order to drive out the entrant, it is said to be capable of *predation*, which discourages entry. Dodgson and Katsoulacos (1988a) analyze when a rational monopolist would respond in this way, showing that informational asymmetries can lead to successful predation.

Indeed, the limited empirical evidence suggests that transit markets are not fully contestable. Evans (1988) describes the experience in Hereford, UK, where transit service was deregulated beginning in 1981. Following a brief period of intense competition, the dominant firm drove out all its rivals except in one small segment of its market. Fares ultimately returned nearly to the levels that prevailed prior to the experiment, but service levels remained substantially higher. Evans suggests that potential entry constrains a monopolist's service levels, which cannot be quickly increased in response to entry, but does not constrain its fares. As we will see in Section 6.3.4, higher prices and more frequent service were consistent results of deregulation of local bus service in Great Britain (outside of London) starting in 1986.

Such experience is consistent with the theory of competition with differentiated products – in this case, service at different times of day (Schmalensee 1978). In such a market, the threat of potential entry will typically cause a monopolist to offer an excessive number of products in order not to leave an open niche for a competitor. The reason is that the monopolist can protect its high profits on each product through price predation, giving it a strong incentive to maintain dominance in each product; but it cannot so easily protect against new products because doing so would require immediately matching an entrant's product characteristics.

Van der Veer (2002) performs numerical simulations to compute the results of such behavior on a prototype bus line. He finds that, as expected, a profit-maximizing monopolist would like to offer service that is *less* frequent than would be optimal – even less than would be second-best optimal subject to a breakeven constraint. But if the monopolist wants to deter entry, it will instead offer service that is *more* frequent than optimal. Van der Veer also finds inefficiencies regarding other dimensions of service quality, which can be partly ameliorated if the government offers a per-rider subsidy. A greater improvement can be achieved by combining a per-rider subsidy with a lump-sum payment required of the firm, which is what could result from a competitive franchising system. The idea here is that the ridership-related subsidy encourages a lower price and better quality of service, while the lump-sum tax (assumed to apply equally to a potential entrant) reduces the incentive to oversupply service because it makes entry more difficult.[12]

The models described above mostly assume constant returns to scale in producing intermediate outputs. Furthermore, most implicitly assume that any economies of scale due to user-supplied time are at a system level rather than a firm level: that is, the traveler cares only about total bus frequency on his or her route, not about the frequency provided by a given firm. This, however, raises troubling questions about the viability of a non-integrated system of urban transit. What if it is not feasible for each firm to use the same stops, for example because they use vehicles of different sizes or because major terminals are owned by one firm? What if consumers care about the reputations of firms whose vehicles they are about to enter? What if the unregulated equilibrium entails differentiated products, *e.g.*, high-fare express and low-fare local service, so that travelers with a strong preference for one cannot benefit from the extra service frequency offered by the other? In all these situations, scale economies are lost by allowing multiple providers, because the waiting times of a given firm's riders are not diminished by an increase in service supplied by other firms. Nash (1988) emphasizes the importance of system integration in realizing these user-cost savings and also reminds us of several other sources of economies of scale and scope, such as through ticketing of passengers and scheduling of drivers, that occur in an integrated system. The implication is that efficiency may be lost unless a central authority takes a proactive role in coordinating service.

Klein, Moore and Reja (1997) tackle yet another issue of entry conditions. Part of a firm's set-up requirements for entering the market for local bus service, they argue, is the need for customers to learn that if they show up at a particular bus stop, a bus will appear to take them where they want to go. This requires establishing a reputation for frequency of service, perhaps by initially providing a greater frequency than could be justified otherwise. But once the availability of service at that location is widely known, competing firms can pick up those same waiting passengers, depriving the initial entrant of the returns from its investment. If the potential entrant understands this in advance, entry may never occur. The solution suggested by Klein, Moore and Reja is to establish "curb rights" that allocate a given curb location to a given firm, which would then be able to reap the advantages of its reputation either directly or by licensing the right to others.

The theoretical considerations described here are consistent with more general analyses of privatization of industries mentioned earlier. Those analyses stress the importance of competition and other institutional structures in providing incentives for good management. Neither public nor private ownership guarantees a strong or a weak set of incentives; instead, much depends on specific rules and policies.

6.3.3 Efficiency of public and private providers

Two types of studies have attempted to compare the costs or productivities of public and private transit operators. The first type compares firms across cities, often estimating cost functions to control for factors other than the type of ownership. The second examines the results in a given city when tendering or franchising of transit services is introduced. Frick, Taylor and Wachs (2007) and Karlaftis (2007) review these studies carefully.

Comparisons across areas

Cross-sectional studies have reached varying conclusions about whether or not private operators are more efficient than public operators.[13] These studies are complicated by potential biases that may make private operators falsely appear more efficient. Public operators often experience sharper daily peaks, and a public authority may take over previously failing private firms or spin off its more successful operations, thereby leaving it with less inefficient operations at any point in time. After accounting for these factors, Iseki (2004), in one of the most careful analyses, finds modest cost savings from contracting of around 5% to 8% in the US.

Before-and-after comparisons

Preston (2005) and Karlaftis (2007) review a number of cases where publicly operated bus and rail services switched to a tendering system. Again the evidence is mixed, but generally positive. Cost savings and/or productivity improvements have been reported for several cases in Sweden, Spain, Australia, New Zealand, and the US. For bus services, most cases reported have shown some immediate reductions in unit costs, averaging around 20% if services remained unchanged and more if services were restructured.

The relatively simple but apparently effective practice of *gross cost contracting* (the "Scandinavian model" in Preston's terminology), in which firms bid on the payment at which they will offer specified services, has been used in Sweden, Norway, Copenhagen, London, Helsinki, Rome, Auckland, and Las Vegas (Nevada), among other places. Some studies have suggested that savings are greater with *net cost contracting*, in which the firm collects and keeps fare revenue. Competitive bids then specify the amount of subsidy required or, perhaps, the amount of profits the firm is willing to return to the government. With this arrangement, the risk created by uncertain demand is shifted to the private firm – which has advantages and disadvantages. On the plus side, the firm is given an incentive to provide services that attract users. On the minus side, private firms may be less able to bear risk than a government, resulting in higher bids and less competition for the contract (Estache and Gómez-Lobo 2005).

The experience with tendering service is less favorable with rail than with bus. Rail service has higher fixed costs and involves a more complex relationship between infrastructure and operations. These traits create more scope for strategic bidding and predatory pricing as means for firms to attempt to control the market. Attempts to privatize the infrastructure itself have been the most problematic, as we will discuss in Section 6.3.4.

As with many economic policies, success depends in part on the particular mechanism used and how well it matches conditions of the local market. There are many dimensions for choosing a form of tendering or franchising: for example, contract duration, ownership of vehicles and terminals, types of bonuses and penalties, and location of responsibility for choosing fares and service levels. Thus it is not surprising to find a lot of variation in outcomes.

Furthermore, the results of any real privatization will depend greatly on the extent and nature of regulation of private firms. A comprehensive theory of regulation developed by Laffont and Tirole (1993) emphasizes information asymmetries between a regulator and the regulated firms – typically the firms know more about their own cost structures, which is information the regulator needs in order to set regulatory parameters. A central conclusion of the theory is that one can often design contracts that induce firms to implicitly reveal their information, and to voluntarily make desirable choices, by offering an appropriate menu of contractual options. Gagnepain and Ivaldi (2002) apply this theory by estimating cost functions that include regulatory variables, using a data set drawn from urban transit providers in France. They find significant departures from optimal contracting arrangements, with cost-plus contracts proving to be especially inefficient. There have been a few other attempts to apply this theory to public transit services, described by Estache and Gómez-Lobo (2005).

Conclusions

While results of private transit provision are promising, the evidence is not straightforward. Rather, it supports the conclusion from the theoretical literature, described earlier, that the most important factors are those that affect the nature of management incentives, especially the nature of competition and regulation, rather than the type of ownership itself. This observation provides a useful background as we examine, in the next subsection, the practical experience with institutional changes in public transit.

6.3.4 Experience with privatization and deregulation

A great deal of experience is now available to help assess the implications of privatization and deregulation of public transit services. Nash (2005) is particularly helpful, covering not only urban transit but inter-city modes as well. Here we focus on two special cases that have proven illuminating: Great Britain starting in 1985, and developing nations.

Great Britain since 1985

One of the most far-reaching and varied experiments with privatization of transit services took place in Great Britain following the British Transport Act of 1985. Useful reviews include Glaister (1997), Small and Gómez-Ibáñez (1999, Section 5.5), Darbéra (2004), and Nash (2005, Section 4).[14]

We can distinguish three quite different experiments in British urban areas. Outside London urban bus services were mostly privatized and free entry was permitted, with municipal operators required either to privatize or to operate on a commercial basis. (Subsidies were allowed but had to be made available on equal terms to all firms.) Within London the public bus operator (London Transport) was retained but it was required to tender services through competitive contracts, while maintaining central control over schedules, routes, and fares. The London Underground, by contrast, was unaffected by the 1985 Act, but starting in 2003 its infrastructure maintenance and investment activities were spun off through public–private partnerships (PPPs).

The main results outside London were large service increases (as measured by vehicle-kilometers), higher fares, lower patronage, and substantial cost savings. Real wages for drivers stabilized after a prior increase but have not substantially declined, implying that the cost savings represent improved productivity. Much of the service increase represented a switch to smaller buses, called "minibuses." The higher fares resulted not from the new market structure but from a drastic reduction in government subsidies that was made simultaneously with deregulation.

The patronage decline was the biggest surprise. Several studies from the mid-1990s compare patronage with counterfactual scenarios to see how much of the decline was due to deregulation (Small and Gómez-Ibáñez 1999). Some results suggest that fare increases alone cannot explain the decline, with authors suggesting that lack of integration of service among competing operators may have diminished the quality of service. Neither is the decline explained by transitional difficulties, as it continued throughout the 1990s and, at a slower rate, to the time of this writing.[15]

The nature of competition varied among metropolitan areas. In most cases, any serious competition was soon eliminated by aggressive increases in route frequency, predatory pricing, or mergers. Mackie, Preston and Nash (1995) explain this consolidation, at least in part, as reflecting inherent advantages of incumbents such as local knowledge. Scale economies of the kind described in Chapter 3 may also help explain it.

The experience with London's buses is in some ways similar: more service, higher fares, and dramatic cost reductions. However, patronage did not fall, but instead has shown a steady increase.[16] This last observation offers some support to the hypothesis that users benefit from the integrated planning of service offerings that continues in London, but it also reflects a much more moderate subsidy-cutting program in London than elsewhere.

The public–private partnerships (PPPs) for the London Underground, forced through by the national government over the strenuous objections of the Mayor of London, consist of three extremely detailed contracts with private consortia of firms to maintain and improve the track, stations, rolling stock, and other infrastructure of specific groups of Underground lines.[17] These contracts were competitively bid, and two of them were awarded to the same consortium; thus, in fact, there are two firms with responsibility for the Underground's infrastructure. London Underground, a public agency, retains responsibility for train operations and fare collection, and is given somewhat circumscribed responsibility to monitor the contracts. The contracts call for frontloading of expenditures by the private firms, to speed up needed upgrades to what everyone agreed was a seriously deteriorated system. These expenditures were covered by private financing arranged by the consortia as part of their bids.

Performance of the two "infrastructure companies," called "infracos," inevitably involved some well-publicized problems including a series of braking failures in 2005, which led London Underground to intervene in the responsible infraco's subcontracting arrangements under a safety clause in the PPP. (Financial penalties were subsequently imposed under the PPP's performance-based provisions.) In other aspects, London Underground (2006) reported mostly satisfactory results from the infracos as of March 2006. But only time will tell whether the Mayor's Commissioner for Transport was right in claiming that divided management will undermine the coordination between operations and infrastructure activities needed for some planned major construction projects.

Developing nations

A number of special characteristics of developing nations influence the performance of privately-provided transit. First, gaps in managerial capacity of government agencies typically make it much less likely that regulations will be consistently enforced. This means that a regulated monopoly or a regulated market of private firms may behave quite differently – generally more chaotically – than intended.

Second, the widespread availability of low-wage labor and the difficulty with which small businesses can raise capital create the possibility of very small companies. Thus many developing cities are characterized by hundreds of separate bus companies – estimated for example at 200 on average for a single minibus route in Lagos, Nigeria (Gwilliam 2005, p. 7). At the same time, a third trait of developing cities is a high modal share for bus transit – estimated for example at 61% for Santiago, Chile, far greater than for any European city (Estache and Gómez-Lobo 2005, p. 147). These factors combine to create the potential for huge numbers of individually-owned buses competing for passengers in an unregulated or under-regulated environment.

Fourth, transit riders in any poor country are likely to value their time at a far lower monetary amount than riders in richer countries. This factor tends to lower the optimal frequency, which depends on a tradeoff of value of time against operating costs. (The latter includes capital goods so is not perfectly correlated with value of time.) As we have already seen, a free-entry equilibrium is likely to result in higher than optimal frequency; this tendency is thus even more harmful in developing countries.

Finally, these tendencies toward oversupply of buses interact with a fifth trait: the prevalence of high levels of congestion, air pollution, and traffic accidents in large developing cities. Bus transit accounts for a high proportion of air emissions in many developing cities – for example nearly one-fourth of fine particulates and more than one-third of nitrogen oxides in Santiago in 2000 (Gwilliam 2005, p. 16). Thus in such cities the tendency of free markets toward excess supply exacerbates congestion and pollution, in contrast to developed countries where excess transit service would tend to reduce congestion and pollution by diverting some people from car trips (Estache and Gómez-Lobo 2005, p. 147). As for accidents, transit buses in developing cities are heavily involved in collisions, and any market structure that encourages "on-the-road competition" for passengers, in the form of drivers racing to the next bus stop in order to collect fares from those passengers, makes the situation even worse.

Experience in two South American cities illustrates how policy makers have tried to alleviate these problems. In Bogotá, Colombia, the TransMilenio project begun in 2000 establishes a single public company to design the bus network, to oversee tendering of routes to private operators, and to organize a centralized (and separately tendered) fare collection system (Estache and Gómez-Lobo 2005, pp. 153–55). At the same time, several elements of bus rapid transit were added, including exclusive bus lanes and enclosed bus stops. Operators work on gross-cost contracts so that they have no incentive to compete for passengers. In its first year, very favorable results were reported: a 32% reduction in average trip times, reductions in bus-related accidents and injuries by 89% and 74%, respectively, and 13% to 54% reductions in air-pollutant concentrations. These gains are despite the fact that 85% of bus trips are on parts of the system that are not part of TransMilenio.

A broadly similar project, Transantiago, began operating in Santiago, Chile, in 2006.[18] It has many of the same goals as TransMilenio: faster travel times, fewer operators, integrated fares (including transfers to and from the subway system), and elimination of drivers racing for passengers. It follows an earlier system of competitive tendering based on net-cost contracts, begun in 1991, which reportedly reduced the number of buses in central Santiago by 31% (Kain and Liu 2002, p. 159). Transantiago hopes to further reduce bus proliferation and on-the-road competition by changing to gross-cost contracts, with pollution one of the factors in the criteria for awarding tenders. The system aims to require no public subsidies.

6.3.5 Paratransit

Private entrepreneurs and firms, in addition to providing conventional transit service, sometimes fill market niches with other services that, like public transit, involve strangers sharing a vehicle. Examples include subscription commuter buses, semi-scheduled jitney services by vans or minibuses, airport shuttle vans, demand-responsive services activated by telephone or hailing, shared-ride taxi, and commuter vanpools. These services, known generally as "paratransit," are usually discouraged by competition from subsidized transit systems and are often strongly inhibited or prohibited outright by regulations. Thus one outcome of deregulation or privatization of transit may be the spontaneous emergence of paratransit services.

What market characteristics can we expect of paratransit? Cervero (1997) provides a comprehensive review of experience. Some types, namely subscription vans and airport shuttles, have proven commercially viable in very specialized markets and seem not to provoke a lot of controversy. Others, such as commuter vanpools, are mostly arranged through large employers (often with government pressure to increase employees' average vehicle occupancy) and again thrive in very limited markets. Yet another type, demand-responsive transit or "dial-a-ride," in which specialized vehicles provide shared-ride service with advance reservations, is very expensive (at least with current dispatching technology) and in the US is almost entirely limited to government-mandated service for elderly and physically handicapped riders.

Here, we concentrate on two other types of paratransit – jitneys and shared-ride taxis – that are most likely to arise spontaneously and that seem capable, in certain circumstances, of carrying substantial market shares of urban trips. Both modes have certain supply characteristics that keep costs down: low overhead expense, small general-purpose vehicles, ability to use part-time labor, and flexibility in adjusting to changing demand conditions.

Jitneys are vans or small buses that follow somewhat regular routes but generally not on a published schedule and often with *ad hoc* route deviations to accommodate passenger needs. From Cervero's observations, it appears that cities with long narrow corridors, limited parking, and a major trip generator (like a rail station or compact business district) offer a favorable environment for jitney service. Jitneys tend to be politically favored in emergency situations such as when a city recovers from hurricane or earthquake damage or during fuel supply disruptions. They also perform better and improve their image when they regulate themselves concerning safety, driving practices, customer service, and the like through industry associations. However, jitneys are often eliminated by regulations instigated by hostile competitors, including public transit systems, and they are highly vulnerable to targeted competition from a subsidized transit system. Thus, while jitneys have thrived in many US cities for periods of a few years to several decades, they had almost entirely disappeared by the late 1990s.

In many developing nations, by contrast, jitneys are an important component of urban transportation – especially in Latin America, Southeast Asia, and Africa. Mexico City has an extensive system, accounting for one-third of all motorized trips in the metropolitan area in

1994, with government regulation of fares, routes, and certain performance standards (Cervero 1997, p. 128). In Bangkok, Jakarta, and Manila, jitneys and shared-ride taxis together accounted for 18% to 30% of all motor vehicles in the early 1990s (Cervero 1997, p. 134). In Africa, jitneys have mostly replaced conventional bus transit; and similar trends appear to be under way in eastern Europe and central Asia (Gwilliam 2003, p. 201).

Shared-ride taxi service means that drivers can combine passengers who are not necessarily traveling together but who have origins and destinations in compatible locations or directions. The ability to do this is mostly determined by the nature of taxi regulation. Where permitted, such service is encouraged by a zone fare system (used, for example, in Washington, DC) and by a pay structure that gives the driver all the incremental revenue resulting from carrying additional travelers. Like jitney service, it is vulnerable to competition from cheap bus transit and in the absence of self-regulation it can easily get a reputation for poor service.

6.3.6 Conventional taxi service

Exclusive-ride taxi is an important but somewhat neglected sector in urban transportation. Taxis handle a large number of passenger trips and provide an alternative to car ownership or rental for short occasional trips, including many by low-income people. Service is heavily regulated in most cities, for reasons that are complex and vary with local conditions.

A number of experiments with deregulation have been undertaken during the past three decades, providing evidence about the nature of the industry and, by comparison, about the effects of the prior regulatory regimes. The loosening of entry and price controls has consistently resulted in significant increases in the number of taxis operating: 18% to 127% in seven US cities deregulated in the decade prior to 1985; 15% in Sweden's two largest metropolitan areas (deregulation 1991); and approximately 100% in New Zealand (deregulated 1989) and in Ireland (2000). Fares, however, have not declined as predicted by many analysts who believed that the industry behaves like a monopoly under regulation (due to regulatory "capture" by industry leaders) and like a perfectly competitive market when unregulated. In fact, fares in cities that deregulated have risen as fast or faster than elsewhere. In New Zealand, deregulated fares in real terms appear to have fallen slightly, but in the US they rose about equally in regulated and deregulated cities, and in Sweden (Stockholm and Göteberg) they rose by around 30%.[19] In the Netherlands, deregulation in 1999 was followed in the next four years by a 50% increase in the numbers of taxis and firms, an 11% increase in real fares, and a 17% reduction in the number of rides (TNS/NIPO KPMG 2004).

Service quality seems to have improved in some cases in terms of availability (*e.g.*, an 18% decrease in average access time in Sweden); but in some cases service has also deteriorated in terms of refusals or no-shows. Productivity dramatically declined in several cases as taxi drivers spent more time cruising or simply queuing at cab stands. In the case of the US, these results seem due to a deregulated market structure typically characterized as an oligopoly with a competitive fringe, with the fringe adding unnecessary excess service to dense markets (airports and other large pickup spots), and perhaps with less oversight over the reliability of the drivers. There were also increased passenger complaints over drivers who did not know the city and/or who could not speak the local language well. On the whole, it seems safe to conclude that successful deregulation needs to take close account of the fact that even if the market appears to have many firms, the individual "products" being bought and sold depend on matching a particular provider with a particular origin-destination request, and this makes the actual market behavior far from competitive.

Indeed, taxicab service exhibits scale economies analogous to those for scheduled transit service, both in the cruising sector (where cabs are hailed by sight) and in the dispatch sector (where cabs are routed in real time over a large network). This is because the average waiting time for finding a cab declines with the density of available cabs, which in turn rises with demand in the medium term. These scale economies probably help account for the tendency of the dispatch market, in which passengers can contact the firm of their choice, to be dominated by a few large firms. Scale economies by themselves would imply that an unregulated equilibrium will have too little service; but countering this effect are congestion and pollution externalities.

The basic idea that scale economies arise from the dependence of waiting time on number of available vehicles underlies a number of formal models.[20] All such models produce the result that a first-best optimum involves negative profits. Some also consider oligopolies and entry barriers such as may be created by the need to be part of a radio-dispatch service. The models differ on the viability of a second-best optimum (one with profits constrained to be non-negative), the result depending on what degrees of freedom the firms are assumed to have. For example, Frankena and Pautler (1986) assume that waiting time depends on the number of taxis, and suggest that the second-best optimum could be obtained just through price regulation; whereas Cairns and Liston-Heyes (1996) assume that each driver can determine hours of operation, arguing that even if price and number of vehicles are regulated at second-best optimum levels, drivers will choose to operate too many hours per day and therefore provide too much service in aggregate. It seems that to make more progress, it is crucial to accurately match modeling assumptions to characteristics of a specific regulatory environment, making it likely that quite different outcomes can be expected depending on fine details of the local situation.

One disappointment from past efforts to deregulate taxi service is that little innovation occurred – nothing like the enormous transformation in strategies that have characterized airlines, trucking, and inter-city railroads, for example. However, the onset of on-board guidance and global positioning systems could dramatically change the potential for larger taxi firms to increase their service quality and dispatching efficiency. Thus, in the future we may see significant changes in the industry when regulatory restrictions allow them, and we will need new modeling techniques to help regulators know which such changes should be encouraged.

6.4 Conclusions

Dissatisfaction with publicly provided transportation infrastructure and services has sparked renewed interest in applying free-market principles to urban transportation. Current research suggests that although the transportation sector is far from meeting the conditions under which unregulated markets are fully efficient, selective use of private enterprise can improve incentives and bring about significant cost savings. We are learning a great deal about the effects of specific regulatory measures on market structure and performance, both from more fine-tuned theoretical models and from careful empirical examination of the many experiments being carried out around the world.

7 Conclusion

Our review of transportation economics has revealed several themes that characterize contemporary urban transportation research. We now turn to an assessment of how these themes are likely to evolve and influence the character of urban transportation research in the future.

7.1 Emerging themes

We anticipate that five major themes will emerge as central topics in transportation analysis, led by developments in transportation economics. The first four themes – reliability, safety, design of road-pricing schemes, and institutional reforms – are extensions of ideas already covered in this book, so our prognosis is perhaps biased by the interest in them we have already revealed. Indeed, we hope that our treatment of them will help stimulate the very developments that we are forecasting. The fifth theme – urban goods movement – is something about which we have said little, but urge transportation economists to vigorously pursue in the future.

Reliability

In Chapters 2 and 3, we identified reliability as a significant factor in travel decisions and in the cost of travel. The most difficult step in making it operational has been to develop measurement tools for actual roads sufficient to incorporate reliability into revealed-preference (RP) analyses. Tools are currently available but they require too much effort to replicate widely in applied studies and do not correspond well to the kinds of hypothetical questions that have been developed for stated-preference (SP) studies.

We expect to see several developments on this front. First, researchers are likely to refine tools to extract measures of reliability, of the kind already identified as helping to explain travel behavior, from the plethora of roadway data now being collected as part of congestion management efforts. Second, researchers will find practical ways to generate predictions of reliability in supply models; this will include a more sophisticated way of analyzing incidents that produce unusual delays. Third, travel-demand researchers will further refine SP questions so that the answers can be transformed into the kind of reliability measures used in RP analyses and in supply models. Fourth, the theory connecting cost of reliability with scheduling decisions will be further developed, with attention to finding relationships (for example, between expected travel cost and specific measures of reliability) that are more general than those now known for specific probability distributions. Fifth, both theory and practical measurements will be developed to provide a simpler and more robust picture of reliability for scheduled periodic services such as public transit – for which, as we noted in Chapter 3, current models are extremely complex and case-specific.

Together, these developments will put reliability on an equal footing with average travel time in terms of modeling capability. Both travel time and travel-time reliability will become universally recognized as critical components in all aspects of transportation analysis. Future textbooks, we think, will assume that every student needs to understand the theory and measurement of reliability as part of the basic training for a career in transportation.

Safety

The cost of traffic accidents, a component of transportation cost identified in Chapter 3, is even larger than the cost of unreliability. As economies grow, and especially as developing economies come to more closely resemble today's highly developed economies, people will place even larger values on safety. This will make traffic accidents an even more prominent part of transportation analysis.

Economics now has long experience with analyzing people's willingness to pay for reduced probability of accidental injury or death. It has shorter but useful experience with analyzing the incentives involved and how they interact with the legal system, the healthcare system, driver behavior, congestion, traffic regulations, vehicle characteristics, and safety regulations for vehicles. There is some work in law journals on these topics, and some in journals covering law and economics. Yet the primary outlets for research on transportation safety remain mostly within engineering. Economists have a great deal to add to this topic, and we expect to see them articulate how traffic accidents affect transportation analysis across the board, from travel demand to institutional analysis, properly accounting for the role of insurance which is often supplied in a private market but under asymmetric information. In other words, we expect to see safety analysis, with economic rigor and insights, pervading transportation modeling in a manner similar to what we expect for reliability.

Design of road-pricing schemes

We have seen in Chapter 4 that second-best analysis has become essential to using economic models to inform policy. This is because first-best pricing is largely off the table as a practical policy, but more restricted pricing schemes are of intense interest to policy makers. The problem is that each situation requires a distinct model to deal with it. Because of this, it has been difficult for us to characterize the results of these models in terms of general lessons for policy toward road pricing. We expect to see future researchers address this task by relating summary measures of success of a proposed pricing system to the characteristics of the system. We might call this a meta-second-best analysis: a formal analysis of the results of individual second-best analyses.

At least five elements will characterize the use of such meta-analyses in road-pricing design. The first element is the role of user heterogeneity in creating a demand for niche products. Deregulation in other transportation industries has led to an explosion of new products and services; nothing comparable has occurred in urban transportation, but this may be due to a less supportive institutional structure rather than to a lack of possibilities. Are there trucking firms that would pay for congestion bypass routes during particular hours, or that would use smaller delivery vehicles under certain conditions? Are there enough drivers of passenger cars who would value a parkway-like express road with lane widths, curvature, and bridge clearances unsuitable for trucks? Would enough people pay for a guaranteed travel time to an airport? All these possibilities imply potential situations where road pricing, perhaps combined with road investments, could be used to make such a niche market financially feasible. Given the barriers to private highways that we discussed in Chapter 6, a free market may never develop fully enough to exploit all such possibilities, and so it is more incumbent upon researchers to consider them.

A second element of road-pricing meta-analysis is reliability. Once better measures and analytical tools are developed, as discussed earlier, how will they be used in designing road pricing? One way is to integrate road pricing with traffic information: if real-time information and guidance systems can include the availability of priced options as a response to unforeseen delays, the benefits of pricing may thereby be enhanced. Another way is to offer travelers a warranty against exceeding a stated travel time.

A third element of road-pricing meta-analysis is the role of simplicity. We expect analysts to seek ways to improve the welfare properties of second-best pricing systems while still keeping them understandable to travelers.

A fourth element is the distributional impacts of pricing. The differential impacts on different people is an important component of the politics of pricing – both because of the way politics aggregates individuals' self-interests and because of the way people, acting as citizens, value fairness and equity. Economic models are already quite rich in their ability to measure distributional effects, and we expect that these results will be important components of general guidelines for the design of road pricing.

A fifth element is the role of dynamics. Our discussion has demonstrated that models that are rich enough to represent scheduling decisions generally identify such adjustments as the major source of social welfare gains from optimal pricing. These timing adjustments take place on a much finer time scale than between peak and off-peak, instead involving adaptations *within* peak periods. Toll schedules that exploit the potential benefits from departure-time adjustments, particularly by preventing hypercongested queuing, seem likely not only to provide substantial efficiency gains but also to induce less political opposition – provided the public and policy makers hold the same expectations of a policy's main effects as are predicted by the analysis on which the policy is based. An important task therefore remains to further develop dynamic models of congestion pricing, preferably based on physically sound representations of traffic-flow dynamics with endogenous departure patterns, so that they inform policy debates in an intuitive manner.

Institutional reforms

We have seen in Chapter 6 that policy makers around the world are seeking to increase private-sector participation in providing urban transportation infrastructure and services. This requires them to understand the properties of various kinds of regulations, franchising arrangements, and procurement procedures. Furthermore, the emergence of infrastructure firms that can assemble funds for huge capital investments highlights the need for public officials to understand the financing mechanisms available to both private and public agents.

These considerations point toward a need to more fully incorporate industrial organization into urban transportation analysis. This will be a challenge because many of the theoretical tools from industrial organization are highly specific to individual cases. Nevertheless, those tools are being applied vigorously in other industries, such as electricity generation and distribution, that are also undergoing sporadic deregulation and that share some characteristics with transportation. Therefore we should see some fruitful interaction between studies in those fields and in transportation, leading to a more general understanding of the strengths and weaknesses of various institutional arrangements.

One general conclusion that is already supported by existing evidence is that the key to good institutional design is incentive structure, not ideology. What we mean by this is that the difference between public and private ownership, while no doubt important in many ways, is not the primary determinant of success in organizing large numbers of economic actors into an effective service delivery system. Rather, the primary determinant is the degree to which incentives given to these actors cause them to voluntarily act in ways that promote social goals. Both public and private ownership arrangements are quite capable of providing good incentives leading to widely approved results; conversely, neither is a guarantee against disastrous outcomes. As the saying goes, "the devil is in the details."

Urban goods movement

The explosive growth of world trade has increased the quantity of goods movement, both within and between cities. This in turn has raised the importance of freight movement as a component of urban transportation systems. There are several implications.

First, truckers are probably more sensitive to congestion than many other users, since their lost time represents inefficient use of expensive labor and equipment. Thus road corridors with heavy truck concentrations may have quite different prospects for pricing than other corridors.

Second, ocean ports are big traffic generators because so much international trade takes place through them. Port facilities, and the roads and freight lines serving them, are often inside cities. Thus, for example, the port complex in Los Angeles and Long Beach, California, has generated such an increase in truck and rail traffic that huge investments have been undertaken, or are in planning, for the rail and road facilities leading to these ports. Furthermore, the planning agency serving the Los Angeles region has proposed to add truck-only lanes, financed by tolls, to major highways that carry traffic from the port complex to the rest of the US.

Third, trucks and freight trains are significant contributors to environmental problems, especially air pollution and noise. Environmental concerns can be expected to remain high on citizens' policy agendas as living standards increase; as a result, increases in freight traffic require action to address these environmental effects. Such concerns have already influenced recent road-pricing experiments targeted at trucks in Switzerland and Germany.

For the most part, maritime, inter-city freight, and urban transportation have been separate fields within transportation economics. We think this separation will be overcome in coming years. One instigating factor is that universities in port cities want to develop research that supports port operations and the ancillary problems they generate.

Other themes

Of course these are not the only areas where important new research will occur. The reader may especially wonder about one omission from our list: environmental problems. The reason we do not consider this an emerging research theme is that the economic analysis of environmental issues is already quite mature. We expect the importance of environmental issues to remain high, especially as living standards increase and global warming becomes more fully understood; but we think solving them will become somewhat routine, using well-known tools. Furthermore, technology is successfully addressing many environmental issues, due largely to a combination of regulation and economic incentives; because of this success, we expect environmental policy toward transportation to aim predominantly at fostering further technological measures. While such policy development without question involves some very interesting economics, it is unlikely to bring about fundamental transformations to the way transportation activities are carried out. Lest this sounds overly optimistic, we caution that developing solutions to environmental problems does not necessarily mean that they will be adopted; that depends on political processes and, in some cases, international negotiations.

Another theme is the spatial behavior of firms and households. Like most of the contemporary literature, we have implicitly treated spatial mismatches in demand and supply as the underlying reason for transportation demand. However, our discussions of second-best policies and of applied cost–benefit analysis suggest that if spatial markets are imperfect – for example, because of agglomeration economies or ethnic discrimination – it may be important to make explicit the link between spatial markets and transportation. As with environmental problems, sophisticated conceptual and empirical methods to address spatial markets and transportation are already available; but in the case of spatial markets there is perhaps greater potential for further development because of increased computing power.

A final theme, that we already identified as potentially fertile ground for further research in Section 3.4.5, is parking. We expect that both the modeling of parking search itself and of the interactions with urban traffic congestion will receive continuing and growing attention in future years.

7.2 Implications for transportation research

The themes described above imply the continuation or acceleration of certain trends already observed in transportation economics.

First, theory is becoming more applied. The elegant theoretical framework underlying congestion pricing, illustrated for example by Beckman, McGuire and Winsten (1956), is giving way to theory that is developed specifically to deal with the messy details encountered in practical applications. The same is true with recent "applied theory" in industrial organization, which will probably find its way more into transportation economics in the near future. One implication of this is that theory is becoming more amenable to empirical testing and to guiding the design of empirical studies, including simulation exercises.

Second, economics is incorporating more complexities. For example, economic models of congestion that consider one or two links are giving way to models designed for medium-size networks, as for example the analyses of several European cities by May, Shepherd and Timms (2000) and of the Washington region by Safirova *et al.* (2004). At the same time, researchers are combining economic methods with solution algorithms for large networks, leading to results such as those of Yang, Qiang and Lee (2004) on iterative design of network-wide pricing schemes. Thus, this trend is even further encouraging the already good collaboration between economists and engineers. (Indeed, the list of authors just quoted includes about as many engineers as economists, even though they are all writing about economic policies.) It is also encouraging further collaboration between transportation economists and other economists. Models in transportation economics now incorporate inputs from public economics (*e.g.*, the relation between congested commuting and distorted labor markets); urban and regional economics (*e.g.*, the evaluation of transportation policy with endogenous location); industrial organization (*e.g.*, the analysis of deregulation and privatization in network markets); and other areas. Such collaboration is not new, but we expect it to receive increasing emphasis in coming years.

Increasing complexity also extends to the modeling of behavior of economic actors. Models can now simultaneously consider multiple margins of traveler behavior including choices about departure time, speed, and safety precautions. Furthermore, models can incorporate the strategic behaviors of public and private operators and, simultaneously, the transportation choices of individuals who take operators' decisions as given. Such "bi-level" modeling is of course particularly useful for studying questions related to industrial organization.

A third trend is that academic research in transportation economics is becoming not only more complex but also more practical. Complexity can make abstract research even more esoteric, or it can make applied research more readily applicable to real policy questions. We think the latter is happening. Therefore, academic economists find themselves in a better position to give policy advice and to interact productively with professionals working in agencies that make and implement policy.

These trends may also affect the relationship between transportation economics and other branches of economics – although it is hard to predict exactly how because of the diversity of economic research. In the past, developments in transportation economics, such as analysis of peak-load pricing and the random-utility model for discrete choice, have been generalized for wide applications throughout the field of economics. We see no reason that this should not recur, especially because transportation problems are so pervasive and inherently interesting to so many people. But it is more likely to recur if transportation economics remains open to influence from broader trends in economic research and if it engages researchers who are active in engineering, planning, and other allied fields. Without doubt, this activity will be fueled by an unending stream of new and interesting problems arising from society's mobility needs.

Notes

2 Travel demand

1 On freight demand, see D'Este (2000) and Small and Winston (1999). Collections of more specialized papers on travel demand are found in Hensher and Button (2000) and Mahmassani (2002).

2 See Pisarski (2006, p. 3). He adjusts the 2001 survey tabulation upward to better match the way "trips" were defined in previous years; without that adjustment the figure is 15%. The reason for the adjustment is that the 2001 survey, unlike earlier surveys, counts each person, even a very small child, as a separate trip-maker. In the NHTS, "trips" includes such casual activities as walking the dog, which is probably why it shows a surprisingly high proportion of trips made by walking or bicycling: 9.5% according to Pucher and Renne (2003), compared to just 3.4% according to the journey-to-work Census (calculated from Pisarski 2006, Table ES-2, by dividing the percentages shown by 0.9674 to eliminate those working at home from their denominators).

3 These statistics are, respectively, from Pisarski (2006, p. 6), Van Dender (2001, p. 103), and Giuliano (1994, p. 261).

4 The figures in these paragraphs are computed from Pisarski (2006, pp. xvi, 76–77), which we divide by (1–0.0326) to express them as proportions of work trips rather than of workers, and from Pucher and Renne (2003, Table 6).

5 Calculated from Pisarski (2006), Fig. ES-2 (p. xv).

6 Pisarski (2006), Figures 3-07 (p. 51) and 3-68 (p. 101), the latter using the adjustment of the 1990 figure for measurement change as described by Pisarski.

7 Pisarski (2006), Tables 3-40 (p. 102) and 3-41 (p. 106). Hu and Reuscher (2004, Table 26) document the much higher average travel time for commutes by public transit (47.9 minutes in 2001) compared to private vehicles (22.5 minutes).

8 Statistics Netherlands (2007). These figures refer to trips by people of age 12 or more. There were 3.1 trips per person per day on average with average trip length 11.2 km (6.9 miles).

9 These figures refer to "very heavily urbanized areas," defined as those with more than 2500 addresses per km^2.

10 That is, $\beta'z \equiv \beta_0 z_0 + \Sigma_k \beta_{1k} z_{1k} + \Sigma_k \beta_{2k} z_{2k} + \Sigma_{kl} \beta_{3kl} z_{3kl}$.

11 If the variables Z_k in (2.2) are replaced by their natural logarithms, and the mean values of these logarithms subtracted, then (2.2) becomes the *translog* functional form:

$$f(Z) = \beta_0 + \sum_k \beta_{1k} \tilde{Z}_k + \sum_k \beta_{2k} \tilde{Z}_k^2 + \sum_k \sum_{l \neq k} \beta_{3kl} \tilde{Z}_k \tilde{Z}_l,$$

where $\tilde{Z}_k \equiv \left(\log Z_k - \overline{\log Z_k} \right)$ and the bar indicates a sample average. This function is widely used in cost analysis and regarded as a particularly good approximation to an arbitrary unknown function: see Spady and Friedlaender (1978), Braeutigam (1999), and Chapter 3 of this book.

12 For basic econometric texts, see Pindyck and Rubinfeld (1998) or Johnston and DiNardo (1997). For an advanced text, see Greene (2003).

13 Utility theory is treated in most texts on microeconomic theory. Varian (1992) provides a concise entry-level graduate treatment.

14 Computed as the weighted average of "percent walking to work" for the columns pertaining to Tel Aviv in Plaut's Table 7 (p. 246).

15 The tobit model, also known as a censored model, postulates a "latent" (unobserved) variable x^* that is explained by an ordinary regression equation like $x^* = \beta'z + \varepsilon$, and an observed variable $x = \max\{x^*, 0\}$. The idea is that we observe x^* except when it is below a logical cutoff for observability (zero in this example), in which case we observe only that it fell below that cutoff. See any econometrics text, for example Johnston and DiNardo (1997, Ch. 13).

16 The double-censored tobit model is like that in the previous note except now $x = 0$ if $x^* < 0$, $x = x^*$ if $0 \leq x^* \leq 1$, and $x = 1$ if $x^* > 1$.

17 Equation (2.2) is a special case of (2.3) in which $J = 2$ and we define $x = x_1$, $z = z_1 - z_2$ and $\varepsilon = \varepsilon_1 - \varepsilon_2$.

18 A good example is the study of transit use in US cities by Baum-Snow and Kahn (2000).

19 Luk and Hepburn (1993); Greening, Greene and Difiglio (2000, Section 3.1.4); Graham and Glaister (2002, Table 2). Johansson and Schipper (1997) estimate a useful breakdown of changes of per-capita fuel consumption into changes in vehicle stock, average fuel economy, and average usage per vehicle.

20 Giuliano (2004) provides a good review.

21 See Giuliano (1991), Giuliano and Small (1993), Cervero (1996), and Schwanen, Dijst and Dieleman (2004).

22 See McDonald and Osuji (1995) and McMillen and McDonald (2004).

23 Reviews with a transportation focus include Ben-Akiva and Lerman (1985), Koppelman and Sethi (2000), Ben-Akiva and Bierlaire (2003), and Train (2003).

24 Comparable normalization is accomplished by dividing the logit coefficients by $\pi/\sqrt{3}$ in order to give the utilities the same standard deviations in the two models. In both models, the choice probabilities depend on $(\beta/\sigma_\varepsilon)$, where σ_ε^2 is the variance of each of the random terms ε_{in}. In the case of probit, the variance of $\varepsilon_{1n} - \varepsilon_{2n}$, which is $2\sigma_\varepsilon^2$, is set to one by the conventional normalization; hence $\sigma_\varepsilon^{PROBIT} = 1/\sqrt{2}$. In the case of logit, the normalization $\mu = 1$ in equation (2.13) implies that ε_{in} has standard deviation $\sigma_\varepsilon^{LOGIT} = \pi/\sqrt{6}$ (Hastings and Peacock 1975, p. 60). Hence to make logit and iid probit comparable, the logit coefficients must be divided by $\sigma_\varepsilon^{LOGIT}/\sigma_\varepsilon^{PROBIT} = \pi/\sqrt{3} = 1.814$.

25 In this example there are three such combinations, so z_{in} is a vector with three components: c_{in}/w_n, T_{in}, and T_{in}^2.

26 The fact that (2.14) can be inverted is due to a property of the logit model: if a full set of alternative-specific constants is included, the predicted choice shares for each of the alternatives can be made exactly equal to the observed shares in the sample by setting parameter β to its maximum-likelihood estimate.

27 Chow (1983, pp. 182–83). An asymptotic distribution is one to which the actual distribution converges as sample size increases. Chow's result requires asymptotic convergence of β at a rate proportional to the square root of the sample size. (That is, as the sample size N increases, the difference between the estimated and true values of β tends to diminish proportionally to $1/\sqrt{N}$.) In the case where $v_T = \beta_2/\beta_1$, the standard deviation σ_v of v_T obeys $(\sigma_v/V_T)^2 \cong (\sigma_1/\beta_1)^2 + (\sigma_2/\beta_2)^2 - 2\sigma_{12}/(\beta_1\beta_2)$ where σ_1 and σ_2 are the standard deviations of β_1 and β_2 and where σ_{12} is their covariance. Such an approximation requires that σ_1/β_1 and σ_2/β_2 be small, which in turn helps ensure that the variance of β_1/β_2 exists.

28 This method is described by Armstrong, Garrido and Ortúzar (2001). See Train (2003, Ch. 9) for how to take random draws from distributions.

29 Lam and Small (2001); Brownstone *et al.* (2003); Small, Winston and Yan (2005).

30 A "demand function" describes quantity as a function of price (and perhaps other characteristics). The same relationship can alternatively be represented as an "inverse demand function" that describes price as a function of quantity (and perhaps other characteristics). Holding other characteristics constant, it is conventional in economics to depict these equivalent relationships graphically by plotting them with quantity along the horizontal axis and price along the vertical axis. Such a plot is conventionally called a "demand curve" even though, using normal mathematical conventions, it actually depicts the inverse demand function. Mathematically, then, consumer surplus can be represented either as

$$\int_{p^*}^{\infty} x(p)\,dp \quad \text{or} \quad \int_0^{x^*} \left[p(x) - p^* \right] dx,$$

where $x(\cdot)$ is the demand function, $p(\cdot)$ is the inverse demand function, and p^* and x^* are the current price and quantity. (Other characteristics that are arguments of these functions are omitted for simplicity.) The second formulation can also be written as

$$\int_0^{x^*} p(x)\mathrm{d}x - p^* x^*,$$

which can be characterized as the difference between the consumer's total willingness to pay for consuming x^* (*i.e.*, the area under the demand curve and to the left of current quantity) and the amount actually paid. As an example, consumer surplus in Figure 5.2 (where quantity is notated as Q rather than x) is area GAp^0 at current price p^0 and GBp^1 at current price p^1.

31 If income y_n is included as an explanatory variable, it might be tempting to simply compute $\partial V_{jn}/\partial y_n$ from the discrete-choice model as a measure of λ_n. This would be incorrect because indirect utility is strongly influenced by income, independently of which alternative is chosen, whereas $\{V_{jn}\}$ capture only the *relative* effects of income on utility of the various alternatives. If price c_{jn} is *not* included as an explanatory variable, then there is no way to estimate λ_n and welfare changes cannot be expressed in monetary terms; nevertheless changes in (2.23) are useful indicators of relative changes in the welfare of groups facing unchanged prices and believed to have identical values of λ_n. For example, if travel time is one of the variables, welfare changes can be computed in terms of equivalent time saved, rather than money, by substituting t_{jn} for c_{jn} in (2.24).

32 The income elasticity of a good is the ratio of the percentage change in its consumption to the percentage change in income, holding prices constant.

33 The relationship between the uncompensated and price elasticities, ε^u and ε^c, is given by the Slutsky equation:

$$\varepsilon^u = \varepsilon^c - s \cdot \eta_y,$$

where s is the share of income spent on the good in question and η_y is its income elasticity. Recall that both ε^u and ε^c are negative; hence the negative sign assures that the income effect (the last term) reinforces the compensated price elasticity. See Varian (1992) or any microeconomics textbook for a derivation.

34 A commonly used algorithm, sometimes known as a contraction procedure, adjusts the alternative-specific constants $\{\alpha_i\}$ at each iteration by an amount $\log[s_i] - \log[\hat{s}_i(\alpha_1,...,\alpha_J)]$, where s_i is the observed share and $\hat{s}_i$ is the share predicted by the model (Train 1986, p. 105).

35 Rank-ordered logit, sometimes called "expanded logit" or "exploded logit," is analyzed by Beggs, Cardell and Hausman (1981) and Hausman and Ruud (1987). Beggs *et al.* call it "ordered logit," but that name is now usually reserved for an ordered response model as described here.

36 For additional examples, see McCarthy (2001, Chs. 3–4) and Small and Winston (1999).

37 Calculated as $0.065/0.106 = 0.61$.

38 This is a partial listing of the coefficients in Lam and Small (2001, Table 11, Model 4b), with coefficients of T and R divided by 1.37 to adjust travel-time measurements to the time of the survey, as described on their p. 234 and Table 11, note *a*. Standard errors are in parentheses.

39 The coefficient for women is -0.159, and that for men is $-0.159 + 0.074 = -0.085$.

40 See Small, Winston and Yan (2005) for further discussion of this same issue in a different data set from SR91.

41 Generalized price is also sometimes known as *generalized cost*; but we avoid this term because in our terminology, price includes taxes and tolls, if levied, while cost does not.

42 The variance–covariance matrix of these utility differences has $(J-1)^2$ elements and is symmetric. Hence it has only $J(J-1)/2$ identifiable elements, less one for utility-scale normalization.

43 This is demonstrated by Lindberg, Eriksson and Mattsson (1995, p. 134). For a simpler proof, see Choi and Moon (1997, p. 131).

44 If maximizing the log-likelihood function is numerically difficult, one can start with the sequential estimator and carry out just one step of a Newton–Raphson algorithm toward maximization; this yields a statistically efficient estimate and seems to work well in practice (Brownstone and Small 1989).

45 For a review of these and other GEV models, see Koppelman and Sethi (2000).

46 See Train (1986, Ch. 5), Mannering and Hensher (1987), and Washington, Karlaftis and Mannering (2003, Ch. 12).

47 Supposedly it can be done for the multinomial logit model as well, but it is extremely complex. Dubin and McFadden (1984) specify a usage model conditional on a single choice, i; they include $J-1$ correction terms, and so estimate $J-1$ correlations (between u and ε_j, $j \neq i$). However, they do not discuss how to pool the data with observations of individuals who choose other alternatives.

48 Sign conventions vary in the literature. In the probit case, some references replace $\hat{\beta}'_Z Z$ by the equivalent quantity $\Phi^{-1}(\hat{P}_1)$, where Φ^{-1} denotes the inverse of the standard normal cumulative distribution function.

49 See Kitamura (2000) for a general review, and Pendyala and Kitamura (1997) or Brownstone and Chu (1997) specifically on attrition.

50 The following simplified explanation is adapted from Small and Winston (1999).

51 As Brownstone and Train (1999) point out, the terms in ϕ_1 and ϕ_2 also may be viewed as part of an additive random utility term, but one that is not a constant, *i.e.*, it depends on values of observed variables.

52 Formally, this is because the variable would be perfectly collinear with the alternative-specific dummies: that is, some linear combination of them adds to zero. The inability to include perfectly collinear variables is a well-known limitation on any regression model. Intuitively, the problem is that two different variables (or combinations of variables) would be competing to explain the same dimension of variation in the data, and so their separate effects could not be distinguished.

53 An alternative solution is proposed by Petrin and Train (2004): adding artificial variables to the model to absorb the part of the error term that is correlated with price, an extension of the approach of Heckman described as "Step 2 Version (b)" in Section 2.4.2.

54 Proof of convergence is given by Berry, Levinsohn and Pakes (1995, Appendix I).

55 Specifically Train and Winston (2007) create four instrumental variables. The first two are the sums of differences in measured characteristics between the make/model in question and (1) all other makes/models by the same manufacturer, or (2) all other makes/models by other manufacturers. The other two are formed the same way but using the *squares* of differences in characteristics.

56 The procedure was first developed for aggregate data, using demand functions built up from disaggregate discrete-choice decisions by Berry (1994); Berry, Levinsohn and Pakes (1995); and Bresnahan, Stern and Trajtenberg (1997). In those cases the mixed-logit part of the algorithm is simplified because consumers, not being observed individually, must be treated as observationally identical. Applications to disaggregate data include Berry, Levinsohn and Pakes (2004) for automobiles and Goolsbee and Petrin (2004) for television reception.

57 For example, Timmermans *et al.* (2002) compare data on Japan, Canada, the Netherlands, the US, and UK.

58 See Ettema and Timmermans (1997), Ben-Akiva and Bowman (1998), or Bhat and Koppelman (2003) for reviews. A collection of recent research appears in Miller (2005).

59 Choo, Mokhtarian and Salomon (2005) and Plaut (1997).

60 It is sometimes claimed that the average value of time savings diminishes rapidly as the time savings shrink to zero, which would imply a very low marginal rate. These claims are based on the idea that travelers judge changes in the transportation system relative to some reference point, taken to be the situation before a proposed change. But that idea ignores the fact that travel patterns and other factors affecting travel are in constant flux. This flux means that within a few months of a change, most travelers will no longer view the "before" situation, as defined by an analyst, as a reference point. It is more plausible that travelers will adjust their behavior to their needs at any point in time, subject to the situation that faces them (as measured by current conditions) and not to some arbitrary previous situation. Studies based on consistent definitions have generally not found such dependencies (MVA Consultancy *et al.* 1987, pp. 65–68), and theory refutes the alleged rationale for them (Mackie, Jara-Díaz and Fowkes 2001).

61 According to (2.54), this could happen by the consumer adjusting so as to raise the wage rate w and/or the marginal enjoyment of work U_{Tw}. This reflects the idea that if time is scarce, one is more choosy about the kind of job one will accept. Academics with consulting opportunities will often say that when they are exceptionally busy, they only accept consulting jobs with very high wages or that they find especially interesting, in either case helping them meet the marginal condition (2.54). Similarly, some people busy with small children will take on part-time work only if it pays well or is especially enjoyable.

62 See, for example, MVA Consultancy *et al.* (1987, p. 149); Small *et al.* (1999); and Hensher (2001).

63 The term "0" in this equation arises from differentiating the lower limit of integration:

$$-\left[\,d(\tilde{t}-t_d)/dt_d\,\right]\cdot\left[(t_d+T_r-\tilde{t})\cdot f(T_r)\right]_{T_r=\tilde{t}-t_d}=1\cdot 0=0.$$

64 This equivalence is pointed out by Wardman (2004, p. 364); the equation is also derived by de Palma and Lindsey (2001).

65 Mean gross hourly earnings for the UK were £6.79 and £7.07/hour in spring 1994 and 1995, respectively. Source: UK National Statistics Online (2004, Table 38).

66 Mean gross hourly earnings in 1997 were £7.42/hour, from same source as previous note.

67 Japan Research Institute Study Group on Road Investment Evaluation (2000), Table 3-2-2, using car occupancy of 1.44 (p. 52). Average wage rate is calculated as cash earnings divided by hours worked, from Japan Ministry of Health, Labour and Welfare (1999).

68 See, for example, MVA Consultancy *et al.* (1987, pp. 133–35, 150, 152) and Mackie *et al.* (2003).

69 This statement is based on Calfee and Winston's (1998) summary of the average over the entire sample (p. 91), and on Hensher's (1997) Table 3.7 (p. 274), panel for "private commute," using his preferred VOT of $4.35/hour.

70 See their Table 1, rows 4–5, 13–14.

71 This statement is based on Hensher's (2001) Table 3, Model 3a, the lower panel showing values of time in which the cost coefficient is that on a variable measuring the toll.

72 An updated version of that study is Small, Winston and Yan (2005).

3. Costs

1 See, for example, Murphy and Delucchi (1998), Nash *et al.* (2003), Litman (2005), Jakob, Craig and Fisher (2006), and the papers in Greene, Jones and Delucchi (1997).

2 By joint cost we mean one that depends on the level of two or more outputs and that cannot be disaggregated into output-specific costs. Button (1993) divides these into two types: "joint costs" where the outputs must unavoidably be produced together (*e.g.*, train travel in opposite directions), and "common costs" where it is an economic choice to produce them together (*e.g.*, carrying passengers and cargo on the same train).

3 Boyd, Asher and Wetzler (1978); Mohring (1979); Jansson (1980, pp. 57–58); Cervero (1982, p. 70).

4 These include: 1.1 for Albany, New York (Reilly 1977); 1.1 or 1.9 for eastern San Francisco Bay Area (Cervero 1982; Small 1983, p. 36); 1.3 for Los Angeles County (Cervero 1982); and 2.5 for a number of British operators (McClenahan *et al.* 1978). The latter study also provided a ratio (relative to weekday base period) of 1.1 for Saturday and 1.4 for Sunday.

5 Chomitz and Lave (1984). Their simulations also suggest a typical value for c_b/c_3 of 0.82. These statements are based on cases B and E of their Table 1, p. 67, using the column "13/10," which they indicate is most typical of work rules.

6 From Viton (1980, Table 2, p. 251). We have transformed his definition of economies of density (*ED*) to ours according to $s=1/(1-ED)$.

7 From Viton (1980, Table 3, p. 252), updated using the transportation component of the Consumer Price Index.

8 From Viton (1981b, Table V, p. 300), transforming his *SCE* to our *s* by $s=1/(1-SCE)$.

9 From Button and O'Donnell (1985, Fig. 1, p. 75), using the same definitional transformation as with Viton.

10 For 76 operating agencies, labor costs are not segregated from capital costs in the data. In these cases the left-hand side of (3.6) is replaced by total cost and an additional term $c_{1c}^j\cdot VM^j$, not multiplied by wage, is added to the equation to represent capital cost, with c_{1c}^j estimated.

11 See Mohring (1976, pp. 145–46).

12 Derivation: $s=ac/mc=[(C_B^*+C_W^*)/q]/(c_p/N)=(C_B^*+C_W^*)/C_B^*$. Note however, that $s\leq 2$ in an optimum, because otherwise we would have $C_W^*>C_B^*$, implying that a marginal increase in frequency V would reduce waiting costs by more (namely by C_W/V) than that it would raise the cost to the bus agency (namely by $c_p=C_B/V$) – contrary to the assumption that the agency is minimizing the sum of these costs.

13 Derivation: we want to set generalized price equal to $mc=d(C_B^*+C_W^*)/dq=c_p/N$. But the part of that price paid in the form of user-supplied costs is $C_W^*/q=\alpha^W\cdot N/(2q)$. The fare is the difference.

14 See Jansson (1980) and Nash (1988).

15 A more precise term than "vehicles" is "passenger-car equivalents," a measure that combines vehicles of different sizes and acceleration capabilities, each with a weight indicating its contribution to congestion. See Krammes and Crowley (1986). In some situations it is more accurate to assume that slow vehicles effectively occupy an entire lane, and treat the highway as two separate roadways (possibly interacting if heavy vehicles are allowed to pass each other); see OECD (1983, Ch. IV).

16 Engineers often call the upper branch of the speed–flow relationship "uncongested flow" and the lower branch "congested flow." In our terminology, which is more common in economics, "uncongested" or "free flow" refers instead to the limiting condition as $V \to 0$ on the upper branch. We use the terms "congested" and "normally congested" interchangeably, depending on whether an explicit distinction with "hypercongested" is needed.

17 This is their preferred equation (20), p. 350, converted to units of vehicles per lane per hour by setting $V = 5q$.

18 This is calculated from Inman's equation (2), p. 23, with parameter estimates from the top row of his Table 1, p. 25. The units and the unreported constant X were supplied by Inman, private conversation, Sept. 1989; they are $N = V/500$, $G = S/10$, and $X = 36.488$. The Inman curve is undefined for $S < 7.2$ mi/hr, and can show no backward-bending portion unless the exponent on the right-hand side is constrained to be precisely an even integer, as it is for the special case represented by the Boardman–Lave formula.

19 This tendency is also noted by Banks (1989) for San Diego, California, and by Hall and Hall (1990) for Toronto, Canada, in both cases for short uniform stretches of highway unaffected by a bottleneck.

20 See UK Department for Transport (2002), Transportation Research Board (2000), and Smith, Hall and Montgomery (1996).

21 This is Keeler and Small's equation (12), p. 11, for the Eastshore Freeway, rewritten to make transparent the maximum V/V_K ratio and the maximum speed.

22 Their equation (8), with values $n = 1.58$ and $v_m = 60/1.95$ as indicated just above their equation (6) on p. 6.

23 See US Bureau of Public Roads (1964). The BPR function has been incorporated into the Urban Transportation Planning Process computer software to describe a single link in a network.

24 Cassidy and Bertini (1999) find empirical evidence that discharge rates from bottlenecks fall after queue formation and then partially recover. The constant flow assumption nevertheless appears a reasonable approximation to observed behavior.

25 The data are from Toronto arterials. We used non-linear least squares with the nine data points reported by Dewees. Estimated parameters for equation (3.9), with V_K arbitrarily set to 1000 veh/hr, are $T_f = 2.48$ min, $a = 0.102$, and $b = 4.08$. Estimated parameters for equation (3.10) are $T_f = 3.07$ min, $P = 14.44$ min, and $V_K = 1357$ veh/hr.

26 Akçelik proposes the following parameters $\{V_K, S_f, J_a\}$ for different types of roads, where $S_f = L/T_f$ (mi/hr) and L is the length of the road: freeway $\{2000, 75, 0.1\}$; uninterrupted arterial $\{1800, 62, 0.2\}$; interrupted arterial $\{1200, 50, 0.4\}$; interrupted secondary $\{900, 37, 0.8\}$; high-friction secondary $\{600, 25, 1.6\}$.

27 Equation (3.16) can be understood as follows. Let ΔN denote the change in the number of cars between two locations x and $x + \Delta x$ over the time interval from t to $t + \Delta t$. If Δt is small enough, the flow rates at the two locations can be treated as constant over time; letting ΔV denote the difference in V between the two locations, we see that the number of vehicles between x and $x + \Delta x$ builds up if incoming flow exceeds outgoing flow, i.e., it builds at rate $-\Delta V$. Thus $\Delta N = -\Delta t \cdot \Delta V$. If Δx is small enough, density at the two locations can be treated as equal; letting ΔD denote the change in density over time, we see that the number of vehicles in this space of length Δx changes in proportion to the change in density: $\Delta N = \Delta x \cdot \Delta D$. Because vehicles are conserved, these two expressions for ΔN should be equal, in turn implying $\Delta V /\Delta x + \Delta D /\Delta t = 0$. When the discrete increments become infinitesimal, (3.16) is obtained.

28 After rotating the $V(D)$ curve of Figure 3.1c by 90°, S_w between two states can be found geometrically as the slope of the straight line connecting these states. The traffic speed in a state is given by the slope of the ray from the origin through that state. Under the stated assumptions, S_w is then always smaller than S_u and S_d.

29 Other interesting phenomena include path-dependency of observed speed–density combinations (Zhang 1999), multiple-class traffic (Hoogendoorn and Bovy 1998), and what appear to be

spontaneous phase transitions, analogous to transitions between liquids and gases, observed in simulation results by Kerner and Rehborn (1997) and others. The relevance of the latter to observed traffic is disputed by Daganzo, Cassidy and Bertini (1999).

30 See Verhoef (1999). When applying conventional stability analysis, an equilibrium is stable for flow perturbations if a small increase in flow leads to average cost $c(V)$ above inverse demand $d(V)$, inducing users to reduce their inflow. An equilibrium is stable for price perturbations if a small increase in "price" (average cost) leads to excess supply: *i.e.*, it leads to a "price" where the supply curve is to the right of the demand curve. In conventional markets this would cause suppliers to reduce the price level; but here the "supplier" is a congestion technology rather than a profit-motivated firm, making this stability criterion a questionable one.

31 The same result occurs with the LWR model when discontinuous changes in traffic conditions (V, D, and S) are ruled out. The intuition is that, from equation (3.17), the shock wave between two hypercongested stationary states always travels at a negative speed. This is because, with $V(D)$ downward-sloping between both states, $V_u - V_d$ and $D_u - D_d$ must have opposite signs. Therefore a change in inflow can never cause a transition between two hypercongested stationary states, or, indeed, from the maximum-flow state to any hypercongested state: the boundary to the new state can travel only backward so can never enter the road.

32 A naïve but understandable choice of P, defined by the instants that queuing begins and ends, would imply a time-averaged inflow V equal to capacity V_K. This choice would produce travel delay equal to zero according to the piecewise-linear function and $(1/2)^{1/2} \cdot (PJ_d/V_K)^{1/2}$ according to Akçelik's function.

33 The Arnott, de Palma and Lindsey analysis treats only the special case in which the desired schedule t_d is identical for all commuters: *i.e.*, $Q \equiv V_d \cdot q$ is fixed but $q = 0$ and V_d is infinite. This version, which we call the "basic bottleneck model," is widely used. We achieve more realism at a modest cost in complexity by retaining Vickrey's original assumption of a uniform distribution of t_d with non-zero q and finite V_d. In doing so we also render the assumption of zero travel time before and after the bottleneck relatively innocuous because the varying preference for queue-exit time could be interpreted as arising from individuals having different free-flow times T_f that are outside the model.

34 These theoretical rates of change are compared to actual rates on congested roads in Paris by Fargier (1983, pp. 247–52) in order to estimate the behavioral parameters β/α and γ/α. He gets values much smaller than the direct behavioral estimates of Small (1982), possibly reflecting the limited realism of the model or a relatively wide dispersion in desired arrival times.

35 Somewhat confusingly, the UE is sometimes called a "user optimum," while the socially optimal flow pattern (to be discussed in Chapter 4) is called a "system optimum."

36 The following example is from Arnott and Small (1994). Suppose two bridges A and B, cross a river. When bridge i carries traffic volume V_i, congestion causes its travel time (in minutes) to be $V_i/100$. Two cities a few miles apart and on opposite sides of the river are connected by two routes. Route A uses bridge A and an uncongested road that takes 15 minutes to travel; route B uses bridge B and a different but identical road. (The roads follow the river bank on opposite sides.) Total traffic of 1000 reaches a user equilibrium when traffic divides equally across the two routes, resulting in flows $V_A = V_B = 500$ and travel times $t_A = t_B = 15 + (500/100) = 20$. An engineer notices that the roads along the river banks are circuitous, and proposes a straight causeway connecting the far ends of the two bridges; it takes only 7.5 minutes to traverse, but to do so requires crossing both bridges. It looks like a time saver because currently each bridge has only 5 minutes of congestion, so the new route C covering both bridges and the causeway takes only 17.5 minutes. However, after the causeway is built, congestion on the bridges rises: travel time on route i is now $t_i = 15 + (V_i + V_C)/100$, for $i = A$, B, while that on route C is $t_C = 7.5 + (V_A + V_C)/100 + (V_B + V_C)/100$. Equilibrium requires that all three travel times be equal; this occurs when $V_A = V_B = 250$, $V_C = 500$, and $t_A = t_B = t_C = 22.5$. Because the causeway has enticed half the travelers onto a route with a higher marginal congestion cost than the other routes (due to its including both bridges), its availability raises travel costs for everyone compared to the situation where it had never been built.

37 Shoup (2005, pp. 303–4) describes quantitative estimates of this effect in the UK and Calcutta, India.

38 Interest in this topic is worldwide, resulting in a literature we cannot begin to summarize adequately. Europeans have been especially active in pursuing it, resulting in a number of reviews, models, and policy-related applications. See, for example, European Conference of Ministers of

Transport (ECMT) (1998), Van den Bossche *et al.* (2003), Quinet (2004), De Ceuster *et al.* (2005), Nash and Matthews (2005), and Newbery (2005).

39   These are estimates from the 2001 National Household Travel Survey. See Hu and Reuscher (2004, Table 26).

40   Ward's Communications (2006, p. 65). For earlier years' data in this same series, see Davis and Diegel (2006, Table 10.11).

41   Average US federal and state gasoline tax rates in 2005 were $0.184 and $0.193 per gallon: US FHWA (2006, Table MF-121T). Average fuel consumption for automobiles was one gallon per 22.9 miles (*ibid.*, Table VM-1).

42   The capital recovery factor ρ is the annual expenditure in each year from 1 to T that has a *present value* of 1.0 (computed at interest rate r). The present value of an expenditure C undertaken at some time t years in the future is the amount, invested today, that would provide sufficient funds for that expenditure; if the interest rate is a constant r and compounded annually, the present value is $C/(1 + r)^t$. For an asset whose initial cost is K, ρK is its *annualized cost of capital* (also known as the annuitized cost or annual equivalent of the capital investment); it can be interpreted as interest plus depreciation on the asset's current value, when that current value takes the unique time path keeping interest plus depreciation constant. The formula for the capital recovery factor, given by Meyer, Kain and Wohl (1965, p. 177), can be written as $r/(1-\delta^T)$, where $\delta = 1/(1+r)$. For a clear derivation, see DeNeufville and Stafford (1971, Ch. 8). If interest is compounded continuously, the formula becomes $r/(1-e^{-rT})$. The discrete version is more commonly used; in this chapter, we use it unless T is not an integer.

43   New car price: Ward's Communications (2006, p. 68); earlier years' data are in Davis and Diegel (2006, Table 10.10). Annual miles per vehicle: US FHWA (2006), Table VM-1. Median lifetime: Davis and Diegel (2006, Table 3.8) for a 1990 model car. This lifetime has grown dramatically, from 12.5 years for a 1983 model car, the latter calculated from American Automobile Manufacturers Association (1997, p. 39).

44   This price-level update uses the transportation component of the Consumer Price Index for all urban consumers, from US CEA (2006, p. B-60).

45   Mean hourly wages for metropolitan areas in 2005 were $19.37, from US BLS (2006, Table 1-1).

46   We update using hourly earnings in private industries, which grew by 15.07% between 2000 and 2005 (US CEA 2006, Table B-47).

47   Transport for London (2004, pp. 2–3).

48   Small (2004), using earlier Transport for London estimates of a 9% increase in bus speed, estimates time savings equal to 35% of initial agency operating costs.

49   See, for example, Golob and Regan (2001). The economic effects of congestion are widespread (Weisbrod, Vary and Treyz 2001) but since most of these are manifestations of the delays and uncertainties that we attempt to measure directly, including them would involve a great deal of double-counting. This issue is discussed at greater length in Chapter 5.

50   This calculation is based on the full frequency distribution for schedule delay, which is summarized but not fully reported in Small (1982, Table 1). Of the 527 commuters, 318 arrive an average of 17.0 minutes early and 22 arrive an average of 7.27 minutes late. We assume no schedule-delay cost for the 187 who arrive on time, thus ignoring the penalty indicated by the coefficient of variable DL. As noted in Section 2.3.2, the equation implies that each minute of early or late schedule delay is worth 0.61 min. or 2.40 min. travel time, respectively. Therefore, the average commuter's schedule delay is worth $[(318)(17.0)(0.61) + (22)(7.27)(2.40)]/527 = 7.0$ min. travel time.

51   We assume that congestion accounted for one-third of the average commute trip time of 22.5 minutes, and that schedule delay imposed a cost equivalent to 7.0 minutes; thus the ratio is $7.0/(22.5/3) = 0.93$.

52   The ratio is $1-(V_k/V_d)$, as seen from (3.36)–(3.37).

53   Their cost estimates, in 2000 dollars, are given in their Table 1. To state them in 2005 dollars, we increase them by 14.24%, the average between the growth of hourly earnings and the growth of the Consumer Price Index for all urban consumers and all items (CPI-U); see US CEA (2006, Tables B-47, B-60). Vehicle-miles traveled in 2000 were 2747 billion, from US FHWA (2002, Table VM-1).

54   Blincoe *et al.* (2002, Appendix A) do consider a related measure: willingness to pay for "quality adjusted life years," which they apply to both fatalities and injuries. However, they present this only as side information on alternative approaches.

55   For another review, see Boardman *et al.* (2006, Ch. 15).

56 Mrozek and Taylor report summary figures of $1.5–2.5 million (1998 dollars, p. 253), while Viscusi and Aldy obtain mean predicted values of $5.5–7.6 million for US studies (2000 dollars, last row of Table 8). Viscusi and Aldy also report the median value for all their studies at about $7 million (2000 dollars, p. 18). Day's "best" estimate is $5.63 million in 1996 dollars (p. 24). We update to 2005 as explained in the next note.

57 In our own procedure for updating accident costs, we approximate this finding of Viscusi and Aldy by increasing all accident costs, regardless of type, by the average between growth in the Consumer Price Index and growth in nominal earnings. This is approximately equivalent to assuming that VSL, stated in real (inflation-adjusted) terms, grows at half the rate of real wages, as suggested by studies. Thus, if i is the growth in the Consumer Price Index and g is the growth in nominal hourly earnings, both for 1996–2005, then the latter assumption is

$$\text{VSL(2005\$)/VSL(1996\$)} = (1+i)\cdot\{1+0.5g^R\} = (1+i)\cdot\{1 + 0.5\cdot[(1+g)/(1+i)-1]\} \approx$$
$$1+i+0.5\cdot(g-i)=1+0.5\cdot(g+i)$$

where g^R is the real growth in earnings. For i we use 24.5% for 1996–2005, 19.8% for 1998–2005, 13.4% 2000–2005; for g we use 33.9%, 23.9%, and 15.1%, respectively (US CEA 2006, Tables B-60, B-47).

58 Fatalities and non-fatal injury data are from the Fatality Analysis Reporting System (FARS) and the General Estimates System (GES), respectively. The latter is a less accurate source because its data are derived from field reports of police officers, who do not necessarily observe the victims, much less obtain a medical diagnosis.

59 See Traynor (1994) or Fridstrøm *et al.* (1995). According to Lindberg (2001), Swedish studies find that in urban areas, the net effect of traffic on accident rates (not costs) is negative for crashes between cars and "unprotected" users (pedestrians, bicycles, mopeds), with elasticity ~ -0.5; zero for car crashes between intersections; and positive for multi-car crashes at intersections, with elasticity $\sim +0.20$ to $+0.45$. An interesting implication is that the marginal external cost of a bicycle or moped is negative: by adding to the traffic stream, it lowers the probability of accidents involving vehicles other than itself, perhaps by causing other drivers to be more alert.

60 Parry's (2004) "medium" scenario that we cite below implies that the elasticity of accident cost with respect to traffic is mildly positive. This property of his model results mainly from his assumption that in two-car collisions, each car imposes an external cost equal to half the other driver's injury damages (p. 356); given that each car's occupants bear their own injury damages, this assumption implies that for such collisions the externality is half as large as the cost itself.

61 The 50% proportion, mistakenly stated as 25% in Parry's text (p. 356), is confirmed by personal correspondence, 15 April 2005.

62 We compute the percentage implied by Lindberg as $28/(76\cdot\theta)$, with $\theta = 0.5$ being the fraction of costs incurred by a typical car in a multi-car crash, from Lindberg's Table 4; private average cost in Lindberg's notation is $\theta\cdot r\cdot(a + b)$. A quite different approach to estimating external costs is taken by Edlin and Karaca-Mandic (2003, 2006), who find that traffic density (at the level of a US state) increases insurance premiums, insurers' payouts, and possibly fatalities (with borderline statistical significance) in high-traffic but not low-traffic states within the US. However, this study misses any costs not reimbursed by insurance; that presents a serious problem for fatality costs since they may be over- or under-reimbursed haphazardly. Since fatality costs tend to dominate cost estimates and fatalities respond in uncertain direction to traffic density according to the unpublished estimates in Edlin and Karaca-Mandic (2003), it is unclear whether their findings of high external effects in insurance costs would also apply to a true measure of total accident costs.

63 An even larger ratio is estimated by Miller, Spicer and Levy (1999), based on older data.

64 Similarly, tabulations by Wenzel and Ross (2002) of fatalities from two-vehicle crashes in the US, unadjusted for different driver behaviors, show that light trucks put drivers of other vehicles at much higher risk than do automobiles.

65 White (2004) finds that this perceived safety advantage is more than offset if the driver changes behavior to that typical of drivers of light trucks as a whole. Thus if drivers change their driving habits according to the vehicle they drive, which can be regarded as a kind of compensating risk-taking behavior, their observed accident risk will be unaffected by the size of their vehicle. Even so they still receive a benefit from the larger vehicle, otherwise unaccounted

for, because they can be equally safe while expending less effort in vigilance against accidents (see Steimetz 2004, Ch. 2).

66 Such offsetting behavior was postulated by Peltzman (1975) and has been tested empirically in many contexts, mostly confirming. For a review and recent example, see Winston, Maheshri and Mannering (2006).

67 State registration fee receipts for automobiles in 2005 were $8.484 billion, divided by passenger-car vehicle-miles traveled of 1690 billion (US FHWA 2006, Tables MV-2, VM-1). Fees for driver licenses and certificates of titles were $2.594 billion, divided by total vehicle-miles of 2990 billion (same sources).

68 Bell *et al.* (2004) identify a correlation between mortality and ozone concentrations over very short time periods, using daily data. As with any such study using daily time series, some or all of the correlation may be due to "harvesting," whereby short-term changes in air quality determine the exact timing of a death that was going to occur soon for other reasons (McCubbin and Delucchi 1999). The only reliable way to discern how much of the correlation is due to harvesting is to also measure cross-sectional correlations over longer time spans, for example current annual mortality as a function of exposure over several decades. Such cross-sectional studies have clearly demonstrated mortality effects of particulates but not of ozone.

69 However, they find that it does not vary in strict proportion to remaining life span, an assumption embedded in a broader technique in which risk of injuries and fatalities at different ages and levels of health status are all valued through a single constant measuring willingness to pay for a "quality-adjusted life year" (QALY). For further discussion of the QALY concept, see Krupnick (2004).

70 The US Department of Transportation uses $2.7 million in 1990 dollars. Following the same procedure as with accident costs, we update by the average 1990–2005 growth in nominal wages (58.1%) and in the Consumer Price Index (49.4%).

71 US FHWA (2000, Table 10), increased by 53.8% to convert from 1990 to 2005 prices.

72 We take health damage per vehicle-mile to be 16.7% higher in urban areas than the US as a whole, based on US FHWA (2000, Fig. 6). To account for reduced emissions per car from 2000 to 2005, we extrapolate the 50% reduction in weighted per-mile emissions from a California gasoline car between 1992 and 2000 that was projected by Small and Kazimi (1995, Table 8); we do this by assuming emissions to be exponentially declining at a rate of 8.66% per year, for a five-year reduction of 35%. Although California has tighter emissions standards than the US as a whole, allowable emissions have been declining in tandem so this should be a reasonable estimate of the rate of change in US average emissions rates.

73 The "mid-range" estimate of air pollution costs given by FHWA and used here is roughly the geometric mean of two other estimates, "high" and "low," which they provide (their Table 10). McCubbin and Delucchi give only a high and low estimate, differing by approximately the same factor of 10 as is the case for FHWA. We therefore take as a mid-range estimate for McCubbin and Delucchi the geometric mean of their high and low estimates for light-duty gasoline vehicles (top right entries, their Table 4); we update to 2005 by the average of hourly wages and consumer prices (53.8%); we adjust the US figure upward to reflect urban areas using their urban-to-US ratio of cost per kilogram for PM10, from their Table 5 (40%); and we assume the same extrapolated rate of decline in emissions per vehicle-mile as we did for the FHWA estimate (8.66% per year, or 73% total decline 1990–2005).

74 See US FHWA (2000) and Delucchi (2000). For a good review of literature assessing willingness to pay to reduce noise, see Navrud (2003). For a recent study using stated-preference data, see Arsenio, Bristow and Wardman (2006).

75 The conversion rate of 413 gal/tC is based on National Research Council (2002, p. 85). One metric ton carbon means an amount of carbon dioxide of which the carbon atoms weigh 1000 kg. The average fuel economy of US passenger cars in 2005 was 22.9 mi/gal, from US FHWA (2006, Table VM-1). Global warming cost in other nations would be the same per ton carbon and therefore lower per mile due to the higher fuel efficiency of automobiles outside the US.

76 Additional output distinctions may prove useful in certain circumstances. One may separate high-occupancy from low-occupancy vehicles, both analytically and physically (Mohring 1979; Small 1983). One may separate automobiles from trucks, and consider the additional capital dimension of pavement thickness (Small, Winston and Evans 1989). One could consider the joint costs of using a right of way for highway and rail transit. All these extensions lead to considerations of economies of scope and multi-product economies of scale, an example of which is treated by Small, Winston and Evans (1989, Ch. 6).

77 Larsen (1993) finds that these factors can substantially modify the optimal choice of capacity in practice.

78 See Section 3.4.6, Part (2).

79 This applies their assumed relationship, $60/S = 1 + (V/V_K)^{2.5}$ (p. 544), to the range of peak volume-capacity ratios (V/V_K) in their Table 1 (p. 537).

80 Keeler and Small (1977), Table 5, p. 18, second column. Their assumption of constant returns makes their results independent of demand.

81 In the limiting special case where $q \rightarrow 0$ while keeping $V \cdot q \equiv Q$ finite, only the second regime applies, and its cost becomes $C_g(Q) = c_{bot} \cdot Q$, showing no scale economies or diseconomies in Q.

82 A sufficient condition is that the intercept of the average cost function be no lower in state 1 than in state 0.

83 As Kraus notes, the envelope theorem guarantees that scale economies for a road network are identical whether capacity is expanded by widening existing roads or by adding new ones.

84 Keeler and Small (1977, Table 1), using their log-linear specification. As their discussion on p. 7 makes clear, the estimates of a_6 reported in their paper should have minus signs.

85 This uses their second estimate on p. 4, with w the number of driving lanes and including a dummy variable for curbside parking; returns to scale are $1/b$. Their first estimate, with w the width of the entire roadway in meters and no control for parking, yields scale economies of only 1.05.

86 The degree of scale economies, as defined here, is the inverse of the cost elasticity, estimated by Kraus at 0.84 (1981, p. 20 and n. 4).

87 US OMB (1992) recommends a 7% real interest rate for project evaluation. The corresponding capital recovery factor with 20-year life is 0.0944. We update from 2004 to 2005 using the US Census Bureau price deflator index of new one-family houses under construction (excluding land), which rose 4.1% (US Census Bureau 2006). This value for annualized capital cost of construction is approximately twice as large as current capital outlays in 2005, which were $82.6 billion (including a portion of administration and research), from US FHWA (2006, Table HF-10). Automobile vehicle-miles traveled in 2005 were 1690 billion (US FHWA 2006, Table VM-1).

88 For this calculation, by "passenger vehicles" we mean automobiles, pickup trucks, and vans in US FHWA (1997), and all two-axle four-tire vehicles in US FHWA (2006), the latter accounting for 2750 billion vehicle-miles in 2005.

89 We update Willson's figures from 1995 to 2002 using the ENR (formerly Engineering News-Record) construction cost index, which rose by 19.5%; and from 2002 to 2005 using the US Census Bureau price deflator index for new one-family houses under construction (excluding land), which rose 19.4%. Sources: US Census Bureau (2004, Table 921) and US Census Bureau (2006).

90 The data are for the nine new structures or additions built at UCLA between 1977 and 2002. Based on Shoup's Table 6-1, these include four underground and five above-ground structures, the latter apparently three to eight stories high.

91 Shoup assumes a 40-year life, which at 7% real interest implies a capital recovery factor of 0.0750. For annual operating costs per space, we use the midpoint of the ranges of annual costs implied by Cambridge Systematics *et al.* (1998, Table 9.3, n. 5), updated to 2005 prices using the Consumer Price Index; these updated annual figures are $217 for surface lots and $519 for structures.

92 This assumes tight planning by the employer; the average vacancy rate for all US parking spaces is said to be 50% (Cambridge Systematics *et al.*, 1998, pp. 9–17, n. 15).

93 These figures are slightly higher than the value of 1.9 ECU per space per trip used for Brussels in 1996 by Calthrop, Proost and Van Dender (2000, p. 68). Converted to US dollars (US$1.27/ECU), updated to 2005 in the same way as US figures (38.0%), and adding a 20% vacancy rate, this amounts to $4.16/trip.

94 Shoup (2005, p. 267) estimates that only 5% of automobile commuters pay to park, and it is clear that they usually pay only a fraction of average cost, which we take for illustration to be one-half.

95 In the first category are Boyd, Asher and Wetzler (1973, 1978), Keeler *et al.* (1975), Dewees (1976), and Allport (1981). In the second are Smith (1973) and Skinner and Bhat (1978).

96 These figures are computed from Allport's discussion on p. 638. We have multiplied his two-way weekday 24-hour passenger demands by 0.075, the assumed ratio of peak-direction peak-hour volume to 24-hour volume (Allport 1981, p. 636).

97 See, for example, US GAO (2001), International Energy Agency (2002), Levinson *et al.* (2003), and Hess, Taylor and Yoh (2005).

4 Pricing

1 A sampling of such applications includes Mohring (1965), Smeed (1968), Keeler and Small (1977), Dewees (1979), Gómez-Ibáñez and Fauth (1980), Anderson and Mohring (1997), Nguyen (1999), May and Milne (2000), De Borger and Proost (2001), Li (2002), Niskanen and Nash (2004), Santos (2004), Sato and Hino (2005), de Palma, Lindsey and Proost (2006), and Eliasson and Mattsson (2006). Implementation issues have also been studied extensively: for example, in Britain (UK Ministry of Transport 1964), Singapore (Watson and Holland 1978), Hong Kong (Dawson and Brown 1985), the US (National Research Council 1994), and the European Union (Niskanen and Nash 2004).

2 Formally, total cost is $V \cdot c(V)$, so marginal cost is $mc(V) = c(V) + V \cdot c'(V)$ (by the product rule of differentiation). With rising average cost, i.e., $c'(V) > 0$, we see that $mc(V)$ exceeds $c(V)$ for any positive V.

3 For exit times outside the period $[t_q, t_{q'}]$, the zero tolls shown in (4.23) are more than sufficiently high to support the optimal pattern. Negative tolls would even be allowed so long as $\tau(t') > p^0 - c_S(t')$.

4 It also implies that (4.26) still holds, even when demand is elastic.

5 This is a slight change of notation from Chapter 3, where c_T and c_S are functions of t. Here c'_T refers to (dc_T/dT_D), so that by the chain rule, the time-derivative of $c_T(T_D(t))$ is $c'_T \cdot T'_D$. Similarly for c_S.

6 Because $T'_D = (V - V_K)/V_K$ when there is a queue, equation (4.29) is consistent with the departure rates of (3.25) in the basic bottleneck model, where $c'_T = \alpha$, $c'_S = -\beta$ for early arrivals, and $c'_S = \gamma$ for late arrivals.

7 Proof: We know that c'_T is positive and that c'_S has the same sign as S_D (the latter because c_S is by definition minimized at $S_D = 0$). For early exits, c'_S is therefore negative; so equilibrium condition (4.29) requires that $T'_D(t) > 0$ (growing queue). It also requires that $c'_T > |c'_S|$ – a consistence condition identical to the previously noted requirement $\beta < \alpha$ in the basic bottleneck model, where $c'_T = \alpha$ and $c'_S = -\beta$. For late exits, (4.29) requires that $T'_D(t) < 0$ (shrinking queue).

8 Proof: If c_T, c_S, and F are everywhere differentiable, then $c'_S = 0$ implies $T'_D(t) = 0$; i.e., $T_D(t)$ must be a maximum where c_S is a minimum.

9 To eliminate travel delays, the optimal entry rate must be equal to the lower capacity, and the optimal time-varying toll is set accordingly. The higher-capacity bottleneck therefore remains inactive in the first-best optimum and is irrelevant. In the unpriced equilibrium, the higher-capacity bottleneck may become active when it is located upstream of the other bottleneck; but even so total queuing time is independent of whether or not the higher-capacity bottleneck exists.

10 Two earlier examples are Chang, Mahmassani and Herman (1985) and de Palma, Lefévre and Ben-Akiva (1987). See Mahmassani (2000) for a brief review.

11 Mun (1999) combines Chu's (1995) approach with a downstream pure bottleneck, and finds that the optimal toll is described by (4.30) during the shoulders of the peak where the exit rate is below the bottleneck's capacity, and takes on the basic bottleneck form with slopes β and $-\gamma$ at other times.

12 The toll and travel delay are both zero for the first and last driver arriving, in the unpriced equilibrium as well as in the optimum. The generalized trip price in both regimes, which is equalized for all drivers, must be equal to the sum of the values of free-flow travel time and schedule delay for the first or the last driver. The fourth result therefore follows from the lengthening of the peak under optimal tolling.

13 Pigou (1920) in fact considered the same network, but because he assumed one road to be uncongested, the derivation of the optimal toll on the other road became a matter of first-best optimization.

14 Thus c_T here refers to user cost on the tolled road (route T), not to travel-delay cost in the sense of Section 4.1.2.

15 More precisely, consider a toll increase that results, after a new equilibrium is established with new amounts of congestion, in a change in generalized price $\Delta p \equiv \Delta p_T = \Delta p_U$. Write the ratio of trips added on U to trips removed from T as $-(\Delta V_U / \Delta V_T)$. Because the roads are perfect substitutes, the change in total trips must equal $\Delta p/d'$ in order to be consistent with the overall inverse demand curve $d(p)$. Therefore $\Delta V_T + \Delta V_U = \Delta p/d'$. Also, to be consistent with congestion, the change in generalized price on road U is given by $c'_U \Delta V_U$. (The same is not true on the road T because the toll is also changing.) Therefore $\Delta V_T + \Delta V_U = c'_U \Delta V_U / d'$, which can be solved for $-(\Delta V_U / \Delta V_T) = -d'/(c'_U - d')$.

16 This is a particular application of the so-called envelope theorem, which implies that indirect effects of a marginal change in a choice variable upon the objective are zero when evaluated in the full optimum. For first-best pricing on general networks, the changes in other link flows that would follow from a marginal increase in one of the link tolls have a zero net welfare effect, because all other links in the network are optimally priced and only carry traffic from OD-pairs for which marginal benefits and marginal costs are equated. The reader may verify that if the first-best general network problem of equation (4.16) were solved using the Lagrangian technique of (4.32) and using route-based tolls as policy instruments, all route-specific multipliers would indeed be equal to zero in the optimum. Indirect effects therefore vanish in first-best optima.

17 Total cost, for an overall demand of Q and two equal capacities V_K, can be determined by substituting $\frac{1}{3}Q$ in (4.21) and $\frac{2}{3}Q$ in (4.26) and adding the costs thus obtained, which yields a total of $\frac{1}{3} \cdot \delta \cdot Q^2/V_K$. Total cost in the unpriced equilibrium and in the first-best optimum can be found from (4.21) and (4.26), respectively, with V_K replaced by $2 \cdot V_K$. The results are $\frac{1}{2} \cdot \delta \cdot Q^2/V_K$ and $\frac{1}{4} \cdot \delta \cdot Q^2/V_K$. Thus the relative welfare gain of second-best pricing is $(\frac{1}{2}-\frac{1}{3})/(\frac{1}{2}-\frac{1}{4})=\frac{2}{3}$.

18 Chen and Bernstein (2004) address the same problem with multiple user groups.

19 See May *et al.* (2002) and Sumalee, May and Shepherd (2005). These two studies, as well as Zhang and Yang (2004), use a genetic algorithm to facilitate search through many possible configurations of charge points and toll levels.

20 Mun, Konishi and Yoshikawa (2003, 2005).

21 These results are derived by Verhoef *et al.* (1996) in a static model, and by El Sanhouri and Bernstein (1994) in a dynamic one.

22 Verhoef *et al.* (1996) and de Palma and Lindsey (1998).

23 The aggravating distortions of Pigouvian taxes are explained by Bovenberg and de Mooij (1994). Kaplow (1996) argues, however, that the labor-supply distortion is largely offset by other aspects of public spending, because people with higher earnings also receive more benefits from public services. If that is true, then the deadweight loss is small anyway so the additional impacts on it from Pigouvian taxes become negligible.

24 In particular the Intermodal Surface Transportation Efficiency Act (ISTEA) of 1991 and the Transportation Equity Act for the 21st Century (TEA-21) of 1998.

25 See the Value Pricing website of the Hubert H. Humphrey Institute of Public Affairs, University of Minnesota, at www.hhh.umn.edu/centers/slp/projects/conpric. We discuss here only the first three categories of value pricing distinguished by FHWA, which are those involving time-varying congestion pricing.

26 We rely especially on Bertini and Rufolo (2004), PRoGRESS (2004), Samuel (2005), and Sorensen and Taylor (2005).

27 Peter Samuel, personal communication, 6 July 2006.

28 For formal demand studies, see Young, Thompson and Taylor (1991) and Willson (1992). For case studies see Willson and Shoup (1990, Table 1) and Shoup (1997).

29 See Glazer and Niskanen (1992) and Verhoef, Nijkamp and Rietveld (1995b). One study calibrated on data from Brussels (Calthrop, Proost and Van Dender 2000) suggests that parking pricing might achieve 70% of the benefits of congestion pricing, but excludes departure-time adjustments and route choice.

30 See, for example, Arnott and Yan (2000, Note 3) for the conditions required. Our model is in fact similar to that of Arnott and Yan except that our rail mode is characterized by scale economies instead of congestion.

31 See equations (4.13)–(4.14) and (4.32)–(4.33). From (4.40), we see that the usual symmetry of second derivatives of $B(\cdot)$ imply symmetry of Slutsky matrix of derivatives of the demand functions, $(\partial d_i/\partial q_j)$, $i, j = A, R$, where q_A means the same thing as V_A. This shows that our ordinary (Marshallian) demand functions are also compensated (Hicksian) demand functions–see Varian (1992) and our discussion of income effects below equation (2.24). The benefit function has negative second cross-derivatives if the two types of travel are substitutes, positive if they are complements. In the special case of perfect substitutes, where the two types of travel can be regarded as two alternate sources for obtaining a single homogeneous travel good, all four second derivatives of $B(\cdot)$ are equal to each other and to the slope of the demand curve for that homogeneous travel good; we know this because in that case $B(q_A, q_B)$ can be expressed as a function $\tilde{B}(q)$ where $q \equiv q_A + q_B$, so that the four second derivatives of B are all equal to $\tilde{B}''(q)$. When the two demand functions are independent of each other, the cross-derivatives of $B(\cdot)$ are zero.

32 The logic is similar to that explained in the note following equation (4.35).

33 From line 3b of their Table 4.

34 For example, the European Commission's UNITE project computed cost-recovery ratios (fare revenues divided by operating costs) averaging 50% for 10 European nations in 1998, varying from 25% for Italy to 91% for the Netherlands (UNITE 2003).

35 See Meyer and Gómez-Ibáñez (1981) and Pucher (1984).

5 Investment

1 Euler's theorem states that if a differentiable function $c(\boldsymbol{x})$ of variables $\boldsymbol{x} \equiv (x_i)$ is homogeneous of degree k, *i.e.*, if $c(t\boldsymbol{x}) = t^k c(\boldsymbol{x})$ for all positive scalars t, then $\Sigma_i x_i \cdot (\partial c/\partial x_i) = k \cdot c(\boldsymbol{x})$. In our case, c_h is homogeneous of degree $k = 0$ in its two arguments.

2 To see why, observe that for a given demand function, the short-run optimal congestion toll and the associated road use per unit of capacity are both decreasing in capacity. This can be verified graphically in the left panel of Figure 4.1, by imagining how a larger capacity would imply equality of $d(V)$ and $mc(V)$ at some price p lower than p^1; this in turn would imply an equilibrium user cost c lower than c^1, hence an equilibrium ratio V/V_K lower than V^1/V_K and a lower optimal toll τ. With exact self-financing for the optimal capacity and toll, short-run optimal toll revenues per unit of capacity therefore exceed the unit cost of capacity when total capacity is below optimal, and fall short of it when total capacity is above optimal.

3 Of course, a full network analysis is still necessary in order to predict the traffic volumes that appear in the equation.

4 They also cover any portion of maintenance cost that is non-allocable to usage, which enters the model just like capital cost, so long as these are proportional to capacity.

5 Examples include Henderson (1977, Ch. 7), Wheaton (1978), Wilson (1983), and d'Ouville and McDonald (1990).

6 These terms, plus "induced travel" and "latent demand," tend to be used synonymously. Lee, Klein and Camus (2002) suggest the following useful distinction: induced traffic is a change in traffic resulting in movement along a short-run demand curve, whereas induced demand is a shift in the short-run demand curve (perhaps also a movement along a long-run demand curve). Here "short-run" should be defined as a time period over which demand factors, such as vehicle fleet or land uses, are kept constant. Other authors, notably Cervero (2003), distinguish between the effects of a capacity expansion on traffic on the facility itself ("induced travel") and the effects on all traffic in the region ("induced demand"). We do not attempt here to maintain this distinction rigorously, partly because we use "latent demand" for a particular kind of potential induced traffic.

7 This "law" exemplifies a more general principle, known as the "tragedy of the commons," applying to any public good or environmental amenity that is available at little or no charge and whose quality deteriorates with intensity of use (Hardin 1968).

8 By contrast, Mokhtarian *et al.* (2002) find no evidence of induced traffic when analyzing nine matched pairs of California road segments. They speculate that the reason might be that induced traffic is greater for new roads than for expansion of existing roads, or it may tend to reflect increases in trip length more than in number of trips. Their measures would miss these types of induced demand. However, they also think that econometric studies using aggregate data are plagued by omitted variables that may bias their results.

9 If the revenue objective were entirely dominant ($\lambda_\tau \to \infty$), the toll in (5.16) would be identical to the revenue-maximizing congestion toll that we will encounter in Chapter 6, equation (6.5).

10 Even for a profit-maximizing road operator, to be considered in Chapter 6, we will see that investment rule (5.3) still applies, for essentially the same reason.

11 If they do, then the labor-supply elasticity appearing in the formula for MCF is typically a compensated elasticity; if not, it is an uncompensated elasticity, which is larger in magnitude.

12 Small (1999b) suggests 1.25 as a central result from literature reviewed. Parry and Small (2005, Note 15) choose central assumptions for the uncompensated labor-supply elasticity (0.2) and for the average tax rate (0.35 for the US, 0.45 for the UK), from which we calculate the MCF as $1 + MEB_L$ using their equation (9d); the resulting MCF is 1.12 for the US and 1.20 for the UK.

13 See, for example, Ng (1987). Wendner and Goulder (2007) offer some empirical evidence that relative-status concerns are large enough to greatly reduce the size of the conventionally measured MCF.

14 Kleven and Kreiner (2006, Table 3, Scenarios S5–S9). The nations, in ascending order of the estimated MCF under most scenarios, are the UK, Italy, France, Germany, and Denmark.

15 A fuller treatment is provided by many references including Little and Mirrlees (1968), Mishan (1988), Layard and Glaister (1994), Small (1999b), Moore and Pozdena (2004), Willis (2005), and Boardman *et al.* (2006). Much of this section is adapted from Small (1999b).

16 More precisely, the real interest rate r is implicitly defined by the equation $(1+r) \cdot (1+\pi) = 1+n$. If π is small, the solution to this equation is approximately $r = n - \pi$.

17 Manuals or directives for practitioners include Transport Canada (1994), Austroads (1996), Japan Research Institute Study Group on Road Investment Evaluation (2000), European Commission DG Regional Policy (2002), American Association of State Highway and Transportation Officials (2003), and US OMB (2003). For access to these and others, see the website of the Economic Development Research Group, *Specialized Benefit-Cost Guides*, http://www.edrgroup.com/edr1/library/lib_guides_special/index.shtml. For critiques of US and European practices, see US GAO (2005) and Grant-Muller *et al.* (2001).

18 Boardman *et al.* (2006, pp. 249, 251, and 253).

19 These figures are from their 1996 edition, in which they used 1989 data. The difference between the two results for the real value of the marginal product of capital is partly because market interest rates on corporate bonds were higher in 1989, but partly because in their earlier calculation they adjusted the corporate-bond rate upward to account for corporate income taxes, which by our arguments is appropriate; for some reason they did not do this in the more recent calculation.

20 Actually he uses the continuous-time discount factor, $\exp(-rt)$, which arises in a version of (5.21) that applies when interest is cumulated continuously, namely

$$PV = \int_0^T C(t) \exp(-rt) \mathrm{d}t \; .$$

This equation can be derived from (5.21) as a limiting process.

21 For a rigorous study defining and measuring such benefits, see Shirley and Winston (2004).

6 Industrial organization of transportation providers

1 See World Bank (2006) for a review of recent experience.

2 This result is equivalent to that of Mohring (1985) for a monopolist owner of a congested port (his equation (4), for one time period only). The equivalence involves converting his demand curve (stated as a function of fee τ) to one that is a function of generalized price p.

3 It is derived in a more conventional context, for example, by Oum and Tretheway (1988), who go on to generalize it to handle externalities imposed by the price-setting firm on society in general.

4 The toll formula (6.11) is derived for the case of fixed capacities by Verhoef, Nijkamp and Rietveld (1996). It could be derived alternatively by using the user-equilibrium conditions to translate total demand for the corridor into demand just for the toll road, then applying (6.5).

5 This latter result is closely related to "double marginalization," which occurs with vertically organized monopolistic producers of intermediate and final goods. With double marginalization, however, the upstream firm faces the downstream firm's marginal revenue function as its inverse demand function. With pure complements as discussed in the main text, the firm faces the market inverse demand function, shifted downward by the prices charged by the other firms. Double marginalization in urban transport would occur when a monopolistic transit firm needs to travel on a private highway without substitutes, or when a transit operator cannot do without the services provided by a private station operator.

6 An example is the recent privatization of two separate US toll roads: the Chicago Skyway and the Indiana Toll Road. These roads, in adjacent states, cover parts of the same interstate highway route (I-90) and so carry a lot of through traffic. Perhaps the problem of excessive tolling, illustrated in this paragraph, is part of the reason why the consortia of firms that won the (separate) franchise auctions for the two roads include two large firms in common, Cintra Concesiones de Infraestructuras de Transporte (from Spain) and Macquarie Infrastructure Group (from Australia). These firms have an interest in internalizing the combined revenue potential from the two roads and therefore could have influenced their respective consortia to bid more, on the expectation that such internalization would be realized yielding higher total revenues.

7 De Borger, Dunkerley and Proost (2007) find that similar mechanisms are relevant when different governments control different parts of a corridor.

8 See especially Laffont and Tirole (1993) and the review by Guthrie (2006).

9 Present value is computed using a formula like (5.21).

10 "Sydney Tunnel mired in dispute," *Public Works Financing*, July–August 2006, p. 21.

11 Definitional lines vary. Preston (2005) defines tendering as "firms bidding for the right to operate services" (p. 65) and defines franchising as a particular type of tendering, involving "contracting out some of the tactical ... as well as operational functions" with an emphasis on arrangements that "expose bidders to revenue risk" (p. 66). Halcrow Fox (2000), however, applies a narrower definition of franchising: an arrangement in which "the authority is in the lead in specifying the broad public transport product and is prepared to incur the costs of doing so"; whereas a concession is somewhat closer to a true free market: a situation in which "the authority imposes a few basic requirements and has no financial responsibility" (p. 3).

12 To see why a per-rider subsidy is at least partly passed through in lower prices, consider an example with constant marginal production cost mc and linear demand curve $p = a - bq$, where p is price and q is quantity. Marginal revenue is then $mr = a - 2bq$, and the monopolist chooses q where $mc = mr = a - 2bq$, yielding $q^* = (a - mc)/2b$ which can be achieved by charging price $p^* = (a + mc)/2$. With a per-rider subsidy s, it will set $mc = s + a - 2bq$, which is the new marginal revenue; this yields $q^{**} = (s + a - mc)/2b$, achieved by charging price $p^{**} = p^* - (s/2)$. Thus, in this example, half of the subsidy is passed through in lower fares.

13 For reviews, see Perry, Babitsky and Gregersen (1988) and De Borger and Kerstens (2000).

14 These reviews in turn rely on many earlier studies, of which two of the most comprehensive are Mackie, Preston and Nash (1995) and White (1995).

15 Darbéra (2004, Fig. 10). The decline has continued at least through 2005/06, according to the UK Department for Transport (2006, Table C).

16 Darbéra (2004, Fig. 10). Also this increase has continued at least through 2005/06, according to UK Department for Transport (2006, Table C).

17 See Transport for London (2001) and O'Connor (2002).

18 See Gwilliam (2005, pp. 17–18), for a prospective description.

19 The figures quoted in this paragraph are from Teal and Berglund (1987), Gärling *et al.* (1995), Morrison (1997), Barrett (2001). For the fare statistics, see especially Morrison (pp. 921–24), Teal and Berglund (Table 3), and Gärling *et al.* (Tables 2–4).

20 Examples include Frankena and Pautler (1986), Hächner and Nyberg (1995), Cairns and Liston-Heyes (1996), and Yang and Wong (1998). Some of these authors cite Orr (1969) as an inspiration.

References

Abbas, Khaled A. and Mona H. Abd-Allah (1999) "Estimation and assessment of cost allocation models for main transit systems operating in Cairo," *Transport Reviews* 19: 353–75.

Agnew, Carson E. (1977) "The theory of congestion tolls," *Journal of Regional Science* 17: 381– 93.

Ahn, Kijung (2007) "Road pricing and bus service policies," working paper, Graduate School of Economics, Kyoto University.

Akçelik, Rahmi (1991) "Travel time functions for transport planning purposes: Davidson's function, its time-dependent form and an alternative travel time function," *Australian Road Research* 21: 49–59.

Alberini, Anna *et al.* (2004) "Does the value of a statistical life vary with age and health status? Evidence from the US and Canada," *Journal of Environmental Economics and Management* 48: 769–92.

Allport, R.J. (1981) "The costing of bus, light rail transit and metro public transport systems," *Traffic Engineering and Control* 22: 633–39.

American Association of State Highway and Transportation Officials (2003) *A Manual of User Benefit Analysis for Highways*, Washington, DC: AASHTO.

American Automobile Manufacturers Association (1997) *Motor Vehicle Facts and Figures 1997*, Washington, DC: American Automobile Manufacturers Association.

Anas, Alex (1981) "The estimation of multinomial logit models of joint location and travel mode choice from aggregated data," *Journal of Regional Science* 21: 223–42.

Anas, Alex (1982) *Residential Location Markets and Urban Transportation*, New York: Academic Press.

Anas, Alex (2007) "A unified theory of consumption, travel and trip chaining," *Journal of Urban Economics*, 62: 162–186.

Anas, Alex and Yu Liu (2007) "A regional economy, land use and transportation model (RELU-TRAN©): formulation, algorithm design, and testing," *Journal of Regional Science* 47: 415–455.

Anderson, David and Herbert Mohring (1997) "Congestion costs and congestion pricing," in David L. Greene and Donald L. Jones (eds.) *The Full Costs and Benefits of Transportation: Contributions to Theory, Method and Measurement*, Berlin: Springer-Verlag, pp. 315–36.

Anderson, Simon P. and André de Palma (2004) "The economics of pricing parking," *Journal of Urban Economics* 55: 1–20.

Anderson, Simon P., André de Palma and Jacques F. Thisse (1988) "A representative consumer theory of the logit model," *International Economic Review* 29: 461–66.

Ardekani, Siamak and Robert Herman (1987) "Urban network-wide traffic variables and their relations," *Transportation Science* 21: 1–16.

Armour, Rodney F. (1980) "An economic analysis of transit bus replacement," *Transit Journal* 6: 41–54.

Armstrong, Paula, Rodrigo Garrido and Juan de Dios Ortúzar (2001) "Confidence intervals to bound the value of time," *Transportation Research* 37E: 143–61.

Arnott, Richard, André de Palma and Robin Lindsey (1988) "Schedule delay and departure time decisions with heterogeneous commuters," *Transportation Research Record* 1197: 56–67.

Arnott, Richard, André de Palma and Robin Lindsey (1990a) "Departure time and route choice for the morning commute," *Transportation Research* 24B: 209–28.

Arnott, Richard, André de Palma and Robin Lindsey (1990b) "Economics of a bottleneck," *Journal of Urban Economics* 27: 111–30.

Arnott, Richard, André de Palma and Robin Lindsey (1991a) "Does providing information to drivers reduce traffic congestion?" *Transportation Research* 25A: 309–18.

Arnott, Richard, André de Palma and Robin Lindsey (1991b) "A temporal and spatial equilibrium analysis of commuter parking," *Journal of Public Economics* 45: 301–35.

Arnott, Richard, André de Palma and Robin Lindsey (1993) "A structural model of peak-period congestion: a traffic bottleneck with elastic demand," *American Economic Review* 83: 161–79.

Arnott, Richard, André de Palma and Robin Lindsey (1998) "Recent developments in the bottleneck model," in Kenneth J. Button and Erik T. Verhoef (eds.) *Road Pricing, Traffic Congestion and the Environment: Issues of Efficiency and Social Feasibility*, Cheltenham, UK: Edward Elgar, pp. 79–110.

Arnott, Richard and Eren Inci (2006) "An integrated model of downtown parking and traffic congestion," *Journal of Urban Economics* 60: 418–442.

Arnott, Richard and Marvin Kraus (1998a) "When are anonymous congestion charges consistent with marginal cost pricing?" *Journal of Public Economics* 67: 45–64.

Arnott, Richard and Marvin Kraus (1998b) "Self-financing of congestible facilities in a growing economy," in David Pines, Efraim Sadka and Itzhak Zilcha (eds.) *Topics in Public Economics: Theoretical and Applied Analysis*, Cambridge: Cambridge University Press, pp. 161–84.

Arnott, Richard, Tilman Rave and Ronnie Schöb (2005) *Alleviating Urban Traffic Congestion,* Cambridge, Mass.: MIT Press.

Arnott, Richard and John Rowse (1999) "Modeling parking," *Journal of Urban Economics* 45: 97–124.

Arnott, Richard and Kenneth A. Small (1994) "The economics of traffic congestion," *American Scientist* 82: 446–55.

Arnott, Richard and An Yan (2000) "The two-mode problem: second-best pricing and capacity," *Review of Urban and Regional Development Studies* 12: 170–99.

Arsenio, Elisabete, Abigail L. Bristow and Mark Wardman (2006) "Stated choice valuations of traffic related noise," *Transportation Research* 11D: 15–31.

Austroads (1996) *Benefit Cost Analysis Manual*, Publication No. AP-42/96, Sydney, Australia: Austroads.

Bailey, Elizabeth E. and Ann F. Friedlaender (1982) "Market structure and multiproduct industries," *Journal of Economic Literature* 20: 1024–48.

Banks, James H. (1989) "Freeway speed-flow-concentration relationships: more evidence and interpretations," *Transportation Research Record* 225: 53–60.

Barnes, Gary (2005) "The importance of trip destination in determining transit share," *Journal of Public Transportation* 8: 1–15.

Barnes, Gary and Peter Langworthy (2003) *The Per-Mile Costs of Operating Automobiles and Trucks*, report MN/RC 2003-19, St. Paul, MN: Minnesota Department of Transportation. http://www.lrrb.gen.mn.us/PDF/200319.pdf.

Barrett, Sean D. (2001) "Bus deregulation in Ireland," Trinity Economic Papers, No. 2001/8, Dublin, Ireland: Trinity College Dublin. www.tcd.ie/Economics/TEP/2001_papers/TEPNo8SB21.pdf.

Basso, Leonardo J. and Sergio R. Jara-Díaz (2006) "Are returns to scale with variable network size adequate for transport industry structure analysis?" *Transportation Science* 40: 259–68.

Bates, John *et al*. (1996) "The London congestion charging research programme: 4. The transport models," *Traffic Engineering and Control* 37: 334–39.

Bates, John *et al.* (2001) "The valuation of reliability for personal travel," *Transportation Research* 37E: 191–229.

Baumol, William J. and David F. Bradford (1970) "Optimal departures from marginal cost pricing," *American Economic Review* 60: 265–83.

Baumol, William J., John C. Panzar and Robert D. Willig (1982) *Contestable Markets and the Theory of Industry Structure*, New York: Harcourt Brace Jovanovich.

Baum-Snow, Nathaniel and Matthew E. Kahn (2000) "The effects of new public projects to expand urban rail transit," *Journal of Public Economics* 77: 241–63.

Becker, Gary S. (1965) "A theory of the allocation of time," *Economic Journal* 75: 493–517.

Beckmann, Martin J., C. Bartlett McGuire and Christopher B. Winsten (1956) *Studies in the Economics of Transportation*, New Haven, CT: Yale University Press.

Beggs, S., S. Cardell and J. Hausman (1981) "Assessing the potential demand for electric cars," *Journal of Econometrics* 6: 1–19.

Bell, Michelle L. *et al.* (2004) "Ozone and short-term mortality in 95 US urban communities, 1987–2000," *Journal of the American Medical Association* 292: 2372–78.

Ben-Akiva, Moshe (1974) "Structure of passenger travel demand models," *Transportation Research Record* 526: 26–42.

Ben-Akiva, Moshe and Michel Bierlaire (2003) "Discrete choice methods and their applications to short term travel decisions," in Hall (2003), Chapter 2.

Ben-Akiva, Moshe and John L. Bowman (1998) "Activity based travel demand model systems," in Patrice Marcotte and Sang Nguyen (eds.) *Equilibrium and Advanced Transportation Modelling*, Boston, MA: Kluwer Academic Publishers, pp. 27–46.

Ben-Akiva, Moshe, Michele Cyna and André de Palma (1984) "Dynamic model of peak period congestion," *Transportation Research* 18B: 339–55.

Ben-Akiva, Moshe, André de Palma and Pavlos Kanaroglou (1986) "Dynamic model of peak period traffic congestion with elastic arrival rates," *Transportation Science* 20: 164–81.

Ben-Akiva, Moshe, André de Palma and Isam Kaysi (1991) "Dynamic network models and driver information systems," *Transportation Research* 25A: 251–66.

Ben-Akiva, Moshe and Steven R. Lerman (1979) "Disaggregate travel and mobility-choice models and measures of accessibility," in David A. Hensher and Peter R. Stopher (eds.) *Behavioural Travel Modelling*, London: Croom Helm, pp. 654–79.

Ben-Akiva, Moshe and Steven R. Lerman (1985) *Discrete Choice Analysis: Theory and Application to Travel Demand*, Cambridge, MA: MIT Press.

Ben-Akiva, Moshe and Takayuki Morikawa (1990) "Estimation of travel demand models from multiple data sources," in Masaki Koshi (ed.) *Transportation and Traffic Theory: Proceedings of the Eleventh International Symposium on Transportation and Traffic Theory*, New York: Elsevier, pp. 461–76.

Bento, Antonio M. *et al.* (2005) "The effects of urban spatial structure on travel demand in the United States," *Review of Economics and Statistics* 87: 466–478.

Berechman, Joseph (1993) *Public Transit Economics and Deregulation Policy*, Amsterdam: North-Holland.

Berechman, Joseph and David Pines (1991) "Financing road capacity and returns to scale under marginal cost pricing," *Journal of Transport Economics and Policy* 25: 177–81.

Berger, J.O. and L.R. Pericchi (2001) "Objective Bayesian methods for model selection: introduction and comparison (with discussion)," in P. Lahiri (ed.) *Model Selection*, Institute of Mathematical Statistics Lecture Notes – Monograph Series, Vol. 38, Bethesda, MD: Institute of Mathematical Statistics, pp. 135–207.

Berry, Steven T. (1994) "Estimating discrete-choice models of product differentiation," *RAND Journal of Economics* 25: 242–62.

Berry, Steven T., James Levinsohn and Ariel Pakes (1995) "Automobile prices in market equilibrium," *Econometrica* 63: 841–90.

Berry, Steven T., James Levinsohn and Ariel Pakes (2004) "Differentiated product demand systems from a combination of micro and macro data: the new car market," *Journal of Political Economy* 112: 68–105.

Bertini, Robert L. and Anthony M. Rufolo (2004) "Technology considerations for the implementation of a statewide road user fee system," in Evangelos Bekiaris and Yuko J. Nakanishi (eds.) *Economic Impacts of Intelligent Transportation Systems: Innovations and Case Studies*, Amsterdam: Elsevier JAI, pp. 337–61.

Bhat, Chandra (1995) "A heteroscedastic extreme value model of intercity travel mode choice," *Transportation Research* 29B: 471–83.

Bhat, Chandra R. and Jessica Guo (2004) "A mixed spatially correlated logit model: formulation and application to residential choice modeling," *Transportation Research* 38B: 147–68.

Bhat, Chandra R. and Frank S. Koppelman (2003) "Activity-based modeling of travel demand," in Hall (2003), Chapter 3.

Black, Alan (1990) "Analysis of census data on walking to work and working at home," *Transportation Quarterly* 44: 107–20.

Blincoe, Lawrence J. *et al.* (2002) *The Economic Impact of Motor Vehicle Crashes 2000*, Washington, DC: US National Highway Traffic Safety Administration. http://www.nhtsa.dot.gov.

Boardman, Anthony E. and Lester B. Lave (1977) "Highway congestion and congestion tolls," *Journal of Urban Economics* 4: 340–59.

Boardman, Anthony E. *et al.* (2006) *Cost–Benefit Analysis: Concepts and Practice*, 3rd edition, Upper Saddle River, NJ: Prentice Hall.

Boarnet, Marlon G. and Randall Crane (2001) *Travel by Design: The Influence of Urban Form on Travel*, Oxford: Oxford University Press.

Boiteux, M. (1949) "La tarification des demandes en pointe: application de la theorie de la vente au cout marginal," *Revue Générale de l'Électricité*. Reprinted in English translation as "Peak-load pricing," *Journal of Business* 33 (1960): 157–79.

Borck, Rainald (2007) "The political economy of urban transit," in Kopp (2007), forthcoming.

Borck, Rainald and Matthias Wrede (2005) "Political economy of commuting subsidies," *Journal of Urban Economics* 57: 478–99.

Bovenberg, A. Lans and Ruud A. de Mooij (1994) "Environmental levies and distortionary taxation," *American Economic Review* 84: 1085–89.

Bowman, John L. and Moshe E. Ben-Akiva (2001) "Activity-based disaggregate travel demand model system with daily activity schedules," *Transportation Research* 35A: 1–28.

Boyce, David E. and Hillel Bar-Gera (2004) "Multiclass combined models for urban traffic forecasting," *Networks and Spatial Economics* 4: 115–24.

Boyce, David E., Hani S. Mahmassani and Anna Nagurney (2005) "A retrospective on Beckmann, McGuire and Winsten's 'Studies in the Economics of Transportation'," *Papers in Regional Science* 84: 85–103.

Boyd, J. Hayden (1976) "Benefits and costs of urban transportation: he who is inelastic receiveth and other parables," *Transportation Research Forum Proceedings* 7: 290–97.

Boyd, J. Hayden, Norman J. Asher and Elliot S. Wetzler (1973) *Evaluation of Rail Rapid Transit and Express Bus Service in the Urban Commuter Market*, report DOT-P-6520.1 prepared by the Institute for Defense Analyses for the US Department of Transportation, Washington, DC: US Government Printing Office.

Boyd, J. Hayden, Norman J. Asher and Elliot S. Wetzler (1978) "Nontechnological innovation in urban transit: a comparison of some alternatives," *Journal of Urban Economics* 5: 1–20.

Boyd, J. Hayden and Robert E. Mellman (1980) "The effect of fuel economy standards on the U.S. automotive market: an hedonic demand analysis," *Transportation Research* 14A: 367–78.

Boyer, Marcel and Georges Dionne (1987) "The economics of road safety," *Transportation Research* 21B: 413–31.

Braess, Dietrich (1968) "Über ein paradoxon aus der verkehrsplanung," *Unternehmenforschung* 12: 258–68.

Braeutigam, Ronald R. (1999) "Learning about transport costs," in Gómez-Ibáñez, Tye and Winston (1999), pp. 57–97.

Braid, Ralph M. (1996) "Peak-load pricing of a transportation route with an unpriced substitute," *Journal of Urban Economics* 40: 179–197.

Branston, David (1976) "Link capacity functions: a review," *Transportation Research* 10: 223–36.

Bresnahan, Timothy F., Scott Stern and Manuel Trajtenberg (1997) "Market segmentation and the sources of rents from innovation: personal computers in the late 1980s," *RAND Journal of Economics* 28: S17–S44.

Brice, Stéphane (1989) "Derivation of nested transport models within a mathematical programming framework," *Transportation Research* 23B: 19–28.

Brownstone, David and Xuehao Chu (1997) "Multiply-imputed sampling weights for consistent inference with panel attrition," in Thomas F. Golob, Ryuichi Kitamura and Lyn Long (eds.), *Panels for Transportation Planning: Methods and Applications*, Amsterdam: Kluwer Academic Publishers, pp. 259–73.

Brownstone, David and Kenneth A. Small (1989) "Efficient estimation of nested logit models," *Journal of Business and Economic Statistics* 7: 67–74.

Brownstone, David and Kenneth A. Small (2005) "Valuing time and reliability: assessing the evidence from road pricing demonstrations," *Transportation Research* 39A: 279–93.

Brownstone, David and Kenneth Train (1999) "Forecasting new product penetration with flexible substitution patterns," *Journal of Econometrics* 89: 109–29.

Brownstone, David *et al.* (2003) "Drivers' willingness-to-pay to reduce travel time: evidence from the San Diego I-15 congestion pricing project," *Transportation Research* 37A: 373–87.

Button, Kenneth J. (1988) "Contestability in the UK bus industry, experience goods and economies of experience," in John S. Dodgson and Neville Topham (eds.), *Bus Deregulation and Privatisation: An International Perspective*, Aldershot, UK: Avebury, pp. 69–96.

Button, Kenneth J. (1993) *Transportation Economics*, 2nd edition, Cheltenham, UK: Edward Elgar.

Button, Kenneth J. (2005) "The economics of cost recovery in transport: introduction," *Journal of Transport Economics and Policy* 39: 241–57.

Button, Kenneth J. and David A. Hensher (eds.) (2001) *Handbook of Transport Systems and Traffic Control*, New York: Pergamon.

Button, Kenneth J. and David A. Hensher (eds.) (2005) *Handbook of Transport Strategy, Policy and Institutions*, Amsterdam: Elsevier.

Button, Kenneth J. and K.J. O'Donnell (1985) "An examination of the cost structures associated with providing urban bus services in Britain," *Scottish Journal of Political Economy* 32: 67–81.

Button, Kenneth J. and Erik T. Verhoef (eds.) (1998) *Road Pricing, Traffic Congestion and the Environment: Issues of Efficiency and Social Feasibility*, Cheltenham, UK: Edward Elgar.

Bye, Raymond Taylor (1926) "The nature and fundamental elements of costs," *Quarterly Journal of Economics* 41: 30–62.

Cadot, Olivier, Lars-Hendrik Röller and Andreas Stephan (2006) "Contribution to productivity or pork barrel? The two faces of infrastructure investment," *Journal of Public Economics* 90: 1133–53.

Cairns, Robert D. and Catherine Liston-Heyes (1996) "Competition and regulation in the taxi industry," *Journal of Public Economics* 59: 1–15.

Calfee, John and Clifford Winston (1998) "The value of automobile travel time: implications for congestion policy," *Journal of Public Economics* 69: 83–102.

Calthrop, Edward and Stef Proost (2006) "Regulating on-street parking," *Regional Science and Urban Economics* 36: 29–48.

Calthrop, Edward, Stef Proost and Kurt Van Dender (2000) "Parking policies and road pricing," *Urban Studies* 37: 63–76.

Cambridge Systematics, Inc. *et al.* (1998) *Economic Impact Analysis of Transit Investments: Guidebook for Practitioners*, Transit Cooperative Research Program Report 35, Washington, DC: National Academy Press.

Cardell, N. Scott and Frederick C. Dunbar (1980) "Measuring the societal impacts of automobile downsizing," *Transportation Research* 14A: 423–34.

Cassidy, Michael J. and Robert L. Bertini (1999) "Some traffic features at freeway bottlenecks," *Transportation Research* 33B: 25–42.

Caudill, Steven B. (1988) "An advantage of the linear probability model over probit or logit," *Oxford Bulletin of Economics and Statistics* 50: 425–27.

Cervero, Robert (1982) "Multistage approach for estimating transit costs," *Transportation Research Record* 877: 67–75.

Cervero, Robert (1986) "Time-of-day transit pricing: comparative US and international experiences," *Transport Reviews* 6: 347–64.

Cervero, Robert (1990) "Profiling profitable bus routes," *Transportation Quarterly* 44: 183–201.

Cervero, Robert (1996) "Jobs–housing balancing revisited: trends and impacts in the San Francisco Bay Area," *Journal of the American Planning Association* 62: 492–511.

Cervero, Robert (1997) *Paratransit in America: Redefining Mass Transportation*, Westport, CT: Praeger.

Cervero, Robert (2003) "Road expansion, urban growth, and induced travel: a path analysis," *Journal of the American Planning Association* 69: 145–63.

Cervero, Robert and Roger Gorham (1995) "Commuting in transit versus automobile neighborhoods," *Journal of the American Planning Association* 61: 210–25.

Cervero, Robert and Mark Hansen (2002) "Induced travel demand and induced road investment: a simultaneous equation analysis," *Journal of Transport Economics and Policy* 36: 469–90.

Cervero, Robert and Kang-Li Wu (1996) "Subcentering and commuting: evidence from the San Francisco Bay Area, 1980–1990," working paper, Department of City and Regional Planning, University of California, Berkeley, Berkeley, CA.

Chan, Y. and F.L. Ou (1978) "Tabulating demand elasticities for urban travel forecasting," *Transportation Research Record* 673: 40–46.

Chang, Gang-Len, Hani S. Mahmassani and Robert Herman (1985) "Macroparticle traffic simulation model to investigate peak-period commuter decision dynamics," *Transportation Research Record* 1005: 107–21.

Chattopadhyay, Sudip (2001) "Welfare measurement in the discrete-choice random utility model under general preference structure," unpublished manuscript, Department of Economics, San Francisco State University, San Francisco, CA.

Chen, Mei and David H. Bernstein (2004) "Solving the toll design problem with multiple user groups," *Transportation Research* 38B: 61–79.

Choi, Ki-Hong and Choon-Geol Moon (1997) "Generalized extreme value model and additively separable generator function," *Journal of Econometrics* 76: 129–40.

Chomitz, Kenneth M. and Charles A. Lave (1984) "Part-time labor, work rules and urban transit costs," *Journal of Transport Economics and Policy* 18: 63–73.

Choo, Sangho, Patricia L. Mokhtarian and Ilan Salomon (2005) "Does telecommuting reduce vehicle-miles traveled? An aggregate time series analysis for the U.S.," *Transportation* 32: 37–64.

Chow, Gregory C. (1983) *Econometrics*, New York: McGraw-Hill.

Christensen, Laurits R., Dale W. Jorgenson and Lawrence J. Lau (1973) "Transcendental logarithmic production frontiers," *Review of Economics and Statistics* 55: 28–45.

Chu, Chausie (1981) "Structural issues and sources of bias in residential location and travel mode choice models," unpublished dissertation, Northwestern University, Evanston, IL.

Chu, Xuehao (1995) "Endogenous trip scheduling: the Henderson approach reformulated and compared with the Vickrey approach," *Journal of Urban Economics* 37: 324–43.

Chu, Xuehao (1999) "Alternative congestion pricing schedules," *Regional Science and Urban Economics* 29: 697–722.

Commissariat Général du Plan (2001) *Transports: Choix des Investissements et Coût des Nuisances* [*Transportation: Choice of Investments and the Cost of Nuisances*], Paris, June.

Coombe, R.D. (1989) "Review of computer software for traffic engineers," *Transport Reviews* 9: 217–34.

Corneo, Giacomo G. (1997) "Taxpayer-consumers and public pricing," *Economics Letters* 57: 235–40.

Crane, Randall (2000) "The influence of urban form on travel: an interpretive review," *Journal of Planning Literature* 15: 3–23.

Currie, Graham (2005) "The demand performance of bus rapid transit," *Journal of Public Transportation* 8: 41–55.

D'Este, Glen (2000) "Urban freight movement modelling," in David A. Hensher and Kenneth J. Button (eds.) *Handbook of Transport Modelling*, New York: Pergamon, pp. 539–52.

Dafermos, Stella C. (1972) "The traffic assignment problem for multiclass-user transportation networks," *Transportation Science* 6: 73–87.

Dafermos, Stella C. (1980) "Traffic equilibrium and variational inequalities," *Transportation Science* 14: 42–54.

Daganzo, Carlos F. (1997) *Fundamentals of Transportation and Traffic Operations*, New York: Pergamon.

Daganzo, Carlos F., Michael J. Cassidy and Robert L. Bertini (1999) "Possible explanations of phase transitions in highway traffic," *Transportation Research* 33A: 365–79.

Daganzo, Carlos and Michael Kusnic (1993) "Two properties of the nested logit model," *Transportation Science* 27: 395–400.

Daganzo, Carlos F. and Yosef Sheffi (1977) "On stochastic models of traffic assignment," *Transportation Science* 11: 253–74.

Dagenais, Marcel G. and Marc J.I. Gaudry (1986) "Can aggregate direct travel demand models work?" in *Research for Tomorrow's Transport Requirements: Proceedings of the World Conference on Transport Research, Vol. 2*, Vancouver, BC, Canada: Centre for Transportation Studies, University of British Columbia, pp. 1669–76.

Dahlgren, Joy (1998) "High occupancy vehicle lanes: not always more effective than general purpose lanes," *Transportation Research* 32B: 99–114.

Darbéra, Richard (2004) "L'expérience anglaise de dérégulation des transports par autobus [Bus services deregulation in the UK]," *Cahiers Scientifiques du Transport* 46: 25–44. Lyon: Association Française des Instituts de Transport et de Logistique. (In French with English summary.) http://www.afitl.com/CST/precedents-numeros/article.php?id=18.

Dasgupta, Partha (1994) "Exhaustible resources: resource depletion, research and development, and the social rate of discount," in Layard and Glaister (1994), pp. 349–72.

Davis, Stacy C. and Susan W. Diegel (2006) *Transportation Energy Data Book, Edition 25*, Oak Ridge, TN: Oak Ridge National Laboratory (ORNL). http://cta.ornl.gov/data.

Dawson, J.A.L. and Fred N. Brown (1985) "Electronic road pricing in Hong Kong: a fair way to go?" *Traffic Engineering and Control* 26: 522–29.

Day, Brett (1999) "A meta-analysis of wage-risk estimates of the value of a statistical life," in European Commission, *Benefits Transfer and the Economic Valuation of Environmental Damage in the European Union: with Special Reference to Health*. http://www.cserge.ucl.ac.uk/VOSL.pdf.

De Borger, Bruno, Fay Dunkerley and Stef Proost (2007) "Strategic investment and pricing decisions in a congested transport corridor," *Journal of Urban Economics*, 62: 294–316.

De Borger, Bruno and Mogens Fosgerau (2006) "Discrete choices and the trade-off between money and time: another test of the theory of reference-dependent preferences," research paper 2006–034, Department of Economics, University of Antwerp, Antwerp, Belgium. http://www.ua.ac.be/download.aspx?c=*TEWHI&n=39157&ct=39867&e=114660.

De Borger, Bruno and Kristiaan Kerstens (2000) "The performance of bus-transit operators," in David A. Hensher and Kenneth J. Button (eds.) *Handbook of Transport Modelling*, New York: Pergamon, pp. 577–95.

De Borger, Bruno and Stef Proost (2001) *Reforming Transport Pricing in the European Union: A Modelling Approach*, Cheltenham, UK: Edward Elgar.

De Borger, Bruno, Stef Proost and Kurt Van Dender (2005) "Congestion and tax competition in a parallel network," *European Economic Review* 49: 2013–40.

De Borger, Bruno and Kurt Van Dender (2003) "Transport tax reform, commuting and endogenous values of times," *Journal of Urban Economics* 53: 510–30.

De Ceuster, Griet *et al.* (2005) *TREMOVE 2.30 Model and Baseline Description: Final Report*, Catholic University of Leuven, Belgium, for European Commission, DG ENV, Directorate C, 18 February. http://europa.eu.int/comm/environment/air/tremove/tremove_model_dev.htm.

De Jong, Gerard (2000) "Value of freight travel-time savings," in David A. Hensher and Kenneth J. Button (eds.) *Handbook of Transport Modelling*, New York: Pergamon, pp. 553–64.

Delucchi, Mark (2000) "Should we try to get the prices right?" *Access* 16: 10–14. http://www.uctc.net/access/access.asp.

De Neufville, Richard and Joseph H. Stafford (1971) *Systems Analysis for Engineers and Managers*, New York: McGraw-Hill.

de Palma, André and Richard Arnott (1986) "Usage-dependent peak-load pricing," *Economics Letters* 20: 101–05.

de Palma, André and Philippe Jehiel (1995) "Queuing may be first-best efficient," discussion paper 95-20, THEMA (THéorie Economique, Modélisation et Applications), Université de Cergy-Pontoise, Cergy-Pontoise, France.

de Palma, André and Robin Lindsey (1998) "Information and usage of congestible facilities under different pricing regimes," *Canadian Journal of Economics* 31: 666–92.

de Palma, André and Robin Lindsey (2000) "Private roads: competition under various ownership regimes," *Annals of Regional Science* 34: 13–35.

de Palma, André and Robin Lindsey (2001) "Optimal timetables for public transportation," *Transportation Research* 35B: 789–813.

de Palma, André and Robin Lindsey (2002) "Private roads, competition, and incentives to adopt time-based congestion tolling," *Journal of Urban Economics* 52: 217–41.

de Palma, André, and Robin Lindsey (2005) "Relation between pricing, toll revenues and investment," Task Report 2.1, Project REVENUE, DG-TREN Fifth Framework Programme. Shorter version appeared as Chapter 2 of André de Palma, Robin Lindsey and Stef Proost (eds.) *Investment and the Use of Tax and Toll Revenues in the Transport Sector*, Amsterdam: Elsevier, 2007.

de Palma, André and Fabrice Marchal (2002) "Real cases applications of the fully dynamic METROP-OLIS tool-box: an advocacy for large-scale mesoscopic transportation systems," *Networks and Spatial Economics* 2: 347–69.

de Palma, André, Moez Kilani and Robin Lindsey (2005) "Comparison of second-best and third-best tolling schemes on a road network," *Transportation Research Record* 1932: 89–96.

de Palma, André, C. Lefèvre and M. Ben-Akiva (1987) "A dynamic model of peak period traffic flows and delays in a corridor," *Computational Mathematics Applications* 4: 201–23.

de Palma, André, Robin Lindsey and Stef Proost (eds.) (2006) *Modelling of Urban Road Pricing and its Implementation*, Special issue of *Transport Policy* 13.

de Rus, Ginés and Chris Nash (eds.) (1997) *Recent Developments in Transport Econonomics*, Aldershot, UK: Ashgate.

Deaton, Angus (1985) "The demand for personal travel in developing countries: an empirical analysis," *Transportation Research Record* 1037: 59–66.

DeCorla-Souza, Patrick (2004) "Recent U.S. experience: pilot projects," in Georgina Santos (ed.) *Road Pricing: Theory and Evidence*, Amsterdam: Elsevier JAI, pp. 283–308.

DeSerpa, A.C. (1971) "A theory of the economics of time," *Economic Journal* 81: 828–46.

DeVany, Arthur S. and Thomas R. Saving (1980) "Competition and highway pricing for stochastic traffic," *Journal of Business* 53: 45–60.

Dewees, Donald N. (1976) "Urban express bus and railroad performance: some Toronto simulations," *Journal of Transport Economics and Policy* 10: 16–25.

Dewees, Donald N. (1978) "Simulations of traffic congestion in Toronto," *Transportation Research* 12: 153–65.

Dewees, Donald N. (1979) "Estimating the time costs of highway congestion," *Econometrica* 47: 1499–512.

Dodgson, John S. and Yannis Katsoulacos (1988a) "Models of competition and the effect of bus service deregulation," in John S. Dodgson and Neville Topham (eds.) *Bus Deregulation and Privatisation: An International Perspective*, Aldershot, UK: Avebury, pp. 45–68.

Dodgson, John S. and Yannis Katsoulacos (1988b) "Quality competition in bus services," *Journal of Transport Economics and Policy* 22: 263–81.

Dodgson, John S. and Neville Topham (1987) "Benefit–cost rules for urban transit subsidies," *Journal of Transport Economics and Policy* 21: 57–71.

Domencich, Thomas A. and Gerald Kraft (1970) *Free Transit*, Lexington, MA: D.C. Heath.

Douglas, George W. and James C. Miller III (1974) "Quality competition, industry equilibrium, and efficiency in the price-constrained airline market," *American Economic Review* 64: 657–69.

d'Ouville, Edmond L. and John F. McDonald (1990) "Optimal road capacity with a suboptimal congestion toll," *Journal of Urban Economics* 28: 34–49.

Dowling, R.G., R. Singh and W.W.K. Cheng (1998) "The accuracy and performance of improved speed-flow functions," *Transportation Research Record* 1646: 9–17.

Downes, J.D. and P. Emmerson (1983) *Urban Transport Modelling with Fixed Travel Budgets (An Evaluation of the UMOT Process)*, supplementary report 799, Crowthorne, UK: Transport and Road Research Laboratory.

Downs, Anthony (1962) "The law of peak-hour expressway congestion," *Traffic Quarterly* 6: 393–409.

Downs, Anthony (2004) *Still Stuck in Traffic: Coping with Peak-Hour Traffic Congestion*, Washington, DC: Brookings Institution Press.

Dubin, Jeffrey A. and Daniel L. McFadden (1984) "An econometric analysis of residential electric appliance holdings and consumption," *Econometrica* 52: 345–62.

Dupuit, Jules (1844) "De l'influence des peages sur l'utilité des voies de communication," *Annales des Ponts et Chaussées*. Translated by Elizabeth Henderson as "On tolls and transport charges," *International Economic Papers* 11 (1962): 7–31.

Dupuit, Jules (1849) "De la mesure de l'utilité des travaux publics," *Annales des Ponts et Chaussées* 8. Translated by R.H. Barback as "On the measurement of the utility of public works," *International Economic Papers* 2 (1952): 83–110.

Economides, Nicholas and Steven C. Salop (1992) "Competition and integration among complements, and network market structure," *Journal of Industrial Economics* 40: 105–23.

Edelson, Noel M. (1971) "Congestion tolls under monopoly," *American Economic Review* 61: 873–82.

Edlin, Aaron S., and Pinar Karaca-Mandic (2003) "The accident externality from driving," working paper E03-332, Department of Economics, University of California at Berkeley, June. http:// repositories.cdlib.org/iber/econ/E03–332.

Edlin, Aaron S. and Pinar Karaca-Mandic (2006) "The accident externality from driving," *Journal of Political Economy* 114: 931–55.

Eliasson, Jonas and Lars-Goran Mattsson (2006) "Equity effects of congestion pricing: quantitative methodology and a case study for Stockholm," *Transportation Research* 40A: 602–20.

El Sanhouri, I. and David Bernstein (1994) "Integrating driver information and congestion pricing systems," *Transportation Research Record* 1450: 44–50.

Else, P.K. (1981) "A reformulation of the theory of optimal congestion taxes," *Journal of Transport Economics and Policy* 5: 217–32.

Emmerink, Richard H.M. (1998) *Information and Pricing in Road Transportation*, New York: Springer-Verlag.

Emmerink, Richard H.M. and Peter Nijkamp (eds.) (1999) *Behavioural and Network Impacts of Driver Information Systems*, Aldershot, UK: Ashgate.

Engel, Eduardo, Ronald Fisher and Alexander Galetovic (1997) "Highway franchising: pitfalls and opportunities," *American Economic Review, Papers and Proceedings* 87: 68–72.

Engel, Eduardo, Ronald Fisher and Alexander Galetovic (2004) "Toll competition among congested roads," *Topics in Economic Analysis and Policy* 4: Article 4.

Estache, Antonio (2001) "Privatization and regulation of transport infrastructure in the 1990's," *World Bank Research Observer* 16: 85–107.

Estache, Antonio and Andrés Gómez-Lobo (2005) "Limits to competition in urban bus services in developing countries," *Transport Reviews* 25: 139–58.

Ettema, Dick and Harry Timmermans (1997) "Theories and models of activity patterns," in Dick Ettema and Harry Timmermans (eds.) *Activity-Based Approaches to Travel Analysis*, New York: Pergamon, pp. 1–36.

European Commission DG Regional Policy (2002) *Guide to Cost–Benefit Analysis of Investment Projects*, European Commission, Brussels, Belgium. http://europa.eu.int/comm/regional_policy/ sources/docgener/guides/cost/guide02_en.pdf.

European Conference of Ministers of Transport (ECMT) (1998) *Efficient Transport for Europe: Policies for Internalisation of External Costs*, Paris: OECD Publications Service.

EXTRA (2001) *Getting Prices Right: Results from the Transport Research Programme*, European Commission, DG Energy and Transport, Consortium for EXploitation of TRAnsport Research, Brussels, Belgium. http://europa.eu.int/comm/transport/extra/web/downloadfunction.cfm?doc-name=200406/20040617_110400_88575_pricing.pdf&apptype=application/pdf.

Evans, Andrew (1987) "A theoretical comparison of competition with other economic regimes for bus services," *Journal of Transport Economics and Policy* 21: 7–36.

Evans, Andrew (1988) "Hereford: a case study of bus deregulation," *Journal of Transport Economics and Policy* 22: 283–306.

Fargier, Paul-Henri (1983) "Effects of the choice of departure time on road traffic congestion," in VanOlin F. Hurdle, Ezra Hauer and Gerald N. Steuart (eds.) *Proceedings of the Eighth International Symposium on Transportation and Traffic Theory*, Toronto: University of Toronto Press, pp. 223–62.

Feldstein, Martin (1999) "Tax avoidance and the deadweight loss of the income tax," *Review of Economics and Statistics* 81: 674–80.

Fernald, John G. (1999) "Roads to prosperity? Assessing the link between public capital and productivity," *American Economic Review* 89: 619–38.

Florian, Michael and Marc Gaudry (1980) "A conceptual framework for the supply side in transportation systems," *Transportation Research* 4B: 1–8.

Flyvbjerg, Bent, Matte K. Skamris Holm and Søren L. Buhl (2003) "How common and how large are cost overruns in transport infrastructure projects?" *Transport Reviews* 23: 71–88.

Flyvbjerg, Bent, Matte K. Skamris Holm and Søren L. Buhl (2004) "What causes cost overrun in transport infrastructure projects?" *Transport Reviews* 24: 3–18.

Flyvbjerg, Bent, Matte K. Skamris Holm and Søren L. Buhl (2006) "Inaccuracy in traffic forecasts," *Transport Reviews* 26: 1–24.

Foldvary, Fred (2006) "Streets as private-sector public goods," in Gabriel J. Roth (ed.) *Street Smart: Competition, Entrepreneurship, and the Future of Roads*, New Brunswick, NJ: Transaction Publishers, pp. 305–25.

Forsyth, P.J. (1980) "The value of time in an economy with taxation," *Journal of Transportation Economics and Policy* 14: 337–62.

Foster, Christopher D. (1974) "The regressiveness of road pricing," *International Journal of Transport Economics* 1: 133–41.

Fowkes, A.S. *et al.* (2004) "How highly does the freight transport industry value journey time reliability – and for what reasons?" *International Journal of Logistics: Research and Applications* 7: 33–43.

Frank, M. and P. Wolfe (1956) "An algorithm for quadratic programming," *Naval Research Logistics Quarterly* 3: 95–110.

Frankena, Mark W. (1987) "Capital-biased subsidies, bureaucratic monitoring, and bus scrapping," *Journal of Urban Economics* 21: 180–93.

Frankena, Mark W. and Paul A. Pautler (1986) "Taxicab regulation: an economic analysis," *Research in Law and Economics* 9: 129–65.

Frick, Karen Trappenberg, Brian Taylor and Martin Wachs (2007) "Contracting for public transit services in the US: evaluating the tradeoffs," in Kopp (2007), forthcoming.

Fridstrøm, Lasse *et al.* (1995) "Measuring the contribution of randomness, exposure, weather, and daylight to the variation in road accident counts," *Accident Analysis and Prevention* 27: 1–20.

Gagnepain, Philippe and Marc Ivaldi (2002) "Incentive regulatory policies: the case of public transit systems in France," *RAND Journal of Economics* 33: 605–29.

Gärling, Tommy *et al.* (1995) "A note on the short-term effects of deregulation of the Swedish taxicab industry," *Journal of Transport Economics and Policy* 29: 209–14.

Gaudry, Marc J.I. (1975) "An aggregate time-series analysis of urban transit demand: the Montreal case," *Transportation Research* 9: 249–58.

Gaudry, Marc J.I. and Michael J. Wills (1978) "Estimating the functional form of travel demand models," *Transportation Research* 12: 257–89.

Giuliano, Genevieve (1991) "Is jobs–housing balance a transportation issue?" *Transportation Research Record* 1305: 305–12.

Giuliano, Genevieve (1994) "Equity and fairness considerations of congestion pricing," in National Research Council, *Curbing Gridlock: Peak-Period Fees to Relieve Traffic Congestion. Volume 2: Commissioned Papers*, TRB special report 242, Washington, DC: National Academy Press, pp. 250–79.

Giuliano, Genevieve (2004) "Land use impacts of transportation investments: highway and transit," in Susan Hanson and Genevieve Giuliano (eds.) *The Geography of Urban Transportation*, 3rd edition, New York: Guilford Press, pp. 237–73.

Giuliano, Genevieve and Kenneth A. Small (1993) "Is the journey to work explained by urban structure?" *Urban Studies* 30: 1485–500.

Glaister, Stephen (1974) "Generalised consumer surplus and public transport pricing," *Economic Journal* 84: 849–67.

Glaister, Stephen (1986) "Bus deregulation, competition, and vehicle size," *Journal of Transport Economics and Policy* 20: 217–44.

Glaister, Stephen (1997) "Deregulation and privatisation: British experience," in Ginés de Rus and Chris Nash (eds.) *Recent Developments in Transport Economics*, Aldershot: Ashgate, pp. 135–97.

Glaister, Stephen and David Lewis (1978) "An integrated fares policy for transport in London," *Journal of Public Economics* 9: 341–55.

Glazer, Amihai and Esko Niskanen (1992) "Parking fees and congestion," *Regional Science and Urban Economics* 22: 123–32.

Goh, Mark (2002) "Congestion management and electronic road pricing in Singapore," *Journal of Transport Geography* 10: 29–38.

Golob, Thomas F. (2003) "Structural equation modeling for travel behavior research," *Transportation Research* 37B: 1–25.

Golob, Thomas F. and Amelia C. Regan (2001) "Impacts of highway congestion on freight operations: perceptions of trucking industry managers," *Transportation Research* 35A: 577–99.

Gómez-Ibáñez, José A. (1996) "Big-city transit ridership, deficits, and politics: avoiding reality in Boston," *Journal of the American Planning Association* 62: 30–50.

Gómez-Ibáñez, José A. and Gary R. Fauth (1980) "Downtown auto restraint policies: the costs and benefits for Boston," *Journal of Transport Economics and Policy* 14: 133–53.

Gómez-Ibáñez, José A., William B. Tye and Clifford Winston (eds.) (1999) *Essays in Transportation Economics and Policy: A Handbook in Honor of John R. Meyer*, Washington, DC: Brookings Institution Press.

Goodwin, Phil B. (1989) "The rule of three: a possible solution to the political problem of competing objectives for road pricing," *Traffic Engineering and Control* 30: 495–97.

Goodwin, Phil B. (1992) "A review of new demand elasticities with special reference to short and long run effects of price changes," *Journal of Transport Economics and Policy* 26: 155–69.

Goodwin, Phil B. (1996) "Empirical evidence on induced traffic," *Transportation* 23: 35–54.

Goolsbee, Austan and Amil Petrin (2004) "The consumer gains from direct broadcast satellites and the competition with cable TV," *Econometrica* 72: 351–81.

Gordon, Peter, Ajay Kumar and Harry W. Richardson (1989) "The influence of metropolitan spatial structure on commuting time," *Journal of Urban Economics* 26: 138–51.

Gordon, Peter and Richard Willson (1984) "The determinants of light-rail transit demand – an international cross-sectional comparison," *Transportation Research* 18A: 135–40.

Graham, Daniel J. and Stephen Glaister (2002) "The demand for automobile fuel: a survey of elasticities," *Journal of Transport Economics and Policy* 36: 1–26.

Grant-Muller, S.M. *et al.* (2001) "Economic appraisal of European transport projects: the state-of-the art revisited," *Transport Reviews* 21: 237–61.

Greenberg, H. (1959) "An analysis of traffic flow," *Operations Research* 7: 78–85.

Greene, David L. (1992) "Vehicle use and fuel economy: how big is the rebound effect?" *Energy Journal* 13: 117–43.

Greene, David L., Donald W. Jones and Mark A. Delucchi (eds.) (1997) *The Full Costs and Benefits of Transportation: Contributions to Theory, Method and Measurement*, Berlin: Springer-Verlag.

Greene, William H. (2003) *Econometric Analysis*, 5th edition, Upper Saddle River, NJ: Prentice Hall.

Greening, Lorna A., David L. Greene and Carmen Difiglio (2000) "Energy efficiency and consumption – the rebound effect – a survey," *Energy Policy* 28: 389–401.

Greenshields, B.D. (1935) "A study of traffic capacity," *Highway Research Board Proceedings* 14: 448–77.

Gunn, Hugh F. (2001) "Spatial and temporal transferability of relationships between travel demand, trip cost and travel time," *Transportation Research* 37E: 163–89.

Guthrie, Graeme (2006) "Regulating infrastructure: the impact on risk and investment," *Journal of Economic Literature* 44: 925–72.

Gwilliam, Ken (2003) "Urban transport in developing countries," *Transport Reviews* 23: 197–216.

Gwilliam, Ken (2005) "Bus franchising in developing countries: some recent World Bank experience," revised keynote paper, 8th International Conference on Ownership and Regulation of Land Passenger Transport, Rio de Janeiro, Brazil, June 2003. http://siteresources.worldbank.org/INTUR-BANTRANSPORT/Resources/bus_franch_gwilliam.pdf.

Hächner, Jonas and Sten Nyberg (1995) "Deregulating taxi services: a word of caution," *Journal of Transport Economics and Policy* 29: 195–207.

Haight, Frank (1963) *Mathematical Theories of Traffic Flow*, New York: Academic Press.

Halcrow Fox (2000) *Review of Urban Public Transport Competition: Draft Final Report*, London: Halcrow Group Ltd. http://siteresources.worldbank.org/INTURBANTRANSPORT/Resources/uk_competition_bayliss.pdf.

Hall, Fred L. (2002) "Traffic stream characteristics," in Nathan A. Gartner, Carrol J. Messer and Ajay Rathi (eds.) *Traffic Flow Theory: A State-of-the-Art Report*, Washington, DC: US Department of Transportation, Turner-Fairbank Highway Research Center, Chapter 2. http://www.tfhrc.gov/its/tft/tft.htm.

Hall, Fred L., Brian L. Allen and Margot A. Gunter (1986) "Empirical analysis of freeway flow-density relationships," *Transportation Research* 20A: 197–210.

Hall, Fred L. and Lisa M. Hall (1990) "Capacity and speed flow analysis of the QEW in Ontario," *Transportation Research Record* 1287: 108–18.

Hall, Fred L., V.F. Hurdle and J.H. Banks (1992) "Synthesis of recent work on the nature of speed–flow and flow–occupancy (or density) relationships for freeways," *Transportation Research Record* 365: 12–18.

Hall, Randolph W. (ed.) (2003) *Handbook of Transportation Science*, 2nd edition, Boston, MA: Kluwer Academic Publishers.

Hall, Randolph W. and Cenk Caliskan (1999) "Design and evaluation of an automated highway system with optimized lane assignment," *Transportation Research* 7C: 1–15.

Hardin, Garrett (1968) "The tragedy of the commons," *Science* 62: 1243–48.

Harker, Patrick T. (1988) "Private market participation in urban mass transportation: application of computable equilibrium models of network competition," *Transportation Science* 22: 96–111.

Hastings, N.A.J. and J.B. Peacock (1975) *Statistical Distributions: A Handbook for Students and Practitioners*, London: Butterworth.

Hausman, Jerry A. and Paul A. Ruud (1987) "Specifying and testing econometric models for rank-ordered data," *Journal of Econometrics* 34: 83–104.

Hausman, Jerry A. and David A. Wise (1978) "A conditional probit model for qualitative choice: discrete decisions recognizing interdependence and heterogeneous preferences," *Econometrica* 46: 403–26.

Hearn, Donald W. and Motakuri V. Ramana (1998) "Solving congestion toll pricing models," in Patrice Marcotte and Sang Nguyen (eds.) *Equilibrium and Advanced Transportation Modelling*, Boston, MA: Kluwer Academic Publishers.

Heckman, James J. (1979) "Sample selection bias as a specification error," *Econometrica* 47: 153–62.

Henderson, J. Vernon (1974) "Road congestion: a reconsideration of pricing theory," *Journal of Urban Economics* 1: 346–65.

Henderson, J. Vernon (1977) *Economic Theory and the Cities*, New York: Academic Press.

Henderson, J. Vernon (1992) "Peak shifting and cost-benefit miscalculations," *Regional Science and Urban Economics* 22: 103–21.

Hendrickson, Chris and George Kocur (1981) "Schedule delay and departure time decisions in a deterministic model," *Transportation Science* 15: 62–77.

Hensher, David A. (1986) "Sequential and full information maximum likelihood estimation of a nested logit model," *Review of Economics and Statistics* 56: 657–67.

Hensher, David A. (1994) "Stated preference analysis of travel choices: the state of practice," *Transportation* 21: 107–33.

Hensher, David A. (1997) "Behavioral value of travel time savings in personal and commercial automobile travel," in Greene, Jones and Delucchi (1997), pp. 245–79.

Hensher, David A. (2001) "The valuation of commuter travel time savings for car drivers: evaluating alternative model specifications," *Transportation* 28: 101–18.

Hensher, David A. and Kenneth J. Button (eds.) (2000) *Handbook of Transport Modelling*, New York: Pergamon.

Hess, Daniel B., Brian D. Taylor and Allison C. Yoh (2005) "Light rail lite or cost-effective improvements to bus service?" *Transportation Research Record* 1927: 22–30.

Hicks, John R. (1941) "The rehabilitation of consumers' surplus," *Review of Economic Studies* 8: 108–16.

Highway Research Board (1965) *Highway Capacity Manual*, special report 87, Washington, DC: Highway Research Board.

Hills, Peter (1993) "Road congestion pricing: when is it a good policy? A comment," *Journal of Transport Economics and Policy* 27: 91–99.

Hoogendoorn, Serge P. and Piet H.L. Bovy (1998) "Modeling multiple user-class traffic," *Transportation Research Record* 1644: 57–69.

Horowitz, Joel L. (1980) "The accuracy of the multinomial logit model as an approximation to the multinomial probit model of travel demand," *Transportation Research* 14B: 331–41.

Hotelling, Harold (1938) "The general welfare in relation to problems of taxation and of railway and utility rates," *Econometrica* 6: 242–69.

Hu, Pat S. and Timothy R. Reuscher (2004) *Summary of Travel Trends: 2001 National Household Travel Survey*, Washington, DC: US Federal Highway Administration. http://nhts.ornl.gov/2001/reports.shtml.

Imbens, Guido W. and Tony Lancaster (1994) "Combining micro and macro data in microeconometric models," *Review of Economics Studies* 61: 655–80.

Inman, Robert P. (1978) "A generalized congestion function for highway travel," *Journal of Urban Economics* 5: 21–34.

International Energy Agency (2002) *Bus Systems for the Future: Achieving Sustainable Transport Worldwide*, Paris: International Energy Agency and Organisation for Economic Co-operation and Development.

Iseki, Hiroyuki (2004) 'Does contracting matter? The determinants of contracting and contracting's effects on cost efficiencies in U.S. fixed-route bus transit service', unpublished dissertation, University of California, Los Angeles, Los Angeles, CA.

Jakob, Astrid, John L. Craig and Gavin Fisher (2006) "Transport cost analysis: a case study of the total costs of private and public transport in Auckland," *Environmental Science and Policy* 9: 55–66.

Jansson, Jan Owen (1980) "A simple bus line model for optimisation of service frequency and bus size," *Journal of Transport Economics and Policy* 14: 53–80.

Jansson, Jan Owen (1984) *Transport System Optimization and Pricing*, Chichester, UK: John Wiley & Sons.

Japan Ministry of Health, Labour and Welfare (1999) *Final Report of Monthly Labour Survey: July 1999*, Tokyo, Japan: Ministry of Health, Labour and Welfare. http://www.mhlw.go.jp/english/database/db-l/.

Japan Research Institute Study Group on Road Investment Evaluation (2000) *Guidelines for the Evaluation of Road Investment Projects*, Tokyo, Japan: Japan Research Institute.

Jara-Díaz, Sergio R. (1982) "The estimation of transport cost functions: a methodological review," *Transport Reviews* 2: 257–78.

Jara-Díaz, Sergio R. (1986) "On the relation between users' benefits and the economic effects of transportation activities," *Journal of Regional Science* 26: 379–91.

Jara-Díaz, Sergio R. (2000) "Allocation and valuation of travel-time savings," in David A. Hensher and Kenneth J. Button (eds.) *Handbook of Transport Modelling*, New York: Pergamon, pp. 303–19.

Jara-Díaz, Sergio R. (2003) "On the goods-activities technical relations in the time allocation theory," *Transportation* 30: 245–60.

Jenkins, Glenn P. (1997) "Project analysis and the World Bank," *American Economic Review Papers and Proceedings* 87: 38–42.

Johansson, Olof and Lee Schipper (1997) "Measuring the long-run fuel demand of cars: separate estimations of vehicle stock, mean fuel intensity, and mean annual driving distance," *Journal of Transport Economics and Policy* 31: 277–92.

Johansson, Per-Olov (1991) *An Introduction to Modern Welfare Economics*, Cambridge: Cambridge University Press.

Johnston, Jack and John DiNardo (1997) *Econometric Methods*, 4th edition, New York: McGraw-Hill.

Jones-Lee, Michael W., M. Hammerton and P.R. Philips (1985) "The value of safety: results of a national sample survey," *Economic Journal* 95: 49–72.

Jun, Myung-Jin (2004) "The effects of Portland's urban growth boundary on urban development patterns and commuting," *Urban Studies* 41: 1333–48.

Kahneman, Daniel and Amos Tversky (1979) "Prospect theory: an analysis of decision under risk," *Econometrica* 47: 263–92.

Kain, John F. *et al.* (1992) *Increasing the Productivity of the Nation's Urban Transportation Infrastructure: Measures to Increase Transit Use and Carpooling, Final report,* Report DOT-T-92-17, prepared for US Federal Transit Administration, Washington, DC.: US Department of Transportation.

Kain, John F. (1999) "The urban transportation problem: a reexamination and update," in Gómez-Ibáñez, Tye and Winston (1999), pp. 359–401.

Kain, John F. and Zhi Liu (2002) "Efficiency and locational consequences of government transport policies and spending in Chile," in Edward L. Glaeser and John R. Meyer (eds.) *Chile: Political Economy of Urban Development*, Cambridge, MA: Harvard University Press, pp. 105–95.

Kaplow, Louis (1996) "The optimal supply of public goods and the distortionary cost of taxation," *National Tax Journal* 49: 513–33.

Karlaftis, Matthew G. (2007) "Privatisation, regulation and competition: a thirty-year retrospective on transit efficiency," in Kopp (2007), forthcoming.

Kawamura, Kazuya (2000) "Perceived value of time for truck operators," *Transportation Research Record* 1725: 31–36.

Kay, J.A. and D.J. Thompson (1986) "Privatisation: a policy in search of a rationale," *Economic Journal* 96: 18–32.

Keeler, Theodore E. and Kenneth A. Small (1977) "Optimal peak-load pricing, investment, and service levels on urban expressways," *Journal of Political Economy* 85: 1–25.

Keeler, Theodore E., Kenneth A. Small *et al.* (1975) *The Full Costs of Urban Transport. Part III: Automobile Costs and Final Intermodal Cost Comparisons,* Monograph No. 21, Berkeley, CA: University of California, Institute of Urban and Regional Development.

Keong, Chin Kian (2002) "Road pricing: Singapore's experience," paper prepared for the third seminar of the IMPRINT-EUROPE Thematic Network, "Implementing Reform on Transport Pricing: Constraints and Solutions: Learning from Best Practice," Brussels, October 2002.

Kerali, Henry (2003) "Economic appraisal of road projects in countries with developing and transition economies," *Transport Reviews* 23: 249–62.

Kerner, B.S. and H. Rehborn (1997) "Experimental properties of phase transitions in traffic flow," *Physical Review Letters* 79: 4030–33.

Keyes, Dale L. (1982) "Energy for travel: the influence of urban development patterns," *Transportation Research* 16A: 65–70.

Kidokoro, Yukihiro (2004) "Cost–benefit analysis for transport networks: theory and application," *Journal of Transport Economics and Policy* 38: 275–307.

Kitamura, Ryuichi (2000) "Longitudinal methods," in Hensher and Button (2000), pp. 113–29.

Klein, Daniel B., Adrian T. Moore and Binyam Reja (1997) *Curb Rights: A Foundation for Free Enterprise in Urban Transit*, Washington, DC: Brookings Institution Press.

Kleven, Henrik Jacobsen and Claus Thustrup Kreiner (2006) "The marginal cost of public funds: Hours of work versus labor force participation," *Journal of Public Economics* 90: 1955–73.

Knight, Frank (1924) "Some fallacies in the interpretation of social costs," *Quarterly Journal of Economics* 38: 582–606.

Kockelman, Kara M. (2001) "A model for time- and budget-constrained activity demand analysis," *Transportation Research* 35B: 255–69.

Kopp, Andreas (ed.) (2007) *Privatisation and Regulation of Urban Transit Systems*, Proceedings of Roundtable 138, European Conference of Ministers of Transport, Paris: Organisation for Economic Co-operation and Development.

Koppelman, Frank S. and Geoffrey Rose (1985) "Geographic transfer of travel choice models: evaluation and procedures," in B.G. Hutchinson, P. Nijkamp and M. Batty (eds.), *Optimization and Discrete Choice in Urban Systems: Proceedings of the International Symposium on New Directions in Urban Systems Modelling*, Berlin: Springer-Verlag, pp. 272–309.

Koppelman, Frank S. and Vaneet Sethi (2000) "Closed-form discrete-choice models," in Hensher and Button (2000), pp. 211–27.

Koppelman, Frank S. and Chieh-Hua Wen (2000) "The paired combinatorial logit model: properties, estimation and application," *Transportation Research* 34B: 75–89.

Krammes, Raymond A. and Kenneth W. Crowley (1986) "Passenger car equivalents for trucks on level freeway segments," *Transportation Research Record* 1091: 10–17.

Kraus, Marvin (1981) "Scale economies analysis for urban highway networks," *Journal of Urban Economics* 9: 1–22.

Kraus, Marvin (1991) "Discomfort externalities and marginal cost transit fares," *Journal of Urban Economics* 29: 249–59.

Kraus, Marvin, Herbert Mohring and Thomas Pinfold (1976) "The welfare costs of nonoptimum pricing and investment policies for freeway transportation," *American Economic Review* 66: 532–47.

Kroes, Eric P., Robert W. Antonisse and Sten Bexelius (1987) "Return to the peak?" in *Transportation Planning Methods*, Proceedings of Seminar C held at the PTRC Summer Annual Meeting [University of Bath, England], London: Planning and Transport Research and Computation (PTRC) Education and Research Services, pp. 233–45.

Krupnick, Alan J. (2004) *Valuing Health Outcomes: Policy Choices and Technical Issues*, Washington, DC: Resources for the Future. http://www.rff.org/rff/Publications/Reports.cfm.

Laffont, Jean–Jacques and Jean Tirole (1993) *A Theory of Incentives in Procurement and Regulation*, Cambridge, MA: MIT Press.

Lago, Armando M., Patrick D. Mayworm and J. Matthew McEnroe (1981) "Further evidence on aggregate and disaggregate transit fare elasticities," *Transportation Research Record* 799: 42–47.

Lam, Terence C. and Kenneth A. Small (2001) "The value of time and reliability: measurement from a value pricing experiment," *Transportation Research* 37E: 231–51.

Larsen, Odd I. (1993) "Road investment with road pricing – investment criteria and the revenue/cost issue," in A. Talvitie, D. Hensher, and M.E. Beesley (eds.) *Privatization and Deregulation in Passenger Transportation*, Second International Conference on Privatization and Deregulation in Passenger Transportation, Espoo, Finland: Viatek Ltd., pp. 273–81.

Lave, Charles A. (1991) "Measuring the decline in transit productivity in the U.S.," *Transportation Planning and Technology* 15: 115–24.

Layard, Richard and Stephen Glaister (eds.) (1994) *Cost–Benefit Analysis*, Cambridge: Cambridge University Press.

Lee, Douglass, Jr., Lisa A. Klein and Gregorio Camus (2002) "Induced traffic and induced demand," in US Federal Highway Administration, *Highway Economic Requirements System – State Version: Technical Report, Appendix A*, Washington, DC: US Federal Highway Administration. http://isddc.dot.gov/OLPFiles/FHWA/010945.pdf.

Levine, Jonathan and Yaakov Garb (2002) "Congestion pricing's conditional promise: promotion of accessibility or mobility?" *Transport Policy* 9: 179–88.

Levinson, David M. (1998) "Road pricing in practice," in Button and Verhoef (1998), pp. 14–38.

Levinson, David M. (2001) "Why states toll: an empirical model of finance choice," *Journal of Transport Economics and Policy* 35: 223–38.

Levinson, Herbert *et al.* (2003) *Bus Rapid Transit*, Transit Cooperative Research Program Report 90 (Vols. 1 and 2), Washington, DC: Transportation Research Board.

Levitt, Steven D. and Jack Porter (2001) "How dangerous are drinking drivers?" *Journal of Political Economy* 109: 1198–237.

Lévy-Lambert, H. (1968) "Tarification des services à qualité variable – application aux péages de circulation [Pricing of variable-quality services – application to road tolls]," *Econometrica* 36: 564–74.

Li, Michael Z.F. (2002) "The role of speed–flow relationship in congestion pricing implementation with an application to Singapore," *Transportation Research* 36B: 731–54.

Lighthill, M.H. and G.B. Whitham (1955) *On Kinematic Waves, II: A Theory of Traffic Flow on Long Crowded Roads*, London: Royal Society.

Lindberg, Gunnar (2001) "Traffic insurance and accident externality charges," *Journal of Transport Economics and Policy* 35: 399–416.

Lindberg, P.O., E.A. Eriksson and L.-G. Mattsson (1995) "Invariance of achieved utility in random utility models," *Environment and Planning A* 27: 121–42.

Lindsey, Robin (2006) "Do economists reach a conclusion on road pricing? The intellectual history of an idea," *Econ Journal Watch* 3: 292–79. www.econjournalwatch.org.

Lindsey, Robin and Erik T. Verhoef (2000) "Congestion modelling," in Hensher and Button (2000), pp. 353–73.

Lindsey, Robin and Erik T. Verhoef (2001) "Traffic congestion and congestion pricing," in Button and Hensher (2001), pp. 77–105.

Lipsey, Richard G. and Kelvin J. Lancaster (1956) "The general theory of second best," *Review of Economic Studies* 24: 11–32.

Litman, Todd (2005) *Transportation Cost and Benefit Analysis*, Victoria, BC, Canada: Victoria Transport Policy Institute. http://www.vtpi.org/documents/transportation.php.

Little, I.M.D. and J.A. Mirrlees (1968) *Manual of Industrial Project Analysis for Developing Countries, II*, Paris: Organisation for Economic Co-operation and Development.

Liu, Louie Nan and John F. McDonald (1998) "Efficient congestion tolls in the presence of unpriced congestion: a peak and off-peak simulation model," *Journal of Urban Economics* 44: 352–66.

Lomax, T.J., S.M. Turner and R. Margiotta (2003) *Monitoring Urban Roadways in 2001: Examining Reliability and Mobility with Archived Data*, report FHWA-OP-03-041, Washington, DC: US Federal Highway Administration.

London Underground (2006) *Managing Director's Performance Report to the Underground Advisory Panel: Year Ended 31 March 2006*, London, 23 May. http://www.tfl.gov.uk/tfl/lu_panel.asp.

Louviere, Jordan J. and David A. Hensher (2001) "Combining sources of preference data," in David A. Hensher (ed.) *Travel Behaviour Research: The Leading Edge*, New York: Pergamon, pp. 125–44.

Louviere, Jordan J., David A. Hensher and Joffre D. Swait (2000) *Stated Choice Methods: Analysis and Applications*, Cambridge: Cambridge University Press.

Luk, James and Stephen Hepburn (1993) *New Review of Australian Travel Demand Elasticities*, research report ARR 249, Vermont South, Victoria, Australia: Australian Road Research Board.

Mackett, Roger L. (1985) "Modelling the impact of rail fare increases," *Transportation* 12: 293–312.

Mackie, P.J. and P.W. Bonsall (1989) "Traveller response to road improvements: implications for user benefits," *Traffic Engineering and Control* 30: 411–16.

Mackie, P.J., S. Jara-Díaz and A.S. Fowkes (2001) "The value of travel time savings in evaluation," *Transportation Research* 37E: 91–106.

Mackie, Peter J., John Preston and Chris Nash (1995) "Bus deregulation ten years on," *Transport Reviews* 15: 229–51.

Mackie, P.J. *et al.* (2003) *Values of Travel Time Savings in the UK: Summary Report*, report to the UK Department for Transport, Leeds, UK: Institute of Transport Studies, University of Leeds. http://www.dft.gov.uk/stellent/groups/dft_econappr/documents/page/dft_econappr022708-01.hcsp.

Mahmassani, Hani S. (2000) "Trip timing," in Hensher and Button (2000), pp. 393–407.

Mahmassani, Hani S. (ed.) (2002) *In Perpetual Motion: Travel Behavior Research Opportunities and Application Challenges*, London: Pergamon.

Mahmassani, Hani S. and Robert Herman (1984) "Dynamic user equilibrium departure time and route choice on idealized traffic arterials," *Transportation Science* 18: 362–84.

Mannering, Fred L. and David A. Hensher (1987) "Discrete/continuous econometric models and their application to transport analysis," *Transport Reviews* 7: 227–44.

Manski, Charles F. and Steven R. Lerman (1977) "The estimation of choice probabilities from choice based samples," *Econometrica* 45: 1977–88.

Marchand, Maurice (1968) "A note on optimal tolls in an imperfect environment," *Econometrica* 36: 575–81.

Marcotte, Patrice and Sang Nguyen (eds.) (1998) *Equilibrium and Advanced Transportation Modelling*, Boston, MA: Kluwer Academic Publishers.

Marsden, Greg (2006) "The evidence base for parking policies – a review," *Transport Policy* 13: 447–57.

May, Adolf D. (1990) *Traffic Flow Fundamentals*, Upper Saddle River, NJ: Prentice-Hall.

May, Anthony D. and Dave S. Milne (2000) "Effects of alternative road pricing systems on network performance," *Transportation Research* 34A: 407–36.

May, Anthony D., Simon P. Shepherd and John J. Bates (2000) "Supply curves for urban road networks," *Journal of Transport Economics and Policy* 34: 261–90.

May, Anthony D., Simon P. Shepherd and Paul M. Timms (2000) "Optimal transport strategies for European cities," *Transportation* 27: 285–315.

May, Anthony D. *et al.* (2002) "The impact of cordon design on the performance of road pricing schemes," *Transport Policy* 9: 209–20.

Mayeres, Inge and Stef Proost (2001) "Marginal tax reform, externalities and income distribution," *Journal of Public Economics* 79: 343–63.

McCarthy, Patrick S. (2001) *Transportation Economics: Theory and Practice: A Case Study Approach*, Malden, MA: Blackwell.

McCarthy, Patrick S. and Richard Tay (1993) "Economic efficiency *vs* traffic restraint: a note on Singapore's area license scheme," *Journal of Urban Economics* 34: 96–100.

McClenahan, J.W. *et al.* (1978) *Two Methods for Estimating the Crew Costs of Bus Service*, special report 364, Crowthorne, UK: Transport and Road Research Laboratory.

McCubbin, Donald R. and Mark A. Delucchi (1999) "The health costs of motor-vehicle-related air pollution," *Journal of Transport Economics and Policy* 33: 253–86.

McDonald, John F., Edmond L. d'Ouville and Louie Nan Liu (1999) *Economics of Urban Highway Congestion and Pricing*, Boston, MA: Kluwer Academic Publishers.

McDonald, John F. and Clifford I. Osuji (1995) "The effect of anticipated transportation improvement on residential land values," *Regional Science and Urban Economics* 25: 261–78.

McFadden, Daniel (1974) "Conditional logit analysis of qualitative choice behavior," in Paul Zarembka (ed.) *Frontiers in Econometrics*, New York: Academic Press, pp. 105–42.

McFadden, Daniel (1978) "Modelling the choice of residential location," in Anders Karlqvist *et al.* (eds.) *Spatial Interaction Theory and Planning Models*, Amsterdam: North-Holland, pp. 75–96.

McFadden, Daniel (1981) "Econometric models of probabilistic choice," in Charles F. Manski and Daniel McFadden (eds.) *Structural Analysis of Discrete Data with Econometric Applications*, Cambridge, MA: MIT Press, pp. 198–272.

McFadden, Daniel (2001) "Economic choices," *American Economic Review* 91: 351–78.

McFadden, Daniel and Fred Reid (1976) "Aggregate travel demand forecasting from disaggregated behavioral models," *Transportation Research Record* 534: 24–37.

McFadden, Daniel and Kenneth Train (2000) "Mixed MNL models for discrete response," *Journal of Applied Econometrics* 15: 447–70.

McFadden, Daniel *et al.* (1977) *Demand Model Estimation and Validation. Urban Travel Demand Forecasting Project Phase I*, report UCB-ITS-SR-77-9, Berkeley, CA: University of California, Institute of Transportation Studies.

McMillen, Daniel P. and John McDonald (2004) "Reaction of house prices to a new rapid transit line: Chicago's Midway Line, 1983–1999," *Real Estate Economics* 32: 463–86.

Meland, Solveig (1995) "Generalised and advanced urban debiting innovations: the GAUDI Project 3 – the Trondheim Toll Ring," *Traffic Engineering and Control* 36: 150–55.

Meyer, John R. and José A. Gómez-Ibáñez (1981) *Autos, Transit, and Cities*, Cambridge, MA: Harvard University Press.

Meyer, John R., John F. Kain and Martin Wohl (1965) *The Urban Transportation Problem*, Cambridge, MA: Harvard University Press.

Miller, Eric J. (ed.) (2005) *Recent Advances in Activity-Based Modelling: Selected Papers from the Lucerne IATBR Conference*, special issue of *Transportation* 32(4).

Miller, Ted R. (1993) "Costs and functional consequences of U.S. roadway crashes," *Accident Analysis and Prevention* 25: 593–607.

Miller, Ted R., Rebecca S. Spicer and David T. Levy (1999) "How intoxicated are drivers in the United States? Estimating the extent, risks and costs per kilometer of driving by blood alcohol level," *Accident Analysis and Prevention* 31: 515–23.

Mills, David E. (1981) "Ownership arrangements and congestion-prone facilities," *American Economic Review* 71: 493–502.

Milne, David S., Esko Niskanen and Erik T. Verhoef (2000) *Operationalisation of Marginal Cost Pricing within Urban Transport*, research report 63, Helsinki, Finland: Government Institute for Economic Research (VATT). http://data.vatt.fi/afford/reports-dell.html.

Mishan, Edward J. (1988) *Cost–Benefit Analysis: An Informal Introduction*, London: Unwin Hyman.

Mogridge, M.J.H. *et al.* (1987) "The Downs/Thomson paradox and the transportation planning process," *International Journal of Transport Economics* 14: 283–311.

Mohktarian, Patricia L. *et al.* (2002) "Revisiting the notion of induced traffic through a matched-pairs study," *Transportation* 29: 193–220.

Mohring, Herbert (1965) "Urban highway investments," in Robert Dorfman (ed.) *Measuring Benefits of Government Investments*, Washington, DC: Brookings Institution Press, pp. 231–75.

Mohring, Herbert (1972) "Optimization and scale economies in urban bus transportation," *American Economic Review* 62: 591–604.

Mohring, Herbert (1976) *Transportation Economics*, Cambridge, MA: Ballinger.

Mohring, Herbert (1979) "The benefits of reserved bus lanes, mass transit subsidies, and marginal cost pricing in alleviating traffic congestion," in Peter Mieszkowski and Mahlon Straszheim (eds.) *Current Issues in Urban Economics*, Baltimore, MD: Johns Hopkins University Press.

Mohring, Herbert (1985) "Profit maximization, cost minimization and pricing for congestion-prone facilities," *Logistics and Transportation Review* 21: 27–36.

Mohring, Herbert and Mitchell Harwitz (1962) *Highway Benefits: An Analytical Framework*, Evanston, IL: Northwestern University Press.

Mohring, Herbert and Harold F. Williamson, Jr. (1969) "Scale and 'industrial reorganisation' economies of transport improvements," *Journal of Transport Economics and Policy* 3: 251–71.

Moore, Terry and Randy Pozdena (2004) "Framework for an economic evaluation of transportation investments," in Evangelos Bekiaris and Yuko J. Nakanishi (eds.) *Economic Impacts of Intelligent Transportation Systems: Innovations and Case Studies*, Amsterdam: Elsevier, pp.17–45.

Morlok, Edward K. and Philip A. Viton (1980) "Self-sustaining public transportation services," *Transport Policy and Decision Making* 1: 169–94.

Morlok, Edward K. and Philip A. Viton (1985) "Recent experience with successful private transit in large U.S. cities," in Charles A. Lave (ed.) *Urban Transit: The Private Challenge to Public Transportation*, Pacific Studies in Public Policy, Cambridge, MA: Ballinger, pp. 121–49.

Morrison, P.S. (1997) "Restructuring effects of deregulation: the case of the New Zealand taxi industry," *Environment and Planning A* 29: 913–28.

Mrozek, Janusz R. and Laura O. Taylor (2002) "What determines the value of life? A meta-analysis," *Journal of Policy Analysis and Management* 21: 253–70.

Mun, Se-il (1999) "Peak-load pricing of a bottleneck with traffic jam," *Journal of Urban Economics* 46: 323-49.

Mun, Se-il (2002) "Bottleneck congestion with traffic jam: a reformulation and correction of earlier result," working paper, Graduate School of Economics, Kyoto University, Kyoto, Japan.

Mun, Se-il, Ko-ji Konishi and Kazuhiro Yoshikawa (2003) "Optimal cordon pricing," *Journal of Urban Economics* 54: 21-28.

Mun, Se-il, Ko-ji Konishi and Kazuhiro Yoshikawa (2005) "Optimal cordon pricing in a non-mono-centric city," *Transportation Research* 39A: 723-36.

Munizaga, Marcela A. *et al.* (2006) "Valuing time with a joint mode choice–activity model," *International Journal of Transport Economics* 33: 193–210.

Murphy, James J. and Mark A. Delucchi (1998) "A review of the literature on the social cost of motor vehicle use in the United States," *Journal of Transportation and Statistics* 1: 15-42.

MVA Consultancy *et al.* (1987) *The Value of Travel Time Savings: A Report of Research Undertaken for the Department of Transport*, prepared by the MVA Consultancy, Institute for Transport Studies, University of Leeds and Transport Studies Unit, University of Oxford, Newbury, Berkshire, UK: Policy Journals.

Nagurney, Anna (1999) *Network Economics: A Variational Inequality Approach*, 2nd edition, Boston, MA: Kluwer Academic Publishers.

Nash, Christopher A. (1974) "The treatment of capital costs of vehicles in evaluating road schemes," *Transportation* 3: 225–42.

Nash, Christopher A. (1988) "Integration of public transport: an economic assessment," in J.S. Dodgson and N. Topham (eds.) *Bus Deregulation and Privatisation*, Aldershot, UK: Avebury, pp. 97–118.

Nash, Christopher A. (2005) "Privatization in transport," in Button and Hensher (2005), pp. 97–113.

Nash, Christopher A. and Walter Bryan Matthews (eds.) (2005) *Measuring the Marginal Social Costs of Transport*, Research in Transportation Economics, Vol. 14, Oxford: Elsevier JAI.

Nash, Christopher A. *et al.* (2003) *UNITE (UNIfication of accounts and marginal costs for Transport Efficiency) Final Report for Publication*, Report for European Commission – DG TREN, Fifth Framework Programme, Brussels, November. http://www.its.leeds.ac.uk/projects/unite/downloads/FinalReport.doc.

National Research Council (1994) *Curbing Gridlock: Peak-Period Fees to Relieve Traffic Congestion*, TRB Special Report 242, Washington, DC: National Academy Press.

National Research Council (2002) *Effectiveness and Impact of Corporate Average Fuel Economy (CAFE) Standards*, Washington, DC: National Academy Press.

Navrud, Ståle (2003) "State-of-the-art on economic valuation of noise," paper prepared for the WCE/WHO Pan-European Program on Transport, Health, and Environment, Stockholm, Sweden, June 2003. http://www.fhi.se/pdf/navrud.pdf (accessed 19 May 2004).

Newbery, David M. (1988) "Road damage externalities and road user charges," *Econometrica* 56: 295–316.

Newbery, David M. (1989) "Cost recovery from optimally designed roads," *Economica* 56: 165–85.

Newbery, David M. (2005) "Road user and congestion charges," in Sijbren Cnossen (ed.) *Theory and Practice of Excise Taxation: Smoking, Drinking, Gambling, Polluting, and Driving*, Oxford: Oxford University Press, pp. 193–229.

Newell, Gordon F. (1971) *Applications of Queueing Theory*, London: Chapman & Hall.

Newell, Gordon F. (1987) "The morning commute for nonidentical travelers," *Transportation Science* 21: 74–88.

Newell, Gordon F. (1988) "Traffic flow for the morning commute," *Transportation Science* 22: 47–58.

Newman, Peter W.G. and Jeffrey R. Kenworthy (1989) *Cities and Automobile Dependence: An International Sourcebook*, Brookfield, VT: Gower.

Ng, Yew-Kwang (1987) "Relative-income effects and the appropriate level of public expenditure," *Oxford Economic Papers* 39: 293–300.

Nguyen, Kim Phi (1999) "Demand, supply, and pricing in urban road transport: the case of Ho Chi Minh City, Vietnam," *Research in Transportation Economics* 5: 107–54.

Niskanen, Esko and Chris Nash (2004) *MC-ICAM (Implementation of Marginal Cost Pricing in Transport – Integrated Conceptual and Applied Model Analysis): Final Report*, Leeds, UK: Institute for Transport Studies, University of Leeds. http://www.strafica.fi/mcicam/reports.html.

Noland, Robert B. (2001) "Relationships between highway capacity and induced vehicle travel," *Transportation Research* 35A: 47–72.

Noland, Robert B. and Kenneth A. Small (1995) "Travel-time uncertainty, departure time choice, and the cost of morning commutes," *Transportation Research Record* 1493: 150–58.

O'Connor, Robert (2002) "London underground: wrestling with privatization, officials are divided while the public leans toward public control," *Mass Transit* 28: 22–31.

Ohta, H. (2001) "Probing a traffic congestion controversy: density and flow scrutinized," *Journal of Regional Science* 41: 659–80.

Olszewski, P. and W. Suchorzewski (1987) "Traffic capacity of the city centre," *Traffic Engineering and Control* 28: 336–43, 348.

Oort, C.J. (1969) "The evaluation of travelling time," *Journal of Transport Economics and Policy* 3: 279–86.

Orr, Daniel (1969) "The taxicab problem: a proposed solution," *Journal of Political Economy* 77: 141–47.

Organisation for Economic Co-operation and Development (OECD) (1983) *Impacts of Heavy Freight Vehicles*, Paris: OECD.

Oum, Tae Hoon and Michael W. Tretheway (1988) "Ramsey pricing in the presence of externality costs," *Journal of Transport Economics and Policy* 22: 307–17.

Parry, Ian W.H. (2004) "Comparing alternative policies to reduce traffic accidents," *Journal of Urban Economics* 56: 346–58.

Parry, Ian W.H. and Antonio M. Bento (2001) "Revenue recycling and the welfare effects of congestion pricing," *Scandinavian Journal of Economics* 103: 645–71.

Parry, Ian W.H. and Kenneth A. Small (2005) "Does Britain or the United States have the right gasoline tax?" *American Economic Review* 95: 1276–89.

Patriksson, Michael (2004) "Algorithms for computing traffic equilibria," *Networks and Spatial Economics* 4: 23–38.

Payne, Harold J. (1984) "Discontinuity in equilibrium freeway traffic flow," *Transportation Research Record* 971: 140–46.

Pels, Eric and Piet Rietveld (2000) "Cost functions in transport," in Hensher and Button (2000), pp. 321–33.

Peltzman, Sam (1975) "The effects of automobile safety regulation," *Journal of Political Economy* 83: 677–725.

Pendyala, Ram M. and Ryuichi Kitamura (1997) "Weighting methods for attrition in choice-based panels," in Thomas F. Golob, Ryuichi Kitamura and Lyn Long (eds.) *Panels for Transportation Planning: Methods and Applications*, Boston, MA: Kluwer Academic Publishers, pp. 233–57.

Perry, James L., Timlynn Babitsky and Hal Gregersen (1988) "Organizational form and performance in urban mass transit," *Transport Review* 8: 125–43.

Petitte, Ryan A. (2001) "Fare variable construction and rail transit ridership elasticities," *Transportation Research Record* 753: 102–10.

Petrin, Amil and Kenneth Train (2004) "Omitted product attributes in differentiated product models," working paper, University of California, Berkeley, CA. http://elsa.berkeley.edu/~train/pt42504.pdf.

Pickrell, Don H. (1983) "Sources of rising operating deficits in urban bus transit," *Transportation Research Record* 915: 18–24.

Pickrell, Don H. (1989) *Urban Rail Transit Projects: Forecast versus Actual Ridership and Costs*, Cambridge, MA: US Department of Transportation, Transportation Systems Center.

Pickrell, Don H. (1992) "A desire named streetcar: fantasy and fact in rail transit planning," *Journal of the American Planning Association* 58: 158–76.

Pigou, Arthur C. (1920) *The Economics of Welfare*, London: Macmillan.

Pindyck, Robert S. and Daniel L. Rubinfeld (1998) *Econometric Models and Economic Forecasts*, 4th edition, Boston, MA: Irwin/McGraw-Hill.

Pipes, L.A. (1953) "An operational analysis of traffic dynamics," *Journal of Applied Physics* 24: 271–81.

Pisarski, Alan E. (2006) *Commuting in America III: The Third National Report on Commuting Patterns and Trends*, National Cooperative Highway Research Program report 550 and Transit Cooperative Research Program report 110, Washington, DC: Transportation Research Board.

Plaut, Pnina O. (1997) "Transportation–communications relationships in industry," *Transportation Research* 31A: 419–29.

Plaut, Pnina O. (2004) "Non-commuters: the people who walk to work or work at home," *Transportation* 31: 229–55.

Polinsky, A. Mitchell (1972) "Probabilistic compensation criteria," *Quarterly Journal of Economics* 86: 407–25.

Prashker, Joseph N. (1979) "Direct analysis of the perceived importance of attributes of reliability of travel modes in urban travel," *Transportation* 8: 329–46.

Pratt, Richard H. *et al.* (2000) "Transit pricing and fares," in *Traveler Response to Transportation System Changes: Interim Handbook*, Online Web Document 12, Washington, DC: Transportation Research Board. http://onlinepubs.trb.org/onlinepubs/tcrp/tcrp_webdoc_12.pdf.

Preston, John (2005) "Tendering of services," in Button and Hensher (2005), pp. 65–81.

PRoGRESS (2004) *PRoGRESS Main Project Report*. PRoGRESS (Pricing ROad use for Greater Responsibility, Efficiency and Sustainability in citieS) Project 2000-CM.10390 (July), European Commission, DG TREN. http://www.progress-project.org/Progress/report.html.

Proost, Stef, Bruno De Borger and Pia Koskenoja (2007) "Public finance aspects of transport financing and investment," in André de Palma, Robin Lindsey and Stef Proost (eds.) *Investment and the Use of Tax and Toll Revenues in the Transport Sector*, Research in Transport Economics, Vol. 19, Amsterdam: Elsevier JAI, pp. 59–80.

Proost, Stef and Kurt Van Dender (1998) "Variabilization of car taxes and externalities," in Button and Verhoef (1998), pp. 136–49.

Prud'homme, Rémy and Chang-Woon Lee (1999) "Size, sprawl, speed and the efficiency of cities," *Urban Studies* 36: 1849–58.

Pucher, John (1984) "Allocating federal transit subsidies: a critical analysis of alternatives," *Transportation Research Record* 967: 14–23.

Pucher, John and Anders Markstedt (1983) "Consequences of public ownership and subsidies for mass transit: evidence from case studies and regression analysis," *Transportation* 11: 323–45.

Pucher, John and John L. Renne (2003) "Socioeconomics of urban travel: Evidence from the 2001 NHTS," *Transportation Quarterly* 57: 49–77.

Quandt, Richard E. and William J. Baumol (1966) "The demand for abstract transport modes: Theory and measurement," *Journal of Regional Science* 6: 13–26.

Quinet, Emile (2004) "A meta-analysis of Western European external costs estimates," *Transportation Research* 9D: 465–76.

Ramjerdi, Farideh, Harald Minken and Knut Østmoe (2004) "Norwegian urban tolls," in Santos (2004), pp. 237–49.

Ramsey, Frank P. (1927) "A contribution to the theory of taxation," *Economic Journal* 37: 47–61.

Ran, Bin and David Boyce (1996) *Modeling Dynamic Transportation Networks: An Intelligent Transportation System Oriented Approach*, 2nd edition, Berlin: Springer-Verlag.

Reilly, John M. (1977) "Transit costs during peak and off-peak hours," *Transportation Research Record* 625: 22–26.

Richards, Martin G. (2006) *Congestion Charging in London: The Policy and the Politics*, Basingstoke, Hampshire, UK: Palgrave Macmillan.

Richards, Paul I. (1956) "Shock waves on the highway," *Operations Research* 4: 42–51.

Rotemberg, Julio J. (1985) "The efficiency of equilibrium traffic flows," *Journal of Public Economics* 26: 191–205.

Roth, Gabriel J. (1996) *Roads in a Market Economy*, Aldershot, UK: Avebury Technical.

SACTRA (Standing Advisory Committee on Trunk Road Assessment) (1994) *Trunk Roads and the Generation of Traffic*, London: Her Majesty's Stationery Office.

Safirova, Elena *et al.* (2004) "Welfare and distributional effects of road pricing schemes for metropolitan Washington DC," in Santos (2004), pp. 179–206.

Safirova, Elena *et al.* (2006) *Congestion Pricing: Long-Term Economic and Land-Use Effects*, discussion paper 06-37, Washington, DC: Resources for the Future. http://rff.org/rff/Documents/RFF-DP-06-37.pdf.

Samuel, Peter (2005) "Technologies will work in parallel," *World Highways*, 19 April. http://www.worldhighways.com/features/article.cfm?recordID=1748.

Santos, Georgina (ed.) (2004) *Road Pricing: Theory and Evidence*, Research in Transportation Economics, Vol. 9, Amsterdam: Elsevier JAI.

Santos, Georgina, David Newbery and Laurent Rojey (2001) "Static versus demand-sensitive models and estimation of second-best cordon tolls: an exercise for eight English towns," *Transportation Research Record* 1747: 44–50.

Sato, Tetsuji and Seiichi Hino (2005) "A spatial CGE analysis of road pricing in the Tokyo metropolitan area," *Journal of the Eastern Asia Society for Transportation Studies* 6: 608–23.

Savage, Ian (1988) "The analysis of bus costs and revenues by time period: I. Literature review," *Transport Reviews* 8: 283–99.

Savage, Ian (1989) "The analysis of bus costs and revenues by time period: II. Methodology review," *Transport Reviews* 9: 1–17.

Savage, Ian (1997) "Scale economies in United States rail transit systems," *Transportation Research* 31A: 459–73.

Savage, Ian (2004) "Management objectives and the causes of mass transit deficits," *Transportation Research* 38A: 181–99.

Schafer, Andreas (2000) "Regularities in travel demand: an international perspective," *Journal of Transportation and Statistics* 3: 1–31.

Schmalensee, Richard (1978) "Entry deterrence in the ready-to-eat breakfast cereal industry," *Bell Journal of Economics* 9: 305–27.

Schrank, David and Timothy Lomax (2005) *The 2005 Urban Mobility Report*, College Station, TX: Texas Transportation Institute. http://mobility.tamu.edu/ums/report/.

Schwanen, Tim, Martin Dijst and Frans M. Dieleman (2004) "Policies for urban form and their impact on travel: the Netherlands experience," *Urban Studies* 41: 579–603.

Shefer, Daniel and Haim Aviram (2005) "Incorporating agglomeration economies in transport cost–benefit analysis: the case of the proposed light-rail transit in the Tel-Aviv metropolitan area," *Papers in Regional Science* 84: 487–507.

Sheffi, Yosef (1985) *Urban Transportation Networks: Equilibrium Analysis with Mathematical Methods*, Englewood Cliffs, NJ: Prentice-Hall.

Sherret, Alistair (1975) *Immediate Travel Impacts of Transbay BART: Technical Memorandum*, document TM 15-3-75, Burlingame, CA: Peat, Marwick, Mitchell & Co., and Berkeley, CA: Metropolitan Transportation Commission, Springfield, VA: National Technical Information Service.

Shiftan, Yoram and John Suhrbier (2002) "The analysis of travel and emission impacts of travel demand management strategies using activity-based models," *Transportation* 29: 145–68.

Shinghal, Nalin and Tony Fowkes (2002) "Freight mode choice and adaptive stated preferences," *Transportation Research* 38E: 367–78.

Shirley, Chad and Clifford Winston (2004) "Firm inventory behavior and the returns from highway infrastructure investments," *Journal of Urban Economics* 55: 398–415.

Shoup, Donald C. (1982) "Cashing out free parking," *Transportation Quarterly* 36: 351–64.

Shoup, Donald C. (1997) "Evaluating the effects of cashing out employer-paid parking: Eight case studies," *Transport Policy* 4: 201–16.

Shoup, Donald C. (2005) *The High Cost of Free Parking*, Chicago, IL: American Planning Association, Planners Press.

Skabardonis, A. and R. Dowling (1996) "Improved speed–flow relationships for planning application," *Transportation Research Record* 1572: 18–23.

Skinner, Louise E. and Kiran Bhat (1978) *Comparative Costs of Urban Transportation Systems*, report by the US Department of Transportation, Federal Highway Administration, Washington, DC: US Government Printing Office.

Small, Kenneth A. (1982) "The scheduling of consumer activities: work trips," *American Economic Review* 72: 467–79.

Small, Kenneth A. (1983) "Bus priority and congestion pricing on urban expressways," in T.E. Keeler (ed.) *Research in Transportation Economics, Vol. 1*, Greenwich, CT: JAI Press, pp. 27–74.

Small, Kenneth A. (1987) "A discrete choice model for ordered alternatives," *Econometrica* 55: 409–24.

Small, Kenneth A. (1992a) *Urban Transportation Economics*, Fundamentals of Pure and Applied Economics, Vol. 51, Chur, Switzerland: Harwood Academic Publishers.

Small, Kenneth A. (1992b) "Using the revenues from congestion pricing," *Transportation* 19: 359–81.

Small, Kenneth A. (1994) "Approximate generalized extreme value models of discrete choice," *Journal of Econometrics* 62: 351–82.

Small, Kenneth A. (1999a) "Economies of scale and self-financing rules with noncompetitive factor markets," *Journal of Public Economics* 74: 431–50.

Small, Kenneth A. (1999b) "Project evaluation," in Gómez-Ibáñez, Tye and Winston (1999), pp. 137–77.

Small, Kenneth A. (2004) "Road pricing and public transport," in Santos (2004), pp. 133–58.

Small, Kenneth A. *et al.* (1999) *Valuation of Travel-Time Savings and Predictability in Congested Conditions for Highway User-Cost Estimation*, National Cooperative Highway Research Program report 431, Washington, DC: National Academy Press.

Small, Kenneth A. and Xuehao Chu (2003) "Hypercongestion," *Journal of Transport Economics and Policy* 37: 319–52.

Small, Kenneth A. and José A. Gómez-Ibáñez (1998) "Road pricing for congestion management: the transition from theory to policy," in Button and Verhoef (1998), pp. 213–46.

Small, Kenneth A. and José A. Gómez-Ibáñez (1999) "Urban transportation," in Paul Cheshire and Edwin S. Mills (eds.) *Handbook of Regional and Urban Economics, Vol. 3. Applied Urban Economics*, Amsterdam: North-Holland, pp. 1937–99.

Small, Kenneth A. and Camilla Kazimi (1995) "On the costs of air pollution from motor vehicles," *Journal of Transport Economics and Policy* 29: 7–32.

Small, Kenneth A. and Harvey S. Rosen (1981) "Applied welfare economics with discrete choice models," *Econometrica* 49: 105–30.

Small, Kenneth A. and Clifford Winston (1999) "The demand for transportation: models and applications," in Gómez-Ibáñez, Tye and Winston (1999), pp. 11–55.

Small, Kenneth A., Clifford Winston and Carol A. Evans (1989) *Road Work: A New Highway Pricing and Investment Policy*, Washington, DC: Brookings Institution Press.

Small, Kenneth A., Clifford Winston and Jia Yan (2005) "Uncovering the distribution of motorists' preferences for travel time and reliability," *Econometrica* 73: 1367–82.

Small, Kenneth A., Clifford Winston and Jia Yan (2006) "Differentiated road pricing, express lanes, and carpools: exploiting heterogeneous preferences in policy design," *Brookings-Wharton Papers on Urban Affairs* 7: 53–96.

Small, Kenneth A. and Jia Yan (2001) "The value of 'value pricing' of roads: second-best pricing and product differentiation," *Journal of Urban Economics* 49: 310–36.

Smeed, R.J. (1968) "Traffic studies and urban congestion," *Journal of Transportation Economics and Policy* 2: 33–70.

Smith, Edward (1973) "An economic comparison of urban railways and express bus services," *Journal of Transport Economics and Policy* 7: 20–31.

Smith, Tony E., Erik Anders Eriksson and Per Olov Lindberg (1995) "Existence of optimal tolls under conditions of stochastic user-equilibria," in Börje Johansson and Lars-Göran Mattsson (eds.) *Road Pricing: Theory, Empirical Assessment and Policy*, Boston, MA: Kluwer Academic Publishers, pp. 65–87.

Smith, W. Spencer, Fred L. Hall and Frank O. Montgomery (1996) "Comparing speed-flow relationships for motorways with new data from the M6," *Transportation Research* 30A: 89–101.

Sorensen, Paul A. and Brian D. Taylor (2005) *Review and Synthesis of Road-Use Metering and Charging Systems*, report commissioned by the Committee for the Study of the Long-Term Viability of Fuel Taxes for Transportation Finance, Washington, DC: Transportation Research Board. http://www.trb.org/publications/news/university/SRFuelTaxRoad-MeterPaper.pdf.

Spady, Richard H. and Ann F. Friedlaender (1978) "Hedonic cost functions for the regulated trucking industry," *Bell Journal of Economics* 9: 154–79.

Starrs, Margaret M. and Christine Perrins (1989) "The markets for public transport: the poor and the transport disadvantaged," *Transport Reviews* 9: 59–74.

Starrs, Margaret M. and David N.M. Starkie (1986) "An integrated road pricing and investment model: a South Australian application," *Australian Road Research* 16: 1–9.

Statistics Netherlands (2007) *Mobility of the Dutch Population*, User-defined tables produced at http://statline.cbs.nl/ (accessed 8 January 2007).

Steimetz, Seiji S.C. (2004) "New methods for modeling and estimating the social costs of motor vehicle use," unpublished dissertation, University of California, Irvine, Irvine, CA.

Steiner, Peter O. (1957) "Peak loads and efficient pricing," *Quarterly Journal of Economics* 71: 585–610.

Stockholmsförsöket (2006) *Facts and Results from the Stockholm Trial – Final Version – December 2006*. http://www.stockholmsforsoket.se/upload/Sammanfattningar/English/Final%20Report_The%20Stockholm%20Trial.pdf.

Storchmann, Karl (2004) "On the depreciation of automobiles: an international comparison," *Transportation* 31: 371–408.

Strelow, Hans (2006) "Passenger transport in the European Union," *Statistics in Focus*, Luxembourg: Eurostat, European Communities. http://epp.eurostat.ec.europa.eu/cache/ITY_OFFPUB/KS-NZ-06-009/EN/KS-NZ-06-009-EN.PDF.

Strotz, Robert H. (1965) "Urban transportation parables," in Julius Margolis (ed.) *The Public Economy of Urban Communities*, Washington, DC: Resources for the Future, pp. 127–69.

Sullivan, Edward *et al.* (2000) *Continuation Study to Evaluate the Impacts of the SR91 Value-Priced Express Lanes: Final Report*, San Luis Obispo, CA: California Polytechnic State University, San Luis Obispo. http://ceenve.calpoly.edu/sullivan/sr91/sr91.htm.

Sumalee, Agachai, Tony May and Simon Shepherd (2005) "Comparison of judgmental and optimal road pricing cordons," *Transport Policy* 12: 384–90.

Supernak, Janusz *et al.* (2001) *I–15 Congestion Pricing Project Monitoring and Evaluation Services: Phase II Year Three Overall Report*, San Diego, CA: San Diego State University Foundation. http://argo.sandag.org/fastrak/pdfs/yr3_overall.pdf.

Tabuchi, Takatoshi (1993) "Bottleneck congestion and modal split," *Journal of Urban Economics* 34: 414–31.

Teal, Roger F. and Mary Berglund (1987) "The impacts of taxicab deregulation in the USA," *Journal of Transport Economics and Policy* 21: 37–56.

Thill, Jean-Claude and Isabelle Thomas (1987) "Toward conceptualizing trip-chaining behavior: a review," *Geographical Analysis* 19: 1–17.

Thomson, J. Michael (1977) *Great Cities and Their Traffic*, London: Gollancz.

Timmermans, Harry *et al.* (2002) "Time allocation in urban and transport settings: an international inter-urban perspective," *Transport Policy* 9: 79–93.

TNS/NIPO KPMG (2004) *Monitoring en Evaluatie Deregulering Taxivervoer 1999–2003* [*Monitoring and Evaluation of Deregulation of Taxi Transport 1999–2003*], in Dutch, Amsterdam: TNS/NIPO.

Tol, Richard S.J. *et al.* (2000) "How much damage will climate change do? Recent estimates," *World Economics* 1: 179–206.

Train, Kenneth (1978) "A validation test of a disaggregate mode choice model," *Transportation Research* 12: 167–74.

Train, Kenneth (1980) "A structured logit model of auto ownership and mode choice," *Review of Economic Studies* 47: 357–70.

Train, Kenneth (1986) *Qualitative Choice Analysis: Theory, Econometrics, and an Application to Automobile Demand*, Cambridge, MA: MIT Press.

Train, Kenneth (2003) *Discrete Choice Methods with Simulation*, New York: Cambridge University Press.

Train, Kenneth and Daniel McFadden (1978) "The goods/leisure tradeoff and disaggregate work trip mode choice models," *Transportation Research* 12: 349–53.

Train, Kenneth and Clifford Winston (2007) "Vehicle choice behavior and the declining market share of U.S. automakers," *International Economic Review*, 48: 1467–1494.

Transport Canada (1994) *Guide to Benefit–Cost Analysis in Transport Canada*, Ottawa (September). http://www.tc.gc.ca/finance/BCA/en/TOC_e.htm.

Transport for London (2001) *Report to Ken Livingstone on the London Underground PPP*, London, 18 April. http://www.london.gov.uk/mayor/ppp/reportfinal.pdf (accessed 11 October 2006).

Transport for London (2004) *Congestion Charging Impacts Monitoring: Second Annual Report*, London, April. http://www.tfl.gov.uk/tfl/cclondon/cc_monitoring-2nd-report.shtml.

Transportation Research Board (1998) *National Automated Highway System Research Program: A Review*, special report 253, Washington, DC: Transportation Research Board.

Transportation Research Board (2000) *Highway Capacity Manual 2000*, Washington, DC: Transportation Research Board.

Traynor, Thomas L. (1994) "The effects of varying safety conditions on the external costs of driving," *Eastern Economic Journal* 20: 45–60.

Tretvik, Terje (2003) "Urban road pricing in Norway: public acceptability and travel behaviour," in Jens Schade and Bernhard Schlag (eds.) *Acceptability of Transport Pricing Strategies*, London: Pergamon, pp. 77–92.

Tversky, Amos and Daniel Kahneman (1991) "Loss aversion in riskless choice: a reference-dependent model," *Quarterly Journal of Economics* 106: 1039–61.

UK Department for Transport (2002) *COBA 11 User Manual, Part 5: Speed on Links*, Department for Transport, London.

UK Department for Transport (2004) *Feasibility Study of Road Pricing in the UK*, Department for Transport, London, July. http://www.dft.gov.uk/stellent/groups/dft_roads/documents/page/dft_roads_029788-01.hcsp#P57_1651.

UK Department for Transport (2006) *Bulletin of Public Transport Statistics: Great Britain: 2006*, September. http://www.dft.gov.uk/stellent/groups/dft_transstats/documents/page/dft_transstats_612534.hcsp.

UK Ministry of Transport (1964) *Road Pricing: The Economic and Technical Possibilities*, London: Her Majesty's Stationery Office.

UK National Statistics Online (2004) *Labour Force Survey (LFS) Historical Quarterly Supplement*. http://www.statistics.gov.uk/STATBASE/Expodata/Spreadsheets/D7938.xls.

UNITE (2003) *Pilot Account Results*, Deliverables 5, 8, 12. UNIfication of accounts and marginal costs for Transport Efficiency, European Commission – DG TREN, Fifth Framework Programme. http://www.its.leeds.ac.uk/projects/unite/deliverables.

US BLS (2006) *National Compensation Survey: Occupational Wages in the United States, June 2005*, Bulletin 2581, Washington, DC: US Bureau of Labor Statistics. http://www.bls.gov/ncs/ocs/sp/ncbl0658.pdf.

US Bureau of Public Roads (1964) *Traffic Assignment Manual*, Washington, DC: US Bureau of Public Roads.

US CEA (2006) "Annual report of the Council of Economic Advisers," in *Economic Report of the President*, Washington, DC: US Government Printing Office. http://www.whitehouse.gov/cea/erpcover2006.pdf.

US Census Bureau (1992) *Statistical Abstract of the United States: 1992*, Washington, DC: US Government Printing Office.

US Census Bureau (2004) *Statistical Abstract of the United States: 2004–2005*, Washington, DC: US Government Printing Office.

US Census Bureau (2006) *Construction Price Indexes: Price Deflator Index of New One-Family Houses Under Construction*, Washington, DC: US Government Printing Office. http://www.census.gov/const/price_deflator.pdf.

US Department of Commerce (2005) "Fixed assets and consumer durable goods for 1994–2004," *Survey of Current Business* 85: 19–30. http://www.bea.gov/bea/pub/0905cont.htm.

US Department of Transportation (1997) *The Value of Travel Time: Departmental Guidance for Conducting Economic Evaluations*, Washington, DC: US Department of Transportation.

US FHWA (1997) *Final Report on the Federal Highway Cost Allocation Study*, US Federal Highway Administration, Washington, DC: US Government Printing Office. http://www.fhwa.dot.gov/policy/otps/costallocation.htm.

US FHWA (2000) *Addendum to the 1997 Federal Highway Cost Allocation Study Final Report*, Washington, DC: US FHWA. http://www.fhwa.dot.gov/policy/hcas/addendum.htm.

US FHWA (2002) *Highway Statistics 2001*, Washington, DC: US Government Printing Office. http://www.fhwa.dot.gov/policy/ohpi/hss/index.htm.

US FHWA (2006) *Highway Statistics 2005*, Washington, DC: US Government Printing Office. http://www.fhwa.dot.gov/policy/ohpi/hss/index.htm.

US GAO (2001) *Mass Transit: Bus Rapid Transit Shows Promise*, report GAO-01-984, Washington, DC: US General Accounting Office.

US GAO (2005) *Highway and Transit Investments: Options for Improving Information on Projects' Benefits and Costs and Increasing Accountability for Results*, report GAO-05-172, Washington, DC: US General Accounting Office.

US OMB (1992) *Guidelines and Discount Rates for Benefit–Cost Analysis of Federal Programs*, circular no. A-94, revised, Section 8, Washington, DC: US Office of Management and Budget.

US OMB (2003) *Regulatory Analysis*, circular no. A-4, revised, Washington, DC: US Office of Management and Budget.

Van den Bossche, M.A. *et al.* (2003) *Guidance on Adapting Marginal Cost Estimates*. UNITE (UNIfication of accounts and marginal costs for Transport Efficiency), report for European Commission – DG TREN, Fifth Framework Programme, Brussels, Belgium. http://www.its.leeds.ac.uk/projects/unite/downloads/.

Van Dender, Kurt (2001) "Aspects of congestion pricing for urban transport," Ph.D. dissertation no. 149, Faculty of Economics, Katholieke Universiteit Leuven, Leuven, Belgium.

Van Dender, Kurt (2003) "Transport taxes with multiple trip purposes," *Scandinavian Journal of Economics* 105: 295–310.

Van Dender, Kurt and Stef Proost (2004). "Optimal urban transport pricing in the presence of congestion, economies of density and costly public funds," working paper, Department of Economics, University of California, Irvine, Irvine, CA.

Van der Veer, Jan Peter (2002) "Entry deterrence and quality provision in the local bus market," *Transport Reviews* 22: 247–65.

Van Ommeren, Jos, Gerard J. Van den Berg and Cees Gorter (2000) "Estimating the marginal willingness to pay for commuting," *Journal of Regional Science* 40: 541–63.

Van Wissen, L.J.G. and H.J. Meurs (1989) "The Dutch Mobility Panel: experiences and evaluation," *Transportation* 16: 99–119.

Varian, Hal R. (1992) *Microeconomic Analysis*, 3rd edition, New York: Norton.

Verhoef, Erik T. (1999) "Time, speeds, flows and densities in static models of road traffic congestion and congestion pricing," *Regional Science and Urban Economics* 29: 341–69.

Verhoef, Erik T. (2001) "An integrated dynamic model of road traffic congestion based on simple car-following theory: exploring hypercongestion," *Journal of Urban Economics* 49: 505–42.

Verhoef, Erik T. (2002a) "Second-best congestion pricing in general static transportation networks with elastic demands," *Regional Science and Urban Economics* 32: 281–310.

Verhoef, Erik T. (2002b) "Second-best congestion pricing in general networks: heuristic algorithms for finding second-best optimal toll levels and toll points," *Transportation Research* 36B: 707–29.

Verhoef, Erik T. (2003) "Inside the queue: hypercongestion and road pricing in a continuous time–continuous place model of traffic congestion," *Journal of Urban Economics* 54: 531–65.

Verhoef, Erik T. (2005) "Transport infrastructure charging and capacity choice," paper presented to the 135th Round Table of the OECD/ECMT Transport Research Centre on Transport Infrastructure Investment Charges and Capacity Choice, ECMT, Paris.

Verhoef, Erik T. (2007) "Second-best road pricing through highway franchising," *Journal of Urban Economics*, 62: 337–361.

Verhoef, Erik T. *et al.* (1996) "Information provision, flat- and fine congestion tolling and the efficiency of road usage," *Regional Science and Urban Economics* 26: 505–29.

Verhoef, Erik T., Peter Nijkamp and Piet Rietveld (1995a) "Second-best regulation of road transport externalities," *Journal of Transport Economics and Policy* 29: 147–67.

Verhoef, Erik T., Peter Nijkamp and Piet Rietveld (1995b) "The economics of regulatory parking policies: the (im-)possibilities of parking policies in traffic regulation," *Transportation Research* 29A: 141–56.

Verhoef, Erik T., Peter Nijkamp and Piet Rietveld (1996) "Second-best congestion pricing: the case of an untolled alternative," *Journal of Urban Economics* 40: 279–302.

Verhoef, Erik T., Peter Nijkamp and Piet Rietveld (1997) "The social feasibility of road pricing: a case study for the Randstad area," *Journal of Transport Economics and Policy* 31: 255–67.

Verhoef, Erik T. and Jan Rouwendal (2004) "A behavioural model of traffic congestion: endogenizing speed choice, traffic safety and time losses," *Journal of Urban Economics* 56: 408–34.

Verhoef, Erik T. and Kenneth A. Small (2004) "Product differentiation on roads: constrained congestion pricing with heterogeneous users," *Journal of Transport Economics and Policy* 38: 127–56.

Vickers, John and George Yarrow (1991) "Economic perspectives on privatization," *Journal of Economic Perspectives* 5: 111–32.

Vickrey, William S. (1963) "Pricing in urban and suburban transport," *American Economic Review, Papers and Proceedings* 53: 452–65.

Vickrey, William S. (1965) "Pricing as a tool in coordination of local transportation," in John R. Meyer (ed.) *Transportation Economics: A Conference of the Universities – National Bureau Committee for Economic Research*, New York: Columbia University Press, pp. 275–96.

Vickrey, William S. (1968) "Automobile accidents, tort law, externalities, and insurance: an economist's critique," *Law and Contemporary Problems* 33: 464–87.

Vickrey, William S. (1969) "Congestion theory and transport investment," *American Economic Review, Papers and Proceedings* 59: 251–60.

Vickrey, William S. (1973) "Pricing, metering, and efficiently using transportation facilities," *Highway Research Record* 476: 36–48.

Viscusi, V. Kip and Joseph E. Aldy (2003) "The value of a statistical life: a critical review of market estimates throughout the world," *Journal of Risk and Uncertainty* 27: 5–76.

Viton, Philip A. (1980) "On the economics of rapid-transit operations," *Transportation Research* 14A: 247–53.

Viton, Philip A. (1981a) "On competition and product differentiation in urban transportation: the San Francisco Bay Area," *Bell Journal of Economics* 12: 362–79.

Viton, Philip A. (1981b) "A translog cost function for urban bus transit," *Journal of Industrial Economics* 24: 287–304.

Viton, Philip A. (1983) "Pareto-optimal urban transportation equilibria," in T.E. Keeler (ed.) *Research in Transportation Economics, Vol. 1*, Greenwich, CT: JAI Press, pp. 75–101.

Viton, Philip A. (1995) "Private roads," *Journal of Urban Economics* 37: 260–89.

Voith, Richard (1997) "Fares, service levels, and demographics: what determines commuter rail ridership in the long run?" *Journal of Urban Economics* 41: 176–97.

Vovsha, Peter (1997) "The cross-nested logit model: application to mode choice in the Tel-Aviv metropolitan area," *Transportation Research Record* 1607: 6–15.

Waddell, Paul (2002) "UrbanSim: modeling urban development for land use, transportation, and environmental planning," *Journal of the American Planning Association* 68: 297–314.

Walters, A.A. (1961) "The theory and measurement of private and social cost of highway congestion," *Econometrica* 29: 676–99.

Walters, A.A. (1968) *The Economics of Road User Charges*, World Bank staff occasional papers, no. 5, Baltimore, MD: Johns Hopkins University Press.

Ward's Communications (2006) *Motor Vehicle Facts and Figures 2006*, Southfield, MI: Ward's Communications.

Wardman, Mark (1998) "The value of travel time: a review of British evidence," *Journal of Transport Economics and Policy* 32: 285–316.

Wardman, Mark (2001) "A review of British evidence on time and service quality valuations," *Transportation Research* 37E: 107–28.

Wardman, Mark (2004) "Public transport values of time," *Transport Policy* 11: 363–77.

Wardrop, John G. (1952) "Some theoretical aspects of road traffic research," *Proceedings of the Institute of Civil Engineers* 1: 325–78.

Washington, Simon P., Matthew G. Karlaftis and Fred L. Mannering (2003) *Statistical and Econometric Methods for Transportation Data Analysis*, Boca Raton, FL: Chapman & Hall.

Waters, William G., II (1996) "Values of travel time savings in road transport project evaluation," in David Hensher, Jenny King and Tae Hoon Oum (eds.) *World Transport Research: Proceedings of 7th World Conference on Transport Research, Vol. 3*, Oxford: Pergamon, pp. 213–23.

Watson, Peter L. and Edward P. Holland (1978) *Relieving Traffic Congestion: The Singapore Area License Scheme*, World Bank staff working paper no. 281, Washington, DC: World Bank.

Weisbrod, Glen, Donald Vary and George Treyz (2001) *Economic Implications of Congestion*, National Cooperative Highway Research Program Report 463, Washington, DC: National Academy Press.

Weitzman, Martin L. (2001) "Gamma discounting," *American Economic Review* 91: 260–71.

Wendner, Ronald and Lawrence H. Goulder (2007) "Status effects, public goods provision, and the excess burden," working paper, Department of Economics, Graz University, Graz, Austria. http://www.kfunigraz.ac.at/vwlwww/forschung/Wendner_Goulder.pdf.

Wenzel, Tom and Marc Ross (2002) "Are SUVs really safer than cars?" *Access* 21: 2–7. http://www.uctc.net/access/access.asp.

West, Sarah E. (2004) "Distributional effects of alternative vehicle pollution control policies," *Journal of Public Economics* 88: 735–57.

Wheaton, William C. (1978) "Price-induced distortions in urban highway investment," *Bell Journal of Economics* 9: 622–32.

White, Michelle J. (2004) "The 'arms race' on American roads: the effect of sport utility vehicles and pickup trucks on traffic safety," *Journal of Law and Economics* 47: 333–55.

White, Peter (1995) "Deregulation of local bus services in Great Britain: an introductory review," *Transport Reviews* 15: 185–209.

Wigan, Marcus *et al.* (2000) "Valuing long-haul and metropolitan freight travel time and reliability," *Journal of Transportation and Statistics* 3: 83–89.

Williams, Huw C.W.L. (1977) "On the formation of travel demand models and economic evaluation measures of user benefit," *Environment and Planning A* 9: 285–344.

Willis, Kenneth G. (2005) "Cost–benefit analysis," in Hensher and Button (2005), pp. 491–506.

Willson, Richard W. (1992) "Estimating the travel and parking demand effects of employer-paid parking," *Regional Science and Urban Economics* 22: 133–45.

Willson, Richard W. (1995) "Suburban parking requirements: a tacit policy for automobile use and sprawl," *Journal of the American Planning Association* 61: 29–42.

Willson, Richard W. and Donald C. Shoup (1990) "Parking subsidies and travel choices: assessing the evidence," *Transportation* 17: 141–57.

Wilson, John D. (1983) "Optimal road capacity in the presence of unpriced congestion," *Journal of Urban Economics* 13: 337–57.

Winston, Clifford (2000) "Government failure in urban transportation," *Fiscal Studies* 21: 403–25.

Winston, Clifford and Chad Shirley (1998) *Alternate Route: Toward Efficient Urban Transportation*, Washington, DC: Brookings Institution Press.

Winston, Clifford, Vikram Maheshri and Fred Mannering (2006) "An exploration of the offset hypothesis using disaggregate data: the case of airbags and antilock brakes," *Journal of Risk and Uncertainty* 32: 83–99.

World Bank (2006) *Toll Roads and Concessions*, Washington, DC: World Bank. http://www.worldbank.org/transport/ roads/toll_rds.htm.

Wunsch, Pierre (1996) "Cost and productivity of major urban transit systems in Europe," *Journal of Transport Economics and Policy* 30: 171–86.

Yang, Hai (1999a) "System optimum, stochastic user equilibrium, and optimal link tolls," *Transportation Science* 33: 354–60.

Yang, Hai (1999b) "Evaluating the benefits of a combined route guidance and road pricing system in a traffic network with recurrent congestion," *Transportation* 20: 299–321.

Yang, Hai and Hai-Jun Huang (1999) "Carpooling and congestion pricing in a multilane highway with high-occupancy-vehicle lanes," *Transportation Research* 33A: 139–55.

Yang, Hai and Qiang Meng (2002) "A note on 'Highway pricing and capacity choice in a road network under a build-operate-transfer scheme'," *Transportation Research* 36A: 659–63.

Yang, Hai, Qiang Meng and Der-Horng Lee (2004) "Trial-and-error implementation of marginal-cost pricing on networks in the absence of demand functions," *Transportation Research* 38B: 477–93.

Yang, Hai and S.C. Wong (1998) "A network model of urban taxi services," *Transportation Research* 32B: 235–46.

Young, William, Russell G. Thompson and Michael A.P. Taylor (1991) "A review of urban car parking models," *Transport Reviews* 11: 63–84.

Zhang, H. Michael (1999) "A mathematical model of traffic hysteresis," *Transportation Research* 33B: 1–24.

Zhang, Xiaoning and Hai Yang (2004) "The optimal cordon-based network congestion pricing problem," *Transportation Research* 38B: 517–37.

Index